MUSIC AND MUSICIANS

ALBERT LAVIGNAC

Professor of Harmony in the Paris Conservatory

With 94 illustrations and 510 examples in musical notation

TRANSLATED BY

WILLIAM MARCHANT

Translator of Chevrillon's "In India," Bazin's "Italians of To-day," etc.

FOURTH EDITION, REVISED AND EDITED, WITH AN APPEN DIX ON MUSIC IN AMERICA AND THE PRESENT STATE OF THE ART OF MUSIC

BY

H. E. KREHBIEL

Author of " How to Listen to Music," etc., etc.

NEW YORK

HENRY HOLT AND COMPANY

Stanhope Press
F. H. GILSON COMPANY
BOSTON, U.S.A.

PREFACE.

This work has the twofold aim of presenting, in the most condensed form possible, well-defined notions concerning the things which must form the substratum of every musician's serious studies, and of interesting all those who cultivate or love the musical art in whatever degree by unveiling to them its machinery and its methods, many of which are but little known to even the most enlightened public.

It is, then, at once a guide for the *student musician*, who will find here laid out a plan for the direction of his labours— more abstruse and more complex than is generally believed— and a popular treatise on Music for the use of the general reader, the intelligent and curious *amateur*.

The former will find information here as to the nature and importance of the studies through which his path lies, in the pursuit of his proposed aim, and an indication of the works of instruction that will be most useful to him in every branch of the musical art,—for this book *has not* in itself, *a didactic character*.

The lover of Music will, however, learn from it the elements of our special technology, which may interest him, and will find here, also, much information, of a nature sometimes to surprise him, and often to gratify his legitimate and sympathetic curiosity.

Such are the reasons which have decided me to publish this work.

TABLE OF CONTENTS

CHAPTER III.—GRAMMAR OF MUSIC.

CHAPTER IV.— ESTHETICS.

CHAPTER V.— HISTORY OF THE ART OF MUSIC.

APPENDIX.

LIST OF ILLUSTRATIONS.

MUSIC AND MUSICIANS.

CHAPTER I.

A STUDY OF MUSICAL SOUND.

A.—Production of the Sound.

All natural phenomena are produced by vibrations.

Sound, like light and heat, is nothing more than a *phenomenon of vibration.*

According to the latest researches, *sound* vibrations — that is to say, vibrations perceived by the ear, *audible* vibrations — have a rapidity which ranges from 16 to 36,500 per second.

Heat vibrations begin at 134 trillions (134,000,000,000,000) per second; and *light* vibrations — those perceived by the eye, *visible* — at 483 trillions. The following table shows the vibrations of the ether producing the seven colours of the rainbow, the gamut of colours:

Red	483,000,000,000,000
Orange	513,000,000,000,000
Yellow	543,000,000,000,000
Green	576,000,000,000,000
Blue	630,000,000,000,000
Indigo	669,000,000,000,000
Violet	708,000,000,000,000

More rapid still are chemical vibrations, which are altogether beyond the reach of any of our senses; these are shown only by certain reactions, as of prepared photographic plates. Vibrations of this order have the extraordinary rapidity of 1017 trillions to the second, or even, according to some scientists, of 1429 trillions.

I give these figures,—of which the mind can form no conception,—not for the purpose of astonishing the reader, but in this way to lead him to regard as nothing extraordinary the vastly inferior figures representing the vibrations called *sonorous,* which are the slowest of all that the senses take cognisance of. It is with these only that we shall be concerned in this volume, and not, even, with all of these, for the limit of the ear's appreciation of sounds *having musical character* (a limit which varies, indeed, in different individuals) rarely extends beyond a minimum of 16 and a maximum of 4138 vibrations to the second, which are respectively the rates of vibration of the lowest tone of the great organ (a pipe of thirty-two feet) and the highest note of the piccolo.

Within these limits lies the domain of sounds purely musical; having thus indicated it, I shall henceforward confine myself strictly to it.

In respect to acoustics also, we shall have to examine only the sound phenomena which are directly of interest to the musician, namely:

1. The production of sound;
2. Its transmission through the air;
3. Its perception by the ear;
4. Its combinations, successive or simultaneous,— scales, intervals, chords, consonances, and dissonances;
5. The acoustic properties of halls;
6. The relations between acoustics and musical rhythm.

We will begin by seeking to obtain a perfectly clear idea of a *vibration.* For this purpose we can do nothing better than examine attentively the way in which a pendulum oscillates. From a string just a metre in length, suspend a weight, having securely fixed the other end of the string;

this makes a pendulum which will answer our purpose (Fig. 1). In a state of rest, it hangs vertically; it is a

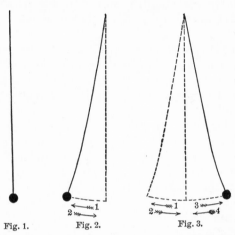

Fig. 1.   Fig. 2.   Fig. 3.

plumb line. Draw it aside and its weight will cause it to fall back again; this is a simple oscillation (Fig. 2). But our pendulum does not stop here; its motion continuing, it goes beyond its position of equilibrium, and then again falls back to it; this is a double oscillation (Fig. 3). And these movements back and forth will continue, so long as the impulse lasts which has been given to it.

The oscillations of a pendulum have this remarkable characteristic, that they are strictly isochronous; that is to say, they have all the same *duration*. According to the greater or less force of the original impulse the extent of the oscillations will vary, but their rapidity will remain the same; they will gradually die out, growing shorter and shorter, but from the first oscillation to the last, even to those so slight as to be imperceptible to the eye, each will occupy exactly a second of time; and this *because* the supposed pendulum is a metre in length.[1] If it were four

---

1 The exact length of a pendulum marking a second of time is, in Paris, 0.994; at the pole, it would need to be 0.996; at the equator, 0.991. [A metre = 3.28 feet; i.e. about 3 feet, 3 inches. Tr.]

metres long, each oscillation would require two seconds; on the other hand, it would make two oscillations to the second if it were reduced to one-fourth its present length, namely, to 25 centimetres.1

Now these oscillations are *vibrations*.

They produce no sound, because a pendulum is not a *sonorous* body, and especially because their motion is much too slow. It is this very slowness, however, which enables us to see them, and to study them with the eye.

We can now, by analogy, easily understand how *sound vibrations* — that is to say, *sounds* — are produced.

Instead of the pendulum we shall take a long piece of

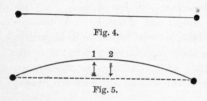

Fig. 4.

Fig. 5.

string, and fix it at both ends without stretching it too much. In its position of equilibrium, it represents a straight line (Fig. 4). Draw it aside from this position and its elasticity will cause it to return; this is a simple vibration (Fig. 5). But it does not stop here; it goes beyond in the opposite direction, and then returns to its equilibrium again; this is a double vibration (Fig. 6). And this movement to and fro will continue so long as there remains a trace of the impulse which was given to it.

The vibrations of the string have this in common with the oscillations of the pendulum, that they also are isochronous, each occupying exactly the same length of time; and that they

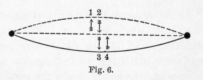

Fig. 6.

grow less and less in amplitude for the same reasons; and that their rapidity is determined by the *length* of the vibrating body, although in a different ratio. A string of

1 The number of oscillations is *inversely proportional to the square of the length of a pendulum.*

double length gives vibrations of half the rapidity, and inversely; and with increased or diminished tension, the same rule applies.

Now, for the moment, let us suppose that, either by shortening the cord, or by increasing its tension, we bring it to make 16 vibrations to the second;[1] these movements will have become too rapid to be detected separately by the eye, the string now appearing as a transparent spindle. Now, however, begins the phenomenon of sound; the ear perceives, though indistinctly, the lowest note in the musical scale. Straining the cord tighter, we shall find the sound becoming higher, by insensible gradations. Finally, — to carry out the hypothesis,— if we suppose that we could, without breaking the string, increase its tension indefinitely, we should obtain sounds higher and higher in pitch, but still retaining their musical character, up to the point where the string gave 4224 vibrations to the second, *which is the limit of musical sounds appreciable by the human ear.*

Beyond this point (that is to say, with a tension still increased) we should cause the string to produce sounds of extreme shrillness, sharp, piercing, hissing, painful to hear, and entirely destitute of musical character. And, finally, could we pass the degree of tension necessary to give 36,-500 vibrations to the second, the string would no doubt go on vibrating, but we should no longer hear it, for at that point the auditory power of the ear ceases completely.

To study more closely the vibrations of strings, we will now have recourse to an instrument well known to all scientists, and known for a very long time, since its invention is attributed to Pythagoras.

This instrument is called the monochord, and consists of a long, narrow wooden box, upon which is stretched a string or wire, either by means of two pegs, or of one peg and a

[1 Following the French method, the author regards as *one vibration*, the movement which he has called *une vibration simple*, that is, the movement to *or* fro; in America, as in England and Germany, it is the movement to *and* fro, which makes the vibration. The latter method is adopted in translation. TR.]

weight. The string passes over two bridges, a metre apart; underneath it is inscribed upon the box the division of this metre into centimetres and millimetres. A movable bridge may be added, by which can be limited at will the portion of string which we desire to use (Fig 7).

The following are a few of the experiments that may be made with this useful and simple apparatus, to be found in every physical laboratory.

The string being suitably stretched, we cause it to vibrate by drawing a bow across, by plucking it with the finger, or by striking it. The sound emitted is produced by the vibrations of the string in its entire length, namely, a metre. Now, if we place the movable bridge exactly in the middle, and excite either half of the string, the sound produced will be precisely an octave higher than that produced by the whole length. This proves that *the number of vibrations of strings is inversely proportional to their length.*

If we now remove this string and substitute another, of

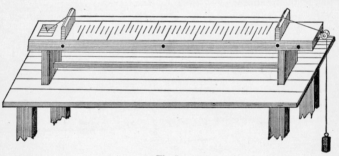

Fig. 7.

equal length, of the same material, but of *twice the diameter*, and give it the same tension as the former had, we shall find it sound an octave lower than the other. This shows that *the number of vibrations of strings is in inverse ratio to their diameters.*

Experimenting successively with two wires of the same length, the same diameter, subject to the same tension, but made of metals differing in *density*, it will appear that *the number of vibrations of strings is inversely proportional to the square root of their density.*

Finally, by varying the stretching weight, it will be shown that *the number of vibrations of strings is directly proportional to the square root of their stretching weights.*

These four fundamental laws, a thorough knowledge of which is indispensable to makers of musical instruments, may be thus summed up for the use of musicians:

The longer, thicker, heavier, and slacker a string is, the slower are its vibrations; hence, the deeper is its tone.

The shorter, finer, lighter, and tenser it is, the more rapid its vibrations; hence, the higher is its tone.

The sound produced by a string vibrating in its entire length, is its *fundamental or natural* tone. It can, however, produce many other sounds at the same time, subdividing as it vibrates; these are called *harmonics,* also *over-tones* (German, *Obertöne*), *partial sounds,* and *concomitant sounds.* To study these, we again have recourse to the monochord.

By means of its pegs we bring the string to the pitch of ![music notation], which requires 129.3 vibrations a second. Touched near the middle with the bow, it vibrates, appearing as a transparent spindle, which may be thus represented (Fig. 8):

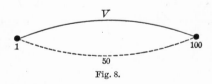

Fig. 8.

and emits its fundamental, which we already know. At the two *fixed* extremities of the string, the motion is necessarily *nil.* These are its nodes, and the vibrating portion of the cord is called its ventral segment.

With a finger of the left hand, or with the feather end of a quill, touch the centre of the string very lightly, just enough to prevent the ventral segment from forming; then draw a bow across at the 25th centimetre; a new motionless

point will have formed under the touch, a node, and the
string will vibrate in two ventral segments (Fig. 9).

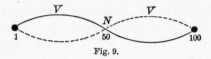

Fig. 9.

Each of these will be but half of the string, hence will produce twice as many vibrations (258.7 a second), and will
emit a sound an octave higher than its fundamental, namely,
: this is called the second harmonic.[1]

In the same way, touch the string at the 33d centimetre;
draw the bow across at the middle point of the string, the
50th centimetre, and we have the third harmonic or partial
tone . The number of vibrations is now 387.5 a
second, and the string will have assumed this form (Fig. 10):

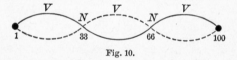

Fig. 10.

We may now observe that besides the node formed by the
touch of the finger or the feather at the 33d centimetre, a
second node has formed spontaneously at the 66th centimetre. This fact is verified by drawing the bow across
at the 16th, 50th, and 82d centimetres, which are, approximately, the middle points of three ventral segments:
the third harmonic will be distinctly heard at each. But,
if we draw the bow across at the 66th centimetre,— which
is a node,— a motionless point,— there will be no sound.

Touching the string at the 25th centimetre, and drawing
the bow across the 12th, 37th, 62d, or 87th, all of which

---

1 A different system of numbering calls the fundamental, *zero*, and its octave,
the *first harmonic;* but since the fundamental gives really only a part of the
sound called by its name, which sound is completed by the higher tones,— the
Obertöne,— it seems logical to call it the first harmonic or partial tone; this
method, moreover, is convenient for mathematical uses, and is the one adopted
by the great physicists of the present time.

are middle points of ventral segments, you will have the
fourth harmonic ♯ which has 517.25 vibrations, and
the string will have the form shown in (Fig. 11); here
two nodes have formed spontaneously.

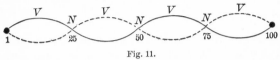

Fig. 11.

In this way are easily produced upon the monochord (especially if a fine string is used) the first ten harmonics; the
table given below represents them with the fundamental C.
The line of figures just below the staff (50, *etc.*) indicates
in centimetres the point of the string to be touched or
stopped for the production of each harmonic; and in the
third row of figures (at right angles to the staff) we have
what is called for convenience the *vibration number* of each.

1	2	3	4	5	6	7	8	9	10
	50	33.3	25	20	16.6	14.2	12.5	11	10 cent.
129.3	258.6	387.5	517.7	646.5	775.8	905.1	1034.5	1163.7	1293

Theoretically, the series of harmonics may be regarded
as infinite, since a string can be indefinitely subdivided,
but the first ten are sufficient for the purposes of this
book.

The series gives occasion for the following remarks, which
should receive careful attention:

1. The harmonics are numbered in accordance with the
number of vibrating segments (called also *ventral segments*
and *loops*).

2. The nodes are always one more in number than the
loops (counting the two fixed ends of the string as nodes).

3. The *fundamental*, vibrating with one loop, is the first
harmonic of the tone.

4. Taken in their numerical order the harmonics are

constantly nearer and nearer together, the successive intervals being an octave, a fifth, a fourth, third, second.

5. The first, second, fourth, and eighth harmonics have the ratio of octaves. (If the series were continued it would be the same with the sixteenth, the thirty-second, sixty-fourth, and so on.) The same relation of octaves occurs between the third and sixth, and the fifth and tenth.

6. The ratio of vibrations for two sounds in the relation

of octaves is as	1 : 2
of perfect fifths, as	2 : 3
of perfect fourths, as	3 : 4
of major thirds, as	4 : 5
of minor thirds, as	5 : 6
of major seconds, as	8 : 9

7. The vibration number of any harmonic is obtained by multiplying the number indicating its place (1, 2, 3, and so on) by the vibration number of the fundamental.

This subdivision of the string which produces the upper harmonics,— *i. e.*, all the harmonics with the exception of the first, the fundamental,— which we have now explained theoretically, can be shown visibly with the monochord. Place at different points on the string little "riders" of thin paper (Fig. 12), and repeat the preceding experiments. Those which have been placed on the nodes will remain undisturbed when the bow is drawn across the string, while those upon the ventral segments will be violently agitated or thrown off.

Fig. 12.

For example, to demonstrate the formation of the fourth harmonic, place riders of white paper at or near the middle of the four ventral segments (which will be, approximately, at the 12th, 37th, 62d, and 87th centimetres) and three of coloured paper, at the 25th, 50th, and 75th centimetres. Touch the string at the 25th centimetre, draw the bow across the string near its end, and at the moment the sound

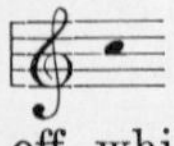

is heard you will see the four white riders thrown off, while the three coloured ones remain undisturbed.

The eighth harmonic unseats eight riders placed on the

middle point of the vibrating segments, and will respect seven others placed on the nodes.

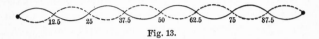

Fig. 13.

We shall have frequent occasion to recur to the monochord for other and more delicate experiments.

What we have studied thus far is the mode of vibration of strings in their entire length, and when divided into sections by the light touch of the finger or a feather.

In the first case there is emitted a single tone, called the *fundamental,* whose loudness is in proportion to the amplitude of its vibrations, and whose pitch depends upon the length, thickness, tension, and density of the string; and in the second case (when subdivided) there are produced other sounds, its *harmonics,* consisting of vibrations from twice to ten times more rapid, and rising correspondingly in pitch.

We have now, however, to take into account the fact that a string never does vibrate simply as a whole, but that to this vibration as a whole, partial vibrations are always added in varying numbers. It is even probable that the partial vibrations are the first in order of time, and that it is their sum which produces the general vibration of which alone we have a clear perception. That is to say, we never hear an absolutely pure tone, but always one accompanied in greater or less degree by certain of its harmonics.

The ear does not always distinguish the partial tones, both from lack of practice and because the attention is not called to them; but there is no doubt that they are there, however difficult it may be to recognise them in any direct way.

Listening attentively, however, the experienced ear can distinguish those of the partial tones which are not octaves of the fundamental (a relation causing them to blend too closely with it), — for instance, in the note ⨏, the harmonics of the unequal numbers 3, 5, 7

The piano and harmonium are particularly well suited for this experiment. One should strike, very softly, the harmonic whose presence it is desired to prove, in order to have the tone clearly in the mind; then, after it has entirely died away, strike vigorously the fundamental, and listen long, for it is often just at the moment when the first tone is about to cease that the overtones become distinguishable.

Another method is this: produce a nodal point on the monochord, as before, either with the finger, or the feather of a quill, or a small camel's hair pencil, so as to obtain by plucking the string, one of the partial tones; continue plucking the string, at the same time gradually diminishing the light touch which has caused the node to form, and the fundamental will by degrees become audible. As you reduce the touch more and more, the fundamental will assume predominance, while still you will not have lost the idea of the overtone, even at the moment when the string has been entirely left free.

The same experiment can be made with the string of a piano or a 'cello; here the point to be stopped must be ascertained by measurement, taking the whole length of the string, and dividing it by three, five, or seven, according to the overtone you may desire to obtain.

Later, in speaking of resonators and of sympathetic vibrations, other experiments will be described which show the complexity of vibrations. At present, however, we shall merely say that this indisputable fact can be as clearly demonstrated to the senses as its mathematical theory is proved to the mind.

We now come, and as a direct sequence from what has just been said, to an explanation of one of the things most interesting to musicians, namely, the cause of *timbre*, or quality of sound.

It being understood that the loudness of a sound depends upon the amplitude of the vibrations, and the pitch of it

upon their number, the question as to what it is that produces differences of timbre long remained unanswered. The
answer is, that it is the *shape of the vibrations;* or, to express
the idea in other words, it is the presence of various harmonics produced simultaneously with the fundamental tone.

And an idea may be formed of the infinite variety possible in timbre, when it is remembered that the slightest
difference in the manner of causing the string to vibrate, or
in the exact point where the impact is made, is enough to
cause or to prevent the formation of this or that partial tone.

For example, a string made to vibrate near its middle
point can have neither its second harmonic, the octave, nor
any harmonic of the even numbers, because these all
require a node at the middle point of the string; and a
vibrating segment has been produced there. In the same
way, by exciting the string at a point one-third or two-thirds
of its length, the third, sixth, and ninth overtones are sup-
pressed, which leaves an evident preponderance to the
others. Evidently it favours the production of harmonics
to excite the string near *one of its fixed extremities.* The
material of the hammer which strikes and the rapidity of its
stroke, the tension of the bow and the manner in which it
was resined, the smoothness or roughness of the finger
which plucks the cord, are all causes which modify the
form of the vibration. Besides this, it is a fact that
the higher overtones are more readily produced where the
string is long and fine. Thus we have enumerated the
principal conditions which produce variations in the quality of tones, their timbre, in all cases where the sounds are
produced from strings.

Now a sound fails to produce an agreeable impression,
regarded musically, unless it has a suitable timbre, colour,
and character resulting from the presence of some of its
harmonics. A theoretically *pure* tone would be insipid,
lacking in timbre.

What is called a *rich, warm* sound, whether of a voice
or instrument, is one which is accompanied, naturally, by
a certain number of overtones which we do not distinctly

perceive, but from which the tone receives its characteristic colour.

Strings, however, are not the only sources of sound at the command of the musician; and we have yet to examine two other modes of producing it, namely, by pipes, and by plates or membranes.

The selection of strings for consideration first was not made at random, for only strings admit of visible and tangible experiment. Having obtained some knowledge as to the production of the sound in their case, we can more readily understand the manner in which it is formed in pipes.

Here, also, vibrations are isochronous; they vary in rapidity according to the length of the pipe; they are subdivided, as in the case of strings, producing harmonics. Here, also, are nodes and vibrating segments; here pitch, loudness, and timbre, depend upon the rapidity, amplitude, and form of the vibrations. The resemblance, therefore, is very close between the phenomena with which we have just been occupied and those which we are now to examine; but the laws are not absolutely the same in the two cases.

And first, we have to notice that the sonorous body, which, in the former case, was the string, palpable and visible, is now something invisible and intangible, namely, the air, — the column of air, contained inside the pipe, whose metal, wood, or other material has no office whatever, except that of determining the form and dimensions of this mass of air imprisoned within it, which is itself, and itself alone, the vibrating body.

The recognition of this fact is of the highest importance in understanding the subject; it has been but recently demonstrated, and many musicians, even among those who play on wind-instruments, have great difficulty in accepting it. But it is certain that four pipes, — one of boxwood, one of ebony, a third of brass, a fourth of porcelain or of any material whatsoever, if they have exactly the same length, diameter, degree of interior polish and of resistance, and in every respect, are *exactly alike,* will produce sounds which have no difference whatever, in pitch, loudness, or timbre. The *material* of the pipe has no influence upon the vibrations; its *dimensions* are everything, for the pipe itself has no share in the production of the sound.

Two famous instrument-makers, Sax at Paris and Mahillon at Brussels, for the purpose of demonstrating this fact, have constructed, the one *brass* clarinets, the other a trumpet of *wood*. But not even this has been enough to eradicate the false ideas entertained upon this point by many musicians. More recently, a well-known scientist and a designer, Reghizzo and Columbo, working together at Milan, have built an organ whose pipes are made of pasteboard. I myself possess several Alpine horns, which are made of rolled birch-bark, and a kind of shepherd's horn, of Finnish origin, which is of wood and sounds exactly like a trumpet or some other of the brass wind-instruments. An even stronger proof is this, that in certain organ-stops, for motives of economy, it is usual to make the lower pipes of wood, while the middle and higher pipes of the same register are of metal, without producing any appreciable difference in timbre.

We must, therefore, accustom ourselves to the idea that in wind-instruments *the only sonorous body is the air which they contain*.

A pipe may be open at one end only, or, at both ends, and the column of air within it behaves differently in the two cases. We shall accordingly examine them separately.

We will begin with tubes open at the ends, as being the simpler form. Tubes of this kind are called *open pipes*.

Here, by an inversion of what we have observed in the case of a string, the single vibration,—that which produces the fundamental tone,—has a node midway in the tube, and a vibrating segment at each end. A little reflection shows the natural reason of this. What is it that causes sound vibrations in the pipe? A light, regular breath directed across one end, as when one whistles with a key; this breath, striking against the sides of the tube causes the flutter of air from which the vibrations begin; naturally they would be most vigorous at the place where the breathing produces them, that is to say, at the extremity of the tube. This gives the middle of a vibrating segment, the point of strongest vibration, and the node, forming spontaneously in the middle of the pipe, divides the vibrating column of air into two half-segments whose sum is equal to the one vibrating segment of the string, emitting its fundamental tone (Fig. 14). The string is set in vibration in the middle to produce its fundamental, but the pipe, at one end; hence the difference in form of the vibrations, to which is due, as we know, the difference in quality of sound.

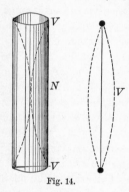

Fig. 14.

This is no mere hypothesis, but a fact, susceptible of demonstration. Take a glass tube, or an organ-pipe of which one side is glass, and let down into it by a string a thin membrane stretched over a hoop, and covered with a thin layer of sand. Set in vibration the air within the pipe; if the hoop hangs just at the middle of the pipe the sand will remain undisturbed, showing a node at this point; if you now let the hoop down to the lower end of the pipe or draw it up to the top, you will see the sand set in violent motion, proving the presence of energetic vibrations in certain parts of the column of air and repose in another part, as was shown in the case of strings by the little riders on the monochord.

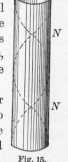

Fig. 15.

By blowing a little harder, the column of air can be divided further, so that there will be two nodes, a ventral segment between them, and the two half-segments at the ends (Fig. 15), and this will produce the second harmonic.

Blowing harder still the whole series of overtones can be obtained, the vibrating mass of air dividing still further, and the rapidity of vibrations proportionally increasing.

The longer the pipe, the deeper is its tone; doubling its length you have a note an octave lower; which proves that here, as in the case of strings, the number of vibrations *is inversely proportional to the length of the vibrating body.*

To examine *stopped pipes* (those of which one end is closed) we may take the open pipe just now used and close it with a cork at one end. Pushing the cork no further than the middle of the tube, we have now, with a difference

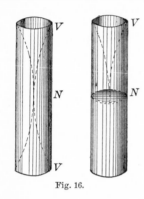

Fig. 16.

in the quality of the sound, the *same note* that we had from the pipe open at both ends. From this we can infer the behaviour of the air; at the point where the impulse was given, that is to say, at the open end, there is the point of strongest vibration, and the closed extremity corresponds to a node, the same which before was half-way in the open pipe (Fig. 16). The stopped pipe behaves like the half of an open pipe.

The experiment shows that at the bottom of the tube is always a nodal point, and its top, the centre of a ventral segment. Hence, if we blow more strongly, in order to cause the stopped pipe to produce harmonics, the simplest form of division for the column of air is that represented in Fig. 17. Here are three vibrating half-segments, and the sound produced is the third harmonic.

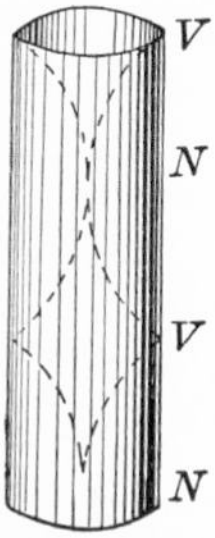

Fig. 17.

Forcing the breath still more, there being always a node at one end of the pipe and a vibrating segment at the other, the column of air must divide as shown

Fig. 18.

in Fig. 18, with three nodes, four ventral points, and five

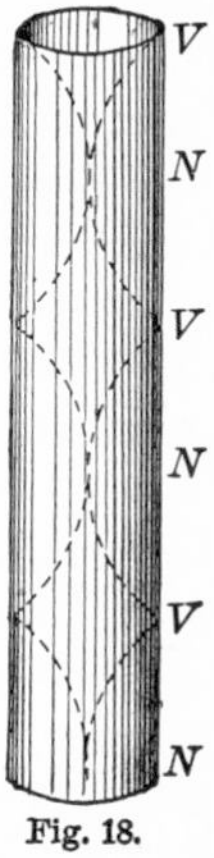

vibrating half-segments. The sound produced will be the fifth harmonic.

It is evident, therefore, that a stopped pipe cannot produce the second harmonic, or the fourth, or indeed any of the harmonics of the equal numbers, which require the presence of a node midway in the column of air.

While, therefore, an open pipe can produce all the partial sounds in the natural order of their succession, the stopped pipe gives only those of the unequal numbers.[1]

1　　2　　3　　4　　5　　6　　7　　8　　9　　10

Harmonics of an open pipe 1.314 metres in length, giving 128 vibrations for its fundamental tone.

1 .　　3　　5　　7　　9

Harmonics of a closed pipe 0.657 in length, giving the same number of vibrations.

In the preceding figures representing pipes complete accuracy has been sacrificed to clearness, and we should be possessed of an erroneous idea if we did not examine more in detail the condition of the air inside the sonorous tube. It does not vibrate transversely, like strings,—as our illustrations seem to indicate,—but longitudinally. The vibrations here consist in consecutive pulsations, whence result alternate condensations and rarefactions of each portion of the mass of air. The first molecules of air set in motion fall upon those adjacent, to which they communicate their motion, with slightly lessened force; the next act in the same way upon their neighbours, and so on, the longitudinal oscillation diminishing constantly in amplitude as far as the nodal point, where we may regard it as *nil*. But here, where there is no motion, the density is greatest, the air being strongly compressed, and this compression becomes, in its turn, by reason of the elasticity of the air,

---

[1] This is the principle of construction of the clarinet, one of the finest instruments of the orchestra.

the cause of a like pulsation impressed upon the contiguous portion of air.

If the air contained in pipes could be seen, if it were coloured, this is the aspect it would present in open and in closed tubes, of the same dimensions, producing their fundamental tone, as each pulsation began (Fig. 19).

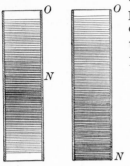

Fig. 19.

Open pipe.   Stopped pipe.

The distance between the orifice O and the node N being twice as great in the stopped as in the open pipe, it produces but half as many vibrations as the other, and its tone is an octave lower.

In the same way we can imagine the condition of the air as each harmonic is produced, bearing in mind that where the harmonic requires a node, the air is compressed between the vibrating portions which act upon it from each side, and in each ventral segment, the air, which moves to and fro, creating the vibration and determining its period, is extremely dilated.

In Fig. 20, we see the same pipes producing their third harmonic.

And here again we see that the stopped pipe behaves like a half of an open pipe. It must do this; hence, it produces only half the possible number of harmonics, and, if we call the fundamental tone the first, there will be the third, fifth, and so on.

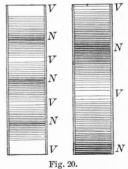

Fig. 20.

Open pipe.   Stopped pipe.

These facts can be verified experimentally by making a minute orifice in the side of a tube, exactly at a ventral point; whether it be an open or a closed tube, the sound will leap at once to that one of its harmonics corresponding to the division thus set up.

Thus, in an open tube, if the minute hole[1] be pierced in the centre, this aperture, establishing communication between the central point and the external air, will render impossible, at this point, the compression of air which forms the node; this node being indispensable for the formation of the fundamental sound and of the harmonics numbered three, five, etc., this pipe remains capable of producing only the second, fourth, sixth, etc.

Likewise, in a stopped tube, if the puncture be made at a point one-third, one-fifth, or one-seventh of the whole length, the third, fifth, or seventh harmonic can be produced, but not the fundamental tone, which requires the column of air undivided.

We have now to consider the different methods by which tubes can be made to produce vibrations.

The vibration of strings may be produced by plucking, by bowing, or by striking with a hammer. The vibration of the air in tubes is produced in two ways: by the brushing of a current of air over an orifice, or by the play of a reed. Without this brushing of the current of air, there would be nothing to cause vibration. In the case of strings, instead of a bow, use an ivory bâton, polished, scraped, absolutely smooth; you may draw it back and forth indefinitely without the slightest sound resulting. But the horse-hair bow, rough to begin with, is further roughened with resin; it thus grips the string and induces vibration. Similarly, a current of air passing evenly over the mouth of a pipe, meeting no obstacle, will incite no vibration in the column of air within it; it is necessary that the current be vibrating, so that the pipe may choose from this vibration impulses corresponding to one of its own vibration-periods.

The reed is a little supple tongue of wood or metal, fitted to the opening of a pipe, so that no air can penetrate into the pipe without disturbing its equilibrium, and producing vibrations more or less rapid, according to its length,

[1] This hole must be very minute, or it will merely have the effect of shortening the tube, and giving it a higher fundamental tone.

width, and thickness.　Of itself, it emits only a dull, almost imperceptible sound; it is not the sonorous body, but only a contrivance for setting in vibration the sonorous body, which is the column of air contained in the pipe.　We have to distinguish between the *striking reed,* which entirely closes the wind-passage, and beats against the sides of it at each pulsation, adding to the musical tone a disagreeable noise; and the *free reed* which has been described above, and is represented (Fig. 21), in section and in perspective.

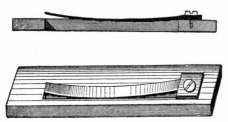

Fig. 21.

A common straw, six or eight inches long, with a little tongue cut in it about an inch distant from a node (Fig. 22), will emit[1] a musical sound, and may be regarded as the

Fig. 22.

simplest and most rudimentary type of the free reed.　The human larynx is the perfect model for this type, the voice being nothing else than a marvellous reed instrument, whose perfections no maker has ever attained.

[1 "The most simple example of this is the common whistle. A thin, flat current of air is caused to impinge on a sharp knife-edge, which cuts it in two, the effect being to set up a sort of fluttering, or beating action, and so to put the air in regular vibration, producing a musical note. In most cases this apparatus forms the foot of a pipe, and the sharp cutting edge is so placed that part of the air enters the tube, setting the whole column it contains into vibration, and so producing a powerful tone." Pole's *Philosophy of Music.* London, 1879.

" According to a more recent theory advocated especially by M. Cavaillé-Coll, Herr Schneebeli, and Mr. Hermann Smith, the vibrations excited in the aerial column are produced by the sheet or blade of air issuing from the slit acting as a reed. Cavaillé-Coll styles this air-blade a free aerial reed (*anche libre aerienne*); Herr Schneebeli calls it a *Luftlamelle,* an aerial lamina ; while Mr. Smith denominates it an 'aëro-plastic reed,' or simply an 'air-reed.' Novel as it may

Lastly, it should be noted that in the brass wind-instruments the player's lips act as a double reed, their pressure against the cap of the mouthpiece modifying their tension, which in its turn, determines the mode of subdivision of the column of air.

In oboes and bassoons the air penetrates the tube by passing between two reeds which strike against each other, and are pressed by the player's lips.

Later on we shall recur to these various applications of the reed principle.

Membranes, or pieces of parchment stretched in a circular form, emit sounds which are higher in proportion as their tension is greater, and their size smaller. I do not think that the exact laws of their vibrations have ever been discovered, nor would they concern us greatly, for the tones of instruments thus made are always confused and indistinct, and rather approaching the quality of noise than of music. We ought to make an exception, however, in favour of kettle-drums, which can really be tuned by means of numerous screws placed around their rims.

The only peculiarity of these instruments which we must here note (because later on we shall make use of it), is that a membrane is capable of producing, simultaneously or successively, many different sounds, more or less true or false, and often of great volume.

Something like this is also the case with *metallic plates*, although the sounds they produce are generally more distinct; their fundamental tone is generally accompanied by harmonics, which are very high and are discordant with

appear, this view seems to have a solid foundation in fact, and the many and ingenious experiments made in support of the theory, are apparently inexplicable on any other assumption. According to Mr. Smith, the air-reed on issuing from the slit does not strike the edge of the lip, as the old theory maintains, but passes very near its outer surface. Like a metal reed, whose action we shall study presently, the air-reed oscillates backwards and forwards, and generates in the air-column within the pipe the alternate condensations and rarefactions which are essential to the production of a musical note. Judging by the experiments appealed to in corroboration of it, — time forbids our discussing them here, — it would appear that the new theory is virtually established, and on a basis that is unassailable. As a working hypothesis, I think we are justified in regarding it as the more probable of the two theories which now generally prevail." Zahm's *Sound and Music*. Chicago, 1892. Tr.]

each other, from which results a special timbre which the listener may, or may not, enjoy.   In general terms we may say that the vibrations of such plates are *in direct ratio to their thickness*, and in *inverse ratio to their surface*.

The vibrations of *metallic rods* or *blades* are more interesting, for they, in many cases, emit perfectly defined musical sounds.

Whether struck by a hammer or set in vibration by the use of a bow, a rod varies its pitch *in inverse ratio to the square of its length*: thus, supposing that the C of 517 vibrations is produced by a rod eighteen centimetres in length, another rod of the same metal, the same thickness, but of only half the length, that is to say, nine centimetres, will give, not the octave above — which would be the case if rods obeyed the laws which govern strings — but a tone two octaves higher, the C of 2069 vibrations.

Of course the thickness of a rod must have its effect: in this case we may consider the number of vibrations to be *in direct ratio to the thickness of the vibrating body*.

The most important use of the principle of vibrating rods is in the tuning-fork, an instrument of but one note, practically invariable, which is employed to tune together the different instruments of an orchestra.

Theoretically, the tuning-fork is a steel rod, fixed in the middle, where, consequently, the nodal point is formed, and free at both ends.   Its simplest mode of vibration (Fig. 23)

Fig. 23.

represents a node in the middle, a half ventral segment at each end, its fundamental tone being produced by the two vibrating half-segments.   (The analogy between the rod and the open pipe is remarkable.)   Fig. 24 will make it clear how this rod can be bent and brought into its usual prong shape without affecting its system of vibrations.

A tuning-fork will write out its own history of vibrations; we need only attach to one of the prongs the

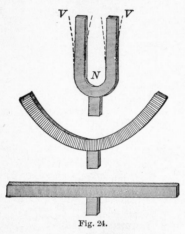

Fig. 24.

point of a needle or steel pen, fixing it with a drop of wax; then having set the tuning-fork in vibration, draw this metal point gently over a piece of smoked glass. The line that it traces will not be straight but wavy; it is in fact a written record of the sound vibrations (Fig. 25).

By reason of the laws which govern vibrating rods, the larger and coarser a tuning-fork, the deeper its note; hence, to raise its pitch, we have only to file down its prongs in length, and to lower it, reduce them in thickness.

For physical experiments, tuning-forks are made of all

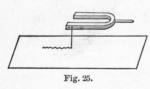

Fig. 25.

sizes and every variety of pitch. But the standard of pitch for orchestras and instrument makers is far from being the same in all countries; in France since 1859 the A of 435

vibrations has been officially adopted as the standard (*diapason normal*), and all the calculations in this book have been made according to it.

All musical instruments obey the laws which we have now investigated, and the following classification will show to which law each instrument is subject:

Strings played with a bow . . . {
Violin.
Viola.
Violoncello.
Double-bass.
}

Strings plucked by the hand . . { Harp. / Guitar. / Mandolin.

Strings struck by a hammer . . { Pianoforte. / Dulcimer.

Open pipes . . . . { Flageolet. / Flute. / Piccolo.

Stopped pipes . . . . { Pan-pipes / (often also with open pipes)

Open reed-pipes . . . . . . Saxophone.

Closed reed pipes . . . . . { Clarinet. / Basset horn or alto clarinet. / Bass clarinet.

Open pipes with double reed . . { *Human voice.* / Oboe. / English horn. / Bassoon. / Double bassoon. / Sarrusophone.

Opens pipes with mouthpiece (lips serving as reeds) . { Horn. / Trumpet. / Trombone. / Tuba. / Ophicleide. / Clarion. / Cornet. / Bugle.

The organ has all varieties of pipes, open and stopped, with and without reeds.

Rods or blades . . . . { Tuning-fork. / Carillon, Glockenspiel. / Harmonica. / Xylophone. / Music-box. / Triangle.

Plates . . . . { Cymbals. / Castanets. / Tam-tam or gong. / Bells.

Membranes . . . . { Kettle-drums. / Tambourine. / Side drum. / Bass drum.

To whatever category it belongs, each one of these instruments occupies a certain place in the general musical scale. Below is given a complete table of the vibration numbers for all the C's in the musical scale; also that for all the notes in the middle octave, the one containing the Λ of the tuning-fork. These figures being known, it is easy to obtain, by multiplication or division, the number of vibrations in any note; these are the row of figures placed between the two staves. Above are given, in feet, according to the usage of organ manufacturers, the length of the open pipe corresponding to each C. The small figures placed below each C are those by which physicists are accustomed to designate the octaves.

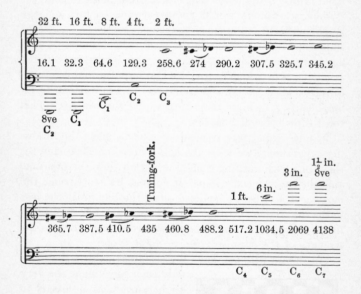

By the use of this table, readers wishing to study special works belonging to the different technical schools, will be able to grasp the relative pitch, notwithstanding the different nomenclatures adopted by physicists, musicians, and instrument-makers.

B.—Transmission of Sound by the Atmosphere.

Around the point where sound is produced by one or other of the processes we have just described, the molecules of air are displaced, and are forced to move to and fro, in a manner exactly similar to the movements of the vibrating body itself; in these movements they strike against contiguous molecules, obliging them also to vibrate, and in their turn to transmit the impulse; and so on. Thus sound is propagated, and not in the air only, but in gaseous, liquid, or solid mediums, which are all, like air, composed of molecules.

It is very important to understand that it is not the air itself which is disturbed and moved from point to point; if it were so, sounds would cause currents of air, and the neighbourhood of a musical instrument might be dangerous to persons liable to colds in the head. Each molecule does no more than reproduce exactly the movement of the vibrating body which caused the first impulse, and it returns to repose after having communicated this movement to its neighbours, which, in their turn repeat the process. This constitutes molecular motion.

To understand this transmission let us make the following experiment: we will take half a dozen checkers and set them in a row touching each other; draw back the first one, and then very gently impel it against its neighbour; the movement will be transmitted along the line until the last in the row, having no other beyond upon which to expend its force, will go off a few inches more or less according to the strength of the impulse given to the first one.

The others will not have stirred appreciably; they will

Fig. 26.

only each have made the very slight movement necessary to pass on the impulse. The experiment is still better, made with billiard balls, but either gives us a very correct idea of the action of molecules.

We may remark in passing that light and heat vibrations to which reference was made in the beginning of this work, are transmitted in the same way, with this difference, that the latter are *atomic* vibratory phenomena, while sound vibrations are *molecular ;* atoms are the final constituent elements of matter, molecules are agglomerations of atoms; and it is evident that vibrations which are numbered by trillions must affect portions of matter incomparably more minute than those which give musical vibrations.

Sound waves, corresponding to the vibrations which caused them are, like the vibrations themselves, composed of alternate compressions and expansions of air. When the first molecule strikes the second, there is a compression ; when it returns to its point of repose, while the second goes towards the third, the first and second part, and expansion results, while at the same time a new compression is produced between the second and the third; and so on. These pulsations therefore propagate the sound through the air *without the air itself being displaced ;* and as each process is but the imitation *ad infinitum* of the original oscillation of the vibrating body, its pitch and timbre are carried in all directions. But of course all these transmissions cannot be made without molecular friction, gradually reducing the amplitude of the vibrations until they become imperceptible and finally extinct, the volume of sound becoming correspondingly diminished and finally disappearing.

We shall shortly see the laws, which are very simple, by which this decrease of sound takes place, but first we shall find a new comparison — opportune, nay almost indispensable.

When a stone is thrown into the water, there forms at once around the spot where the stone falls, a sort of liquid ridge, constituting the first wave; to this soon succeeds a second, wider, but strictly concentric ; then a third, then a multitude of others, forming a vast halo around the central point. All these rings are *circular waves.* If, instead of one stone, two or more are thrown in, some distance apart, their waves will be seen to meet, to cross, to pass over each other, but never to blend; a steamboat passes, producing furrows or undulations of a different kind; there is a rainfall on the water, each drop disturbing the surface of the water—still the eye can follow out these various crossing and recrossing undulatory movements, each pursuing its regular course without interfering or being confounded with any other. Reaching the shore they are thrown back, as rays of light are reflected from a mirror, and resume, though enfeebled by the shock, their now reversed course undisturbed by newly formed circles on their way towards the shore.

In mechanics, this is called the superposition of petty movements. When two or more systems of waves meet each other, the pulsations add themselves algebraically; but the alternating series of condensations and rarefactions is transmitted faithfully from molecule to molecule, until the original force is entirely exhausted.

Thus instruction can be gained by throwing stones into the water; thus, also, we can imagine the atmosphere of a concert hall, furrowed in every direction by regular waves which meet and intersect each other in all possible ways, without any one of them losing, from all these contacts, its own individuality.

But there is this difference, that the sound waves give rise to combinations much more complicated than the superficial liquid waves of which we have just spoken. The shock caused by a body falling into the water manifests itself to the eye only where the air and water meet, and the undulations to which it gives rise all move in the same horizontal plane; for this reason we have called them *circular waves*. But sound waves produced in the midst of the atmosphere extend symmetrically in every direction, upwards and downwards no less than to right and left, entirely surrounding the sonorous body from which they emanate; that is to say, they are spherical. The loss of force is, therefore, in direct ratio to the square of the distance which separates the hearer from the first cause of the sound; or, to put it in other terms, the loudness of a sound decreases in proportion to the mass of air acted upon by its vibrations.

In the open air, in calm weather, a sound heard at a distance of two metres is of one-fourth the intensity it would be if one had the instrument at his ear; at three metres it is one-ninth; at four metres, one-sixteenth; and so on. (This is demonstrated mathematically; but, as a matter of fact, it is evident that some sounds carry much further than others, which must result from the presence of high overtones, rendering the timbre piercing.)

If, in any way, the lateral diffusion of the sound waves can be avoided, the range of the sound can be very greatly increased; the celebrated physicist, Biot, tells us that in speaking in an ordinary tone through a succession of empty water-pipes of the city of Paris, his voice could be heard at the distance of more than a kilometre. M. Regnault found that the sound waves extended further in large pipes than in small ones, showing that part of the force was wasted on the sides of the pipe.

Using a gramme of powder, a pistol-shot can be heard at 1159 metres in a pipe whose diameter is 0.108 metres; in a pipe of 0.300, its sound reaches a listener at the distance of 3810 metres; and if the pipe be 1.100 metres in diameter, the same sound can be heard 9540 metres. On this principle speaking-tubes are constructed.

But there are other ways of giving direction to sound waves. Rays of sound, like rays of light, have the property of being reflected and refracted; the wall behind an orchestra and the arch of the ceiling above it are really mirrors for sound, which is reflected from a polished surface exactly as light is, and like light, has an angle of reflection equal to the angle of incidence.

The feeblest sound of a tuning-fork, or even the ticking of a watch, placed at one focus of an elliptic reflector, converges towards the other focus, where it is distinctly heard. Instead of the elliptic reflector, use one of parabolic form, and all the rays will be sent back in parallel lines following the axis of the parabola. A sound also may

receive many successive reflections from walls suitably constructed, acting upon it as a series of mirrors acts upon
rays of light. To this property is due the production of
echoes, of which we shall speak later, and also the rolling
of thunder, or at least in great part; in this latter case the
clouds furnish reflecting surfaces.

Sound can, likewise, be *refracted,* in traversing media of
unequal density, and although this property has never as
yet received any artistic application, it may be easily
demonstrated, as follows: at a few inches' distance from a
tuning-fork in a state of vibration, suspend a balloon of

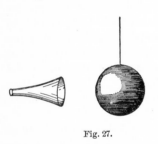

Fig. 27.

gold-beater's skin, filled
with carbonic acid gas,
which is denser than the
air; then, holding a funnel
at your ear, as an ear-
trumpet, move away grad-
ually to a distance of four
or five feet, keeping the
balloon between your ear
and the tuning-fork (Fig.
27). You will soon find the point at which the sound of
the tuning-fork reaches its maximum of intensity. Then,
if a watch be substituted for the tuning-fork, you will hear
its ticking as plainly as if it were close to your ear, and
you will recognise the fact that the balloon has made
the rays of sound converge just as a lens collects rays of
light.

This effect is due to the differences in elasticity and
density between carbonic acid gas and atmospheric air.
The refraction of the rays is due to the lessened speed of
their motion through the denser medium contained in the
balloon.

The greater the elasticity as compared with the density,
the greater is the speed of transmission. In iron, this
rapidity is of about 5127 metres; in lead, 1228; in fibres of
acacia, 4714; in those of the pine, 3322; in sea water, 1453;
in fresh water, 1436; in rectified alcohol, 1453; in hydro-

gen, 1269; in carbonic acid, 261. (At the sea-shore, in calm weather, a bather who is near a pier, can hear three times any violent noise on shore, like the firing of a gun: once by leaning his head against the side of the pier, a second time by putting his head under water, and a third time through the air.)

The figures given above are only approximate, and vary quite perceptibly according to the temperature. In the atmosphere, with which alone we are at present concerned,[1] the exact rapidity of sound motion is 332.8 metres a second when the centigrade thermometer marks zero[2] [32° Fahr.] and it increases at the rate of about 60 centimetres to each degree centigrade of heat. It would seem there is here a contradiction, for as the temperature rises the air expands, and the speed should diminish, whereas it increases; this, however, is because the rarefaction is accompanied by a large increase in elasticity, the importance of which must not be overlooked in considering the transmission of vibrations. Experimentally and mathematically, the following law has been established: the rapidity of sound in its passage through the air is *directly* proportional to the square root of the elasticity, and *inversely* proportional to the square root of the density: an entire absence of density would involve the suppression of all elasticity, that is to say, sound cannot be propagated in a vacuum. One of the simplest experiments in physics is that of a bell, moved by clockwork, vibrating *silently* in an exhausted receiver; the air being removed, there are no molecules to transmit vibrations.

Each tone has its own number of vibrations per second; but all tones are transmitted by the air with an equal rapidity, of 340 metres in a temperature of 15° C [58 1-2° Fahr.] The distance through which the sound passes during *one* vibration of the sonorous body is called a *wave-length*.

---

1 The transmission of sound through solid walls should always be considered in the construction of buildings destined for music, like opera-houses, and concert-halls.

2 For Paris this is exact at a barometrical pressure of 760 millimetres.

If there were but one vibration to a second, the wave-length would be 340 metres; with two vibrations, it is 170 metres; the standard tuning-fork of 435 vibrations gives a wave-length of $\frac{340}{435} = 0.780$; which means that the wave has gone a distance of 78 centimetres when the prongs of the tuning-fork have made one vibration.

The wave-length varies necessarily with the speed of transmission through different media.

When the tone is produced by the column of air contained in a pipe, it is easy to understand how all the surrounding air can be set in vibration by the quite large bulk of the sonorous body. But it is not the same with strings; the very small surface of a string can displace but very few of the adjacent molecules, and communicates to them oscillations that are very feeble and musically insufficient. Here art utilises a phenomenon of the highest interest, which is called *resonance*.

Certain substances, notably wood, enter into vibration with extreme facility; of it are made boxes and tables, over which strings are strained; by the points of attachment, and especially by means of the bridge, vibrations are transmitted to the table, which, with its large surface, communicates them forcibly to the surrounding air.

Resonance is manifested not only when the sonorous body is directly in contact with the reinforcing organ, but in a multitude of other cases, of which a few will suggest the rest. A 'cello or a guitar hanging on the wall of a room, will vibrate strongly, without being touched, if a voice of fine quality emits, at some little distance from it, a tone corresponding to one of its strings, or, even, having merely an affinity with it through the overtones. Open the lid of a piano, press the pedal that raises the dampers, and leaning over the strings vocalise with energy the chord

or some other; you will at once hear those strings whose period of vibration is identical with that of the notes you have sung reproduce the same chord.

Take two tuning-forks that are in unison, and both mounted
on sounding-boards; cause one of the two to vibrate by
drawing a bow across it, and its mate, even at some distance, will vibrate untouched. The air will have transmitted its vibration to the mass of air contained in the
sounding-board of the second tuning-fork, and this air will
have vibrated forcibly enough to move the heavy bent bar
of steel. Take one of the tuning-forks off from its board,
and, striking it with a hard body, set it in vibration: holding it in the hand, you can scarcely hear its sound; bring
it near any vase or pipe, thirty-nine centimetres in height,
and the sound will be considerably reinforced, because a
pipe of that length is exactly in unison with an A of 435
vibrations.[1] In this case it is the column of air which is
set in motion by the vibrations of the prongs of the tuning-
fork. With two pianos standing side by side, press the
pedal of one, and play a scale on the other; you will have
a horrible jumble of sound. I once had a small petroleum
lamp which would never allow me to play on the piano the
march in *Tannhäuser.* As soon as I reached the chord
B, D♯, F♯, in the trumpet-call, at the beginning,

 it went out,

as if by magic. It is evident that this chord corre-
sponded to the modes of division in the glass chimney, and
threw the air contained in it into such a flutter that the
flame was blown out. I was obliged to submit to this;
and when I wished to play the march, I had to use another
lamp. Every person must have noticed that certain bodies
which are not musical instruments, notably candle stick
sconces and the pendants of chandeliers, will vibrate un-
seasonably under the influence of certain notes, while other
notes will not disturb them at all. All these manifestations
are referable to one and the same cause, *sympathetic vibration.* Small and feeble as are the air-waves, they are able,
acting together, and by reason of their perfect regularity, to

1 This tube could be made of pasteboard, or even of strong paper.

set in motion bodies relatively heavy, on this condition, the only, but also the indispensable one,— that these bodies can mate with them, that is to say, conform to their period of vibration. Such is the phenomenon of resonance.

An inexperienced person, endeavouring to ring the great bell of a church, will probably expend much unnecessary strength; while a little choir-boy, wise from experience, instinctively pulls the rope down with a kind of cadence, according to a regular rhythm, waiting patiently until these feeble oscillations add themselves together and set the great mass in motion. It is thus that the alternate condensations and rarefactions of the sound-waves succeed, with their persistent isochronism, in compelling bodies often very massive to submit to their influence.

We will now return to the monochord, and this time will give it two strings, tuned in unison, which will afford us opportunity, by several pleasing experiments, for further study of this interesting phenomenon of sympathetic vibrations. We will arrange, as before, three white riders at the points twenty-five, fifty, and seventy-five centimetres, and four others of some coloured paper in the intervening spaces, upon one only of the two strings, *which, then, we shall not touch again.* Now pluck the *other* string, at one of the points, 12.5, 37.5, 62.5, or 87.5, while touching it at twenty-five or at seventy-five, so that it shall produce the fourth harmonic; whereupon the coloured riders *on the first string* are thrown off. Touch the string at fifty, pluck it at twenty-five, or at seventy-five, and the first string will lose its remaining riders with the exception of the middle one. Finally draw the bow over the second string at its middle point, and this last one will finally be unseated.

Remembering the theory of the vibrating segments, the nodes and loops, we find that the second string imposed upon its neighbour not merely the obligation to vibrate, but to vibrate precisely like itself, even adopting the same mode of subdivision.

Replacing the riders on the first string, we will lower by

a little, a semi-tone merely, the pitch of the second string;
the first will now be undisturbed, the two strings being no
longer in unison. If we now lower the pitch of the
second string until it is a perfect fifth below the first, and
cause it to emit its sixth overtone, by touching it at one of
its sixths (16.5, for example), the coloured riders of the
first string will be much agitated, for the sixth harmonic
of the second string will now be in unison with the fourth
harmonic of the first:

These experiments can be varied indefinitely, and the
phenomenon that they exhibit is of capital importance in
the study of musical acoustics, as will be shown a few
pages further on.

Membranes, which, as has already been said, vibrate
without emitting a perfectly definite note, have, for this
very reason, the property of entering into sympathetic
vibrations under the influence of an infinity of different
sounds, while fine sand spread upon their surface reveals its
slightest movement. For this reason they were the object
of profound study on the part of the celebrated Helmholtz.
For analysis of sound, however, specially of timbre, nothing
equals, in precision and in
simplicity, the resonators invented by this eminent scientist. They are hollow spheres
of glass or of brass, their
dimension being so calculated
as to furnish a given sound.
They have two orifices, the
larger intended to communicate

Fig. 28.

with the surrounding air, the smaller, funnel-shaped, to be
introduced into the ear (Fig. 28).

The air within the sphere vibrates through sympathy whenever the sound proper to the resonator is part of the compound sound whose analysis is desired. It thus produces to the ear a sort of musical humming which is so strong as almost entirely to efface the fundamental tone by the predominance given to the particular overtone thus isolated and reinforced.

With a resonator having the pitch of 𝄞, this sound is clearly detected, even by quite an unpracticed ear, as the second overtone of 𝄞, as the third overtone of 𝄞, as the fourth overtone of 𝄞, and so on, perhaps even, with careful attention, as the tenth of 𝄢.

Resonators are a kind of isolators, which aid in fixing the attention upon some one of the constituent elements of a compound sound, and in disengaging this overtone from the sonorous mass which we are accustomed to consider as the simple sound.

With a series of these instruments we can verify, experimentally and indisputably, the theoretical statements which have been made in the preceding pages; namely, that open pipes possess all the harmonics, that stopped pipes have only the overtones of unequal number, that strings never emit sounds strictly simple; many other things, also, can be established, into the details of which I cannot enter here without exceeding the scope of a purely musical work.

C.—Perception of Sound.

Aided by the knowledge we possess as to the nature of sound, its constituent elements, its mode of propagation in elastic media, the properties of membranes and resonators, and sympathetic vibrations, we can now understand the mechanism of the act of hearing,— the mysterious action of the ear.

But first, it is necessary to examine the anatomical structure of that organ.

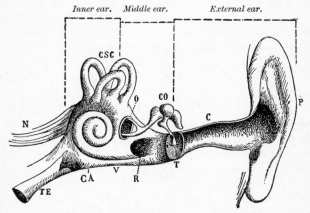

Fig. 29.— TRANSVERSE SECTION OF THE EAR.

External ear: P, pinna; C, auditory canal; T, tympanic membrane. *Middle ear:* T, tympanic membrane; CO, ossicula auditus; O, oval window; R, round window. *Inner ear:* V, vestibule; CA, Cochlea; CSC, semi-circular canals; N, acoustic nerve; TE, Eustachian tube.

The visible part, the external ear, is that of least importance: it consists of the auricle which acts as an ear trumpet, and of the auditory tube, partly cartilaginous, partly bony, which ends at the tympanic membrane.

Behind this membrane is the middle ear, a cavity, which may be compared to a drum, having four openings; the largest of these is closed by the tympanic membrane, whose outer side is in communication, through the auditory channel, with the external air; in the bony wall of the opposite side is the "round window" and just above it the "oval window," both closed by very thin and very elastic membranes; the fourth opening, the only one which is not

entirely closed, is the Eustachian tube, a sort of conical
duct, connecting the middle ear with the
pharynx; this tube opens in the act of
swallowing. Inside this drum, a curious
series of little bones stretches across between the tympanic membrane and the
oval window (Fig. 30); these are four
in number, and are named in accordance
with their forms: the *malleus* (hammer),
which is attached by its handle to the
tympanic membrane; second, the *incus*
(anvil), connected by a joint with the
hammer; third, a little bone almost round, which is called
the *os orbiculare;* and, lastly, the *stapes* (stirrup), the
bottom of which almost entirely covers the oval window,
only a narrow rim of the membrane being left uncovered.

Fig. 30.
OSSICULA AUDITUS.

S, stapes; O, os orbi-
culare; IN, incus;
M, malleus.

By the round and the oval windows the middle ear con-
nects with the inner ear. This is the marvellous *labyrinth,*
a cavity in the hardest part of the cranium, the *petrous bone,*
which is entirely filled with an aqueous liquid. The
labyrinth consists of the vestibule, in direct communication
with the oval window, the cochlea, a cartilaginous organ
shaped like a snail-shell, and three semi-circular canals.[1] In
the peculiar liquid which the cavity contains, floats a kind
of membranous sac, attached to the bony walls only by
blood vessels and by bundles of nervous fibres which traverse the liquid (Fig. 31).

Both in the vestibule and in the cochlea, the microscope
shows a multitude of little hairs or filaments, which are
nothing else than prolongations or ramifications of the extremities of the acoustic nerve or of its appendixes;
these minute organs bear the name of their discoverers:
those of the vestibule are the *bristles of Schultze;* those of the
cochlea are *Corti's fibres,* of which 3000 have been counted.

---

[1] These semi-circular canals, although making part of the ear, do not seem
to be solely useful in the act of hearing. They are the special organs of a sense
not as yet catalogued, the sense of *equilibrium,* of *verticality.* When one of these
is accidentally destroyed, the man or the animal can no longer stand or walk
straight, but staggers as if intoxicated.

Such, briefly (perhaps too briefly) described, is the instrument. We will now examine its action.[1]

A vibration reaches the external ear; it produces, in the auditory tube, a condensation, followed by a rarefaction.

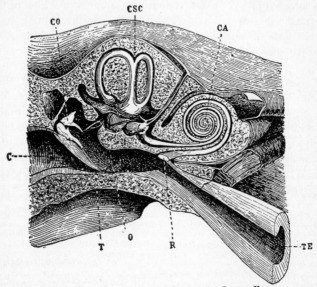

Fig. 31.—SECTION OF THE MIDDLE AND INNER EAR.

C, auditory canal (the pinna is omitted); T, tympanic membrane; CO, ossicular auditus; O, oval window; R, round window; CA, cochlea; CSC, semi-circular canals; TE, Eustachian tube.

The tympanic membrane is first driven in, then drawn outwards (we should here remember that membranes respond to vibrations of every kind); by the chain of little bones, the tremor traverses the middle ear and is communicated to the membrane of the oval window. The liquid of the inner ear vibrates, and stimulates the vibration of the fibres

1 [The following is a more minute description of the inner ear, from Tyndall's *Sound*, pages 369, 370.

" Behind the bony partition, and between it and the brain, we have the extraordinary organ called the *labyrinth*, filled with water, over the lining membrane of which are distributed the terminal fibres of the auditory nerve. When the tympanic membrane receives a shock, it is transmitted through the series of bones above referred to, being concentrated on the membrane against which the

that it surrounds; but only those respond whose period of vibration corresponds to the fundamental sound or to one of its overtones, for each fibre has its own pitch.

The bristles of Schultze and the fibres of Corti constitute a microscopic, yet giant, stringed instrument of which each string vibrates *sympathetically* with a certain sound, and transmits the sound-impression to the brain, by the acoustic nerve, of which it is the ramification.

Having thus broadly sketched the general scheme of the auditory apparatus, it is fitting to take up, more in detail, each one of its organs, were it only to make clear that each has its special function, that there is not one too many, and also to make clear the simplicity that there really is in all this apparent complexity.

What is the purpose of the Eustachian tube? At each

base of the stirrup bone is fixed. The membrane transfers the shock to the water of the labyrinth, which, in its turn, transfers it to the nerves.

"The transmission, however, is not direct. At a certain place within the labyrinth exceedingly fine elastic bristles, terminating in sharp points, grow up between the terminal nerve-fibres. These bristles, discovered by Max Schultze, are eminently calculated to sympathise with such vibrations of the water as correspond to their proper periods. Thrown thus into vibration, the bristles stir the nerve-fibres which lie between their roots. At another place in the labyrinth we have little crystalline particles called *otolithes* — the *Hörsteine* of the Germans — imbedded among the nervous filaments, which, when they vibrate, exert an intermittent pressure upon the adjacent nerve-fibres. The otolithes probably serve a different purpose from that of the bristles of Schultze. They are fitted by their weight to accept and prolong the vibrations of the water as corresponding, which might otherwise escape attention, while the bristles of Schultze, because of their extreme lightness, would instantly yield up an evanescent motion. They are, on the other hand, eminently fitted for the transmission of continuous vibrations.

"Finally, there is in the labyrinth, an organ, discovered by the Marchese Corti, which is to all appearance a musical instrument, with its chords so stretched as to accept vibrations of different periods and transmit them to the nerve filaments which traverse the organ. Within the ears of men, and without their knowledge or contrivance, this lute of three thousand strings (according to Kölliker, this is the number of fibres in Corti's organ) has existed for ages, accepting the music of the outer world, and rendering it fit for reception by the brain. Each musical tremor which falls upon this organ selects from the stretched fibres the one appropriate to its own pitch, and throws it into unisonant vibration. And thus, no matter how complicated the motion of the external air may be, these microscopic strings can analyse it and reveal the constituents of which it is composed. Surely, inability to feel the stupendous wonder of what is here revealed, would imply incompleteness of mind; and surely, those who practically ignore or fear them, must be ignorant of the ennobling influence which such discoveries may be made to exercise upon both the emotions and the understanding of man." TR.]

movement of swallowing, it opens, and in this way it enables the air contained in the middle ear to remain in equilibrium of pressure with the external air; without this perfect and constant equilibrium, the tympanic membrane would not be in good condition to receive vibrations. This is so true that when it happens by accident, as, for instance, in sneezing, that the air becomes compressed in the drum of the ear, the membrane is for the moment forced outwards, there is a buzzing sound and a temporary deafness, which disappears at the first natural swallowing.

The membrane of the oval window, situated between a liquid body and a gaseous body, is less easily set in vibration than the tympanic membrane; hence, the utility of the chain of little bones, which, stretched between the two membranes, delivers a blow upon the inner, the membrane of the oval window; it is noteworthy that the point of attachment of the hammer-bone upon the tympanic membrane is exactly at its centre, its point of greatest vibration. Perhaps, in the absence of these bones, the sound could be transmitted by the air contained in the drum of the ear, but it would certainly be much more feeble in comparison; for, by the chain of little bones, the tympanic membrane is in close connection with the membrane of the oval window.

We have now to consider the object of the round window. To understand this, we must consider that, in the act of hearing, the liquid of the inner ear, influenced by the vibrating air contained in the auditory tube, is constantly in a state of molecular condensation or rarefaction; if the wall surrounding it were inflexible at every point, there would be either a rupture of this wall or there would be an end to vibration, for without elasticity vibration cannot take place. In order, therefore, that the liquid mass may oscillate synchronously with the membrane which incites its vibration, it must have somewhere another elastic surface which will yield under pressure. This it has in the round window, placed between the middle and the inner ear.

The number of fibres constituting what has been called the sympathetic harp of the inner ear may seem incredibly great; but as many as 3000 have been counted under the microscope, and it is certain there are even more. But assume that this is the whole number. Helmholtz very acutely remarks, on this subject, that if we estimate at 200 the variety of *non-musical* sounds of which the pitch is only imperfectly defined, there remain 2800 fibres for the seven octaves of musical instruments, that is 400 to each octave, 33 1-2 to each semi-tone, which is enough to account for the perception by the ear of fractions of semi-tones, to the extent to which we know that this perception actually does take place.

In respect to the transmission of the sound-impression to the brain by the auditory nerve, we have no more cause to wonder than we have in an infinity of analogous physiological phenomena. The network of nerves in the human body has been often compared to a system of electric wires; and this comparison seems to be most appropriate.

In the wires circulates one and the same fluid, which we call electricity; it is the same fluid, whether the wires convey power or transmit language or carry light in every direction. This depends on the different apparatus employed. Likewise the nerves of the body, conductors of the nervous fluid, according to the different organs, carry to the brain — their central station — sensations of taste, smell, touch, sight, and hearing. But a wonder indeed is this,— although science explains it,— namely, the marvellous faculty of the human ear to decompose and analyse with entire precision the extremely complicated movements of vibrating air, having to work upon so very small a portion of air as that which comes in contact with the drum of the ear. It is, however, in this way that the phenomena of hearing are produced.

D.— Relations of Successive Sounds. Tonality.

It being admitted that the ear perceives clearly sounds varying in rapidity from 16 to 4224 vibrations to the second, we must now recognise the fact that *the number of the sounds really produced between these two limits* cannot be expressed by any figure. The finer the ear, the better constituted, the more experienced, the better able it will be to divide and subdivide this range, to grasp and to take account of the very slightest differences; accordingly the estimate of the degree of sensibility of the auditory nerve for differences of pitch varies extraordinarily with different authors.

In the noise made by the wind in a chimney on a windy day, or, as it blows through the reeds, the sound rises and falls, changing incessantly from one pitch to another; now in this infinite variety of pitch, no degree can possibly fix the attention and become a point of comparison. No ear is capable of perceiving in such a succession of sounds, changing every instant, a precise degree of pitch. This is the " raw material " of music.

While poetry finds its material ready made in the words of a language, and painting in the hues of nature, and sculpture and architecture in animal and vegetable forms, music, in every civilisation, has been obliged to create its own alphabet, by choosing out of the infinity of sounds a certain number, fixed and definite, to serve as starting points for its combinations of more or less scientific or artistic merit. It is, therefore, perfectly natural that— according to the epochs, the degrees of civilisation of different peoples, their tastes, barbaric or refined, the climates and the temperatures in which they live — a great number of different scales should have been established, and should continue to this day. This subject will be treated in a later chapter on the history of music, and I shall speak of it by anticipation only so far as to say that there is one singular fact, invariable in all countries where there is a germ of music however rudimentary, namely, the presence *in every scale* of the *octave*, the *fifth*, and the *fourth*.

The reason is easily found and is conclusive, being derived from the simplest laws of acoustics.

Excluding from the consideration timbre, with which we

are not concerned here, any sound finds its counterpart in another sound in unison; this is the ratio of one to one.

Here we have the embryo of music; thus reduced to a single note, it would be too monotonous to excite enthusiasm in the multitude. Elements of variety must therefore be sought in other tones, but in such as shall have manifest affinities with the original tone.

If a man's voice sings a C and another man wishes to do likewise, he will sing the same note; but if it is a woman's voice that seeks to imitate the pitch, this note being too low for her, she will sing what is most like it, and find the C an octave higher; mathematically this is in the ratio of one to two.

After the ratio 1 to 2, the simplest would evidently be that of 2 to 3. Now, in the series of harmonics this ratio, it will be remembered, represents the perfect fifth.

Some years ago being at Mont San Michel at Easter, I heard the peasants sing, without any accompaniment, the familiar sequence: *O filii et filiae ;* the bass voices chanted in deep tones:

; the voices of the women and
O fi - li - i   et fi - li-ae

children accompanied them an octave higher:

; while the old women, and
O fi - li - i   et fi - li-ae

the boys whose voices were changing, finding one register too low and the other too high for them, struck bravely in between, making fifths with the bass voices and fourths with the trebles: . The result, to my
O fi - li - i   et fi - li-ae

ear, was atrocious:

In the Middle Ages, it would have appeared satisfactory and correct. It is derived, indeed, from a perfectly true and natural law: after the ratio 1 to 2, which is the octave, the simplest ratios are those of 2 to 3, which is the

fifth, and 3 to 4, which is the fourth, and the peasants in question acted in a logical, though primitive, manner.

We must, therefore, first of all admit and comprehend that both mathematically and physiologically, there exists a great analogy among the sounds which are an octave, a fifth, and a fourth apart, a resemblance so great that the uncultivated ear can, and readily does, take one for the other.

The sound most resembling C is, first, C, and then, G; hence a person of but slight musical experience may, up to a certain point, confuse these three sounds, and the mathematical theory furnishes a very natural excuse for this error by demonstrating that the ratios between these sounds are the simplest that can be. We need only refer to the scale of harmonics mathematically established and verified by experiment upon the monochord, to prove this:

$$= \frac{2}{1}; \qquad = \frac{3}{2}; \qquad = \frac{4}{3}.$$

8ve   5th   4th

These three intervals, the octave, the fifth, and the fourth, have been, therefore, in all countries, as I have already said, the basis of every rudimentary scale, — the first to be discovered, even without seeking for them, in the mere attempt to imitate a primitive sound, — and, consequently, the first to be associated and combined in various ways because they were the easiest to grasp and to compare one with another.

This being well established, we will place these three intervals above the same note (which we will call C always, for convenience in reasoning) and it will become very

easy, without the use of any other theories than those with which we are already familiar, to explain the formation of the diatonic scale, major and minor, and then, by extension, the formation of the chromatic scale.

We have now three sounds bound by unquestionable kinship: C, F, and G; emitted with some force by a voice of good quality, or by a powerful instrument, they develop with themselves, in some degree, their overtones, of which every ear, even though untrained, will have a more or less conscious perception. This is a matter of demonstration.

It is therefore among these overtones, or harmonics, that the musician will be led to seek his new elements. And he will find them there, or rather, to speak more accurately, there he has found them, without being obliged to carry his search beyond the fifth harmonic of each of the three principal sounds, D, F, G; and without other guide than the natural resonance of sonorous bodies.

The natural overtones of C are:

as we have demonstrated, and those of F and of G are necessarily:

and these three groups taken together furnish ample material for the major scale:

The C occurs four times in the three groups;

The D occurs once;

The E occurs once;

The F occurs twice;

The G occurs four times;

The A occurs once;

The B occurs once; and it is to be observed that each note is represented more or less frequently, according to its relative importance in the scale, as will be shown later, when we examine the theory of harmony.

The major diatonic scale may be considered, then, as a rational product of the resonance of sonorous bodies, having for origin a single note which is the base of the system, but we must also recognise the fact that it is a product, *which has been moulded by human agency*, and shaped, as to its definitive form, by human genius, in accordance with human tastes and aptitudes.

We do not intend to say that this system has been organised by mathematicians, or in obedience to their formulas; it has been created empirically, by musicians, without other guide than their own instinct, leading them to choose notes whose relations seemed to them agreeable; but the theory of acoustics comes in to explain in what way *their artistic feeling was unconsciously guided*, and proves that the result of their attempts, of their blind groping for centuries, constitutes a normal system, admirably in accordance with the severest logic.

There are many ways of stating the numerical relations of the notes of the scale. I will give the one that seems to me simplest.

Let us first take up the series of partial-tones, carrying it further now than we did before, namely, to the fifteenth harmonic; the table here presented must contain at least once every one of the intervals to be measured. It is as follows:

Now the major scale is formed of seven notes, , plus the octave: , and it is the relations among these notes that we desire to demonstrate.

The first two (C–D) form what musicians call a major second; a little interval is found in the series of harmonics, between the eighth and ninth notes (C–D). If it be remembered that the harmonics are so numbered that these numbers express exactly the ratio of their vibration-number to that of the fundamental tone, and consequently, also, of the overtones to each other, it will be readily perceived that while C (8) makes eight vibrations, D (9) is making nine; hence, while C is making one, D makes one plus an eighth; that is to say, $\frac{9}{8}$. The relation between these two notes then, or any notes that form a major second, is expressed by $\frac{9}{8}$.

The same reasoning applies to all the intervals; we will now abridge it.

The major third (C–E, first and third degrees of the scale) is represented in the series of harmonics by the numbers 4 and 5, which is to say that while C is produced by four vibrations, E requires five; if we suppose C made but one ($\frac{4}{4}$) E then would make $\frac{4}{4} + \frac{1}{4} = \frac{5}{4}$. The relation $\frac{5}{4}$ therefore represents the major third.

The third and fourth harmonics (G–C) give us an instance of a perfect fourth, and teach us that this interval is formed by two tones in the relation of 3 to 4; it is the same, of course, for any other perfect fourth, and the one between the first and the fourth note of the scale (C–F) will be expressed by the fraction $\frac{4}{3}$.

The perfect fifth (C–G, first and fifth degrees of the scale) is represented in the scale of harmonics by the notes numbered 2 and 3; its ratio, then, is $\frac{3}{2}$.

The third and fifth notes (G–E) give us a major sixth; the ratio of the major sixth in the scale between the first degree and the sixth (C–A) is consequently $\frac{5}{3}$.

Finally, and it is to include this that we have extended the series of harmonics from the eighth to the fifteenth, comes the major seventh (C–B), the same presented in the scale between the first and the seventh notes, whose ratio is expressed by $\frac{15}{8}$.

The octave given by the first and second notes is formed, as we have seen long since, by two tones, of which one produces one vibration while the other is producing two: $\frac{2}{1} = 2$.

We will now sum up these results in a table:

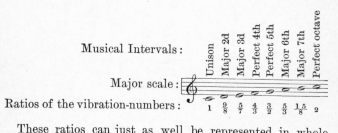

These ratios can just as well be represented in whole numbers, multiplying them all by twenty-four, which is the least common multiple of the denominators 2, 3, 4, 8; we thus obtain the ratio of vibrations for each note of a perfectly true major scale:

C	D	E	F	G	A	B	C
1	$\frac{9}{8}$	$\frac{5}{4}$	$\frac{4}{3}$	$\frac{3}{2}$	$\frac{5}{3}$	$\frac{15}{8}$	2
24	27	30	32	36	40	45	48

The minor scale, which has, moreover, various forms, is a more artificial product. It is, in truth, a major scale in which art has altered certain ratios, still always preserving the three generator-tones , immutable bases of the tonal principle.

It is upon the fifth harmonics of these three tones that the modifications are made, which consist in lowering them, either all three, or two of them, or even sometimes one only, by a given quantity. In the following table appears the major scale, by these modifications becoming, so to speak, more and more minor:

	C	D	E	F	G	A	B	C
Major Scale.	1	$\frac{9}{8}$	$\frac{5}{4}$	$\frac{4}{3}$	$\frac{3}{2}$	$\frac{5}{3}$	$\frac{15}{8}$	2

	C	D	E$\flat$	F	G	A	B	C
	1	$\frac{9}{8}$	$\frac{6}{5}$	$\frac{4}{3}$	$\frac{3}{2}$	$\frac{5}{3}$	$\frac{15}{8}$	2

	C	D	E$\flat$	F	G	A$\flat$	B	C
Minor Scales.	1	$\frac{9}{8}$	$\frac{6}{5}$	$\frac{4}{3}$	$\frac{3}{2}$	$\frac{8}{5}$	$\frac{15}{8}$	2

	C	D	E$\flat$	F	G	A$\flat$	B$\flat$	C
	1	$\frac{9}{8}$	$\frac{6}{5}$	$\frac{4}{3}$	$\frac{3}{2}$	$\frac{8}{5}$	$\frac{7}{4}$	2

The new sounds thus introduced have a kinship less direct, a less simple relation to the tonic, the key-note, whence results that sensation of vagueness that character-ises the minor, and gives it its rather sad charm. The minor mode is an invalid mode, certain of whose members are intentionally atrophied by musicians, as gardeners do with plants when they desire to create new varieties more beautiful, in their opinion, but assuredly less natural and less robust.

We will now explain the chromatic scale. I shall do this in accordance with a theory imparted to me personally of M. Barbereau, a modest, great scholar, to whom his con-temporaries have never done justice.

Let us consider again the major scale, regarding it under

a new aspect, more familiar to musicians, the tones of
which it is composed, and whose affinity or relationship
with a principal sound called the *tonic*, we have demonstrated, are unequally spaced among themselves. They
present five intervals, *nearly* alike, and two others, manifestly smaller; these are the tones and semitones thus
distributed:

Tones :
Semitones : 　C　D　E　F　G　A　B　C

These two semitones being admitted, it is natural that
musicians, always desirous of enriching their system by
the addition of new tones, should have formed the idea of
introducing others, into the five larger intervals, so as to
obtain a discontinuous succession of semitones. But, further, it was necessary, in order to satisfy a musical ear,
that the new sounds should be so chosen that there might
be a certain tie between them and the tonic. In the following ingenious manner, Barbereau has made this tie
apparent:

The seven notes of the natural scale, ranged in a certain
order, present a series of perfect fifths:

F　C　G　D　A　E　B

Continuing this series further, or to the right (still by
perfect fifths) five new sounds are produced:

F　C　G　D　A　E　B　F♯　C♯　G♯　D♯　A♯

which intercalated among the seven, exactly fill the spaces
between the tones:

C　C♯　D　D♯　E　F　F♯　G　G♯　A　A♯　B　C

On the other hand, carrying this series backward, or to the
left:

G♭　D♭　A♭　E♭　B♭　F　C　G　D　A　E　B

the same spaces are again filled, this time, however, with
flats:

C　D♭　D　E♭　E　F　G♭　G　A♭　A　B♭　B　C

The two series, one with sharps, the other with flats, give us, in each case, a succession of absolutely perfect fifths — Pythagorean fifths [1], with the exact ratio of $\frac{3}{2}$. Comparing among themselves the corresponding intercalated notes by a mathematical process, we find that they differ by that small quantity called *comma*,[2] which comes so near the limit within which the human ear can distinguish difference of pitch that, while recognising it mathematically, one may consider it, musically, of no importance. There is a singular divergence here between musicians and physicists : the latter, depending upon actual figures, insist that the C sharp is lower than the D flat, while musicians, guided by their artistic feeling, with no less energy affirm the contrary. In the mean time, however, by reciprocal concessions, justified by the tolerance of the ear, it has been admitted that $C\sharp = D\flat$ (and by extension to the other interpolated notes $D\sharp = E\flat$, $F\sharp = G\flat$, $G\sharp = A\flat$, $A\sharp = B\flat$), whereby results the only true chromatic scale which is really practical, called the tempered scale :

$$C \begin{cases} C\sharp \\ D\flat \end{cases} D \begin{cases} D\sharp \\ E\flat \end{cases} E\ F \begin{cases} F\sharp \\ G\flat \end{cases} G \begin{cases} G\sharp \\ A\flat \end{cases} A \begin{cases} A\sharp \\ B\flat \end{cases} B\ C$$

This scale is formed of twelve tones following each other at equidistant intervals, among which are the seven of the diatonic scale and five others, of which each has two names, necessary from the point of view of musical orthography, for which reason these have been called *enharmonic notes.* No one of them is strictly perfect in intonation, but there is so little lacking to this that the most delicate ear finds nothing offensive.[3]

Such, with its faults and its merits, is the scale system

[1] See later, *History of Music.*

[2] Musicians say that the *comma* is the ninth part of a tone. To physicists the relation is $\frac{81}{80}$. The Pythagorean comma is $\frac{531447}{524138}$. *about* $\frac{13}{72}$

[3] The slight value of the Pythagorean comma $\frac{531447}{524138}$ is divided into twelfths among the twelve fifths.

evidently a mistake for $\frac{531441}{524288} = \left(\frac{3}{2}\right)^{13} \times \frac{1}{2^6}$

accepted at the present time in countries the most advanced in civilisation. It is called the *equal temperament*. Thus, pianos and organs are tuned, and all instruments having fixed tones. Stringed instruments, voices, and in certain cases, wind instruments are able to make the enharmonic notes differ.

E.—Relations of Simultaneous Sounds.

INTERVALS; CHORDS; CONSONANCE AND DISSONANCE.

We now come to simultaneous combinations of sounds, that is to say, to the principle of consonance and dissonance. We at once see that its explanation lies in the very phenomenon of the production of the sound, with its *natural* accompaniment of overtones, and that the key to this explanation will be given us by the monochord, which will thus have been, from first to last, the instrument of our investigations.

The ideal of consonance would be an absolutely pure tone, without any alloy whatever of overtones; but tones like these, as we have already said, exist in theory only; at the same time, the tuning-fork, certain flute tones and some organ pipes (flute-stops) give us the idea of a sound that is almost simple. Outside of this ideal consonance, every tone is a compound tone, coming so much the nearer to theoretic purity as the harmonics composing it are simpler in their numerical relation to itself. The nearer the overtones are to the fundamental tone, the better they accompany it, producing upon our organisation that agreeable sensation we call consonance. On the other hand, when the overtones are very remote from their fundamental, and hence are very near each other, we no longer have the sensation of a homogeneous whole, but of a tone in itself poor, and accompanied by a sharp and disagreeable noise; this is dissonance. It is absolutely the same in the case of those aggregations of notes that we call chords, in which art does nothing more than imitate nature. The nearer we come, in these groupings, to the simple theoretical tone, the more consonant — in the musical sense of the word — is the result obtained.

In reality, there is no absolute limit between consonance and dissonance; it varies with the degree of sensibility of each individual, and also according to the habit resulting from education; it is a question of the ear's tolerance, what appears harsh to one often seeming most agreeable to another.

But, while it is impossible to say where consonance ends and dissonance begins, it is perfectly easy to establish a gradation, leaving each person free to set the barrier where he pleases.

This is what we shall now do, taking again the monochord, and studying anew the series of overtones, the inexhaustible source whence, in the main, is derived the whole material of the musical art. This time I will present the overtones of *C*, uniting them consecutively, two by two, in a way to obtain from them all the groupings which present different relations.

The ideal of consonance, absolute purity, being expressed by the ratio 1 : 1, which is, in fact, that of unison, it is certain that the nearer we come to it, that is to say, the simpler the ratio, the more consonance we hear; in reading the fractions of the above example, in the order in which they present themselves, we find, therefore, a series of groups of two tones, less and less consonant, more and more dissonant.

We will pursue our experiment by grouping the tones, no longer consecutively, but skipping one or more, so as to

exhaust all the really different combinations which can be
formed with the first ten harmonics:

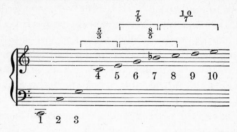

This gives us but four new groups which are, successively, more and more remote from consonance.

If now we classify all these fractions, beginning with
those that present the simplest relations, we shall determine
with certainty the degree of comparative sweetness or
harshness of all the intervals which they represent.[1]

I have added to this table, so that it may contain all the intervals of the
major scale, the relations $\frac{16}{9}$, $\frac{15}{8}$, and $\frac{16}{15}$, corresponding to the intervals of
the minor seventh, the major seventh, and the minor second, which have been
previously determined. It is easy to verify their exactness by continuing the
series of harmonics as far as the sixteenth:

On the other hand, I have omitted the relations $\frac{8}{7}$ and $\frac{10}{9}$, which represent
varieties of tone greater or less than that of the tempered scale, which is invariably $\frac{9}{8}$.

This, in my opinion, is the simplest and most accurate
method of measuring the degree of consonance or dissonance
between two sounds.

---

[1] P signifies perfect; M, major; m, minor; /, diminished; +, augmented.

Though I have established in the beginning the fact that there is no sharply drawn line between consonances and dissonances, regarded from the purely physical point of view, and that the question is merely what the ear will tolerate, what degree of harshness it will consent to endure, I have, nevertheless,— as I shall be obliged later, in speaking of harmony, to employ the classification adopted in music,— indicated, in the table given above, by means of a dotted line, the limit which is generally admitted.

What I have said of compound sounds and their intervals applies necessarily to chords, which are merely groups of intervals. The nearer the chord is to the absolute purity of unison, the stronger the impression of consonance.

Take the tone 1, accompany it by its harmonics, 13, 14, 15, which are very remote:

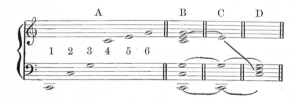

It is evidently a dissonance.

On the other hand, choose and consort with it its nearest overtones, those which have the simplest ratio with it, and the chord will be essentially consonant:

This constitutes the common chord. In A is a succession of the first six harmonics, the most perfect consonants; in B, they are heard simultaneously; in C, the three repetitions are left out, one G and two Cs; in D, they are grouped in the simplest manner, and present among themselves the ratios $\frac{2}{3}$, $\frac{5}{4}$, $\frac{6}{5}$.

But if we venture further, and add the 7th partial tone, B♭, we come into the region of dissonance:

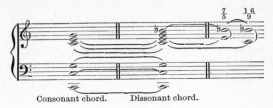

Consonant chord.   Dissonant chord.

because of the ratios $\frac{7}{5}$, and $\frac{16}{9}$ (E–B♭ and C–B♭) which are too remote from theoretic purity, and produce on the ear a slight sensation of harshness, perhaps by causing a vibration of nerve-fibres that are too near together and interfere as they move.

Helmholtz has developed, on this subject, quite a different theory, which is admirably ingenious, based on *resultant sounds*, but has the defect of not being quite in agreement with musical feeling. I therefore give my adherence to the one explained above, at the same time advising the reader to study also that of Helmholtz, most interesting in its subtlety and — even though not fully satisfying to the artistic sense — containing elements useful as guides to sincere seekers after truth.

F.—Acoustic Qualities of Halls.

That branch of acoustic science which is least developed, notwithstanding the great interest which it presents, is undoubtedly the one treating of the acoustic properties of halls,— a subject very closely allied to architecture. We have long been in possession of the facts in the case, but no one has yet been able to construct with certainty, on mathematical principles, a hall whose acoustic properties were perfect.

Not long since, one of our most famous architects, having a theatre to build in Paris, made the tour of Europe to study in every country the acoustic conditions of theatres thought to have best fulfilled these unknown laws; notwithstanding all his fidelity, the result was in no way remarkable,— from this point of view, I mean to say. The same architect, employed in a restoration of the hall of the Conservatory, which is an acoustic marvel, though no man can say exactly why, dared not displace the partition of a box, add drapery, or make the slightest modification, in the well-founded fear that he might impair this unexplained perfection.

In building a concert hall or theatre, two perils must be specially guarded against: too great or too little resonance; generally the architect falls into the second of the two.

A hall is, in its nature, a closed place, where the sound-waves are not propagated as freely as in the open air, in concentric zones, but must encounter every possible reflection, from partitions, walls, floor, ceiling. Nor is the complication ended here, for, according to their substance, the material of which they are made,— stone, more or less hard, woods of divers kinds,— and the hangings with which they are covered, the walls offer different degrees of resistance, and also of conductivity, producing most unexpected effects. More than this: a hall whose resonance is too great when it is empty, becomes satisfactory when filled with an audience, whose garments deaden the sound as carpets or drapery might do.

The worst of all faults for a hall, where destined for music or the voice, is to give echoes. Now it is almost as much beyond our power to avoid an echo as it is to produce one. I have read somewhere the story of an Englishman who, finding in some foreign country a house in which there was a remarkable echo, bought the house, numbered the stones, caused the building to be transported piecemeal to England, and there had it rebuilt on his estate,— the identical house. But the echo was no longer in it; as a matter of course, the Englishman blew his brains out. Whether it be true or not, this story is quite probable. There are a multitude of famous echoes; some are natural, produced in valleys or caves, where they have been discovered; others are made by the hand of man, in buildings, but involuntarily; they have been explained minutely, but no man has ever succeeded in copying them.

The famous hall of the Conservatoire des Arts et Métiers in Paris presents only phenomena of sonority reinforced by the reflection of sound-waves from surfaces whose curve has been planned for that effect, as can be done in optics for combinations of mirrors; these are not echoes, in the true sense of the word.

The foyer of the old opera house in Berlin, which was built in 1743, and was destroyed by fire a century later, presented a like phenomenon.

What we know with certainty, or with a very close approach to certainty, on the subject is this : sound is reflected from any surface, as light is from a polished surface, and according to the same law (the angle of incidence and the angle of reflection are equal); it moves at the rate of 340 metres a second; on the other hand, we can scarcely utter more than ten syllables, or ten distinct musical sounds, in a second, that is to say, a syllable in the tenth of a second; during this period the sound has gone 34 metres; if it meets at that distance a reflecting surface it returns, with the same velocity, that is to say, in another tenth of a second, and we perceive it as an echo. An echo, then, requires a distance of 34 metres, and with this, there can be only one syllable or one sound repeated; for two sounds, the distance must be doubled. This is frequently the case among the mountains.

At a distance of less than 34 metres, if there is no echo well marked as such, distinctly repeating articulations, there may be reverberations, quite as disagreeable; that is to say, a kind of incomplete echo, too short, in which the reflected sound is sent back so quickly that it blends with the direct sound, appearing to prolong and reinforce it with a disagreeable and wearisome humming. Cathedral vaulted roofs almost always produce echoes and reverberations which are not without a certain majesty, but often render spoken words unintelligible and destroy the effect of all musical combinations. There are but very few large churches that can be considered really good for music; for this reason it has been usual to avoid, in compositions destined for the church, any rapid successions of sounds, which would increase the chances of confusion at the same time that they destroyed the character of solemnity.

It is well known that rigidity of walls is not an indispensable condition for the production of echoes; at sea, a sail swollen by the wind; in the open country, a screen of trees and even low lying clouds are frequent causes of this phenomenon.

Also it is well known that plane surfaces cause the sound-rays to diverge, scatter them apart; that parabolic surfaces render the rays parallel; and that elliptic surfaces cause them to converge towards one focus (Fig. 32), from

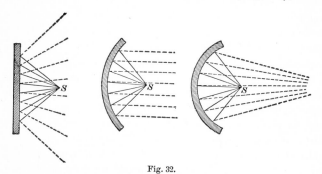

Fig. 32.

PLANE SURFACE.   PARABOLIC REFLECTOR.   ELLIPTIC REFLECTOR.
S. Sound-producing object.   ———Rays emitted.   - - - - - -Rays reflected.

which we infer that the elliptic form should be avoided for ceilings as well as walls, since it would be advantageous only for the one spectator placed exactly at the focus. It is known that the nature of the wall is a matter of importance, since sound rebounds and is reinforced from elastic surfaces. It is known that bare walls are much more resonant than those hung with drapery. A few other things are also known; but that which no man 'knows is how practical advantage may be derived from this knowledge.

The ancients, whose theatres and amphitheatres were open to the sky, doubtless lost, in this way, a vast number of vibrations, but, on the other hand, they had no cause to dread reverberations from ceilings: hence, all their efforts were with the aim of reinforcing the sound, so that the actor's voice, notwithstanding its loss in the open air, should reach with sufficient power the highest rows of seats. The Greeks, whose amphitheatres accommodated many thousand spectators, employed for this purpose a method which Vitruvius describes at some length : they placed in niches made under the benches great bells of brass or of terra cotta, of a pitch carefully adjusted to reinforce certain sounds. These bells were especially in use at Corinth, whence they were brought home to Rome by Mummius, after his victory in 145 B. C.

Shall we not say that these Greeks had discovered resonators ?

The famous organ-maker, Cavaillé-Coll, a great acoustician, has employed in the contrary intention, namely, to diminish a too great resonance, the following curious method, which I describe in accordance with notes which he has kindly given me. Threads of common knitting cotton are stretched, with very slight tension, across the hall, half-way up the walls, parallel to the floor, forming a sort of network against which the sound-waves break, somewhat as waves of the sea break against the piles or other obstacles, relatively very feeble, which are opposed to them for the defence of threatened coasts. These threads, being so fine and of the same colour as the walls and placed so high, are invisible, and the improvement they make in the acoustic quality of the hall is the more mysterious because the cause is not observable. No known law regulates the number or arrangement of these threads, and they are placed in such a way as successive trials show to be best.

This plan seems to have been invented in Great Britain, where Mr. Robert S. Greeg has employed it successfully in correcting the disagreeable reverberation of sound in the new cathedral of S. Finn Barr (Cork), whose nave is very high. It has also been put in practice in the Palace of Industry in Amsterdam, where the acoustic conditions were faulty and it was feared the effect of the organ would be always confused and veiled by the unfortunate reverberation. "Threads of common cotton, quite fine and nearly unelastic, were stretched in different directions across the upper part of the hall. As these threads were placed, it was perfectly evident that the resonance diminished. The impression produced from the first was that of a sort of tranquillity established in the atmosphere, and accidental noises, occurring while the work was going on, were evidently less and more isolated than heretofore. Trials made with an orchestra, first in the empty hall, then in many concerts with varied programmes, confirmed this first result in a manner so evident as to strike not only the audience but also the performers, who perceived, with surprise, that they now heard themselves much more distinctly than they had done before." [1]

With a success more or less noteworthy, but never with complete failure of result, the same system has been tried in Paris, in the church of Notre-Dame des Champs, in the hall of the Trocadéro, and, more recently, in the hall of the Society of Horticulture.

G.— Relations between Acoustics and Rhythm.

Certain halls, then, being more or less unsuited, by echoes or reverberations, for musical use, it is also to be noted that this fault increases in proportion to the rapidity with which sounds are produced. In a place having too great resonance, chords isolated, or separated by sufficient length of silence, may have a harmonious and imposing reverberation, while a succession of sounds with shorter intervals between, will end in being a horrible confusion, each sound

[1] C. M. Philbert, *l'Orgue du palais de l'Industrie d'Amsterdam;* 1876.

being mingled with its predecessors and then with those that follow it.

This fact — which, by the way, explains why public speakers, and especially preachers, utter their words slowly, separating even syllables from each other, to lessen the chance of confusion between the emitted and the reflected sounds — enables us to show the connection between the three principal qualities of sound due to acoustic laws, namely, *loudness*, *pitch*, and *timbre*, on the one side, and on the other, *duration*, a fourth quality, which seems arbitrary, abandoned to the caprice of the composer or the performer, but subject in reality also to certain natural laws,— those, namely, of *rhythm*, which are but little known or studied.

The origin of the feeling for rhythm has been sought in the successive steps made in walking, in the pulsations of the heart, in the sounds of respiration, and, more mathematically, in the invariably isochronous oscillations of a pendulum.

Walking gives the simplest idea of the binary division. A person awake breathes regularly, in double measure; but in sleep the inspiration is twice as long as the expiration, which gives the ternary division, making triple measure.

The metronome, an instrument measuring musical rhythm as the monochord measures vibrations, is really a clock which marks the fractions of a minute, as the pendulum would do if its length could be varied at will. Now observe that it was in the movements of the pendulum that vibration was most simply demonstrated.[1] Thus we are brought back, by this excursion into the domain of rhythm, exactly to the point from which we set out in our researches into acoustic phenomena having musical character.

Whatever its origin may be, it is certain that the sentiment of the division of time into equal parts is natural to us — within narrow limits, however, since we perceive with precision and certainty only these two simple modes of division, namely, by twos and by threes, the binary division and the ternary division. It is true, indeed, that we recognise the equality in duration of eight or of sixteen sounds

1 Page 3.

emitted successively, but this is by means of the unconscious mental operation $16 \div 2 \div 2 \div 2 = 2$. And in nine
we recognise in the same way three times three.

The proof of this is that we do not recognise the number
with the same facility, in groups formed of ten, of fifteen,
or of seventeen sounds. To have a clear perception of the
division of time, we must bring it down to one or other of
the two points of comparison: $\frac{2}{1}$ or $\frac{3}{2}$, which are the bases
of the rhythmic system no less than of the harmonic.

The combinations which are derived from these two
modes of division are almost inexhaustible, and we by no
means employ them all; with the Arabs and other Orientals,
who have no idea of the use of simultaneous sounds, rhythm
has acquired a much greater importance and an altogether
greater development, for this is their only means of enriching an accompaniment.[1]

This is not the point where, according to the order of
arrangement adopted for this little work, a study of
rhythm has its place; I speak of it here only to call the
reader's attention to the remarkable fact that all the constituent elements of the musical art are connected with
mathematics, or properly speaking, are derived therefrom.
Is it for this reason that, in general, scientific men, mathematicians, physicists, physiologists, are passionate lovers of
music? However this may be, the converse of it (as they
would say) is not true, for it is rare, unfortunately rare,
to see a musician take pleasure in the study of the positive
sciences, even so far as to seek in them the first cause of
natural phenomena which are of everyday familiarity to
him.

This, however, is true, that in music, numbers and relations of numbers are not everything.

———————

I must express the hope that no one will suppose that I
have aspired to present in these few pages, a treatise upon

[1] A singular fact is that they call it the *harmony*, which must, of course, be
understood to mean the *accompaniment*.

acoustics. I have merely wished to demonstrate that those who are interested in the musical art can find a real pleasure in the scientific analysis of the raw materials of this art; if I have succeeded in opening to them new horizons, my end is attained, and I have only to point out to them certain of the books in which they may make a serious study of acoustics, works from which I have drawn most of my material:

HELMHOLTZ, *On the Sensations of Tone.* (New York, Longmans.)
TYNDALL, *Sound.* (New York, Appleton.)
ZAHM, *Sound and Music.* (Chicago, McClurg.)
RADAU, *l'Acoustique.* (Paris, Hachette, 1870.)
MAHILLON, *Éléments d'acoustique.* (Bruxelles, 1874.)
G. KASTNER, *la Harpe d'Éole et la musique cosmique.* (Paris, 1856.)

I shall proceed in the same way in the chapters to follow, making no attempt to have them take the place of Treatises on Instrumentation, or Courses of Harmony and of Fugue; they will not assume to teach Composition or the History of Music; but merely to diffuse among the musical public true and definite ideas upon each one of these branches of artistic erudition, of a nature to interest amateurs and persons of intelligent curiosity, as well as to guide young students in the direction of their work.

CHAPTER II.

THE MATERIALS OF SOUND.

A. — Of Instrumentation.

SOUNDS WHICH CONSTITUTE THE MATERIAL ELEMENT

OF MUSIC.

The sounds which form the musical material can be produced only by three classes of instruments:

> Wind-instruments,
> Stringed Instruments,
> Instruments of Percussion,

the human voice being considered as belonging in the first
class, of which it is the highest type.

The knowledge of these different instruments, that is
to say, of the compass, particular timbre, construction,
and mechanism of each, constitutes the science called
Instrumentation, [1] the term Orchestration being specially
applicable to the art of grouping, managing, and combining
them, using them as a painter uses the colours on his
palette.

We shall therefore examine them, one by one, beginning

---

[1] Knowledge of instruments; application of their individual qualities to the
translation and interpretation of the musical idea.

with the human voice, which, later, will often be of use to us for purposes of comparison.

The best way of getting an idea of the mechanism of an instrument which one does not play is by a careful reading of a well-written Method; accordingly, we shall append to a description of the principal instruments the names of several of the most valued Methods for each.

THE HUMAN VOICE.

Every person has a voice of some kind, good or bad, strong or weak, of wide range or of narrow, true or false, — commonly true and of small compass, — but something that can be called a "voice," that is to say, the power of producing sounds having musical character. The male voice in temperate climates is generally a baritone, the female (and also the voice of children) a mezzo-soprano; and it is rare to find a person *aphonous,* incapable of uttering, according to age and sex, one or other of the two following series of sounds:

Men.   Women and children.

Study, developing the rudimentary voice, not only augments its volume, but has the effect also of improving its quality as well as extending its compass in one direction or the other.   Hence results, for trained voices, the following classification, which is only approximative, varying considerably according to different schools and individual opinions, but appearing to me, on the whole, to give a sufficiently exact idea of the range of each kind of well-defined voice.

(And by "well-defined," I mean, voices in some degree trained, as contrasted with natural, uncultivated voices, concerning whose possibilities there can be, at first, only conjecture.)

The same table is now given a second time, in the usual notation, and presented in a form which will make it easier to grasp the classification of voices on a common scale, presented on a double stave of piano-music, at the foot of the page.

It is interesting to compare these tables of trained voices (pp. 69, 72) with the table of theoretical voices which is used in the study of Harmony, and will be given later.

It will be noticed also that, according to the present method of writing, tenor voices are represented an octave above their real sound, a practice truly irrational.

This classification, I would repeat, is by no means absolute; but it is impossible to give one that would be more exact, since the great teachers of singing have, almost as a rule, each his own, in the matter of voice-compass.

For classifying voices, a surer and more characteristic thing is their *timbre*. There are no words, it is true, with which to describe it, but with any capacity for observation it can easily be recognised. The timbre of a soprano or of a tenor voice is clearest in the upper registers of the voice, the tones growing duller and less resonant as they descend in the scale; on the contrary, the contralto and the bass possess more homogeneity and *retain their timbre in the low notes*. It is more difficult to differentiate the tenor voice from the baritone, and the soprano from the mezzo-soprano, these intermediate voices presenting numerous varieties, and admitting of different valuations; but here the compass of the voice can serve as a guide.

The voice is, then, we may say, an essentially personal and elastic instrument; there are no two voices alike in all respects, and absolute, unvarying classification is impossible.

A word as to exceptional voices. It is not uncommon in Russia to hear *double-bass* voices, that can produce the A♭ , a fifth below the E♭, which is the extreme limit of our *bassi profundi*.

In the high register, no male voice, so far as known, has ever exceeded the famous chest-note, C♯, of Tamberlik.

In the voice of Faure is united the range of the "singing bass" and the tenor; but the timbre of the voice is, *par excellence*, that of a baritone.

The admirable voice of Alboni, the most perfect type of

a contralto, while preserving the same rich timbre, had this enormous compass :[1]

Madame Nilsson, and, after her, Mlle. Bilbaut-Vauchelet, have let us hear F in alt: without apparent effort in the aria of the Queen of Night, in the

---

[1] I once asked Alboni to tell me the exact compass of her voice ; in reply, she wrote me the following interesting letter, which I cannot deny myself the pleasure of inserting here, with the suppression only of some passages absolutely personal in character :

Paris, 29 March, 1892.

My dear Lavignac,

. . . .

. . . . . At the age of eight, I had a contralto voice already formed ; and a person hearing me sing, without seeing me, would have supposed it to be a young man, sixteen or eighteen years of age, who was singing. I found it very easy to remember pieces I had heard : very often I sang contralto soli, and then soprano soli in the soprano register. This was an amusement that might have cost me dear, for when, at the age of eleven, I began to study music and singing seriously, there was really a gap between the two registers. I applied myself most carefully to the correction of this fault by studies and exercises, and finally I got the middle notes from B♭ to D, of great sweetness, but they had never the strength of the lower notes ! And it has been by method of singing only that I have been able in some degree to conceal this defect.

When, after many years of study, my voice had attained its complete development, I could very easily sing a scale from low G to the high C of soprano ; sometimes in these exercises I went from low F to high D and to E♭ ; but this was for my amusement. In public I limited myself to G and C.

With my two registers I could sing both contralto and soprano parts ; especially out of France where I was obliged to select my repertoire as best I could, Rossini's music not being always appreciated at its true value.

I sang " La Sonnambula," " Norma," " Don Pasquale," " Anna Bolena," " La Fille du Regiment," etc., etc., etc! Also I sang the part of Elena in the " Donna del Lago," " Ninetta in " La Gazza Ladra," etc., etc., etc. Of course, I also sang all the contralto roles in these same operas.

In London, in 1848, at Covent Garden, I sang the part of Don Carlos in Verdi's "Ernani," to facilitate the debut of a comrade, the troupe having at that moment no baritone ! ! !

The contralto voice being in itself monotonous, I introduced my own cadenzas, but always in the style of the music I was singing. Often I went up to high C ; but I was always careful to finish with a note in the true contralto register, for these were my richest and most velvety tones !

In this way I was sure of my effect ! ! ! This, my dear Lavignac, is my answer to your question.

. . . .

MARIE ZIÉGER ALBONI.

an octave
lower than
the notation

Notes commo

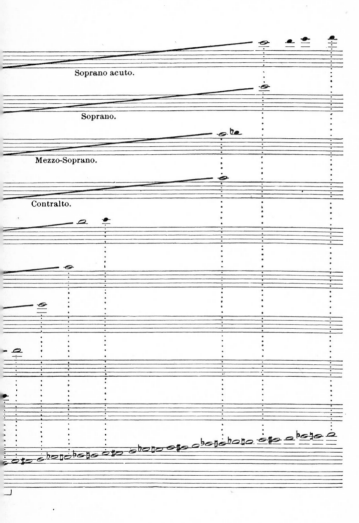

Soprano acuto.

Soprano.

Mezzo-Soprano.

Contralto.

Magic Flute, which note must have been also possible to the singer — whose name is unknown to us [1] — who first created the rôle. Miss Sibyl Sanderson, the brilliant Esclarmonde of Massenet, runs up easily to G in alt :

These are indeed extraordinary voices; what then can we say of the voice of Lucrezia Agujari, called "La Bastardella," heard by Mozart in 1770, who executed in his presence a passage running up to the C in altissimo of 2069 vibrations per second? [2]

Between the low A♭ of the Russian basses, and the C in altissimo of the Bastardella, there is a range of five octaves and a major third. This, then, is the ultimate limit of the vocal organ in its rarest manifestations.

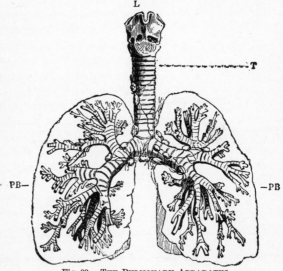

Fig. 33.— THE PULMONARY APPARATUS.
PB, lungs and bronchial tubes; T, trachea; L, larynx.

1 [She was Madame Josepha Hofer, Mozart's sister-in-law. ED.]
2 But it should be remembered that in 1770 the pitch was a little lower than at present in France.

Let us now analyse the physiological operation of this model instrument.

The human voice, the only instrument which has life, originates in the larynx by means of an expulsion of breath with more than usual force. The air thus expelled from the lungs makes its way through the bronchial ramifications to the trachea, which is a tube, at first quite broad, then abruptly narrowing, so that the air is compelled to pass through a very small aperture, the glottis; the edges of this aperture are vibratory, elastic membranes, the lips of the glottis, which act as reeds and now permit, now prevent the passage of the breath (Fig. 34).

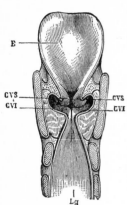

Fig. 34.—VERTICAL SECTION OF THE LARYNX.

Lg, larynx and glottis; CVS, upper vocal chords; CVI, lower vocal chords; E, epiglottis.

By this variable tension they determine the rapidity of vibrations, upon which the pitch of the sound depends, its timbre being afterwards modified strongly by the conformation — differing in different individuals — of the palate, the trachea, the nasal orifices, as well as by the position of the tongue and the lips in emitting sound (Fig 35).

Comparatively narrow in women and children, the opening of the glottis enlarges considerably as the boy attains maturity, whence it results that the grown man has a deeper voice,— averaging an octave lower than a woman's; at the same time the glottis does not lose the power of contracting, and can suddenly go an octave higher, producing what is called the *head-voice* or *falsetto*, in distinction from the *chest-voice*, which is the ordinary tone. These two expressions are both alike inexact, since it is the whole of the pulmonary laryngial and buccal apparatus acting in concert, which produces all kinds of vocal sound. At the same time these expressions are so consecrated by usage in all countries, and at the same time they so well give the impression of the difference of timbres, that it would be unreasonable to attempt to substitute for them designations more rational; but there is no physiological objection to considering head-tones, with their flute-like timbre, as in some degree analogous to the second harmonic of pipes or wind instruments, a kind of relic, so to speak, of the childish voice.

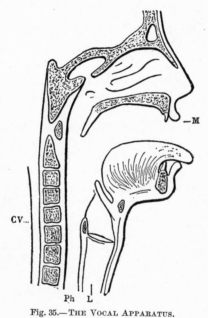

Fig. 35.—THE VOCAL APPARATUS.

M, mouth; L, larynx; Ph, pharynx; CV, vertebral column.

In the chest-voice, the lips of the glottis vibrate in their entirety; in the head-voice, on their edges only, as has been demonstrated by laryngoscopic examination.

METHODS OF SINGING.

Besides the famous Method of the Conservatoire, prepared by GARAT, GOSSEC, MÉHUL, CHERUBINI, and other masters of that date, there are the Methods of Carulli, Mme. Cinti-Damoreau, Crosti, Delle-Sedie, Duprez, Faure, Garaudé, Garcia, Jules Lefort, Stéphen de la Madelaine, Madame Marchesi, etc., all valuable from different points of view.

WORKS ON VOCAL PHYSIOLOGY.

Mandl, *Hygiène de la voix* (1879).
Manuel Garcia, *Observations physiologiques sur la voix humaine.*
Bataille, *Recherches sur la phonation.*
Gougenheim et Larmoyer, *Physiologie de la voix et du chant.*
Faure, *la Voix et le chant.*
Dr. Castex, *Hygiène de la voix parlée et chantée* (1894).
Morel Mackenzie, *The Hygiene of the Vocal Organs.*
Lennox Browne and Emil Behnke, *Voice, Song, and Speech.*

The great superiority of the voice over all the instruments that human ingenuity has constructed lies in this, that to it is added language, whereby it expresses with precision the sentiments to which it is giving musical utterance, and fully explains their nature. Without this incomparable faculty the human voice would be manifestly surpassed — in compass, flexibility, and power — by many of the instruments of music which we are now about to examine.

THE ORGAN.

Shall we consider the organ as *an instrument,* or as *an orchestra,*— an aggregation of instruments manipulated by one man ? I am much inclined to the second definition. It is, at least, *par excellence* the great polyphonic instrument ; it represents infinite power ; nothing is impossible to it.

If the violin is the king, it may well be said that the organ is the god of the orchestra ; wherever it deigns to add its voice, it protects, rules, supports ; it can appear in no other way than as master, hovering in tranquil majesty above the tone-masses which seem to melt at its feet.

It is more difficult to describe the organ than any other instrument, not only because it is the largest, most powerful, as well as the most complicated, but especially for the reason that no two organs are alike. A single series of pipes tuned chromatically, controlled by a key-board and

furnished with bellows, constitutes an organ of a rudimentary kind, the organ of one manual; but that of S. Sulpice
has 118 stops, that of Notre-Dame 110, and there are even
larger instruments, notably that of the Cathedral of Riga

Fig. 36.—Organ (proposed) of S. Peter's at Rome.

which has 124 stops, and that of the Town-hall of Sydney,
with 128; now it must be remembered that a single organ
stop is equivalent in itself to a perfect orchestral instrument, even one of the most powerful, having a compass of
five octaves.

It is said in the Bible that God made man in his own image; and now when man proposes to create an instrument for the praise of God, it seems as if he took his own vocal organ for a model, and, in turn, in his own image, makes the organ,—vastly increased and enlarged, however. In truth, in this giant instrument we find, in suitable proportion, all the elements which constitute the human voice: the bellows represent the lungs; the great wind-trunks which distribute the wind to the different stops are the bronchial tubes and the trachea; each reed represents the glottis and each pipe the larynx, many times repeated, for that which man cannot imitate is the suppleness and the elasticity of the living instrument, which, contracting or dilating, can change at will both pitch and timbre, and the maker of an organ must employ as many pipes of unequal length as he desires to have tones, and vary the forms of these pipes as often as he wishes a difference in timbre, thus substituting quantity for quality.

The longest organ-pipes ever made are of thirty-two feet, producing the $C-_2$ of 16.15 vibrations. (Made of tin, such a pipe exceeds nine hundred pounds in weight.) There is no object in making pipes longer than this, for their tones would not be perceptible, musically speaking; the vibrations would strike upon the ear separately, as a succession of shocks, not as a musical sound. The shortest organ-pipes are no larger than toy whistles, half an inch long or less, extremely shrill, touching the opposite extreme, the high limit of musical sounds.

That is to say, the organ goes over the entire extent of the musical scale, and knows no limits other than those which its physical organisation assigns to our organ of hearing.

The forms of the pipes, which may be *cylindrical, conical, widened* at the top, or *narrowed* (pyramidal), *rectangular, varying in diameter* in proportion to their length, *open, stopped, pierced, surmounted by a bell,* etc., and, *to a certain extent,* the material of which they are made, giving interiors more or less smooth, more or less resistant, cause infinite variety in the form of the column of air within the pipe; hence result differences of timbre, whose richness may be regarded as inexhaustible, depending only on the degree of skill and ingenuity possessed by the maker.

The materials used are, in woods, oak, red deal, walnut, maple, pear-tree wood ; in metals, pure tin, a composition of tin and a little lead known under the name of " metal," and a composition of tin with one per cent. of copper, called " alloy."

Pipes may be divided into two distinct classes, *flue-pipes* and *reed-pipes*.

The *flue-pipes* themselves are of two kinds : *flute* or *open* stops, in which the column of air vibrates either without subdivision in its entire length, producing only the fundamental tone of the pipe, or again, is divided into vibrating segments, emitting the second or the third partial tone[1] (in which case the pipes are called *octaviants* or *harmonics*); and *Bourdons*, or stopped pipes, whose extremity opposite to that by which the air enters is hermetically closed.

In consequence, the vibrating column of air is reflected from the bottom of the pipe, and must vibrate through its length doubled; hence the tone produced is the octave below that which an open pipe of the same length would emit, as the theory of acoustics easily proves.

The sound from stopped pipes is less clear, it is duller and more muffled than that of the open stops; but the former occupy less space, which is a consideration of importance in building an organ. Moreover, by the very fact of their dullness of tone they make an important contribution to the variety of timbres, which is one of the most precious qualities of the instrument.[2]

Speaking in general terms, the larger the pipes are, the more breadth, majesty, calm, and fullness has the sound; on the other hand, pipes comparatively narrow, favouring the development of harmonics, give the timbre a char-

[1] See page 16.

[2] They can have only the harmonics of the uneven numbers. See p. 17.

acter more incisive, more penetrating, yet without completely excluding from it the sweetness and serenity especially belonging to the flue-stops.

In the *reed-stops* we also find two principal categories : the *free* reeds, which move in the opening where they are placed without touching its sides; and the *striking* reeds, which, as they vibrate, strike with more or less force against the walls of the tube which they command. [1] It is needless to say that reeds of the former class have vastly more gentleness, fineness, and distinction than those of the latter, to which belong extreme brilliancy of tone, and a penetrative power, sometimes almost violent.

In the reed-stops, the pitch is determined by the length and thickness of the reed itself; the length of the pipe must, however, be in suitable proportion, and has an important influence in modifying the timbre. Here the pipe acts as a powerful resonator.[2]

Omitting, as a matter of choice, a great number of the imaginative designations which organ-makers of different countries have assigned to varieties of stops, I give below only the names of those which are usually to be found in organs of the more important rank, classing these stops according to the divisions established above. Opposite each name, I indicate the *usual* diapason of each stop, putting in parenthesis lengths of pipes that are only occasionally met. It must be remembered that these figures represent in feet the length of the longest pipe in each stop; [3] that is to say, we should read as follows : eight feet, sixteen feet, thirty-two feet, for the low C of each stop.

FLUE — PIPES.

Large *open pipes.*

Principal or montre	8.	16.	32.
Flûte . . . . 4.	8.	16.	(32).
Flûte douce . . . . 4.	8.		
Prestant . . . . 4.			

1 See page 21.
2 See page 36.
3 See page 26.

Doublette . . . . 2.
Contrebasse . . . . 16.   32.
Diapason . . . . 8.
Unda Maris . . . . 8.
Piccolo . . . . 1.
Flûte harmonique . . . . 4.   8.
Flûte octaviante . . . . 4.

Smaller pipes.

Gambe . . . . (4).   8.   (16).
Salicional . . . . (2).   4.   8.   (16).
Violoncelle . . . . 8.
Violon . . . . (4).   8.
Basse de violon . . . . 16.
Viola d'amore . . . . 4.   8.
Voix céleste . . . . 8.
Eolien . . . . 8.   (16).
Kélaurophone . . . . 8.

Stopped pipes.

Bourdon . . . . 4.   8.   16.   32.
Flûte bouchée . . . . : . 4.   8.   16.   32.
Quintaton . . . . 8.   16.   (32).
Bourdon harmonique . . . . . . 4.   8.

REED – STOPS.

Free reeds.

Hautbois . . . . 8.
Basson . . . . 8.   (16).
Musette . . . . 8.
Clarinette . . . . 8.
Voix humaine . . . . 8.
Cromorne . . . . 8.
Cor anglais . . . . 8.
Euphone . . . . 8.   16.

Striking reeds.

Trompette . . . . 8.   16.
Bombarde . . . . 16.   (32).
Trombone . . . . 16.   (32).
Clairon . . . . (2).   4.
Tuba . . . . 8.   16.
Trompette harmonique . . . . 8.
Clairon harmonique . . . . . 4.
Cromorne harmonique . . . . 8.

MUTATION—STOPS.

Plein-jeu.
Fourniture-cymbale.
Nazard ou quinte.
Etc.[1]

It will be noticed that at the end of the above table is a class of stops entitled *mutation-stops* (in English, *mixtures*).

Formerly too much valued, perhaps at the present day too much decried, these stops, whose principle may appear barbaric at first sight, illustrate, nevertheless, one of the most judicious applications of our knowledge as to the constitution of musical sound. Their pipes are so tuned as

---

[1] [For purposes of comparison, the following specification is given of an English organ, from Mr. H. Heathcote Statham's *My Thoughts on Music and Musicians*. London, Chapman & Hall, 1892. This really includes all the main classes of stops; it is but of fifty, and still, those of eighty or a hundred must really make up their number largely by repetition.

Specification for Organ of 50 stops with three manuals and pedal:

Great Organ.
1. Bourdon, 16-foot tone.
2. Open diapason, 8-foot.
3. Small open diapason, 8-foot.
4. Gamba, 8-foot.
5. Stopped diapason, 8-foot tone.
6. Principal, 4-foot.
7. Flute, 4-foot.
8. Twelfth.
9. Fifteenth, 2-foot.
10. Sesquialtera (3 ranks).
11. Mixture (3 ranks).
12. Trumpet, 8-foot.
13. Clarion, 4-foot.

Swell Organ.
14. Bourdon, 16-foot tone.
15. Open diapason, 8-foot.
16. Stopped diapason, 8-foot tone.
17. Salicional, 8-foot.
18. Spitzflöte, 4-foot.
19. Dulciana, 4-foot.
20. Fifteenth, 2-foot.
21. Flageolet, 2-foot.
22. Contra-oboe, 16-foot.
23. Oboe, 8-foot.
24. Cornopean, 8-foot.
25. Clarion, 4-foot.
26. Vox humana, 8-foot.

Choir Organ.
27. Geigen Principal, 8-foot.
28. Lieblich Gedacht, 8-foot tone.
29. Dulciana, 8-foot.
30. Vox angelica, 8-foot.
31. Viol d'amore, 8-foot.
32. Clarabella, 8-foot.
33. Harmonic flute, 4-foot.
34. Gemshorn, 4-foot.
35. Lieblich Gedacht, 4-foot tone.
36. Piccolo harmonique, 2-foot.
37. Corno di Bassetto, 8-foot.
38. Orchestral oboe, 8-foot.

Pedal Organ.
39. Sub-bass, 32-foot tone.
40. Open diapason, 16-foot.
41. Bourdon, 16-foot tone.
42. Violone, 16-foot.
43. Principal, 8-foot.
44. Violoncello, 8-foot.
45. Flute bass, 8-foot.
46. Fifteenth, 4-foot.
47. Mixture (5 ranks).
48. Contra-fagotto, 16-foot.
49. Trombone, 16-foot.
50. Posaune, 8-foot.

T꜀ʀ.]

to utter, not the written sound, the note played, but one or more of its harmonics; thus the *jeu de nasard* or *quinte* when a C is played, emits a G ; the cornet stop gives with three rows of pipes the perfect chord C, E, G, an octave below; the *plein jeu* or the *fourniture* contains almost all the overtones. Why, you say, this cacophony ?

To understand it we must remember that a sound, to have a satisfactory musical character, must be accompanied by a certain number of its overtones or harmonics;[1] without this, it appears feeble, lacking in character, deficient in timbre. Now this is the case with the many of the flue-pipes, notably with the Bourdons ; they produce a sound far too pure to please us, too destitute of harmonics, a sound which we consider insipid and colourless ; but if to them are joined by means of a mutation-stop, a mixture, *which is perfectly appropriate*, the overtones which they lack, the ear does not perceive the subterfuge, and simply receives the impression of a fundamental tone, rich, warm, well-coloured. This is the utility of the mixtures, which have been abused, but in their fitting employ are of musical and logical use.

Other stops are constructed on a surprising principle; in the Vox Humana and the Voix Céleste, for example, each key commands two pipes, slightly discordant, that is to say, so tuned that one is a little above, the other a little below, the true pitch, — very slightly, of course. This no doubt is false, but so little that one is not conscious of it unless he knows that it is so ; and the undulating, iridescent sound which results from this singular arrangement has a peculiar, mysterious charm, a sort of vacillation and balancing of the sound.

Only a limited and discreet use, however, should be made of these stops. Their excessive use is fatiguing to the ear. Also it is usual to avoid mingling these stops with others, as the discord would then be conspicuous.

The Unda Maris has the same peculiarity of tone.

1 See pp. 13 and 14.

The pipes belonging to the different stops are placed in rows lengthwise over the *wind-chest*, a shallow, air-tight box. In the wind-chests the air sent by the bellows through the wind-trunks accumulates and is compressed, having no outlet except through the pipes. This outlet, however, is closed in two ways, by the *sliders* and by *valves*, whose working we shall explain.

The *sliders* are long, thin strips of wood, slipping in grooves under each row of pipes; they are pierced with holes designed to permit the air in the wind-chest to enter the pipes. By means of draw-stops at the right and left of the key-board, or above it, the organist makes these sliders move, so that their holes correspond or do not correspond with the apertures of the pipes, and he thus opens or shuts off at once all the pipes of the stop.

But when a stop is open, still the air cannot yet enter the pipes, for each is shut off by a valve which closes the opening from the wind-chest to the mouth of the pipe. This valve is opened by the pressure on a key of the manual, and the same touch opens the valve of every pipe speaking the same note on all the stops belonging to the key-board.

The stops are divided among the different key-boards without any absolute rule; as has been said, no two organs are alike. In most cases, where an organ has five key-boards, the first (counting from the lowest upwards), which has been called the *Positif*, and also the *Choir Organ*, contains the stops suited for light and rapid utterance and specially adapted for the accompaniment of a choir;[1] the second is the manual of the Great Organ, and commands the most powerful stops; the same is very nearly true of the third, the Swell Organ; the fourth, the Solo Organ, consists of stops of a special character, fine, expressive, melodious, useful to be employed in solos; and the fifth, the Echo Organ, is connected with stops placed far in the back of the Organ, or above it, so as to produce the effect

[1] In the early organs, the stops of the Positif occupy a little shelf by themselves, quite separate from the rest of the instrument, and in front of it.

of distant sounds. The arrangement then is as follows:

> 5th, Echo ;
> 4th, Solo ;
> 3d, Swell ;
> 2d, Great Organ ;
> 1st, Choir Organ.

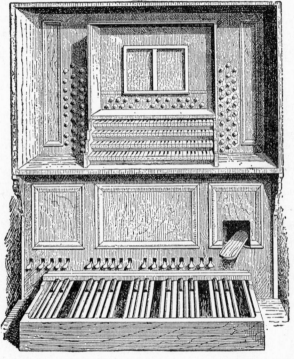

Fig 37.— ARRANGEMENT OF KEY-BOARDS IN THE ORGAN OF SAINT-EUSTACHE.

When there are but four key-boards the Echo or the Swell is omitted ; the arrangement then is either :

4th, Echo ;	or : 4th, Solo ;
3d, Solo ;	3d, Swell ;
2d, Great Organ ;	2d, Great Organ ;
1st, Choir Organ	1st, Choir Organ.

In instruments of less vast proportions the Great Organ and the Swell will have but one manual; the same is the case with the Solo and the Echo; hence results this very frequent combination:

> 3d, Solo ;
> 2d, Great Organ ;
> 1st, Choir Organ.

And if there are but two key-boards, the first usually serves for Choir Organ and Grand Organ combined, and the second has the more characteristic stops:

> 2d, Solo ;
> 1st, Choir Organ.

But these arrangements are extremely variable.

It often is the case, and indeed this arrangement is usual in organs of modern construction, that a certain number of the stops are inclosed in a box having venetian blinds which can be gradually opened or closed by a pedal; when these shutters are wide open, the sounds have their greatest intensity, and in closing them a marked effect of gradually increasing distance is produced. It is to the Solo Organ that this mechanism is generally applied; though in some instruments it is arranged for several or even all of the manuals (Fig. 38).

The ordinary extent of the key-boards of an organ is four octaves and a half, from C_1 to G_5 :

It is needless to repeat that this is by no means the actual limit of the instrument, since each key of the manual can call into utterance, together or separately, five different octaves, according as the sliders of the 2-, 4-, 8-, 16-, or 32-foot tone are open or shut. Besides this there is the pedal key-board.

This key-board has generally two octaves and a half, from C to F ; placed under the feet of the organist, it is formed of keys arranged like those of a manual,

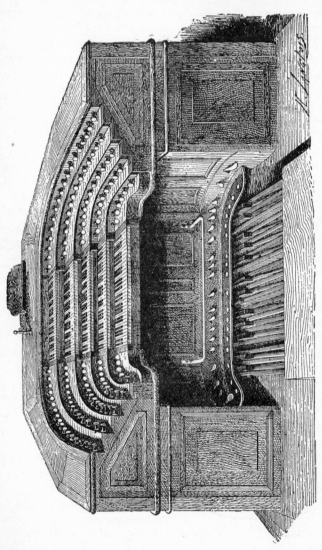

Fig. 38.— BANKS OF KEY-BOARDS AT SAINT-SULPICE.

but so wide that for the fingering can be substituted the alternate use of the heel and toe, which is called *pedal playing,* and requires much study.

Since the pedal key-board supplies the bass of the harmony, it is evident that it must be rich in grave stops of every timbre and every kind, of 16-foot — and even of 32-foot tone, if the instrument contains them,—which does not exclude the presence of other lighter stops which may be used either for solos, or to reinforce, accentuate, and add brilliancy to the deeper tones.

As accessories, and not without importance, there are also *combination-pedals* of different kinds ; these are placed just over the pedal key-board, and have some resemblance to the pedals of a piano. The following are the principal varieties, those most frequently employed :

1. The *Couplers.* These unite two manuals, that is to say, they give to one key-board the command of all the stops belonging to two or more. Thus, upon an organ with five key-boards, if the Echo be coupled to the Solo, then the Solo to the Swell, then the Swell to the Great Organ, finally the Choir Organ to the Great Organ, there is concentrated upon this last manual all the power of the instrument.

2. The *Tirasses* (pedal-couplers). These have the effect of putting a manual, or more than one, in communication with the pedal key-board, so as to increase the power or the variety of timbre of the latter. Thus if to the preceding combination we add the *tirasse* of the Great Organ, the pedal key-board acquires the power of all the united stops of the five manuals, plus the stops peculiar to itself. To have a part of this strength only, the *tirasse* of the Swell only, or of the Choir Organ only, may be employed.

3. *Composition pedals for the reeds.* In many modern organs the loudest reed-stops, though open, remain silent until thrown in by the use of a corresponding pedal, which gives the opportunity to prepare them in advance, and have them ready at the desired moment. Releasing this pedal,

they are again thrown out. There may be one of these pedals for each key-board or one only for the whole instrument.

4. The *Swell pedal*, which opens or closes the shutters for the Swell.

5. Some other pedals have an artistic character of more doubtful value, the *tremolo* or *tremblant*, for instance, by which the tone of the Vox Humana is made to flutter (not very flattering to the singers it purposes to imitate); the *storm*, which depresses at once all the low pedal-keys, thus producing an imitative, but anti-musical, uproar, etc.

It would not be worth while for me to call the reader's attention farther to the formidable complication of diverse mechanisms which are required in a great organ, where all the stops, to whichever key-board they belong, must be able to be grouped, two by two, three by three, without any other limit than that of the composition of the instrument. It requires clockwork and locksmith's work, and with its multiplicity of divers movements, traces, sliders, levers, valves that he must employ, the art of the organ builder demands as much knowledge of mechanics as of acoustics. Also, until very lately, as instruments of early date attest, the use of the key-boards was more and more difficult in proportion as the organist desired to employ simultaneously more and more stops. At the present time, owing to the use of pneumatic levers (invented by Barker, about 1832), owing also to electric transmissions which have simplified marvellously the mechanical contrivances needed, the touch of a large organ has become as light as that of the most docile piano. But an extremely ill-judged use of electricity has also been attempted, while placing the key-boards far distant from the wind-chests and the pipes, for instance the key-board in the chancel, the pipes over the main entrance to the building. Nothing could be more attractive; the organist being thus close beside the officiating priest; moreover, the same performer could thus command in turn the Choir Organ and the Great Organ, which never require to be played together. The result would be a decided economy for organ builders. But unfortunately it had not been considered that while electric transmission is instantaneous, it is no less true that waves of sound move only at an average rapidity of 1115 feet a second, whence it results that the unfortunate organist, with his instrument thus at long range, never hears the chord or the note that he is playing, but the chord that he has just played, the note just now produced, which is nothing less than a torture for the ear, only to be endured by a deaf man.

And organists are not deaf. On the contrary, of all performers, they are those whose art demands the most intelligence and rapidity of thought, as well as the largest store of erudition. A profound knowledge of his complex instrument; its handling, which requires a finish of execution of which the pianist has no idea; the grouping of the stops, which is truly an orchestration; a special study of the pedal key-board; an acquaintance with the rich musical literature of the organ,— all this is but a small part of what the organist must know, for he is required also, by the exigencies of the liturgy, to improvise almost constantly; it is but rarely, in the church, that any written piece is played; all must spring on the instant from his brain and his fingers, following upon the action of the celebrant. So that, if the organ is the *instrument of instruments,* as its Latin name declares *(organa),* the organist is the *musician of musicians ;* besides his technical knowledge in harmony, counterpoint, fugue, he must have nothing less than *inspiration,* the genius creative of musical forms, and a special readiness of mental action without which all his knowledge would be but a barren store.[1]

Organ music is written on three staves, the upper two for the hands, the third for the feet. In regard to the choice of stops, the composer, if he is not himself the organist, would do well not to go beyond general indications, such as: *8-foot, 16-foot, flue-stops, reed-stops,* which, united with signs of expression, will be interpreted by the

[1] See the chapter on *Improvisation.*

performer according to the effect desired, and the resources of his instrument.

Where shall we seek for the origin of the organ ?

The Bible tells us that it was invented by Jubal, and it seems from the Talmud that an instrument similar to it was known to the Hebrews under the name of *magrepha.* By others the invention is attributed to Archimedes or Ctesibius, both of whom lived about 200 B.C. Many Latin authors mention the organ; notably Tertullian, who, writing in the second century of our era, gives a description which, inconceivable as it may seem, really is applicable to the modern instrument: "Observe," he says, "the extraordinary genius of Archimedes. I mean the water-organ : so many members, so many parts, so many joinings, so many roads or passages for the sounds, such a compendium of sounds, such an intercourse of modes, such troops of pipes, and all composing one great whole ! "

This was the hydraulic organ, in which water served to equalise the pressure of the air furnished by the bellows, in a manner long uncomprehended, but recently explained by M. Cl. Loret from a text of Vitruvius. Organs of considerable size, on this plan, were in use in the East and in Constantinople in the fourth century. Later, the pneumatic organ, *Organum pneumaticum,* was invented, in which nature's abhorrence of a vacuum was utilised as it is in our own time.

In its earliest form, the instrument was very small and movable, the *Portative Organ;* when larger ones were made that required fixed *position* they were called *Positifs;* [1] and this name remains to a manual of the present instrument which commands a group of independent stops.

Thus we see that without doubt the organ was known to remote antiquity. If we now ascend the stream of time, and seek the primitive idea, the germ, we shall find it in three very rudimentary instruments (Fig. 39, 40, 41).

The Pan's-pipes or syrinx is the earliest example of a

[1] From the Latin *ponere.*

graduated series of open pipes, with a very obvious resemblance to a flute-stop. All the Greek authors speak of this as something *ancient in their time.* The *cheng* or Chinese organ is described in Chinese books, and has remained the same from its origin to the present day. It is a row of reed-pipes, blown directly, like the syrinx, by the human breath. Lastly, the bagpipe or its precursors, known to

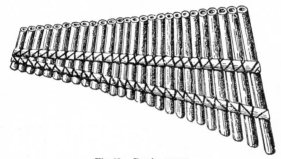

Fig. 39.— PAN'S-PIPES.
Width, 15 in.

the ancients under the generic name of *tibiae utriculariae* (bag-pipes), offer the first example of the storage of compressed air. These three elements united undoubtedly gave rise to the first attempts at organ-building; there was lacking only the key-board, which seems to have appeared about the sixth or seventh century in the rudimentary form of keys several inches wide, which had to be struck with the clenched fist, like the Flemish carillon; and thus we have a rude sketch of the giant instrument which has now been hurriedly and insufficiently described.

WORKS ON ORGAN—BUILDING.

Dom Bédos de Celles, *l'Art du facteur d'Orgue.*
Cavaillé-Coll, *De l'Orgue et de son architecture.*
Hopkins & Rimbault, *The Organ, its History and Construction.*
Edwards, C. A., *Organs and Organ Building.*

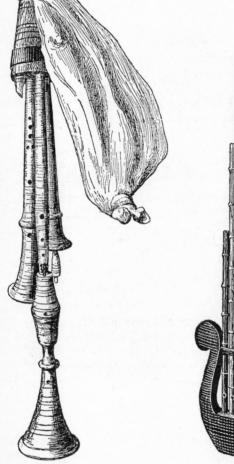

Fig. 40.— BAGPIPE.
Length, 3 ft. 10 in.

Fig. 41.— CHENG OR CHINESE ORGAN.
Length, 19 in.

HARMONIUM, OR CABINET ORGAN.

The harmonium,[1] or cabinet organ is designed as a substitute for the organ in places where there is insufficient

Fig. 42.— HARMONIUM.
Breadth, 4 ft. 6 in.

space, and up to a certain point it has its use. It produces no effect of grandeur, its thin, nasal tone, its narrow com-

---

[1] Most of the illustrations have been designed from models courteously furnished by the principal instrument-makers, Cavaillé-Coll, Erard, Pleyel, Mustel, Alexandre, Gaud, Colin-Mézin, Thibouville-Lamy & Co., Couesnon, Evette & Schaeffer, Besson, and others. A few instruments in the Musée du Conservatoire are represented here; the others belong to the author personally.

pass, the lack of the pedal key-board which gives the organ
a third hand, so to speak, the monotony in its timbre, and
other deficiencies, render the imitation extremely feeble; but
in small chapels, to accompany sacred song, or in parlours,
especially with other instruments, such as the violin, the
violoncello, the piano, the harp, etc., it is not without
charm. It is often used in the theatre also, *incognito*,
behind the scenes, to guide, sustain, and even strengthen
an unaccompanied chorus. It is, therefore, a useful,
serviceable instrument, which it is well to know.

The key-board of the harmonium has but five octaves

 ; but (and it is in this that consists its

closest resemblance to the organ) each key by means of
registers commands, not only the stops giving the written
note (as of the 8-foot of the organ), but other stops, lower
or higher by an octave (as the 16-foot and the 4-foot), which
enables the one finger to produce at will from the one key,
one, or two, or three tones, either the octave or the 15th :

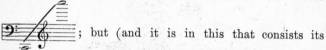

The chords are multiplied, strengthened, and doubled in

the same way  , which, joined to the

continuity of the sound, produces, in restricted space, some
small suggestion of the organ.

The sonorous principle of the harmonium is the free
reed, without the pipe.[1] It would seem then that the
timbre would be always very nearly the same; but the
skill of the makers has succeeded in creating, by ingenious
arrangements, stops having quite an appreciable variety in
this respect.

Each stop is divided into two half-stops; there is a
register for the higher notes of the manual and another for

[1] See, p. 81, the difference as to the reed-stops of the organ.

the lower, which allows one combination of stops for the right hand and another for the left; numbers placed upon the draw-stops show the correlation between these half-stops; the division generally is made the middle E and F:

The following is the ordinary composition of a harmonium of four stops, which is regarded as the type:

(S)	(0)	(4)	(3)	(2)	(1)	(G)	(E)	(1)	(2)	(3)	(4)	(0)	(T)
Sourdine.	Forte.	Bassoon.	Clarion.	Bourdon.	Cor anglais.	Grand jeu.	Expression.	Flute.	Clarinet.	Fife.	Hautbois.	Forte.	Tremblant.

The numbers 1 and 4 produce the written note.

The numbers 2 produce it an octave lower.

The numbers 3, an octave higher.

There is, in general, very little relation between these stops and the instrument they are supposed to represent. There will be observed at the extremities of the list registers that we have not yet explained: at the left, the Sourdine (S) which is number one (low) softened; at the right, the Tremblant (T), of which I prefer not to speak, and of which persons of taste will avoid the use; next, two zeros (0) which augment the power of the stops 3 and 4 by a system of venetian shutters resembling the Swell of the organ; in the centre, the Grand jeu (G) which opens all the stops at once, and the Expression (E) which allows the volume of sound to be increased or diminished by the pressure of the feet on the bellows; hence the instrument has been called *l'orgue expressif*. In the harmonium as a percussion instrument, the stop 1 is strengthened by a series of hammers which strike upon the reed when the key is pressed, producing a rapid and noisy emission of sound.

An improvement of the greatest importance is the *Double Expression*, invented by Mustel in 1854, which makes it possible by means of two knee-swells to vary the shades of intensity independently in the two halves of the key-board.

There are rudimentary harmoniums of a single stop; others have been constructed with twelve, fifteen, or even more stops; also with more than one key-board, and even with a pedal key-board, and of course with greatly increased power; but all are made on the same principle.

METHODS FOR THE HARMONIUM: *Renaud de Vilbac, Lefébure-Wély, Clément Loret.*

FREDERIC ARCHER, *A Complete Method for the American Reed Organ,* August Reinhard (Ger., Fr., and Eng.)

The organ and the harmonium are, among wind instruments, the only autonomous ones; by their range and by their reservoir of air they form, in themselves, a complete whole, as in the other families do the piano and the harp.

THE FLUTE FAMILY. INSTRUMENTS WITH OPEN MOUTH-HOLE.

FLUTE.

Bore open and cylindrical, the only one in which the vibratory motion is produced from a lateral mouth-hole. It is made of wood, of silver, or of German silver. Its total

range, chromatically, is three full octaves . The

sounds of the first low octave are rather faint; those of the second (2nd harmonics), produced by the same fingering and a stronger use of the breath, are more vigorous; those of the third (the 3d, 4th, and 5th harmonics), obtained by still augmenting the force, become shrill and piercing; they are only suited to *forte* or *fortissimo* passages. All the others have the characteristic gentleness and suavity of this instrument, which also has an incomparable volubility, so to speak: arpeggios, grace notes, diatonic and chromatic scales with notes slurred or detached, rapid repetitions obtained by double-tonguing,—all are common to the flute, and it is above all things a warbling instrument.

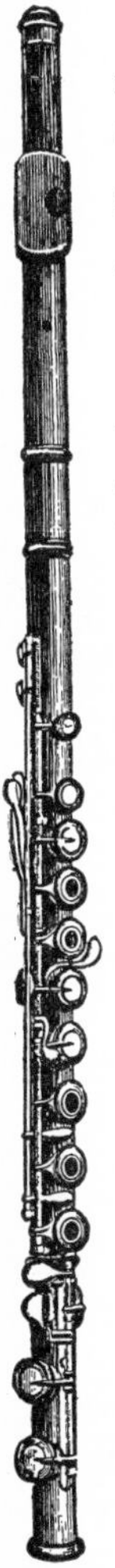

The trill alone ♪ is prohibited to it by the mechanism of its keys, which the German Boehm (1847) especially perfected; the major trills on the notes ♪ or their synonyms are very difficult.[1]

PICCOLO.

Music for the piccolo is written like that for the large flute, but sounds an octave higher (the *octava* is understood); the mechanism and fingering are the same also.

Its sound is brilliant and hard, only suited to effects of force and agility; is lacking in charm and sweetness. It is the highest instrument of the symphonic orchestra, the most clamorous also.

PICCOLO FLUTES IN E♭ AND IN F.

These are used only in military music. They give the highest sound of any instruments. Their written compass is ♪, but the actual sound, by transposition, is

for the E♭ piccolo, and for the F.

Their sound, of course, is extremely shrill and piercing.

Fig. 44.
PICCOLO
Length,
13 in.

Fig. 43.
FLUTE.
Length,
26 1-2 in.

1 We speak of the flute of the orchestra in its present form. The origin of this instrument is lost in the night of time; but it is only at a comparatively recent date that the idea occurred of placing the mouth-hole laterally, whence its name, *traverse flute*, in contrast to the early *beak-flutes*, which were held like the oboe or clarinet. (See later, *Flageolet.*)

[As early as the 16th century, the traverse flute was in use. ED.]

FLAGEOLET.

This is the flute of the *pifferari*, the ancient beak-flute, quite out of style at the present day, owing to its too great imperfections, but used by Gluck, Handel, and Mozart, nevertheless, in the guise of a piccolo. It was written a twelfth below the actual note.

The instrument is no longer heard except in some dance-hall or tea-garden orchestras of the lowest rank, and even from these it is now disappearing.

Oboe Family. Instruments with Double Reed.

OBOE.

Conical tube, in which the column of air is made to vibrate by means of a double reed, that is to say, two reeds placed opposite to each other. It is made of wood, as its name (*hautbois*) indicates, usually of grenadilla. Its compass is,

chromatically : the oboes of some

French makers have also a B♭ below. The fingering is much like that of the flute. The timbre is thin and nasal, very piercing in *forte* passages, of exquisite refinement in its *piano*, harsh and of bad quality in its very high and its very low notes. The oboe is artless and rustic in its expression; it is easily pastoral and melancholy; if it is gay, the gayety is frank and almost excessive, exaggerated, but its natural tone is of a gentle sadness, a resigned endurance. It is unrivalled in depicting simple, rural sentiments of whatever kind, and, on occasion, can even become pathetic.

Fig. 45.
OBOE.
Length,
24 1-2 in.

It certainly has not the agility of the flute, but it can, however, especially in its middle notes, venture upon certain formulas comparatively rapid, scales and arpeggios, if simple in contour.

The major trills upon  or their synonyms must, however, be avoided; their execution is either impossible or of excessive difficulty.

METHODS : *Brod, Verroust, G. Parès.*

COR ANGLAIS.

This is the same instrument as the oboe, but a fifth below. Its tone is essentially sad, melancholy, sorrowful; it suits the expression of mental suffering; this is its characteristic note.

It is really an oboe in F. It is written a fifth above its actual sound:

Notation.   Actual Sounds.

hence results for the performer (who is always an oboeist) great ease in execution, but for the reader, the necessity of reading in the mezzo-soprano clef, transposing to the lower fifth, as the instrument itself does automatically.

The cor anglais, which is a very ancient instrument, was originally, and for a very long time, constructed in a curved form, which was considered, on account of its length, as a convenient arrangement; furthermore, it was generally covered with a sort of bag of skin; all contributed to give it a certain resemblance to a horn, a sort of Alpine horn; hence, probably, its singular name of cor (horn), which is justified neither by the timbre of the instrument nor the family to which it belongs. Now, why *English?* For this

Fig. 46.

COR ANGLAIS.

Length, 2 ft. 11 1-2 in.

I can offer no reason, although I have sought to find one.

OBOE D'AMORE.

Intermediate between the oboe and the cor anglais, the oboe d'amore, an instrument now fallen into neglect, was very much used in the time of Sebastian Bach. This is an oboe in A.

Its compass was [musical notation] written [musical notation]

according to the principle that rules all transposing instruments. Its timbre gentle and veiled, less incisive than the oboe, less cavernous than the cor anglais, had a great charm, and its neglect may well be regretted.

BASSOON.

Open pipe with conical mouth-hole and double reed; may be considered the bass of the oboe.

Its compass is very large for a wind-instrument, namely, three octaves: [musical notation] with

all the chromatic degrees. Like the flute and the oboe, its deep notes are fundamental tones, those of the middle register are second harmonics, and its highest are third, fourth, and fifth harmonics, obtained with the same fingering as for the fundamentals by forcing the breath so that the column of air divides into two, three, or four vibrating segments. From this result varieties of timbre. In its lowest tones it is solemn and pontifical like an organ pedal; its medium has a sweet sonority of some richness but little strength; and its high register is the most expressive, but painful, distressed, and dejected.

Fig. 47.
OBOE
D'AMORE.
Length,
2 ft. 4 in.

At the same time this instrument has comic possibilities; in the medium or lower registers certain staccato notes which have been often used have a certain grotesqueness which almost borders on impropriety.

These four major trills should be avoided 𝄢, as well as those which go below 𝄢, or above 𝄢.

They are extremely difficult or even impossible.

METHODS : *Jancourt, Cokken, Beer, G. Parès, Charles Almenraeder* (Ger. and Fr.).

DOUBLE BASSOON.

This instrument figures more frequently on scores than in orchestras, where a sarrusophone or some reed bass is generally used instead.

Its normal range would be an octave lower than the bassoon, but there are generally used only the notes between 𝄢 and 𝄢, which sound, of course, an octave lower.

Even with this limited compass, it is the deepest-toned instrument in the orchestra.

SARRUSOPHONE.[1]

A brass instrument, with conical tube and double reed, having a resemblance to the oboe and the bassoon, though with a richer timbre;

Fig. 48. — BASSOON.
Length, 4 ft. 3 1-2 in.

[1] From the name of the inventor, Sarrus, a bandmaster in the French army under the Second Empire.

it has been made in different voices, soprano, alto, tenor, etc. The only one used in orchestras is the double-bass sarrusophone, which gives the grave octave of the note

Fig. 49. — SARRUSOPHONE.
Length, 2 ft. 11 1-2 in.

written ; it is used with great advantage in place of the double bassoon.

The fingering much resembles that of the saxophone.

METHOD : *Coyon.*

INSTRUMENTS WITH DOUBLE REED AND AIR RESERVOIR.

CORNEMUSE, BINIOU, ZAMPOGNA, BAGPIPE, MUSETTE, ETC.

These various instruments, of which representative types may still be found in the south of France, in Brittany, in Italy, and in Scotland, belong to the same family, which is of very ancient origin.

They consist, essentially, of a leathern bag (or else a bladder) which is filled with air; into this bag are fixed the ends of sonorous pipes of different sizes, of which some give a certain definite sound, a pedal in the harmonic sense of the word, more frequently, however, a double pedal, tonic and dominant, while the others, pierced with holes and having the reed of an oboe, give the performer opportunity for playing varied and rapid melodies, but within a a very limited compass.

The Breton binious and the Highland bagpipes often present a gamut which appears to us grotesque, without subdominant, or incomplete, manifestly vestiges of ancient tonalities now abandoned, and in this aspect they are historically of interest.

It is impossible also not to see in this grouping of pipes around a reservoir of air, in the case of instruments unquestionably of very ancient origin[1], an idea which may have preceded that of the organ, and may have led to it. These instruments have been used in the orchestra. In Great Britain the military band of certain Scottish regiments is formed entirely of bagpipes and fifes.

CLARINET FAMILY.
INSTRUMENTS WITH SINGLE REED.

CLARINET.

This instrument, the richest in compass and in variety of timbre of all the wind instruments, is subject to a special and very curious law. Its tube

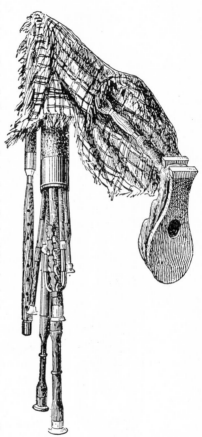

Fig. 50. — HIGHLAND BAGPIPE.
(Musée du Conservatoire, No. 525.)

---

1 Traces of these are found among the Jews. The Romans called them *Tibia utricularis.* In Persia the bagpipe is found under the name "nay ambânah."

is absolutely cylindrical, open, and its column of air is set in vibration by a single flexible reed. Now a peculiarity in pipes of this construction is that the vibrating segment forms, not at the middle point, but at the end where the

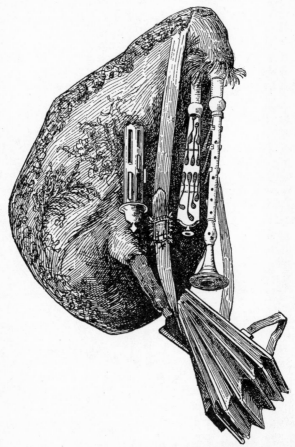

Fig. 51.—MUSETTE. (Musée du Conservatoire, No. 521.)

reed is, so that the mode of subdivision of the aerial column is the same as if the pipe were stopped.[1] The clarinet has

1 See pp. 16-20.

therefore only the harmonics of unequal numbers, which renders its fingering very different from that of the flute, the oboe, and the bassoon. It would seem that this might place it below them; on the contrary, this instrument lends itself with admirable suppleness to the expression of all sentiments which the composer may wish to entrust to it.

Its compass, the greatest possessed by any wind instrument , chromatically, (and being able even, according to the skill of the player, to go higher) has a great share in giving it this richness of expression; but the diversity of timbre belonging to its lower, middle, and higher registers, must be regarded as the true superiority of this instrument.

The sonority of the lower register, produced by the fundamental tones (which are also called *chalumeau* tones, in memory of the rudimentary instrument, precursor of the clarinet, which had only these low notes), is vibrating, hollow, and incisive, almost cavernous at the bottom of the scale; this register extends from to .

The high register obtained by the same fingering, but *quintoyant*, that is to say, giving the 3d harmonic, possesses incomparable power, brilliancy, and warmth. It is called the *clarion register*,[1] and gives the instrument its name: the clarinet is a *chalumeau* (English: shawm) endowed with the power of uttering these high notes up to the twelfth from the fundamental to .

Fig. 52.
CLARINET.
Length, 25 in.

Between the low notes of the *chalumeau* and the

[1] There is no possible connection here with the instrument of that name used for military calls.

brilliant notes of the *clarion* there is a range of four notes
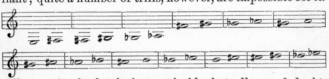 which is the feeble part of the instrument. Then,
above the *clarion* come the very high notes,[1] of a piercing
character, often disagreeable, only to be used in *fortissimo*

passages of the orchestra ▬▬▬▬.

Thus we see the extreme multiplicity of effects of which
the clarinet is capable. Almost as agile as the flute, it can
venture upon the most complicated passages, even those containing abrupt digressions; its arpeggios are especially brilliant; quite a number of trills, however, are impossible for it.

All are not absolutely impracticable, but all are of doubtful execution.

Equally it must be observed that tonalities nearest the
key of C are most suitable for rapid or complicated designs,
and that tones burdened with more than two or three alterations involve difficulties of execution.

In order to render it possible to use the clarinets for
movements in any key, this instrument has been made in
three different sizes: the one of which we have been speaking is the C clarinet, which plays the notes as they are
written.

Somewhat longer is the clarinet in B♭, which is written
in the same way, but sounds a major second lower:

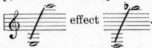

It must then be read in the tenor clef, an octave higher
being supposed, with the appropriate change of signature.

The longest tube furnishes the scale of the A clarinet,

<hr />

1 Twelfths from those of the middle register, and obtained by the same
fingering.

which sounds a minor third below the written note:

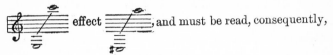 effect , and must be read, consequently,

by means of the soprano clef.

The two latter are, then, transposing instruments.

Independently of the differences in actual compass, and independently also of the qualities of timbre belonging to their different registers, the three clarinets, the C, the B♭, and the A, possess each a special, well-defined character.

The C clarinet is brilliant, merry, violent, and sometimes trivial.

The B♭ clarinet has a rich, warm, velvety timbre, energetic and passionate.

The A clarinet is tender and elegiac, penetrating, but sombre.

It thus appears that the B♭ clarinet is the richest and noblest of the whole family; hence it is almost universally adopted by the great virtuosi who are able, by force of skill, to execute upon this one instrument whatever is written for the others, with the exception, of course, of the lowest note of the A clarinet which remains beyond reach.

In doing this, for their own personal convenience and to simplify their material, they will not acknowledge even to themselves that, to a certain point, they falsify the composer's thought, not furnishing to it exactly the timbre which he desired.

METHODS : *Beer, Klosé, Parès, Carl Baermann.*

ALTO-CLARINET OR BASSET-HORN.

This is a clarinet in F which sounds a fifth below

the written note: effect . It has the

same principle of construction and the same fingering as the ordinary clarinet, although the handling is a little heavier. The dominant character of this instrument is an eloquent gravity, a great charm allied with dignity.

For reading, the mezzo-soprano clef (C on the second line) must be assumed, as for the cor anglais.

BASS-CLARINET.

This instrument is written like the clarinet in B♭, but sounds an octave lower, that is to say, a major 9th below the written note:

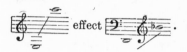

A person reading the score must employ the tenor clef.

The size of the tube and the pontifical character of the timbre of this instrument forbid the use of compositions too light and rapid, except, however, certain arpeggios which it executes not without a degree of suppleness, especially in its best tonalities which are, as for all the clarinets, those which contain the largest number of naturals in the written key.

Fig. 53.—BASSET-HORN.
Length, 2 ft. 10 in.

SMALL CLARINETS.

Clarinets have been made in D, in E♭, and in F. Only the one in E♭ is in constant use, and this only in military music. It has all the merits of the large clarinets in point of agility; but its timbre is always crude and shrill.

Its written compass is the same as that of the clarinet

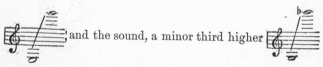

and the sound, a minor third higher

(Gluck, Berlioz, and Wagner have *exceptionally* introduced this instrument into the orchestra.)

SAXOPHONE.

The saxophone[1] resembles the clarinet by its reed, but its tube is conical, which renders its fingering like that of the oboe, and it is generally a brass instrument.

Its timbre cannot be mistaken for that of any other; it is perhaps like that of the alto clarinet and the cor anglais, though with much more volume; it is, however, far more conspicuous and noticeable.

Its written compass is that of the oboe; but, in varying the size of the instrument, there is obtained, as in the case of the clarinet, an actual difference in the range.

The one which, up to the present time, has been most frequently employed in the orchestra, is the contralto saxophone in E♭; the following is its written compared with its real compass:

Endowed with a penetrating and

intense sonority, this instrument can perform, though with a little heaviness, all the passages of agility of which the other wind instruments are capable.

In military music, the saxophones hold an important place:

Fig. 54.— Bass Clarinet.
Length, 3 ft. 1 in.

1 From the inventor's name, Adolph Sax.

Sopranino in E♭ ;
Soprano in B♭ ;
Contralto in E♭ ;
Tenor in B♭ ;
Barytone in E♭ ;
Bass in B♭.

Fig. 55. — SAXOPHONES.

Soprano.	Alto.	Tenor.	Bass.
Length, 15 3-4 in.		Length, 2 ft. 7 1-2 in.	Length, 3 ft. 9 in.

All have the same fingering; from the lowest note of the bass saxophone in B♭ to the highest of the sopranino in E♭, there is this enormous range :

METHODS · *Kokken, Klosé, Mayeur, G. Parès.*

FAMILY OF THE BRASS–WIND.

HORN.

The simple horn consists of a tube bent into a spiral (for convenience in holding), comparatively narrow near the mouthpiece, and gradually enlarging to the bell; it is therefore a conical pipe. There is no hole pierced in it; accordingly the column of air contained vibrates in its whole length. It has no reed, but a simple mouthpiece, and the lips of the performer serve as reeds. It is therefore, in acoustic principle, and also in appearance, the simplest of instruments; but it is not the easier to handle on that account.

Fig. 56. — HORN.
Length, 22 3-4 inches.

According to the length of the tube, a horn is in C, D, E♭, etc., which means that its fundamental tone, the tone emitted by the tube when its column of air vibrates undivided, is C, or D, or E♭, etc.

By a slight modification in the pressure of the lips on the mouthpiece the performer causes the column of air to divide into two, three, four, up to fifteen or sixteen vibrating segments, and thus to produce all the harmonics of its fundamental. The natural scale of the horn is then, theoretically, the series of harmonics to which so frequent reference has already been made. But the dimensions of the pipe render the emission of the fundamental sound very doubtful and of a weak, indeterminate character: it is, therefore, never used, and the lowest note a horn gives is in reality its second harmonic.

Below is given the scale, or as is sometimes said quite improperly, the gamut of the C horn, whose (impractica-ble) fundamental is low C , with the actual pitch of each sound as heard:

And it is written thus:

This gives occasion for two interesting remarks:

1. It is usual, I do not know why, to write always the lowest note (and only that one) in the F-clef, while the others are written in the G-clef, but an octave above the actual sound, as is usual for tenor voices.

2. The tones 7, 11, 13, and 14, are not absolutely true; the two B flats are sensibly too low; this fault is reduced in playing with some force, but remains very conspicuous in soft effects, where they should be employed only as passing notes, or else alone, without any harmony; as to the F♯ (11), it is quite as much like F natural as F sharp, for which reason, in special works, it is regarded as an F which is too high. All these sounds require to be corrected by the skill of the performer; in their natural state they would be discordant with the other elements of the orches-tra, and even alone they surprise the ear unpleasantly; they are never employed except with a slight alteration

made by partly closing the bell with the hand, thus lowering them and at the same time dulling the timbre. They belong therefore in the category of *stopped sounds*, as contrasted with *natural*, or *open sounds*.

The same procedure can be applied to all the other notes of the natural scale, and by this artifice the horn obtains for itself a sort of artificial chromatic gamut, where the open notes alone are brilliant and energetic, while the closed notes are more and more vague and timid as the bell is more nearly closed.

In the following example these inequalities are represented by difference of values; the whole notes sound clearly, the half notes are dull, the quarter notes still more so.

(Certain shades of detail useful only to the player are omitted here.)

The difficulty of playing complicated or rapid passages with means of execution so delicate, has led the makers of every date to construct instruments of many keys, or, which amounts to the same thing, to construct movable pieces of tubing, called crooks, which, inserted in the length, alter the pitch, according as they are longer or shorter. In this way the mute fundamental is varied, and all its harmonics with it. There are crooks for all the keys, but the following are those used by the classic masters; in the table are given the actual sounds produced and their notation; if to those be added the closed sounds, which are the same as for the horn in C, we shall have the whole number of notes accessible to these instruments with their degree of vigour or of attenuation.

Effect produced.   Notation.

The timbre of the horn may be utilised in many ways, but great skill is necessary to use it to advantage. It is by turns heroic or rustic, savage or exquisitely poetic; and it is perhaps in the expression of tenderness and emotion that it best develops its mysterious qualities.

In melodic formulas which require force and rapidity, the open notes are alone sure to be successful. The closed notes must be uttered guardedly, and are never very loud. Their production is facilitated by having them follow an adjacent open sound.

METHODS: *Dauprat, Gallay, Domnich, Meifred, Richard Hofmann (Ger.).*

COR À PISTONS, OR CHROMATIC HORN.

If we suppose the ordinary horn to have many crooks permanently attached, and the performer to be able to pass from one to the other merely by pressing the finger on one, two, or three pistons, we shall have some idea of the construction and advantages of this instrument. A cor à pistons in F (the key most used) can produce with equal facility the seven series of harmonics belonging to common horns in F, E, E♭, D, D♭, C, and B; thus it has from

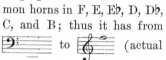 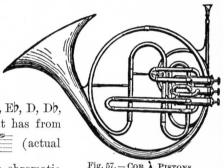

Fig. 57. — COR À PISTONS.
Length, 22 3-4 in.

to (actual notes), a complete chromatic scale of three octaves and six notes, many of which are obtained by many fingerings, a very important advantage, and besides this, the faculty of transforming each one of these sounds into a closed sound, just as an ordinary horn would do.

With all these incomparable merits it is not equally appreciated by all composers; by some the common horn is preferred, from the point of view of timbre, of poetical quality; this perhaps is due to the fact that performers, once in possession of this perfected implement, too generally abandon early procedures and the use of closed sounds, which by their very vagueness communicated to the primitive instrument a sort of timidity which was not without its charm.

METHODS : *Meifred, Gounod, Garigue, G. Parès.*

COR DE CHASSE. (HUNTING–HORN.)

This is a simple harmonic horn in D, without pistons or crooks, perhaps less carefully made than the others, but in all points similar to them. Most blowers of the hunting-horn are unaware, however, that their instrument can pro-duce naturally a B flat (which sounds C) and is the

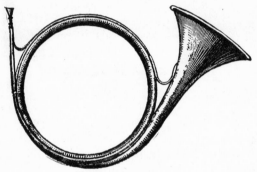

Fig. 58. — COR DE CHASSE.
Length, 23 1-2 in.

seventh harmonic; as also they have no idea of using the hand to produce closed sounds. The only notes employed for fanfares are these:

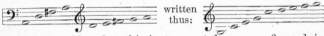

I have an idea that this instrument has never figured in orchestra except in Méhul's overture to *Le jeune Henri*, where, with its noisy rendering of a well-known fanfare, it produces one of the most picturesque and captivating effects.

TRUMPET.

This fine instrument tends, alas! to disappear from the orchestra, where its place is invaded by the chromatic trumpet, or, still more unfortunately, by the cornet à pis-tons, the type of triviality; now the simple trumpet is, on the contrary, the especially stately and heraldic instrument.

To describe it in brief, we may say it is the soprano of the horn: it has nearly the same harmonic scale, but moves in a region at once higher and more restricted; it differs from the horn farther in that it produces only the open sounds; closed sounds are unknown to it, and if attempted would produce only an unpleasant effect.

Like the horn, the trumpet is a transposing instrument;

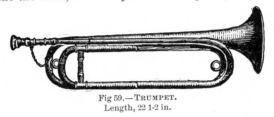

Fig 59.— TRUMPET.
Length, 22 1-2 in.

it has a number of crooks or lengthening pieces; those of C, D, E flat, E, F, G, B flat, B, are the most used.

The following scales show the notes of value in each of these keys:

It must always be remembered that here, as in the case of the horn, the seventh and eleventh harmonics (B♭ and F♯ of the notation) are only approximately true, and also, that they cannot be corrected by the partial closing of the bell. It is, therefore, wise to avoid them. However, the most classic masters have often used this false F♯ as an F natural, trusting, without doubt, to the skill of the performer to conceal the fault.

Of great agility, the trumpet is admirably suited to rapid figures, arpeggios, especially to repetitions of notes. Besides noisy fanfares and strident calls, it is able to produce, in *piano* or *pianissimo*, effects either fantastic or of extreme sweetness.

METHODS: *Dauverné, Richard Hofmann* (Ger. and Eng.), *F. L. Schubert* (Ger.).

TROMPETTE À PISTONS, OR CHROMATIC TRUMPET.

The trompette à pistons is to the ordinary trumpet as the chromatic horn to the simple horn: the transformation is

Fig. 60. — TROMPETTE À PISTONS.
Length, 22 1-2 in.

the same. It has crooks like the simple trumpet, and it embraces the written compass of $\bumpeq$ to $\bumpeq$, chromatically, of course.

It is written like the ordinary trumpet of the same key. As in the case of the horn, the timbre of the instrument seems to have been slightly modified by the addition of the pistons; it is less brilliant, a little more pasty (*empâté*), but these defects, not very conspicuous, and perhaps to be easily remedied, are largely compensated by facility and sureness of execution, and still more, by the richness and extends of the scale.

METHODS: *Dauverné, Guilbaut, G. Parès.*

CORNET À PISTONS.

The instrument requiring least study; also the most

Fig. 61. — CORNET À PISTONS.
Length, 13 3-4 in.

commonplace of instruments. Its very short tube allows it to produce only the lower harmonics, from the 2d to the 8th at most, and its timbre is entirely lacking in dignity and distinction. Its chief merit is an astonishing facility of utterance; it triumphs in the execution of repeated notes, trills, rapid passages of every kind, even chromatic, and it sings with ease every kind of melody, at the same time giving to all its own common and trivial character; on occasion it assumes to imitate the horn and the trumpet, the heroic instruments; but this imitation is often a caricature. This instrument is the *gamin de Paris* of the orchestra,[1] more at home in dance-halls and café-concerts

---

[1] In the chapter on Orchestration, there will be explained some good uses of the cornet à pistons in association with other brass instruments.

than in grand opera or symphonies, whence it would be well that it should disappear.

The cornet à piston in B flat, the most readily used, has for its actual compass, chromatically, the interval from

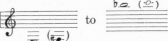

which is naturally written a tone higher, as shown by the notes in brackets.

It is made in other keys, especially in A, but the cornet in B♭ is the type of the instrument, the great soloist in popular fanfares and in military music.

METHODS : *Forestier, Arban* (also in English), *Gérin, Guilbaut* (elementary).

THE SLIDE TROMBONE.

There are three varieties of the instrument, the alto, the tenor, and the bass trombone ; each is written in the proper key of the voice whose name it bears (C_3, C_4, F_4). Trombones differ from other brass-winds in that they are not transposing, but render the note as it is written.

Below is represented the range of each, chromatically :

Fig. 62.
TROMBONE.
Length,
3 ft. 9 1-2 in.

with its translation into the more familiar clefs. The

principle of construction which gives this extensive compass will now be explained, taking the tenor trombone as a type; the others have the same effects, the one being a fourth higher, the other a fourth lower.

The slide being entirely closed, that is to say, the tube reduced to its shortest dimension, the instrument produces (modifying, as with the horn, the breath and the pressure of the lips) the harmonics of  from the second to the

eighth :  ; this is called the first position.

By pulling out the slide a little, which increases the length of the tube, we have the second position; the fundamental is now : , and its harmonics are:

A further extension gives the third position, producing the harmonics : , whose fundamental would be : .

And so on, at each new extension of the slide; the fundamental being lowered, the whole series of harmonics is lowered also.

The fourth, fifth, sixth, and seventh positions give the following tones :

Fourth:

Fifth:

Sixth:

Seventh:

Bring these notes together in order, and you have the complete chromatic scale of the tenor trombone. Skilful performers are able to produce, in the treble, the ninth and tenth harmonics, thus enriching the instrument with two more notes  hard and frail in timbre; and in the bass, the fundamentals of the first two or three positions, ; but these are exceptional cases, and, unless with a special effect to produce, it is better not to use them. The same is true of the lower notes of the bass trombone; for, this instrument being very fatiguing to play, even by persons of the strongest lungs, a second tenor trombone often is used in its place, which, of course, cannot produce these notes.

When the three trombones play together, which is usually the case, it is more convenient to unite them on a single stave, in the key of one of them; instead of

which takes much space, it is simpler to write

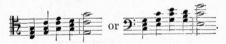

The timbre of the trombone is in its nature majestic and imposing. It is sufficiently powerful to dominate a whole orchestra; it produces, above all, the impression of power, a power superhuman. In *fortissimi* there is no instrument more stately, noble, imposing, but it can also become terrible, or rather terrific, if the composer has so decreed; in *pianissimi*, it is mournful and full of dismay, or it may have the serenity of the organ; it can also, according to the shades of meaning, become fierce or satanic, but still with undiminished grandeur and majesty.   It is a superb instrument of lofty dramatic power, which should be reserved for great occasions when, properly introduced, its effect is overwhelming.

It is a matter of good taste, by reason of the solemnity of its character as well as to diminish the difficulty of execution, not to commit to this instrument too rapid figures — unless, indeed, the passages are formed of notes belonging to the same position; it would be almost a lack of respect. But in a moderate movement it can make the needed evolutions with much ease.

METHODS : *Beer and Dieppo,   Chlodomir,   G. Parès.* In English, *Otto Langley,* "Tutor for Slide Trombone."

TROMBONE A PISTONS.

This is a tenor trombone having instead of the slide a system of pistons, like those of the horn and cornet,— which renders it much more manageable.

It is used as an ordinary trombone, with this difference, however, that there can be assigned to it much more rapid

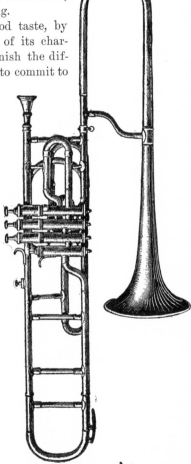

Fig. 63. — TROMBONE À PISTONS.
Length, 25 1-2 in.

designs; moreover, it goes a semi-tone lower, to E♭ 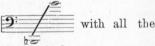.

Very rarely an orchestra has alto and bass trombones à pistons; but usually three tenor trombones take the three parts.

METHODS: *Carnaud, Chlodomir, G. Parès.*

OPHICLEIDE.

Although it has a few higher notes, the practical range of this instrument must be limited thus:

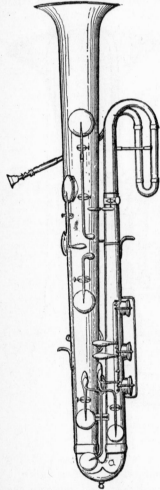

Fig. 64. — OPHICLEIDE.
Length, 3 ft. 7 in.

with all the chromatic degrees.

Its tone is rude and coarse; it has little suppleness, and it lacks in precision of tune. The ophicleide tends to disappear from the orchestra, where it reinforced the third trombone or sometimes took its place, and instead, we have the tuba, an instrument vastly its superior.

It is written in the F clef like the bass trombone.

The ophicleide[1] is derived from the *serpent*, which anciently accompanied the plain song in the churches, and is still to be found in the provinces.

METHODS: *Guilbaut, Cornette.*

[1] Etymology: Keyed serpent.

TUBA, OR BASS TUBA.

A brass instrument of the sax-horn family. If too rapid passages are not required from it, the tuba may be employed in this range :

having pistons it possesses all the chromatic degrees ; but it is better to abstain from the highest notes and from the whole lowest octave. Its timbre is vigorous, very solemn, mysterious, and lugubrious in *pianissimi*, and in all circumstances furnishes a superb bass to the brass-wind.

Fig. 65. — BASS TUBA.
Length, 3 ft. 3 in.

It is the only representative, in the orchestra, of the group of the sax-horns, whose numerous varieties figure in military bands. I will enumerate them and indicate the really available compass of each.

Small saxhorn in E♭ (or small bugle).

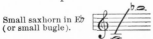

Soprano saxhorn in B♭ (or soprano bugle).

Alto saxhorn in E♭ (or alto bugle).

Tenor saxhorn in B♭ (or tenor or barytone bugle).

Bass saxhorn in B♭ (or bass tuba).

Bass saxhorn in E♭ (or bombardon).

Contrabass saxhorn in B♭ (or contrabass tuba).

Fig. 66. — ALTO SAXHORN.
Length, 15 3-4 in.

METHODS FOR SAXHORNS OR KEY-BUGLE: *Arban, Chlodomir, Fessy and Arban, Forestier, Guilbaut, Sax* (Saxhorns and Saxotrombas), *G. Parès.*

FAMILY OF STRINGED INSTRUMENTS PLAYED WITH THE BOW.

VIOLIN.

This is without question the king of the orchestra. No instrument can compare with it, either in richness of timbre, or variety of intensity, or rapidity of articulation; still more extraordinary is the almost living responsiveness of the string vibrating directly under the finger which presses it. It shares with the human voice the inestimable advantage of being able to vary infinitely the absolute pitch of sounds, and with the organ, the power of prolonging them indefinitely.

These incomparable qualities belong also, it is true, to the other instruments of this family (the viola, violoncello, and double-bass); but in the violin only do they find their maximum of intensity.

All that it has, however, is but four catgut strings, stretched by means of common wooden pegs and tuned thus:

1st¹ 2d 3d 4th

the fourth string being covered with wire to make it heavier.¹

When these strings vibrate in their entire length under the bow, —as "open strings," that is to say,— only these four notes are produced; but if the vibrating portion be shortened by the pressure of a finger of the left hand, there can be obtained a continuous succession of tones, passing through all the degrees of the scale, diatonic, chromatic, or enharmonic, and all the most delicate subdivisions of these tones up to the very highest notes, without other limit than that assigned by the personal skill of the performer. Of fixed notes, invariably true when the instrument is in perfect tune, there are but those of the four open strings; all the other notes must be *made* by the player himself, and he can vary them infi-

Fig. 67. — VIOLIN.
Length, 23 1-2 in.
Length of bow, 29 1-2 in.

¹ The name *chanterelle* is given to the first, or highest, string.

nitely. In a word, the violinist has the privilege of *playing out of tune,*—a privilege which he sometimes abuses, but one which, rightly used, constitutes an inexhaustible wealth of varying intonations, a power of expression and of communicative emotion which is entirely without equal. The violin truly sings; it laughs also, and weeps, and screams ; it lacks only articulate speech to equal the human voice, and it has a compass far greater than that of the voice.

The bow, rubbed with rosin, grips the string, either with up or down movement (to which correspond signs of notation, ◗ or ◖ for the down-bow, ∧ or ∨ for the up),[1] and determines thus with admirable feeling the shades, the punctuations of the musical discourse ; on it depend, also, in great part, the variations of timbre ; the bow determines the vibration, rules its intensity, and modifies its timbre, while the left hand, as we have seen, determines the pitch.

In addition to these *ordinary* or *natural* tones, of which we have now been speaking, the violin is capable of producing *harmonics,* which are peculiarly sweet and celestial in character, somewhat resembling the timbre of the flute, or the head-notes of the human voice, and having a fair degree of loudness.[2] To produce these tones, the player no longer *presses* the string to shorten its vibrating length ; he *touches* it only, at certain points,[3] just enough to destroy the natural sound, and the harmonic is then produced in absolute purity.

The *natural harmonics* are those of the four open strings :

(In the written music they are indicated by a small zero above the note :) *Artificial harmonics,* however,

---

1 French terms : *tirez,* draw , *poussez,* push.

2 These have been called flageolet-tones.

3 Its natural divisions, the half, third, fourth, and so on. See pp. 7-9

can be produced by pressing with one finger to determine a fundamental, then touching with another to sub-divide the

vibrating portion. To do this requires much skill; it is not within the power of every player, and the composer himself not a violinist should use it with the greatest discretion.

If, ceasing to use the bow, the player plucks the string with his finger (*pizzicato*) he obtains a dry, rapid sound, never loud, having a resemblance, though the sound is duller, to that of the stringed instruments which are always played in this manner (the guitar and mandolin). The use of the *pizzicato* is limited, but it adds to the resources of the instrument. To indicate the close of the passage, the composer introduces the words : *col' arco*, "with the bow."

Finally, the violin, although essentially a melodic instrument, principally destined to the production of phrases having a vocal character, is capable, under certain conditions, of making two sounds heard at once, or even arpeggios composed of three or four sounds *almost* simultaneous ; this is the limit of its polyphonic capabilities, which are to it only an accessory of secondary importance.

I must not forget the *sordino* or mute. This is an appliance of metal, or other material, which, being clipped on to the bridge, impedes in a degree the transmission of the vibrations of the strings to the sound-board, that is to say, the body of the violin, an admirable resonator,[1] of which the energy is thus reduced.

The use of the mute is called for by the words *con sordino*, or *avec sourdine;* and its cessation, by *senza sordino* or *sans sourdine.* A rest of a few seconds is sufficient for this manipulation.

By the simplicity and the suppleness of its organs, by the richness and variety of their effects, also by its slender size and light weight, and still more by its freedom from

[1] See page 36.

all mechanism interposed between the resonant string and the player's will, the violin is certainly the most docile of instruments, the one which permits the fullest development of virtuosity.

It will not be expected that we should give here the fingering of the violin, or any sketch, however rapid, of the innumerable formulas that are familiar to it. These are matters for Violin Methods, and Treatises on Instrumentation. All that can be done here is to indicate what should be considered as impossible for the violin, or so difficult that it is wise not to require it, at least in orchestral music, for, since Paganini, to the violinist virtuoso nothing is impossible.

In the orchestra, then, it is wise not to exceed, as the high limit, the A ♪, and this gives, indeed, a fine range ♪.

Where the pizzicato is used, a good effect cannot be anticipated from notes above C or D, ♪; they become far too dry and snapping.

The natural harmonics are the only ones that can be safely used, and these only in a moderate movement; for any further use of them, the composer must himself be a player, either of the violin or of some other stringed instrument. The same is true as to *double stopping*, and of course, with greater reason, as to *triple* and *quadruple ;* these can be safely used, especially in rapid movements, only by a person who understands the fingering of the instrument. Unless, then, the composer is himself somewhat of a violinist, he should avoid writing the intervals enumerated below:

1. All those in which both notes are below D ♪, as, for instance, ♪, which are absolutely imprac-

ticable, for the simple reason that the *two* notes composing them belong to the one bass string G, which can produce them only successively; 2. Seconds higher than [♪] ;

3. Thirds above [♪], and also these [♪],

which are not free from difficulty; 4. Fourths above [♪] ;

5. Fifths above [♪]; 6. Sixths above [♪]; 7. Sevenths

above [♪]; 8. Octaves above [♪], and also these,

[♪], which are difficult of execution.

Beyond the octave, any interval which has not an open string for its bass note, like [♪], must be considered impracticable, or at least dangerous of execution.

For chords of three and of four notes, which, on account of the convexity of the bridge, can be emitted only by an arpeggio more or less rapid, the most convenient are naturally those which contain open strings, as [♪],

etc.; outside of this it is wise to write only chords disposed in mixed fifths and sixths, such as [♪].

Sevenths can be employed also, thus disposed upon the upper three strings, from [♪] to [♪]; but it is

rarely except in accompaniments or, on the other hand, in solos (two cases exactly the opposite of each other) that there is occasion to employ frequently two, three, or four strings. The violin is pre-eminently a melodic instrument,— the splendid, sparkling soprano of the stringed tribe, the richest in varied effects, the most agile, the most expressive, and the most impassioned of orchestral elements.

All tonalities are within its reach, but it is more at ease in the frequent use of the open strings. Consequently the most convenient keys, as well as the most musical, are those which contain few alterations; at the same time, such is the extreme skill of violinists at the present day, that this scarcely requires to be considered except in rapid movements.

There is no other instrument a thorough knowledge of which is so useful to any one wishing to work intelligently in instrumentation. Every composer who seeks to write well for the orchestra must have had a violin in his hands, were it but for a few months, and no treatise upon instrumentation, however perfect it may be, can replace the practical ideas thus obtainable.

The origin of the violin and of the other instruments of the family at whose head it stands, must be sought in India. In the time of Ravana, king of Ceylon, who lived about five thousand years before Christ, the *ravanastron*[1] was invented, which seems to be the most ancient type of instruments played with the bow. (It is still found in its primitive form in the hands of the poor Buddhist monks belonging to the mendicant orders.) This rudimentary instrument had, in fact, all the constituent elements of the violin — the catgut strings, the bridge, the resonant box, the neck, the pegs; also the bow,— whose development we shall examine later. Its earliest improvement upon the *ravanastron* was the *omerti*, which served as model for the *kemangh-a-gouz* of the Arabs and Persians, and later, for their *rebab*. It is not difficult to trace the arrival of the rebab in Europe, during the Middle Ages, and the derivation from it, successively, of instruments which figure in all the museums,— the

1 See pp. 136, 137.

rubèbe, rebelle, rebec, rebecchino, whose names alone would suffice, in the absence of historic documents, to establish the affiliation. Then came the great epoch of the Italian *lutherie*, creating the definitive types which the makers of our day strive to imitate; its most illustrious representatives are, in order of date[1]:

	Birth.	Period of work.		Death.
Gasparo da Salo		*circ. 1560*	*1610*	
Paolo Maggini		*circ. 1590*	*1640*	
Andrea Amati	1520			1580
Geronimo Amati	?	?		1638
Antonio Amatio	*circ.* 1550			1635
Nicolo Amati	1596			1684
Geronimo Amati	1649			1672
Andrea Guarnerius		1650	1695	
Joseph Guarnerius (del Gesù)		1683	1745	
Francesco Ruggieri		1670	1720	
Peter Guarnerius of Cremona		1690	1725	
Vincenzo Ruggieri		1700	1730	
Giambattista Ruggieri . . .		1700	1725	
Pietro Ruggieri		1700	1720	
Peter Guarnerius of Venice .		1725	1740	
Ant. Stradivarius	1644			1737
Carlo Bergonzi		1725	1750	
Michel-Angelo Bergonzi . .		1725	1750	
Lorenzo Guadagnini . . .		1695	1740	
Giambattista Guadagnini . .		1755	1785	
Carlo Landolfi (Landolphus) .		1750	1760	

Then followed the Tyrolese school, derived from the Italian:

	Birth.	Period of work.		Death.
Jacob Stainer	1620			1670
Matthias Albani	1621			1673
Matthias Albani the younger .		1702	1709	
Matthias Klotz		1670	1696	

Sebastian Klotz and his brothers, sons of Matthias, etc.

(The most celebrated names are in italics.) Guarnerius, Stradivarius, and Stainer were pupils of Nicolas Amati.

---

1 These dates are not given as in every case strictly exact but as approximately so. When the dates of birth and death are not to be obtained, the period of production of each artist-*luthier* is given.

The elder Albani was the pupil of Stainer, as also was Klotz.

Many pupils of Stradivarius spread abroad through Europe the traditions of the Italian *lutherie*; of these, the most famous are:

	Period of work.		Place of work.
Médard	*1680*	*1720*	Lorraine
Decombre	*1700*	*1735*	Belgium
Fr. Lupot	*1725*	*1750*	Stuttgart
Jean Vuillaume	*1700*	*1740*	Mirecourt

It is useless to speak of contemporary *luthiers* whose merits are well known.

The primitive bow of the *ravanastron* resembled that now used by the Arabs and the Tunisians, and also that employed by the Chinese,[1] races to whom progress is almost unknown, among whom traditions are perpetuated indefinitely.

A piece of bamboo forms the stick; at the heel this bamboo is pierced with a hole through which is passed a mesh of hair secured by a knot; at the other extremity of the stick a little cleft is made, and here the other end of the lock of hair is fixed, again by a knot; in this way the stick is curved, whence its name, a bow.

Although somewhat improved in Arabia, this implement remained a very rude one until the twelfth century when, losing its curve, it became almost straight; and, finally, it received a slight curve inwards, was grooved, and acquired the form familiar to us at the present day, nearly the opposite of that which it at first had.

The principal artists who have contributed to this curious

---

1 I had the opportunity of hearing the Marquis Tseng, Chinese ambassador in Paris, on a *ravanastron* or Chinese violin, which belongs to me (Fig. 68). The instrument has this peculiarity, that the bow remains constantly entangled, interlaced, as it were, in the two strings, which are tuned in fifths, but upon which the bow plays alternately, according as it is moved forwards or back. Saint-Saëns heard it to satiety in China; he even essayed, unsuccessfully, to play it, and considers it as having a charm " essentially Chinese," but to which one becomes habituated. " It is sometimes atrocious, it is not discordant," he wrote to me on the subject.

transformation are: Corelli (born about 1653), Vivaldi (about 1700), Tartini (1692); finally, Tourte, a Frenchman (1747–1835), who brought the violin-bow to its present perfection. He determined its length (75 cent. for the violin, 74 for the viola, 72 for the 'cello); he established the fact that Brazil-wood (until then solely employed in dyeing) was the best material to use; he determined the exact curve which gives it its admirable lightness, balance, suppleness, and energy; finally, he invented a method of keeping the hairs flat like a ribbon, by pinching them at the nut with a ferule, thus materially increasing the volume of sound and the force of expression.

Fig. 68. RAVANASTRON OR CHINESE VIOLIN. Length, 27 1-2 in.

Others regard the violin as derived from the Breton crouth (*crwth*), the *rote* and the *lyra* being intermediate stages; but as nothing proves that the crouth is not itself derived from the Indian *ravanastron*, this opinion does not invalidate what we have already said as to the orign of this king of instruments; its Indian germ may have been transported into various civilisations developing simultaneously in each; but it remains incontestable that in Italy it attained its complete development, and that this occurred in the sixteenth century, since which time nothing more has been added to it, and no change in it has been made.

METHODS : *Baillot,* "l'Art du violon," *Baillot, Rode and Kreutzer,*

Mazas, Jean Comte, Bériot, Alart, Daubé, etc. In English : " Violin
Methods ": *Chas. de Bériot, Ch. Dancla ;* "Violin Schools ": *J. D. Lo-
der, F. David, Louis Schubert, Singer and Seifritz, L. Spohr.* "The
Technics of Violin Playing," *Karl Courvoisier.*

VIOLA (TENOR VIOLIN, ALTO OR QUINTE).

The viola may be considered as a large violin tuned a
fifth lower, or as a small violoncello tuned an octave higher,
which explains its French names : it is the lower fifth
(*quinte*) of the violin, or the high octave (*alto*) of the 'cello :

The extended description that
has been given of the violin will
render it unnecessary to enter
into equally minute detail as to
the other instruments of the same
family.

The viola, resembling the violin in its construction, is played in
the same way, though requiring,
owing to its larger size, a somewhat wider separation of the fingers of the left hand ; every skilful violinist can, in a few weeks,
acquire the ability to play it fairly well ; but the true virtuoso of
the viola must study his instrument long and carefully. By referring to the pages on the violin
and reading the examples a fifth
lower, it will be easily seen what
can and what cannot be done
with the viola.

Fig. 69. — VIOLA.
Length, 26 in.   Length of bow,
29 1-2 in.

But an important difference to be noted is in the character of the timbre ; by as much as the violin is biting, incisive, masterful, the viola is humble, wan, sad, morose ;
accordingly, besides using it to fill the harmony, composers

take advantage of these qualities to obtain expressions of melancholy and resignation, for which the instrument is incomparable, its range of sentiment running from sad reverie to agonised pathos.

Although the viola is written normally in the C-clef, on the third line, the G, or violin-clef, is occasionally employed for its highest notes; the total range of this instrument, as employed in the orchestra, is therefore thus limited:

, though, in fact, in skilful hands, it can go much higher.

By reason of its functions in the orchestra, occupying the centre of the harmony, the use of double and triple stopping is very frequent in accompaniments. (There is no special Method for the viola, its fingering and its handling being manifestly the same as for the violin.)

VIOLONCELLO.

The 'cello (bass-viol) is the only instrument which, on account of its compass, gives occasion for the use of three clefs: the bass-clef, the tenor-clef, and, rarely, the treble-clef. This is the range , as it

Fig. 70. — VIOLONCELLO.
Length, 3 ft. 10 in.
Length of bow, 28 in.

can be used in the orchestra; but the virtuoso can prolong it indefinitely in upper notes, either natural sounds or harmonics, as is the case with all bowed instruments.

It is thus tuned: , an octave below the viola, a twelfth below the violin.

It is rare, except in solos, that double, triple, or quadruple stops are used upon the 'cello; in this case, while referring to what has been set forth as regards the violin, and transposing the examples a twelfth lower, it must be borne in mind that the instrument is far less docile, and that in consequence of the wide separation of the different notes (about double that of the violin) the best chords are those which consist most largely of open strings. The effect must not be overworked.

On the other hand, the harmonics are very effective and are easily produced, the strings being so fine and so long.

The functions of the 'cello in the orchestra are manifold; usually it gives, reinforced by the double-bass, the bass of the harmony; this is its natural place. But sometimes the singing part is committed to it, when — losing its austerity — it becomes a ravishing instrumental tenor, of pure, warm timbre, ecstatic or passionate, but always distinguished and captivating. Its rapid and light utterance, the frequent passage from natural sounds to harmonics, imitating the alternations of chest and head notes, complete its resemblance to the human voice.

Moreover, the violoncello, though moving in another region and awaking other sensations, possesses a richness of varied tones almost as extensive as that of the violin; and its *pizzicati* are better, less dry, than those of the violin.

METHODS : *Baudiot, Romberg, Chevillard, Rabaud.* In English : *Fries* and *Suck, F. A. Kummer, C. Schroeder, Josef Werner.*

DOUBLE—BASS (CONTRA—BASS).

The double-bass differs from the violin in its tuning, which is in fourths: , and it occupies the lowest step of the orchestral scale. Accordingly, to avoid the constant use of leger-lines, it is written an octave above the real sound, thus : [♩] .[1]

The range of the double-bass in the orchestra comprises

eighteen degrees : [♩] .[2]

Its almost constant rôle in the orchestra is to reinforce and re-double the 'cellos, or, at least, the bass of the harmony; notwith-standing the great size of the in-strument, and the long distance over which the left hand must travel from one note to another, the double-bass player is able to execute either in connected or in *detached* tones, pas-sages of some rapidity, if they are not too com-plicated. Its *tremolo* produces excellent dra-matic effects, and its *pizzicato* is fuller and richer in tone than that of any other instru-ment. Double notes are almost unknown

[1] The same device, inversely, is used in the notation of the piccolo.

[2] There have been made, and are still sometimes to be met with, double-basses with three strings which only go as low as G, and are tuned in fifths : [♩] , like the one represented in the illus-tration.

Fig. 71. — Double Bass.
Length, 6 ft. 6 in. Length of bow, 26 in.

to it, and would be moreover as difficult as they are useless and injurious in this region of the scale where it is not desirable to heap notes together, but, on the contrary, to separate them. The harmonics would be easy for the double-bass, but have been used only rarely up to the present time.

Many of the classic masters, notably Gluck, Haydn, Mozart, and even Beethoven, have written scores for the double-bass, descending as low as C [musical notation] (written note).

What shall we infer from this? That in their lifetime and in Germany, the double-bass was tuned differently from what it now is? This can hardly be, for no author mentions the fact. Shall we believe in any general and persistent negligence on their part? This is still more improbable. This question is one to which I can offer no answer.

METHODS: *Verrimst, Labro, Gouffé, Bottesini.* In English: *C. Bottesini, John M. Flockton;* German: *Franz Simandl.*

VIOLA D'AMORE.

This is a curious and interesting instrument, chiefly because it is the only one in which a systematic use is made of *sympathetic vibrations.*[1] It has seven catgut strings tuned in the perfect chord of D-major: [musical notation], and under these strings there are seven metal ones, giving the same sounds, but out of reach of the bow, and vibrating spontaneously under the influence of the upper strings.[2]

Its timbre is strangely poetic; but the sympathetic reinforcement being produced only upon the notes of the perfect D chord, and, besides, the fingering being very peculiar (on account of the manner in which it is tuned), it is one of the most imperfect of instruments; its orchestral use

[1] See pp. 33-5.

[2] The illustration on the next page is on a very much larger scale than in the case of the other stringed instruments, in order to show the interesting details of the construction of the viola d'amore, notably the sympathetic strings and the double row of pegs is required.

is so restricted that I can mention only a single instance of this, namely, in the first act of "Les Huguenots," where, indeed, its place is generally filled without detriment by the first solo viola.[1]

It is chiefly in a small hall, in concerts of chamber-music, that its peculiar charm can be appreciated, but it cannot hold the attention long without becoming wearisome.

FAMILY OF STRINGED INSTRUMENTS PLAYED BY PLUCKING.

HARP.

It is clear from many ancient bas-reliefs that the primitive idea of the harp dates *at least* from the Egyptians of over six thousand years ago! The early harp had from four to eleven or twelve strings, and, in some cases, the

Fig. 72. — VIOLA D'AMORE.
(Musée du Conservatoire, No. 157.)
Length, 30 in.

1 [C. M. Loeffler has composed a symphonic poem, "The Death of Tintagiles" in which two violes d'amour are employed *obbligato* with the orchestra. Ed.]

elegant form which now characterizes this graceful instrument. Then it appears among the Hebrews; then, in all the great civilisations, constantly gaining in size, but still

Fig. 73.—HARP. Height, 5 ft. 8 in.

without mechanism of any kind. Now it was precisely the adaptation of an entirely peculiar and very ingenious mechanism,— a mechanism whose first sketch belongs to

Nadermann (1773–1835), and whose final improvement is due to the famous maker, Sebastian Érard,— which has given citizenship to the harp in the modern orchestra, where, employed appropriately and with discretion it produces effects, now seraphic, now stately, and always of the greatest sweetness. (Fig. 73.)

The following is the curious principle of construction of the double-action Erard harp, the only one that is now in use:

Its forty-six strings are tuned to give the diatonic scale of C♭ major.

Seven pedals surround its base, and can be depressed and fixed at two different notches. If one of these pedals is fixed at its first notch, all the strings F♭ are simultaneously shortened by so much of the length as corresponds to a semi-tone, that is to say, the F♭ becomes F♮, and we have the key of G♭ major; a second pedal acts in the same way on the C♭ which becomes C♮, producing the key of D♭ major; and so on, by lowering the other pedals to their first notch, there are further obtained the keys of A♭, E♭, B♭, F and C, all major.

Returning now to the first pedal, that of F, we lower it to the second notch; all the F strings are raised another semi-tone, becoming sharped, whence we have the key of G; continuing with the other pedals, each time we get a new major key. So that when the seven pedals are all fixed at their second notch, the instrument originally in C♭ is now in C♯ major.

The peculiarity of this mechanism will be remarked. Let us now see what results as to the writing of music for the harp.

First it appears that the chromatic genre is that which suits it least, and the chromatic scales are completely pro-

hibited to it except in extremely slow movements since
every chromatic note requires the shifting of a pedal;
moreover, the effect is bad.

Further, it is seen that the minor scale presents, though
to a less extent, a similar difficulty, by reason of the
variable character of the sixth and seventh degrees, which
causes it to share in the chromatic character.

Finally, it appears that rapid modulations, especially
into remote keys, are dangerous, since they can only be
obtained by altering the position of the pedals, which re-
requires time, since they must be moved consecutively.

The most musical keys for the harp are those which contain the greatest number of flats, since these use the strings
in their greatest length. The major keys are preferable
because the instrument is thus tuned.

Chords, struck at once or in arpeggio, scales, and diatonic
phrases in octaves, thirds, and sixths are the effects most
familiar to the harp.

The strings are so near each other that the hand can
stretch the interval of a tenth as easily as an octave on the
piano; but in chords only four notes should be required of
each hand, since harpists as a rule do not use the fourth
finger.

Trills and repeated notes are not very successful in effect.

Like the instruments played with a bow, the harp has
harmonic sounds; touching the string midway, with the
outside of the hand, which leaves the fingers free for playing, the second partial tone (the octave of the fundamental)
is obtained, a note of exquisite sweetness especially in the
middle register of the instrument; the right hand can
render but one harmonic at a time, the left hand two, and
in a moderate tempo; they are not loud, and can be utilized
only in *piano* or *pianissimo* passages. Their notation is
very simple; it consists in writing the desired sound an
octave lower and with a zero (0) above it.

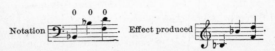

Making allowance for the peculiarities we have here noted, and although the two instruments are developed from principles differing *in toto*, we may consider the music of the harp to be written very nearly like that of the piano; the same clefs are used, and the same system of notation, but the execution is entirely different.

METHODS: *Labarre, Nadermann, Prumier, Bochsa.* In English: *Nadermann, Bochsa, Oberthür.*

GUITAR.

This is not, properly speaking, an orchestral instrument, although it has sometimes been employed as such with a picturesque intention; in Spain and Italy it often accompanies the voice, and, in familiar music, is not without a certain poetic quality. Its tuning suggests that of the lute, from which it is derived: ; it is written an octave above and in the G clef.

Fig. 74. — GUITAR.
Length, 36 1-2 in.

METHODS: *Carulli, Gatayes, Cottin.* In English: *Bayer, Caracassi.*

MANDOLIN.

Of this instrument there are many kinds. The one generally used has eight strings in pairs, tuned like those of the violin: , whence results a similar fingering;

but it will not do to go higher than E: .

The strings of the mandolin are not plucked by the finger directly, like those of the guitar and harp, but with a little quill, or a shell plectrum. The strings are doubled to obviate the feebleness of the sound, but especially to allow of a very rapid *tremolo,* which the player substitutes for sustained notes; it is an effect peculiar to this instrument, and one of which the auditor soon tires.

METHODS: *Cerclier, Cottin, Pietrapertosa, de Sivry, F. de Cristofaro, Patierno.* In English: *Pietrapertosa, Brunzoli, Gargiolo.*

FAMILY OF INSTRUMENTS WITH STRINGS STRUCK.

PIANO.

Though the piano is, above all, an autonomous instrument, it is enough that it has been used by Berlioz in "Lélio"; by Saint-Saëns in his marvellous Symphony, op. 78; by Vincent d'Indy in his "Chant de la Cloche," and by other composers less eminent, to give it rank henceforth among instruments which can, at least exceptionally, make part of the orchestra. There is nothing to prove that it will not take its place here eventually, for it produces effects new and individual which can be obtained from no other musical instrument. The Hungarians have the cembalo in their national orchestra which is a piano minus the key-board; and the ancient Italian, German, and French composers employed its ancestor, the harpsichord,[1] in their scores and as the accompaniment of recitatives, where it was written in figured bass.

Fig. 75.—MANDOLIN.
Length, 23 1-2 in.

In the church,—whence it is excluded only by a sort of prejudice,—associated with the organ, and played with discretion, it assumes a character quite as religious as the harp; and while it cannot be substituted in all cases for the latter, which has peculiar effects and specially hieratic

1 *Clavi-cembalo* (cembalo with a key-board).

appearance, it is capable, nevertheless, of combinations entirely personal to itself. Thus Gounod often employed it.

To describe the piano seems to be needless; let me say,
however, in the rather improbable case that this volume
might drop upon some other planet than our own, that it is

Fig. 76. — GRAND PIANO.
Length, variable; key-board, 4 ft. 3 in.

an instrument having metal strings which are struck by the
hand, and a key-board with the chromatic extent of seven

octaves, from ♩ to ♩, being the largest of all musi-

cal instruments, except the organ. This extent, already

enormous, will probably be still further increased, for the
piano has been increasing steadily up to the present time,
the earliest instruments having the compass of the harpsichord, about five octaves, while the pianos of today usually
extend to the C of 4138 vibrations. It is true that these
extremely high notes have a pitch nearly inappreciable.

There has been sometimes attached to the piano a pedal

Fig. 77. — UPRIGHT PIANO.
Height, variable; key-board, 4 ft. 3 in.

key-board which enriches it with special effects, but necessarily deprives the player of the use of the ordinary pedals
of the instrument.

METHODS : *Adam, Bertini, Le Carpentier, Leduc, Lemoine, Kalkbrenner, Zimmermann, Le Couppey, Anthiome, Decombes, Köhler,*
etc. *De Bériot père et fils,* "la Clef du piano" (to teach singers to
accompany themselves). *Lavignac,* "l'Ecole de la pédale." *Falkenberg,* "les Pédales du piano."

In English : *E. Pauer,* "The Pianoforte ;" London, 1877. *T. R.
Prentice,* "The Musician ;" London, 1883. *Heinrich Germer,*

"Theoretico-Practical Elementary Pianoforte School"; *William Mason*, "Pianoforte Technics"; *Carl Tausig*, "Daily Studies."

Fig. 78. — PIANO WITH PEDAL KEY-BOARD.
Height of pedal-box, 11 in.

CEMBALO OR ZIMBALON.

This curious instrument which gives a quite peculiar tang to Hungarian and Tsigane orchestras, is composed of

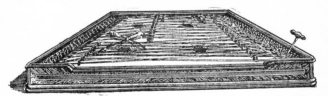

Fig. 79. — HUNGARIAN CEMBALO. (Musée du Conservatoire, No. 311.)
Breadth, 4 ft. 5 1-2 in.

a trapezoidal sound-board, across which are stretched strong metal strings (from three to five for each note) by means of pegs like those of the piano. The strings vibrate under the percussion of two supple hammers which the player manages skilfully with both hands.

It is tuned in the most extraordinary manner,[1] the strings of the lower register vibrating in their full length, while the others are divided by a bridge, or by two or three bridges, so as to produce many different tones. The whole range is four octaves, from 𝄢 to 𝄞 , sometimes more, and the most rapid and complicated passages can be rendered by this instrument; if double strings are used the time must be slower, for only one note can be struck at once, by each hand.

It is not without interest to observe that the very name

---

[1] Tuning of the Hungarian cembalo:

HIGH.— *5 strings to a note* . . . .

The strings 1, 3, 5, are divided into three parts, by two bridges, and produce three tones each.

The strings 2, 4, 7, 9, 11, 13, 15, 17, 19, are divided into two parts, by one bridge, and produce two sounds.

The other strings vibrate in their entire length, and produce but one sound.

1. . . $G\sharp_4$ . . . . . . B_4 . . . . . . E_5.		
2. . . . . C_5 . . . . . . $C\sharp_5$.		
3. . . $F\sharp_4$ . . . . . . A_4 . . . . . . $D\sharp_5$.		
4. . . . . $A\sharp_4$ . . . . . . $D\sharp_4$.		
5. . . F_4 . . . . G_4 . . . . . D.		
6. . . . . $D\sharp_3$.		
7. . . . . E_4 . . . . . $A\sharp_3$.		
8. . . . . $C\sharp_3$.		
9. . . . . D_4 . . . . $G\sharp_3$.		
10. . . . . B_2.		
11. . . . . $C\sharp_4$ . . . . . $F\sharp_3$.		
12. . . . . $A\sharp_2$.		
13. . . . . C_4 . . . . . F_3.		
14. . . . . A_2.		
15. . . . . B_3 . . . . . E_3.		
16. . . . . $G\sharp_2$.		
17. . . . . A_3 . . . . . D_3.		
18. . . . . G_2.		
19. . . . . G_3 . . . . C_3.		
20. . . . . $F\sharp_2$.		

MEDIUM.— *4 strings to a note* . . . . .

21. . . . . F_2.	
22. . . . . E_2.	
23. . . . . $D\sharp_2$.	
24. . . . . D_2.	
25. . . . . $C\sharp_2$.	
26. . . . . C_2.	

LOW.— *3 strings to a note* . . . .

27. . . . . B_1.	
28. . . . . $A\sharp_1$.	
29. . . . . A_1.	
30. . . . . $G\sharp_1$.	
31. . . . . G_1.	
32. . . . . $F\sharp_1$.	
33. . . . . F_1.	
34. . . . . E_1.	

of this instrument proves its relationship to the clavi-
cembalo, or cembalo with clavier, that is to say, the *clavecin,*
the harpsichord, which is the ancestor of the modern piano.

The origin of the cembalo is very ancient and probably
oriental.

Family of Instruments of Percussion Having Definite Pitch.

KETTLE-DRUMS.

Among the numerous percussion instruments in which
the resonant body is a stretched skin, the kettle-drum is
the only one whose pitch is definite.

Fig. 80. — Kettle-drums.
Diameters, 22, 24 and 26 in.

A kettle-drum is a great hemispheric basin of copper, a
sort of cauldron, covered with calfskin strained so tight as
to give musical vibrations. A ring of metal moved by
screws which are turned by a key, regulates the tension of
this membrane, and causes it to produce sounds which are
clearly different in pitch; the intonation can be varied
about a fifth.

It is usual to have two drums of unequal size, sometimes

three, rarely more than that.[1] The tones that they can produce are comprised between $\begin{matrix}9\end{matrix}$ and $\begin{matrix}9\end{matrix}$, that is to say, one complete octave.

When there is a pair of kettle-drums, as is usual, they are generally tuned in fifths or in fourths, furnishing the tonic and the dominant of the key of the composition, the larger drum emitting, naturally, the lower note between $\begin{matrix}9\end{matrix}$ and $\blacksquare$; and the smaller drum, the higher one between $\begin{matrix}9\end{matrix}$ and $\blacksquare$; while if there is a third, it gives a note between the two. The drums will be tuned, of course, within these limits, according to the wish of the composer.

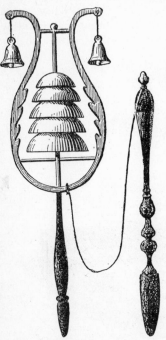

Fig. 81.—ANCIENT CHIME OF BELLS.
(Musée du Conservatoire, No. 737.)

The kettle-drum is available for all rhythmical figures, even the most rapid; the roll is indicated by *tr.* (for *tremolo*). It has also the entire range of shading from the faintest *pianissimo* to the noisiest *fortissimo*.

If it is desired to vary the pitch of the kettle-drums during the performance of a movement, time enough for doing this must be given; there will be written in the score: change to D, or to B♭, F, etc.

METHODS: *Kastner, de Sivry.*

1 [" In order to obtain a certain number of chords in three, four, and five parts, more oɪ less doubled, and, moreover, a striking effect of very close rolls, I have employed in my grand Requiem Mass eight pairs of drums, tuned in different ways, and ten drummers." BERLIOZ. TR.]

CARILLON. GLOCKENSPIEL.

A series of small bars of steel or bronze, so placed that they can be struck by a small hammer, and tuned either diatonically or chromatically, makes an elementary carillon.

Fig. 82. — CARILLON WITHOUT CLAVIER.
Width, 12 in.

By adapting a key-board to a carillon, we obtain an instrument more convenient for use; and, besides, this admits

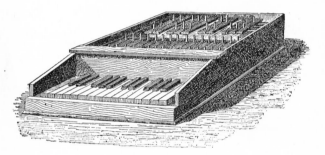

Fig. 83. — CARILLON WITH CLAVIER.
Width, 15 3-4 in.

of chords, arpeggios, trills, and all the rapid passages which would be impossible to the simple carillon.

These instruments may have any desired range; this depends merely on the number and dimensions of the strips of metal.

TYPOPHONE.

A series of tuning-forks, generally having a compass of four octaves, having a manual, and a mechanism of hammers, producing by percussion crystalline sounds of ideal clearness and purity; this instrument, invented by Mustel, or better still, the

CELESTA,

of the same maker, is advantageously substituted for all the old carillons; in the celesta, the resonant body is a bar

Fig. 84. — CELESTA.
Height, 2 ft. 11 1-2 in.

of steel, loaded at each extremity with a little block of brass soldered to the bar; this is its form   ; the timbre is that of a tuning-fork, more energetic however, but of less prolonged duration. The instrument as now made has a compass of five octaves, its lowest note being the C_2; it also has dampers and a soft pedal, like the piano.

XYLOPHONE.

The early forms of this instrument are found among many quite barbarous tribes, among the Malagasy, for in-

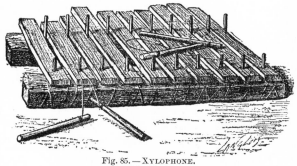

Fig. 85. — XYLOPHONE.
Width, 27 1-2 in.

stance, who call it *mogologondo*,— in Central Africa, and elsewhere. In France, it is called *claquebois*, and in Germany, *Holzharmonica*.

It consists of a series of strips of wood, of length and thickness either calculated or found by actual experiment to produce various notes of a scale; the strips, more or less in number, are supported in a way to isolate them, either on straws or threads of silk, and they are struck with two little mallets.

The dry, flat tone of the xylophone can find use (to a very limited extent) only in imitative, descriptive, or grotesque music.

METHOD (in English) : Fischer.

BELLS.

There can be nothing more false than the saying : "Who hears a bell hears one sound only," for of all sound-producing agents the bell is perhaps the one which develops the greatest number of partial tones, often discordant even, which sometimes causes a difficulty in discovering which is its fundamental tone, regarded musically.

The larger and heavier the bell, and the denser the metal of which it is made, so much the deeper is the sound which

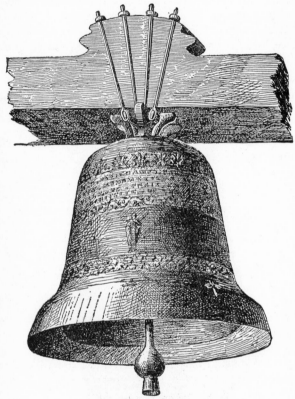

Fig. 86.— BELL.

it produces; to produce the C of the bass clef $\text{\textbf{9:}}$, a bell must weigh about twenty-two and a half tons; for the C an octave higher $\text{\textbf{9:}}$ not quite three tons will be needed, according to this law: *The vibrations of bells are in inverse ratio to the cube root of their weight*; now, good bell-metal costing about thirty-six cents a pound, the larger of these two bells would cost (in round numbers) $18,000, and the smaller, $2,400. The largest bell in the world, that of the Kremlin, which has never been hung, weighs a little over 247 tons.[1] In the theatre, a church bell is usually imitated by a heavy bronze bell struck by a hammer, or else by steel bars, which are cheaper and are perfectly sufficient to produce, in-doors, the effect of the real bell vibrating in the open air, on the top of its tower.

FAMILY OF INSTRUMENTS OF PERCUSSION WITHOUT PITCH.

BASS DRUM.

The bass drum, struck with a padded stick, is the more sonorous, the larger it is. It takes part only in noisy,

Fig. 87. — BASS DRUM.
Diameter, about 2 ft. 7 in.

1 The great bell of Notre Dame de Paris weighs but 16,000 kilos ; and produces a tone a little higher than the D of the bass clef ⨍ (16,192 kilos). It requires eight men to ring it.

rhythmic effects, where it is frequently associated with the cymbals, the same player causing both instruments to sound, one with each hand, which, in general, is easily done.

Employed alone, the bass drum imitates cannon-firing; *in tremolo,* beaten with two drumsticks, it represents thunder; and in the *pianissimo,* it produces effects not destitute of solemnity.

METHOD (in English): *Sousa.*

Fig. 88. — CYMBALS.
Diameter, 13 1-2 in.

CYMBALS

Are often employed simultaneously with the bass drum. This combination may serve in the great, noisy *fortissimi,* where it marks, not without brutality, the accented part of the bar.

The cymbals are thin plates, of a composition of copper and tin, round in form, and slightly concave at the centre. They are clashed together, producing various effects. They furnish mere rhythmic forms; when not damped, their vibration lasts a long time.

SIDE DRUM (TAMBOUR).

This is the military drum, and is used in all rhythmic figures by means of alternate or simultaneous beating with its two drumsticks.

Fig. 89. — SIDE DRUM.
Diameter, about 15 1-2 in.

METHODS (in English): *Chaine, Fischer, Sousa.*

TRIANGLE.

A cylindrical steel bar, bent into an equilateral triangle.

It is struck with a small bar of the same metal. The sound is crystalline, and can vary from the lightest *pianissimo* to *fortissimo*. The pitch is indefinite, so that it can be employed in all keys and with all chords. The most complicated rhythms are within its reach, and also the trill or *tremolo*.

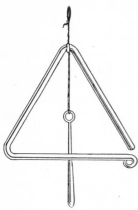

Fig. 90. — TRIANGLE.
Height, about 8 in.

TAMBOURIN.

Though this instrument is in use in the middle and south of France and the Basque country, it must not be confused with the *tambour de basque* (tambourine) hereafter to be described. This is a long and slender drum, which is beaten with one stick; it produces therefore only isolated sounds which have a certain rhythm, but never a *tremolo* or roll. The player will often strike his tambourin with the left hand while with the right he plays a fife or flute.

Fig. 91.—TAMBOURIN PROVENCAL.
(Musée du Conservatoire, No. 701.)
Length, 26 in.

TAMBOURINE (TAMBOUR DE BASQUE).

This is a wooden ring, over which parchment is stretched and around which are hung little disks of metal in pairs, "jingles," or very small bells; it has two kinds of sound, that of the membrane struck with a sharp blow of the knuckles, that of the little cymbals when the tambourine is shaken; sometimes these two effects are united. Furthermore, by drawing the finger in a certain way over the parchment, a sort of roll is produced which, mingling with the metallic sounds of the little bells and jingles, makes a very characteristic effect. This instrument is popular in Spain and Italy.

Fig. 92.
TAMBOURINE.
Diameters, 10 and 12 in.

TOMTOM OR GONG.

The most vigorous and violent of the percussion instruments. It is appropriate only in scenes of terror, and always has that effect, whether the blow, struck upon it with a mallet covered with felt or rags, is heavy or light.

The instrument consists of a disk of bronze, of peculiar composition and temper, the secret of which is known only to the Chinese. The gong is made in a great variety of sizes, of which one of the largest is represented. (Fig. 93.)

CASTANETS.

Two wooden shells, united by a string, clicking against each other in the hollow of the hand,— these are castanets. Their action is purely rhythmic; their only use is in dance-music having a Spanish character.

METHODS (in English) : *Fischer, Salino.*

CROTALA (CLAPPERS).

These were *metallic* castanets, usually, but sometimes of wood, or even shells, whose clicking together was much appreciated by the Egyptians, the Greeks, and the Latins.

The metallic crotala must have produced an effect like that of very small cymbals.

Such are, I believe, very nearly all the musical instruments now at our command and usually to be found in orchestral scores.

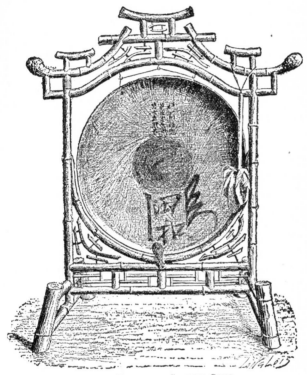

Fig. 93. — Tomtom or Chinese Gong.
Height, 3 ft. 10 in.

B. — Of Orchestration.

Instrumentation, in the sense that we attach to this word, is a science merely; it teaches what can be asked and obtained from each instrument considered by itself. Where science ends, art begins. Orchestration is, then, an art,

that of calling into action the different voices of the collective instrument we call an orchestra, and causing it to
produce emotions by means of combinations of infinite
variety. The word infinite is not an exaggeration, for
there is no reason to suppose that these combinations will
ever be exhausted, as I will now briefly explain.

Two instruments may be associated in unison, or in
octaves,— which constitutes an increased volume, or, a
complex timbre; or they may be associated with a certain
interval, one or the other occupying the higher part; and
thus we have four combinations possible with the use of
two instruments only. The same can be done with three,
with ten, with thirty, or more. An important figure can
be committed to almost the entire orchestra, reserving but
two or three instruments for the harmony; or, on the other
hand, the same figure can be given to one instrument
alone in its brightest tones, giving it for accompaniment all
the others in their more veiled tones. Or one may handle
masses, taking the instruments in families, the strings, the
wood-wind, and the brass-wind, or intermingling them in
certain proportions. And if to this we add the new
elements that the makers are constantly adding, one can
easily see that orchestral art is really infinite. And later
this will be made still clearer.

A system of orchestration based on the idea that intensity
of sound is in direct ratio to the number of instruments
employed, would be simply childish. An absolute *pianissimo* may be obtained by the use of all the instruments
playing together, even those which are considered noisy, if
their comparatively dull sounds are utilised; there may
even result from this a very impressive effect. It is equally
true that a powerful *fortissimo* can be produced with the
use of a very few instruments, if they are well chosen for
that purpose, and the most vigorous portion of their range
is called forth.

Between these two extremes are contained the most delicate shades of orchestration, of musical colouring.

Here all that artistic training can do — after having furnished the student with thorough information as to the extent, the individual character, the mechanical principle, and the powers of expression of each one of the constituent elements of the orchestra — is to call attention to their affinities and their mutual relations in timbre and in pitch; the rest depends upon the spirit of observation, the intuition, and the initiative of each person.

It will now be useful to group methodically, according to their resemblances, their individual character, and their mode of utterance, the various instruments which we have already examined in detail.

The following table, drawn up for this purpose, does not realise an ideal of perfection, but, such as it is, it may serve for a point of departure, and I shall not hesitate, later, to indicate its faults when there appears occasion to do so.

Let us then, for the moment, agree that the instruments which the musician can employ, are thus grouped:

CLASSIFICATION.	INSTRUMENTS.			
	COMPOSING THE CLASSIC SYMPHONIC ORCHESTRA.	OF LESS FREQUENT AND MORE MODERN USE.	OF VERY RARE USE.	NOT USED IN THE ORCHESTRA.
With free mouth.	Flute.	Piccolo.		Flageolet.
With double reed.	Oboe. Bassoon.	Cor anglais. Contrabassoon (Sarrusophone)		Cornemuse.
With single reed.	Clarinet.	Alto-Clarinet. Bass-Clarinet. Saxophone.		
Brass.	Trumpet.	Trumpet à pistons. Cornet à pistons. Trombone. Ophicleide (Tuba).		
	Horn.	Cor à pistons.		Cor de chasse.

CLASSIFICATION.	INSTRUMENTS.			
	COMPOSING THE CLASSIC SYMPHONIC ORCHESTRA.	OF LESS FREQUENT AND MORE MODERN USE.	OF VERY RARE USE.	NOT USED IN THE ORCHESTRA.
Of direct percussion.	Kettle-drums.	Bass drum. Cymbals. Side drum. Triangle. Tomtom.	Tambourin. Tambourine. Carillon. Bells. Castanets. Xylophone.	
Strings plucked.		Harp.	Guitar. Mandolin.	Cembalo (strings struck).
With key-board.		Organ. Typophone.	Piano.	Harmonium.
With bow.	1st violin. 2nd violin. Alto. Violoncello. Double-bass.		Viola d'amore.	

The first column contains the list of instruments which have been of strictly classic use in the symphonic orchestra, since the time of Haydn, Mozart, and Beethoven.

The second gives us those which are of comparatively modern use, and more frequent in opera than in the purely symphonic orchestra, at least, up to the present date.

The third, those which are only exceptionally used in the orchestra, and chiefly for picturesque or descriptive purposes.

In conclusion, the fourth, those which while possessing a purely musical character, are absolutely without value in the composition of the orchestra.[1]

We shall now examine separately the different groups composing this table, in the order of their importance, beginning with the family at the foot of the first column, namely the strings, which are the solid basis of all orchestration.

But first some general considerations are necessary as to

1 This last column might contain many other names of musical instruments, but they are without interest for this work.

the manner in which the composer may bring his musical material into action.

It would be rash, no doubt, to attempt orchestration without having thoroughly mastered the principles of harmony, but it would also be a mistake for a composer to feel that he must render slavish obedience to the letter of its rules, treating the instruments as simply theoretic voices. Much greater liberty is necessary that each instrument may have full scope for its powers of expression and bring out in clear relief its own peculiar traits, at the same time doing its part in the fine sonority of the general effect.

If harmony may be considered as the solid framework, the bony skeleton, of every musical composition, without which it cannot exist, orchestration is the colouring, the external vesture, the garb, now sober, now splendid, of the musical thought. It must, therefore, be regarded from a different point of view, and there must be license for the instrumental parts to be doubled or reinforced, by unison or by octaves, to cross each other, to be divided, to be forced apart, to be entangled in every conceivable manner,— to be silenced, then reappear again, without appreciable harmonic cause; consecutive octaves are permitted between an intermediate and any other part,— the bass only excepted, — although it is better to dispense with them if possible; fifths can be picturesquely employed; a false relation, a friction, a harshness, may often be greatly diminished by diversity in timbre.[1] We can and should allow ourselves all these liberties, if only they are suggested and directed by good taste, and if, through them, be always apparent the solid harmony upon which they rest, without which they would be mistakes, blunders, or incoherencies of style. In a word, it is required that the composition regarded as a whole be able to show itself purely and logically conceived if, despoiled of its orchestral adornment, it be reduced to its simplest expression,— on the piano, for example.

Formerly, this was not permitted. The composers who

---

[1] For all these technical terms, see the following chapter; " Grammar of Music " (Harmony).

preceded Bach, and Bach himself, for the most part, treated the instrumental parts very nearly as if they were voices,— except so far as concerned their compass and their pitch,— and subjected their progression to the rules of counterpoint; but it must be remembered that, at that time, the whole was supported and held together by an autonomous instrument having a key-board — the organ in church, the clavichord or harpsichord in the theatre or concert, which went on continuously, constantly reiterating the fundamental harmony, whence its name, *continuo*. This was written as a figured bass, and complete liberty was left to the performer in the disposition of the chords. By this system, which seems to us now very primitive, there was obtained an orchestration solid, powerful, though quite monotonous, and massive,— all the instruments being employed almost uninterruptedly; it could have been of real interest only to an auditor who was able to enjoy following the ingenious progression of these instrumental *voices*. The present procedure, which attaches more importance to a richness and variety of musical sound than to a strictly correct handling of the parts, has vastly more colour, warmth, and life, and constitutes a notable advance which is alike undisputed and indisputable. Without it, there would be no such thing as modern orchestration.

The *string-band* — the principal mass of the orchestra, in which it holds the chief place, like that of the foundation stops in an organ — is thus composed :

> One part of first violins ;
> One part of second violins ;
> One part of violas ;
> One part of violoncellos.

With the 'cellos are almost always associated the double-basses, reinforcing them an octave lower, thus adding solidity to the base of the musical edifice, without constituting an independent part.[1]

[1] The double-basses are the equivalent of the sixteen-foot pipes of the pedal key-board.

(The available compass of each of these instruments has been stated in the chapter on *Instrumentation ;* we add only, on this subject, the remark that since the second violins naturally fall to the less skilful performers, it is wise to write the part more simply than that of the first, not going higher than F or G above the line  .)

The first violin is the most important part of the orchestra, as to melody and expression ; while as to harmony, this superiority belongs to the part of the 'cello and double-bass, which almost invariably gives the lowest note in the chords. The second violin and the viola are parts comparatively secondary, yet capable of being called upon to fill for a moment an important rôle, whether the two violins reply to each other, or the viola, crossing above them, occupies for a moment the highest part, thus colouring the melody with that melancholy tinge which is the viola's peculiar characteristic.

With the exception of the double-bass all the parts may indeed interchange places, but the crossing is most frequent between the viola and the second violin ; here also is made the principal use of the double stops, especially in accompaniment figures.

The triple and quadruple stops are generally reserved for the great *fortissimi ;* but on the double-bass, as has been already explained, they are never used.

When it is desired to employ the specially sympathetic timbre of the 'cello in bringing out an important melodic figure, a special part is written for it, and the double-bass alone takes the low note. Another method is also employed in the same intention, which does not so much enfeeble the bass,— the 'cellos are divided and the score is written thus :

First violoncellos:

Second 'cellos and double-basses:

But in this case the melodic part (the 'cellos) loses somewhat of its intensity, a defect which can, in turn, be remedied by doubling it with a unison of the violas, a method much used by Beethoven and later composers.

All the parts, indeed, can be doubled by unison, octave, or double octave, either in a few notes or in long passages. Frequently also the double-bass is silenced for a time, in order to lighten the general effect; its return always gives pleasure, as of something that was missed.

The *pizzicato* may be employed simultaneously on all the instruments of the quartet, in simple sounds, in double, triple, and quadruple stops; it may be used in one part only, or in more than one; the same is true as to muting and as to the harmonics.

A single performer may also be detached from his group to render a distinct part; this is then written on a staff by itself and is indicated thus: *Violin solo, viola solo, violoncello solo.*

Lastly, a procedure very much in honour with the present school consists in subdividing each class of instruments, so as to have four parts of violins, two of violas, two of 'cellos, or more, which makes it possible to arrange in steps, so to speak, chords formed by many notes occupying a wide space.

For those especially who know how to use the harmonics, there is here an unexplored mine of etherial sounds to be exploited.

This system of division is especially useful in large orchestras having many stringed instruments.

In a complete orchestra, well balanced, so that the strings may properly counterpoise the two groups of wind-instruments, there should be not less than

> 10 first violins;
> 10 second violins;
> 8 violas;
> 6 'cellos;
> 6 double-basses.

As outside limit, fifteen violins in each part, twelve violas, twelve 'cellos, and ten double-basses; with any larger number the wind instruments would be overpowered.[1]

No group equals in importance the string-band, both by reason of its perfect homogeneity and of the richness and variety of its effects. Hence, it is frequently used alone, sometimes for a few measures only, but sometimes in entire compositions.

In the second rank are the wood-wind (the wind instruments of wood); this group includes, in the classic symphonic orchestra:

> First and second flutes;[2]
> First and second oboes;
> First and second clarinets;
> First and second bassoons;

in all, eight performers; furthermore, we must remember that Mozart and Haydn rarely employed the oboe and the clarinet at the same time, the latter instrument being at that period played by the oboeists; therefore there were six performers only, all soloists.[3]

It will appear at once that this group is very differently constituted from the mass of the string-band. Each part, instead of being performed, as it were, in chorus, by eight or ten similar instruments, is committed to the single performer, and thus acquires a more individual character.

Another fundamental difference is that here the instruments are heterogeneous, not of the same family, producing their sound according to different principles, having only in common the human breath. The flute with its free orifice, the oboes and bassoons with their double reed, the clarinet with its single reed, produce timbres entirely distinct.

The wind instruments must therefore have very different

---

1 It might seem, at first sight, that by proportionally increasing the number of wind instruments the equilibrium could be re-established, however numerous the bow instruments might be; but this would be true only for massed effects; for, according to the true conception of the modern orchestra, the wind instruments must preserve their *individuality*, and each must be a *soloist*, as will be shown later

2 Originally, the flute was made in wood only.

3 By *soloist* in this connection, is meant the player who is alone in the execution of his part.

treatment from that which is suited to the strings. When the whole group is employed, the best effect is generally obtained by distributing the parts according to the natural ranking of the instruments : the flutes for the highest; below them the oboes ; then the clarinets ; lowest, the bassoons, as voices would be treated; and they scarcely ever cross, except with special effects intended.   On the other hand, it is very common for them to speak in unison, as the two flutes together, or the two oboes,— which is indicated by *a due*, *unis*, or *à 2*, or by giving the notes a double stem ; or else, reinforcing the second flute by the first oboe, the second oboe by the first clarinet, and so on, which is richer and better in strong passages.   In soft passages, the second instrument of each kind may be silent, which is indicated thus: *1mo solo*.   Or again, to each of the eight performers may be given a different part, whereby a more diffuse and iridescent sonority will be obtained.

It is by no means necessary to employ all the wood-wind at once ; the effect would be very heavy and poor ; but in suppressing some of them, it is far from being a matter of indifference which timbre it is that is silenced. The absence of the flutes takes from the group something of its sweetness and lightness ; that of the oboes renders the ensemble less bright and luminous ; suppressing the clarinets we diminish the richness and smoothness of the general sonority ; the absence of the bassoons enfeebles the bass, and thus renders the whole effect lighter.   Keeping well in mind the special character of each instrument, the composer will readily perceive the advantage of suppressing this one or that, according to the effect he may desire to produce, as well also as the disadvantages that would result.

Very frequently the timbre of the horns is associated with the wood-wind and the alliance is admirable, especially in *piano* and *mezzo forte* passages.   We must even consider the horns *from a practical point of view*, as belonging (notwithstanding they are of metal and not of wood) almost as much to the wood-wind as to the brass ; or, if this statement is preferred, as in a class by themselves, affiliated to both groups, in which they can by turns be utilised for different effects.

By the addition of the horns the wood-wind, whose voice was perhaps *a little frail,* gain greatly in plenitude; the bassoons are no longer alone in the low region; the horn, sometimes assuming the bass, brings variety into the combinations; at other times, it blends with the clarinets or the bassoons in figures of accompaniment; it can also, with its wide compass, undertake the principal melodic part, if this be placed midway in the general scale (which would be the upper register of the horn), and with its own generous sonority [1] make it more beautiful.

The classic masters employed two horns, first and second, almost always in the same key, which might be changed in the course of the composition.

The remark made earlier as to the range to be given to the first and to the second violin, is applicable to all instruments, of whatever kind, thus numbered; but it acquires special importance as applied to horns (and to all the brass-wind) because the performer employs an orifice more or less narrow, according as he plays the first horn or the second. It is only the first which can easily reach the highest notes, and the lowest notes are denied to it; the converse of this is true as to the second horn.

It is very seldom that the wood-wind is employed alone for more than a few bars; yet the group is a complete one, and, especially with the addition of the horns, can suffice for itself; a proof of this is given by the many quintets, septets, and octets written for wind instruments alone.

The third group in the classic orchestra is at once the least numerous and the least important; it is composed of the noisiest instruments:

> First and second horns (rarely third and fourth);
> First and second trumpets;
> A pair of kettle-drums.

In all, five performers or seven.

[1] In the table of p. 165, I could not represent the horns otherwise than in the group of the brass-wind. This is one of the defects of that table.

It can be employed alone only in rare cases, *fanfares,* military or hunting, and calls, with echo or without.

Usually, the two horns and the two trumpets are in the principal key if the mode is major,[1] and in the relative major key if the mode is minor; the kettle-drums are tuned in fourths and fifths, so as to furnish the tonic and the dominant, or more rarely the tonic and the subdominant. But it often is the case that the brass instruments are tuned in other keys, or even differently among themselves; this depends on the character of the musical design committed to them (it must be remembered that they are *simple* horns and trumpets); likewise the kettle-drums can be tuned to take other intervals than fourths or fifths, although these latter are those most employed by the old masters.

In using the brass instruments the greatest freedom is allowed as to the harmonic progression of the parts, the composer seeking to obtain the greatest possible advantage from the few notes of which they are capable. Thus the early composers *ignored the progression of the seventh* in the chord of the dominant 7th, and followed it by the tonic, when it could not find its natural and normal resolution in the scale of the brass.

Furthermore, the different groups of the classic orchestra may be intermingled; and here, the interlacing of all imaginable combinations becomes really indescribable. We can only give some idea of those most in use, indicating a few and suggesting the immeasurable extent of their possibilities.

If it is desired to reinforce the strings, the first method which presents itself is to double by means of the wood-wind all the constituent parts of the string-band, or those only to which it is desired to give preponderance; thus we may emphasise a design of the first violin by doubling it with a flute, an oboe, a clarinet; a design of the viola, by a few notes of the clarinet or bassoon; this at once attracts

1 In using four horns, the key of the third and fourth usually differs from that of the first two, thus increasing the number of tones at command. Usually, also, the third is high, and the fourth, low.

attention, which can be further compelled by the addition of many instruments either in unison, or an octave higher or an octave lower. If it be desired that each harmonic part of the string-band preserve an equal importance, the ensemble being strengthened alike, it would be natural to couple each instrument of the string quartet with the one corresponding to it in the wood, so far as their comparative extent permits.

Also, the composer must take into account, in these various augmentations, the special character and *resources* of each instrument; for instance, the wind instruments will better reinforce a *tremolo* of the strings by simple holding-notes than by repetitions, in which they lose their strength; the high notes of the violin are rendered more brilliant by association with the flute, while in its middle or lower register, the oboe or the clarinet will be more successful; and so on.

For still more powerful effects, horns are added, and then, trumpets; but here, it is rarely a question of simple redoubling, the natural brasses, with their incomplete gamut, being unable to render the same formulas as instruments of uninterrupted chromatic range. Their action is different, being rather to strengthen the harmony than to aid in designing some melodic figure, unless it be one of great simplicity, and *formed of their good notes,* which would seldom occur unless it had been created for them with this special effect in view.

In general, they proceed by holding-notes more or less prolonged, or else accentuate the rhythm by vigorous chords placed on the beat, accented or unaccented, or by repeated notes; in these latter cases, the kettle-drums are often added, and then the whole orchestra is in action.

A combination frequently used is to make two groups answer each other: strings and wood-wind; or, wood and brass-wind; or, the whole mass of the wind instruments opposed to the string-band, each being harmonically arranged so as to form a complete whole; in this way very strong and well-marked effects of contrast are obtained.

It is very unusual to associate the brass-wind and the

strings; there would be a lack of cohesion; no doubt on occasion certain special effects can be obtained thus, but as a rule, the absence of the wood-wind leaves a gap.

No more when intermingled than when separate are the groups obliged to proceed constantly in a compact mass; most frequently, on the other hand, one instrument (or more) of a group will be associated with others essentially different,— for instance, a passage for the violins will be accompanied by some of the wind instruments,— a melody of flutes or horns, supported by part of the string-band,— a *duo* of oboes or clarinets upon a *pizzicato* of the strings, with a holding-note of the horn to tie them, and so on. It is here that one begins to appreciate the kaleidoscopic variety of symphonic combinations, and the possibility, notwithstanding all that has been already done, of creating new groupings, obtaining effects of musical sound never before heard, as undoubtedly new melodies and new harmonies will continue to be produced with the seven notes of the scale and the seven time-values. And it should be firmly established in the mind that all these combinations, in number incalculable, from the most commonplace to the most grotesque, will have their value if they correspond to the sentiment to be expressed, or will be ridiculous and futile if they are inappropriately employed.

It is in this special tact that the art of handling an orchestra resides; here the talent or the genius of the symphonist is manifested.

In skilful orchestration, nothing is left to chance; everywhere there is design, there is a reason why; in every note, ingenuity and talent are shown, and to read a score finely adapted is, for him who understands it, an intellectual pleasure which has no equal.

Before going further, and entering upon certain considerations as to the use of instruments which have been more recently employed, I have thought it advisable to sum up what has now been said, by presenting to the reader a table of *all the notes* belonging (1) to *each instrument* considered separately; (2) to *each group* taken by itself; and (3) to the *ensemble of the classic orchestra*, which remains, whatever additions may be made to it, the solid foundation of all modern orchestration.

(For details concerning each instrument the reader is referred to the previous chapter on *Instrumentation*.)

Comparative scale, *in actual tones*, of the compass belonging to instruments of each class composing the *classic* symphony orchestra.

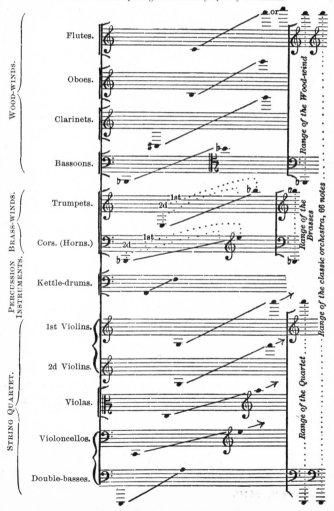

If then, to this classic orchestral material we now add, as *hors d'œuvre* or condiments, some of the instruments of our second column,[1] its richness will be increased; and this is not solely on account of the *number* of instruments being augmented, but rather because of the new *timbres* that these bring to the ensemble.

The addition of the *piccolo* will give brilliancy and keenness, but, unwisely employed, it communicates to the orchestra a certain triviality.

The *trombones* have a pomp and majesty which they never lay aside.

(These two instruments, the piccolo and the trombone, with the double bassoon, are the only additions that Beethoven made to his symphonic orchestra, doing this with great sobriety, and at the same time increasing to four the number of horns.)

The *cor anglais* brings its sad and pensive poetic note; the *alto* and *bass clarinets*, their almost pontifical solemnity; the *saxophone*, its hybrid timbre, which takes such hold upon the attention that the ear seeks and follows it as soon as once it is heard.

The *harp* ought not to appear except where its use is called for in its two-fold character, etherial and hieratic; to use it too frequently is to destroy its effect, which is most impressive and poetic where it has been kept in reserve for the fitting occasion.

The *ophicleide* (now replaced by the *tuba*) is to be considered as the bass of the three trombones, of which it completes the quartet, strengthening it with its own immense volume of sound.

The use of *chromatic horns* and *trumpets* (*à pistons*) enriches the group of the brass-wind, giving it an entirely new freedom of action. In the great modern orchestras, this group is generally composed thus:

> two trumpets à pistons;
> four horns à pistons;
> three trombones;
> one tuba;

1 Pages 165 and 166.

ten performers,— which gives it a fine range and great strength.

The *cornet*, though employed by the masters before the chromatic trumpet was invented, ought to disappear from the symphonic orchestra, where its triviality is too clamorous, and should be reserved for military music only, in which, on the contrary, it is of great use, and where it is in its true place.

The percussion instruments without fixed pitch, the bass drum, side drum, tambourin, tambourine, etc., serve only to mark the rhythm, and each has its conventional character: the drum suggests barracks; the castanets are Spanish; the tambourine, likewise, leads us to the Pyrenees; the silvery triangle calls for mirth, and the tomtom is always gloomy.

These latter are accessions of slight importance, playing but a secondary rôle, purely picturesque.

Quite differently should be regarded the instruments struck with hammers, of which the *typophone* is the most perfect form, and also the *piano*,— both of which may, at some future time, normally make part of the constitution of the orchestra.

The *guitar* and the *mandolin*, serenade instruments, as well as the *viola d'amore*, have never really been accepted, appearing in orchestras only episodically, for the sake of special effects.

As for the great *organ*,— which brings with it, as well in power as in richness of timbres, the equivalent of another army corps,— whether it answers back the symphonic instruments, or adds its elements to their combinations, it is always magnificent and imposing in its effect, in the church or in the theatre, in scenes of a religious character, or, again, in the oratorio.

The use of these additional instruments, or any others that may be invented, is perfectly easy to the composer who knows how to handle those which form the basis of the orchestra, namely, the classic *strings*, the *wood-wind*, and the *brass-wind;* it is, then, these that one ought chiefly to study. The same is true as to the addition of a *chorus* to the orchestra; the chorus may be treated as voices are in the study of harmony or counterpoint, and form in itself a complete whole, to which is added the orchestra, either to reinforce each of the parts, or only certain ones, or — which is more frequently the case — to create a mesh of various ornaments and designs surrounding the choral plot without at all interfering with its development. In this case, the total mass may be considered as containing four distinct groups:

> The chorus;
> The strings;
> The wood-wind;
> The brass-wind;

having each its comparative degree of importance.

When an accompaniment is required for a soloist, vocal or instrumental, to whom the predominance must be given, this is not done by using only a few instruments, but by keeping the instruments used in that region of their compass which is less brilliant than the one occupied by the soloist, and, especially, by choosing for this accompaniment instruments whose timbre could not be confused with the timbre of his own, and be a rival to it.

Thus a flute or clarinet solo will find the best material for accompaniment in the medium or low register of the strings; a phrase for the violoncello will be in better relief against a background of wind instruments than if it be surrounded by the tones belonging to the string-band; while the human voice, itself a wind instrument, contrasts better with the violins, violas, and 'cellos, than with horns, bassoons, and clarinets. But this rule, it must be noted, is not imperative: in fact, there can be nothing imperative in orchestration. In some cases, indeed, it may be desired to establish a sort of intimate cohesion between the soloist and his accompaniment, which must then be selected from his own group, but kept in the least brilliant part of their range. It may also be said, speaking generally, that when an instrumental solo is to receive orchestral accompaniment, it is better not to employ a timbre absolutely identical with that which is to be set in relief,— for example, the orchestra for a clarinet concerto should not contain clarinets, except some special effect is sought. This rule cannot hold in the case of a violin concerto, for an orchestra could not be deprived of its first and second violins ; but here a very subordinate rôle is to be given them, so that the solo player may have his pedestal to himself. A concerto for the piano can admit timbres of every kind, since it could not be confused with any.

What I have just said in regard to the concerto — which is a *solo* prolonged — necessarily applies to any fragment of an orchestral composition where it is desired to call attention, were it but for a few bars, or even a few notes, to some one instrument, which for the moment becomes a soloist; care must be taken not to drown it in waves of similar sound, and there must be sought, in other groups, or on another level, a background against which its melodic contour can be thrown into relief.

The art of orchestration lives only by contrasts, either among diverse timbres employed simultaneously with the design of making one or more of them predominate, or among combinations following one another, for the purpose of attracting and fixing the attention of the auditor, of interesting and gratifying him at every moment by the rapid presentation of new and captivating musical effects, appropriate to the circumstances or to the sentiments that are to be depicted. In this consists the very effective picturesque side of orchestration, its share in giving local colour. I do not here speak of the use of an organ in church scenes, of a horn for the chase, of a harp — the favourite instrument of seraphs — in apotheoses, but of something much more subtle, which can be grasped only by those endowed with a fine and delicate artistic sense.

The painter habitually employs this metaphor, *the gamut of colours,* and the musician may appropriately use this one in return, *the colouring of the orchestra.* Of this colouring I have now to speak.

Too often only the ludicrous side is seen of the anecdote — really a sad one — where a man blind from his birth is instructed by a friend concerning the colour *red*. "It is violent," says the friend, "striking, superb, yet brutal: it kills adjacent tints." "Oh, I understand," rejoins the blind man, "this colour, red, must be like the sound of a trumpet!"

Now it is not unreasonable to maintain that he was quite right, and that each instrument has really *its own* colour, which may be defined as its special character, admitting at the same time that this resemblance may vary with different observers, perhaps owing to differences in the conformation of the eye or of the ear. From this divergence in judgment springs the sole real objection as to the demonstration I propose making.

To most persons, as to myself, the etherial, suave, transparent timbre of the *flute* with its placidity and its poetic charm, produces an auditive sensation analogous to the visual impression of the colour *blue*, a fine blue, pure and luminous as the azure of the sky.

The *oboe*, so appropriate to the expression of rustic sentiments, appears to me distinctly *green*,[1] a rather crude tint.

The warm sound of the *clarinet*, at once rough and velvety, brilliant in the high notes, sombre but rich in the chalumeau register, calls up the idea of a *red-brown*, the *Vandyke red, garnet.*

The *horn* is *yellow*, a brilliant coppery-yellow and the poor *cor anglais*, so melancholy, corresponds to *violet*, expressing affliction, sadness, and resignation.

The family of *trumpets*, *clarions*, and *trombones*, presents all the gradations of *crimson ;* mingled with the horns, it gives *orange ;* while the *cornet*, trivial and braggart, utters a note of a very ordinary red, *ox-blood*, or *lees of wine.*

---

1 I see that, in Gevaert's " Cours d'Orchestration " (p. 107), on one occasion he speaks of the oboe as a red line. (It may be noted that red and green are complementary colours, mistaken for each other by the colour-blind). Later, also, in the same volume (p. 150), the author speaks of " the *verdure* of the oboe " ; which is manifestly the same sentiment differently expressed.

The *bassoon,* sombre, sad, painful, with feeble, timid, and inconspicuous timbre, is certainly a *dark-brown,* not a clean colour, but a little mixed with gray.

The percussion instruments, *kettle-drums,* the *bass drum,* make great *black* holes in the mass of sound; the roll of the *side drum* is *grayish*; the *triangle,* on the other hand, can be nothing else than *silvery.*[1]

Thus at least I *hear them,* which does not prevent other men from *seeing them* differently. But with almost every one the perception of musical timbre is united, perhaps unconsciously, to an idea of colour which needs only to be suggested for each person to be conscious of the fact.

I should not venture to be so explicit in respect to the great family of the bow instruments, for each one of these has its infinite variety of timbres : for instance, the violin, in its harmonics, is as aerial, as blue as the flute ; its fourth string gives the illusion of the grave red-brown of the clarinet; with its mute, it can bring out the rustic character of the oboe, or the profound sadness of the cor anglais, while its *pizzicati* are little specks of black. We may indeed say that the violin, the orchestral king, an instrument whose richness of timbre is unequalled, possesses almost the whole gamut of the musical colours.

In the same way, it would be impossible to assign any one colour to the 'cello; like the violin, it has almost all colours, but they all are graver and darker in tone.

Also, the viola has them all, as it were attenuated and veiled by a general neutral tint, through which the different shades are seen as through a fog. It is very useful in the ensemble, but it has no distinct personality ; the viola is a philosopher, sad, helpful, always ready to come to the aid of others, but reluctant to call attention to himself.

If I did not fear to fatigue the reader by further

---

[1] [H. Heathcote Statham says: " I myself always feel the sound of the trumpets as a bright yellow, that of the horns as orange, that of trombones as a deep, heavy red, and that of the flutes as white." Tr.]

developing this idea, which is not without importance, I would add that the art of orchestration seems to me to have much similarity to the painter's art in the use of colour; the musician's palette is his orchestral list; here he finds all the tones necessary to clothe his thought, his melodic design, his harmonic tissue, to produce lights and shadows, and he mixes them almost as the painter mixes his colours.

From a point of view like this, *military music, concerted music*, the *fanfare*, correspond to different kinds of decorative painting. Like it, they proceed in grand masses, they neglect details, employ strong procedures, and aim specially at effects from a distance. And *chamber music* would be the *aquarelle*, appealing to the sensibilities, and having very tender delicate gradations of colour. And the *organ*, with its tones so warm and so varied, its formidable strength and its seraphic gentleness, is it not, in our cathedrals, the natural associate of the painted windows, where the loudest and most contradictory colours melt into a harmony of light?

As for the *piano*, it is a percussion instrument,— *black*. The music of the piano is, then, black and white, like a drawing in pencil, a charcoal sketch, an engraving. And, as the drawing reproduces a picture, giving, in a way, by comparative values, some idea of its colouring, so the piano is *par excellence* the instrument for transcription, which, in the domain of sounds, is the same thing. In skilful hands, it is able to give an impression of various timbres, and for this reason, the great masters have without hesitation committed to it — even have written specially for it — things conceived and planned for the orchestra. The cross-hatchings are to the sketcher what the *tremolo* is to the pianist, the rôle of the pedal is like that of the stump, mingling, blending, strengthening, or reducing, according to the manner of using it and the occasion for its use.

No one will deny that as manifestations of art there is a great resemblance between the hand-organ and the chromo, between photography and phonography, although the latter has the advantage, since colours are not as yet reproduced in the photograph, while the phonograph, though still imperfect, gives a certain impression of timbre, of *Klangfarbe* (sound-colour), as the Germans say, agreeing with me and the blind man; I feel bound to repeat this here, in support of my theory.

Moreover, is there not a most remarkable similarity between the ear, whose structure we have described,[1] and the organ which has perception of colours. The eyelids protect the eye, as the pinna and the auditory conduit protect the ear; the pupil, first lens, and crystalline second lens correspond well to the tympanum and the oval window; the anterior and posterior chambers of the eye contain each a peculiar liquid, the aqueous and the vitreous humour, which have great resemblance to the liquids of the vestibule and labyrinth of the ear; the eye communicates with the pharynx by the tear-duct, as does the ear by the Eustachian tube; lastly, the optic nerve is spread over the retina in fibres and microscopic rods (the rods of the Jacobean membrane) *of different lengths,* corresponding to the different colours, just as the acoustic nerve ends in ramifications called Schultze's bristles and Corti's fibres, of which each is responsive to a different tone. The two organisms receive, decompose, and transmit to the brain vibrations of very different periods, the one atomic, the other molecular, but in each case they are vibrations.

And the emotion which music produces, who knows but this may be only another vibratory phenomenon, whose receiving organ is the soul? But here we lose ourselves in conjectures.

To remain practical, let us now seek to determine how shall be acquired the skill necessary for handling an orchestra, not losing from sight the fact that this is a most difficult thing for any one who has not the intuition of it. And first, a person desiring to orchestrate well must read many scores, seeking to understand the reasons which led the composer, in each case, to employ such or

1 Chaper I., section C.

such an instrument, group, or combination; he should attend many symphonic concerts, following the score, which he should previously have studied, and should subsequently re-read, recalling so far as possible the actual sounds, and seeking to get a clear idea of the means by which they were produced.

He will then find it an excellent practical exercise to orchestrate, himself, fragments or entire compositions, entr'actes, symphonies, using a good transcription for the piano, and afterwards comparing his work with the composer's own score.

In ways like these, the student will soon be able to write things that could be performed by an orchestra; but real skill, the sure and supple hand which works unerringly in producing that which the author intended to produce, is acquired only by long practice and experience, and belongs only to the chosen few.

An excellent piece of advice for all those who desire to study thoroughly this important branch of the musical art is this: they should themselves learn to play on many instruments belonging to the different groups, even if it be but superficially in each case; a musician who is already a pianist (and everyone is a pianist, to a degree, I mean,— not a virtuoso) and has a good knowledge of harmony, if he will devote some months to the study of each of these three instruments, the 'cello, the clarinet, and the horn, will thus very greatly enhance his ability to assimilate everything connected with instrumentation and orchestration. I do not say this is an indispensable preliminary,— far from it, for many do without this,— but it is of very great advantage, a sure means of gaining time, and of escaping many disappointments.

To associate with the members of an orchestra, to take part personally in rehearsals or performances, develops rapidly the feeling for orchestration, and many composers could be named who have attained great skill after months and years of service in the modest but responsible post of kettle-drummer.

The following list contains the principal works treating of this subject:

KASTNER, *Cours d'instrumentation.*

—— *Traité général d'instrumentation.*

BERLIOZ, *Grand Traité d'instrumentation et d'orchestration modernes.*

GEVAERT, *Nouveau Traité d'instrumentation.*

—— *Cours méthodique d'orchestration.*

GUIRAUD, *Traité pratique d'instrumentation.*

DELDEVEZ, *l'Art du chef d'orchestre.*

LAVOIX FILS, *Histoire de l'instrumentation.*

In English, BARRET, W. A., *Instrumentation*, London, 1879.

DANA, W. H., *Orchestration*, 1875; *Instrumentation*, 1876.

PROUT, G., *Instrumentation*, London, 1876.

MACDONALD, J. D., *Sounds and Colours*, London, 1867.

HUGHES, MRS. F. J., *Harmonies of Tones and Colours*, London, 1883.

CORDER, F., *The Orchestra, and How to Write for it*, London and New York, 1896.

CHAPTER III.

THE GRAMMAR OF MUSIC.

We here enter the domain of pure music. By *grammar* is to be understood harmony and counterpoint, which govern musical orthography.

We suppose the reader to have already some elementary ideas as to music, understanding notation and the technical terms which we cannot avoid using. If this is not the case, he can in no way better obtain this ·knowledge than by the perusal of any one of the books enumerated in the following list :

A. Savard, *Principes de la musique et méthode de transposition.*
E. Durand, *Théorie musicale.*
A. Danhauser, *Théorie de la musique.*
M. Simon, *Cours complet des principes de la musique.*
A. Marmontel, *la 1re année de la musique.*
———— *la 2me année de la musique.*
In English : Hullah, Dr. J., *Grammar,* etc., London, 1876.
Culwick, J. C., *Rudiments,* etc., Dublin, 1881.

I should also mention here the excellent pamphlet of M. P. Rougnon, *Dictionnaire musical des locutions étrangères,* giving the translation and explanation of all terms in Italian, German, Latin, or other languages, employed in editions of music published in the different countries, whose significance many musicians do not fully understand.[1]

[1][Admirable works of the same nature in English are: *Music,* by H. C. Bannister ; and *The Philosophy of Music,* by William Pole ; *The Nature of Harmony and Metre,* by Moritz Hauptmann, translated by W. E. Heathcote. In German : *Elemente der Musik,* by Arrey von Dommer ; and *Populäre Vorträge über Bildung und Begründung eines musikalischen Urtheils,* by Hermann Küster. Ed.]

A.— The Harmonic System.

A series of musical sounds, emitted or heard successively, — for instance, sung by a single voice,— constitutes melody.

For harmony, two or more different musical sounds must be produced or heard simultaneously.[1]

The same notes which placed horizontally upon a single stave form a melodic phrase belong to the domain of harmony if written vertically, whether on one stave or on several staves.

(In composition, especially in instrumental composition, it often happens that the notes composing a chord are emitted not together but successively, and the chord is said to be *broken* or *arpeggio'd.* From the theoretic point of view, however, they should be regarded as simultaneous.)

In the present division of our subject, we have, therefore, (excepting some references to melodic contours) to consider only the simultaneous combination of sounds which are called *chords.*

The simultaneous sounding of *two notes* does not constitute a chord. It is not enough; it is nothing more than a *harmonic interval,* an uncompleted chord, imperfect, lacking one of its elements.

The true chord is composed of *three, four,* or *five notes.*[2]

The *primitive* or *fundamental chord,* also called the *triad,* is formed by superposed thirds; the origin of this chord is easily discovered in the phenomenon of the resonance of sonorous bodies, already examined thoroughly

---

1 [Hauptmann finely elaborates the distinction between melody and harmony. Melody conveys an idea of motion; harmony, of rest. Melody must go on, or cease to be melody; harmony, though stationary, contains a complete musical idea. Progressions in harmony are a succession of distinct ideas; in melody, the idea as a whole develops by the succession of tones. TR.]

2 Certain chords, indeed, consist of *six.* See p. 207.

in Chapter I.,[1] to which we shall have occasion to refer later.

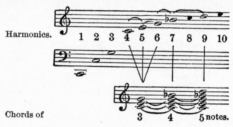

Harmonics. 1 2 3 4 5 6 7 8 9 10

Chords of 3 4 5 notes.

The first harmonics (namely the 4th, 5th, and 6th) furnish the triad or perfect chord; by adding to it the 7th harmonic, we obtain a chord of four notes, called *the chord of the seventh;* and, lastly, the 9th harmonic,[2] added to the preceding, produces the chord of five sounds which is known as the *chord of the ninth.* The triads are the only *consonant chords.* With them this study will begin.

CONSONANT CHORDS.

The most characteristic type is the perfect major chord, composed of a major third and a perfect fifth : This combination of intervals occurring, in the major mode, upon the 1st, 4th, and 5th degrees (root-notes), and, in the minor, on the 5th and 6th, the major triad can occupy these various positions, and no other:

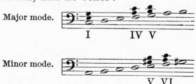

Major mode. I IV V

Minor mode. V VI

By lowering its third, we have the *minor triad* (an artificial product) formed with a minor third and a perfect fifth.

Major. Minor.

Perfect chords.

---

1 Page 9.

2 The 8th (C) would be used twice with 1, 2, and 4. The 10th (E) would be twice used with 5. These are not taken into the account.

These two intervals being found together only, in the major mode, on the 2d, 3d, and 6th degrees, and only, in the minor mode, on the 1st and 4th, it follows that upon these degrees only can the perfect minor chord be built.

If now we lower the fifth of the minor triad, we have a chord of the diminished fifth (a diminished triad) which is a still more artificial product, containing a minor third and a diminished fifth.

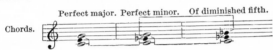

This chord can be built, in the diatonic scale, only upon the 7th degree in the major, and on the 2d and 7th in the minor, which limits it to the following positions:

Each degree of a scale, whether major or minor, can therefore receive, without the intervention of notes foreign to the key, a chord of three notes, a triad, in its fundamental position:

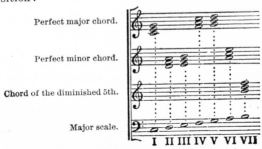

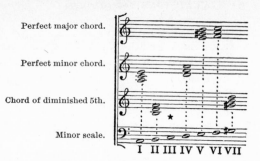

Perfect major chord.

Perfect minor chord.

Chord of diminished 5th.

Minor scale.

I II III IV V VI VII

except the 3d degree of the minor mode (marked with a star) on which can be erected only a chord of *the augmented fifth,* whose inutility most theorists admit. It is besides too harsh to the ear to be admitted into the family of the consonant chords; the chord of the *diminished fifth* even can be received only by a kind of tolerance (with the object of rendering the system more homogeneous by building upon each degree of the major scale a chord of three notes), for its characteristic note, the diminished fifth, is itself **dissonance.**[1]

It is understood then that there are three chords of three tones, *consonant chords, triads,* formed in their fundamental position by two superposed thirds, and these are: the *perfect major chord,* the *perfect minor chord,* and the *chord of the diminished fifth.* Each of these chords belongs exclusively to certain degrees of each mode, outside of which it cannot be used.

Both chords and intervals are capable of inversion; an interval can have but one inversion, and a chord can have as many inversions as it contains distinct intervals. A triad, then, is susceptible of two inversions. These are obtained by setting its lowest note an octave higher:

[1] We should remember that the chord of the diminished fifth has only been admitted with reluctance. Inverted it contains the alarming *tritone,* once absolutely prohibited, and in mediæval times called *diabolus in musica.* (See Chap. V.).

Fundamental chord. 1st inversion. 2d inversion.

The first inversion of a triad is called *a chord of the sixth*, from the name of the interval which it introduces into the system; its second, *a chord of the fourth and sixth* (4–6), for a like reason. Each of these must be examined separately, beginning with the first.

The first inversion of the *perfect major chord* is formed of a minor third and a minor sixth, two minor intervals, which is not surprising when we reflect that inversion *reverses* the relation of an interval.

Perfect major chord.   Chord of sixth.

In the same way the inversion of the perfect minor chord gives only major intervals, a third and a sixth.

Perfect minor chord.   Chord of sixth.

The first inversion of the *chord of the diminished fifth* gives a minor third and a major sixth, the notes of this forming between themselves, within the chord, the interval of the augmented fourth, which is the inversion of the diminished fifth.

Chord of dim. 5th.   Chord of 6th (augm. 4th).

The origin of these chords indicates the place they can occupy in the scale. They are derived from the fundamental chords; they have as their bass the thirds of those chords; they are formed by the same tones differently grouped, inverted; they must stand on the degree which forms an interval of a third with the one on which their fundamental chord stands.

Hence we can build on each degree of the major or minor scale, a chord of the sixth, the first inversion of the fundamental chords:

except on the fifth degree of the minor mode, to which would correspond the inversion of the (unused) chord of the augmented fifth

We will now examine *second inversions*. That of the *perfect major chord* contains a perfect fourth and a major sixth.

Perfect major chord.   Chord of 6th.   Chord of 4 - 6.

That which is derived from the *perfect minor chord*

differs only in having a *minor sixth* instead of a major, and the fourth remains perfect,

Perfect minor chord. Chord of 6th. Chord of 4 - 6.

while in the second inversion of the *chord of the diminished fifth* is found its inversion, the augmented fourth, accompanied by a major sixth.

Chord of dim. 5th. Chord of 6th. (Augm. 4th.)

Hence this last is usually designated by the special name, *chord of the augmented fourth and sixth.*

Every fundamental chord admitting of a second inversion, as it does of a first, simply by changing the position of the tones which compose it, it is plain that on every degree of the diatonic scale can be erected a chord of 4–6 in either mode, by using as bass the fifth of the fundamental chord, which is also the third in chords of the sixth, the first inversion.

This is shown in the table annexed, where each degree of the scales, major and minor, is shown having its chord of 4–6:

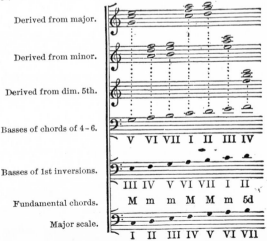

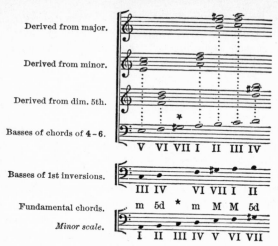

Derived from major.
Derived from minor.
Derived from dim. 5th.
Basses of chords of 4–6.
V VI VII I II III IV

Basses of 1st inversions.
III IV VI VII I II

Fundamental chords.
m 5d * m M M 5d
Minor scale.
I II III IV V VI VII

except the seventh degree of the minor, where now occurs the gap already mentioned, which renders it incapable of carrying a chord of 4–6, which would be a diminished fourth and sixth,

The entire system of the consonant chords, which, for the sake of clearness, we have thus studied, chord by chord, is now summed up and represented in the following tables, in the two modes:

1st and 2d inversions.
Major mode.
Fundamental chords.
Majors. ........M.................M....M...............................–3
Minors. ....m....m...............................m......–3
Of dim. 5th. ....d5.....–1

1st and 2d inversions.
Minor Mode.
Fundamental chords.
Majors. ..................................M....M...............–2
Minors. ......m......................m......................–2
Of dim. 5th. ....d5.........................d5.....–2

We see that it is directly derived from the system of tonality, of which it is, to speak more truly, the extension, the necessary consequence. The same is true as to the system of

DISSONANT CHORDS

which we shall now examine and shall find to be of equal simplicity.

A third and a fifth, that is to say, two superposed thirds, built upon any degree of the scale, have given us chords of three sounds, consonant chords, in their fundamental position. If we build upon these musical constructions by the addition of another third (a higher note, of course) we shall obtain, upon each degree, a new chord formed of four tones, a *chord of the seventh*, also in its fundamental position, differing from the consonant chord upon the same degree only by this *third* third, which has been added to it, forming a *seventh* with the root-note, and bringing into the chord the dissonant element which characterises it.

Consonant chord. Chord of 7th (dissonance).

Thus are constituted, always without the use of tones foreign to the diatonic scale, the chords of *the major seventh*, which, in the major scale, are built upon the first and fourth degrees, and in the minor upon the sixth only,

Major mode. I IV

Minor mode. VI

and are composed of a major third, a perfect fifth, and a major seventh.

The chords of the minor seventh, which are only minor triads, surmounted by a third third, forming with the root an interval of a minor seventh, are built, in the major, on the 2d, 3d, and 6th degrees and, in the minor, upon the 4th only.

Major mode.

II III VI

Minor mode.

IV

If to a perfect major chord we add a minor seventh, we have the chord of the dominant seventh, so called because it can only be built upon the fifth or *dominant* degree of either mode.

Major mode.

V

Minor mode.

V

The chord of the dominant seventh is the most frequently used of any chords of the seventh; it is the least dissonant, being formed by a union of the harmonics **4, 5, 6,** and **7,** while all the other chords of the seventh contain tones foreign to the harmonics of their root.

If, finally, to a chord of the diminished fifth be added a seventh, two different chords are obtained according as this seventh is minor or diminished.

If minor, the following group is formed: , which is called the *seventh* chord of the leading tone, on the seventh degree of the major scale,

Major scale.

VII

and the *minor seventh* and *diminished fifth*, when it is built on the second degree of the minor scale:

Minor scale.

II

Diminished, it forms the *chord of the diminished seventh :* , which can be formed only on the seventh degree in the minor mode:

Minor scale.

There is, then, a chord of the seventh, a dissonant chord of four notes, which can be erected on each of the degrees of the major or minor scale, excepting always the inevitable gap on the third degree in the minor.

Hence, the major scale has :

> 1 chord of the dominant seventh.
> 2 chords of the major seventh.
> 3 chords of the minor seventh.
> 1 chord of the seventh on the leading tone.

Total: 7, one to each degree.

The minor scale has:

> 1 chord of the dominant seventh.
> 1 chord of the major seventh.
> 1 chord of the minor seventh.
> 1 chord of the minor seventh and dim. fifth.
> 1 chord of the diminished seventh.

Total: 5, *but all different.*[1]

This is shown in the following table :

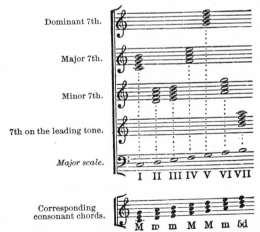

[1] The last major and the last minor in these lists of chords may also be considered, when they are built on the seventh degree, as chords of the ninth deprived of their root-tone. See p. 206.

The perfect correlation between the chords of the seventh and the fundamental consonant chords from which they are derived is noticeable.

Also it will be remarked that the absence of a chord of three notes on the third degree of the minor scale results indirectly in preventing the formation of a chord of the seventh on the first degree also, since it would have within it an interval of the augmented fifth, which, harmonically considered, cannot make part of a chord.

From this it must not be inferred that every combination containing an augmented fifth is absolutely inadmissible; this would be a grave error. Combinations of this kind are in frequent and excellent use, and will be explained in their appropriate place.[1]   But it is suitable, for purposes

[1] Page 253.

of pure classification, to omit them in the enumeration of chords properly so-called, for they have not this character, and call for the application of special rules. It is simply a question of nomenclature.

Chords of the seventh, containing four tones, are susceptible of three inversions.

Fundamental chord. 1st inversion. 2d inversion. 3d inversion.

The first inversion of each is composed of a third, a fifth, and a sixth, whose character differs according to the composition of the fundamental chord. It is called in general terms a chord of 6–5, with the specification, when it occurs, that the fifth is diminished, or that the sixth occupies the seventh degree of the scale, the leading tone.

The table shows these chords, with their names, the indication of the degree on which they can be built, and that of the fundamental chord from which they are derived.

The bass of the first inversions is of course the third from that of the fundamental chords.

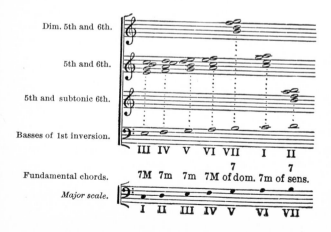

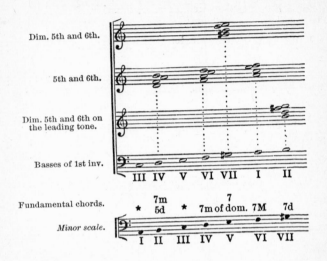

The second inversion contains a third, a fourth, and a sixth, in various relations. In general, it is called the chord of 4-3, because it is the only one containing these two intervals, the third and fourth, which form between them the dissonance of a second. At the same time this inversion is specially designated, whenever among the intervals composing it there is any characteristic one. Thus it may be called : *Sixth on the leading tone, tritone* [1] *with major third; tritone with minor third; augmented fourth and sixth;* being in each case, however, nothing more than the second inversion of a chord of the seventh. These various designations have the effect of characterising it better, and, as a matter of fact, determine precisely the situation that a chord occupies in the scale.

The following table presents all the chords of the seventh in their second inversion. Here their bass-note forms a fifth with the bass of the fundamental chord.

[1] Old appellation of the augmented fourth, which contains *three whole tones.*

The third inversions compose the family of *chords of the second*, whose bass is the seventh in relation to the fundamental chord. According to circumstances these are called *the second* on the leading tone, the *augmented second*, *chord of the tritone*, showing their composition — or their place, which amounts to the same thing, since, each degree being differently constituted, by knowing the formative elements you can find the degree, and *vice versa*.

(This is not absolutely without exception, since certain chords can be built on two or three different degrees; but, as we shall see later, no confusion results from it.)

The third inversions are represented in the following table, with indication of the special name of each, in the major and minor:

As I have already done in the case of consonant chords,[1] I will give a synoptic table for the system of chords of the seventh, taking each mode separately.

[1] Page 196.

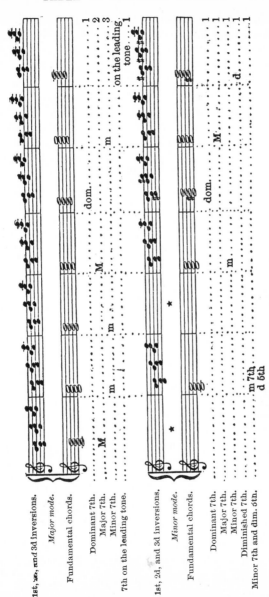

In order to complete our knowledge of chords, we have now only to examine the dissonant chords of five tones, or *chords of the ninth;* this will be speedily done, for they are but two in number, built upon the same degree, which shows, of course, that they belong to different modes.

If we add to a chord of the dominant seventh a higher third, which must of necessity be major or minor according to the mode, we shall obtain either the *major chord of the dominant ninth,* or *the minor chord of the dominant ninth.*

Dominant 7th.   Major 7th.   Minor 7th (dissonances.)

This chord contains two dissonances, the seventh and the ninth.[1]

Inversions of these chords are so infrequent that I merely mention them; the fourth is even impracticable, a *ninth* exceeding the octave, which is the limit of inversions.

The chords of the *dominant seventh,* of the *seventh* of the leading tone, of the *diminished seventh,* of the *major* and *minor* dominant ninth, which constitute, as we shall see later, a special group (that of *natural dissonant harmony*)[2] present an interesting peculiarity. They can all receive the tonic as bass, *below their normal bass,* and in this new form they assume new aspects, without, however, ceasing to be the same chords that they were before.

Take a chord of the dominant seventh, 🎵, a chord of

---

[1] By omitting the bass of a chord of the ninth, we have a chord of the seventh of the leading tone, or of the diminished seventh.   See p. 199, *note.*

[2] Page 242.

the leading tone seventh, , a chord of the diminished

seventh, , a chord of the major ninth, , a chord

of the minor ninth, ; give them all as bass the tonic

C, common to them all, and you have the family of chords
called *sur-tonic.*

			6	♭6
+7	+7	+7	+7	7
	6	♭6	5	5
(a)	(b)	(c)	(d)	(e)

(*a*) Chord of the sur-tonic dominant 7th.
(*b*) Chord of the sur-tonic 7th of the leading tone.
(*c*) Chord of the sur-tonic diminished 7th.
(*d*) Chord of the sur-tonic major dominant 9th,
    which combines the chords *a* and *b*; called also by some
    authors chord of the tonic 11th.
(*e*) Chord of the sur-tonic minor dominant 9th,
    which combines the chords *a* and *d*; called also chord of
    the tonic 13th.

The first three are composed of five tones; the latter two,
of six; none of them can be inverted; for, in displacing the
bass note, this would deprive them of their special character as sur-tonic chords.

This is the entire list of chords, and there are no others;
but these can undergo transformations of a nature to render them almost unrecognisable to the unpractised eye.

Some of these transformations will now be explained,—
those, namely, which are connected with the doubling or
with the omission of certain notes, and with the divers
positions of the chords. Others can not be explained till
later, after an examination of the laws which govern the
associations of chords.

A succession of chords can be written in three, four, five,
six parts, or more, according to the number of voices at
command. (In musical language, the word *voice* is often
used as a synonyme for *part.*[1]) However, as many chords[2]

---

1 [" The practice cannot be recommended." Baker. Tr.]
2 All the dissonant chords.

could never be fully presented with three parts only, and as, on the other hand, there are but a few which require five voices,[1] it has become the general custom to write in four parts, and it is thus that most of the harmonic exercises are presented in all good schools.

The consonant chords containing but three notes, it becomes necessary (to give employment to the four parts) to double one of their constituent notes.

The choice of the tone to be doubled is not a matter of indifference; it is important that the note should be, in itself and in its position, the most important of the chord, so that the equilibrium is not disturbed, but the added predominance will only further accentuate the tonal meaning.

The best notes to be doubled are necessarily the first, fourth, and fifth degree : the *tonic, subdominant,* and *dominant,* that is to say, the tonic notes, the generators of the scale, called also by some authors, the *good notes.*

In addition to these, it would rarely be injurious to double the fundamental of a chord, because its importance is so great.

The notes less useful for doubling are, as a rule, the *modal notes* (with some exceptions); but the note which must never be doubled in any case is that of the seventh degree, the leading tone, as this would involve grave faults of harmonisation.[2]

These general rules are too vague; they will now be made more definite by examining the chords in succession.

In the perfect major or minor chord, the best note to double is the *bass,* first, as being the fundamental ; and then, because these chords have their most frequent and most logical use upon the tonal notes.

Perfect chords
with doubled bass.

I   IV   V   I   I   IV   V   I

---

1 The two chords of the ninth and the sur-tonic chords.
2 See page 223.

Also, their *third* may be doubled, and this is often particularly successful in chords built on the sixth degree,
because then the doubled note is the tonic.

The doubling of the *fifth* is rarely productive of good
effect; at the same time this cannot be absolutely prohibited
especially where the fifth is a tonal note.

The doubling of the bass is so much more advantageous
than that of any other that frequently, instead of doubling
a third or a fifth, it is better to triple the bass (the fifth
then being omitted):

this is, moreover, conformable to the natural order, since,
in the series of ten harmonics, the fundamental tone, the
generator occurs four times, while the third and fifth each
occur but twice.

(I cannot refrain from calling attention again to the
many instructive facts of various kinds that can be derived
from this simple series of over-tones).

Each one of these reduplications, which are in fact only

reinforcements of some one of the constituent elements of the chord, has its own peculiar character.

By doubling the *bass* the chord becomes stronger, more sonorous, more vigorous; its fundamental note is thus accentuated, and the effect of the whole chord rendered rich and energetic. By doubling the *third* the modal character of the chord is emphasised and — except upon the sixth degree, where the note doubled is the tonic — the feeling of tonality is weakened; it gives chords that are sweet and smooth, but not forcible or brilliant when compared to those with doubled bass. On the contrary, the reduplication of the *fifth* produces harshness, a sort of disagreeable hoarseness, and for this reason should be used as rarely as possible. One needs only to play the three following chords, on a harmonium, or on a piano that is in perfect tune, to perceive these divers characters:

The first chord is rich and well-balanced; the second is comparatively feeble, soft; the third, in comparison, is hard and harsh. If they are changed from major to minor by substituting E♭ for E, the impression remains the same.

In the *chords of the diminished fifth* it is impossible to double the fifth, on account of its tendency in resolution, which would inevitably occasion faults of harmonisation.[1] There remain, therefore, only the third and the bass susceptible of reduplication, and of these, the bass must be avoided as much as possible when it chances to be the leading tone, because of its *tendency*, which we shall speak of later.[2]

Hence, in the *chord of the diminished fifth of the seventh degree*, major or minor, we double, by preference, the third;

[1] *Consecutive octaves;* see p. 226.

[2] Page 236.

in that of the second degree, of the minor mode, the bass.

Chords of the diminished fifth with third or bass doubled.

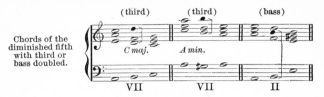

The same reasons which make a reduplication useful or the reverse in a chord in its fundamental position applying equally to its inversions, we shall be able to dismiss the latter with fewer details.

For *chords of the sixth,* derived from perfect chords, the order of preference is as follows: *sixth, third, bass.* For the same class of chords derived from the chord of *the diminished fifth* on the seventh degree: *third,* or *bass;* for that on the second degree: *sixth,* or *bass.*

Various doublings of chords of the sixth.

Fundamental chords.

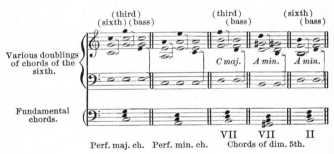

Perf. maj. ch.   Perf. min. ch.   Chords of dim. 5th.

The doubling of the bass being here always the most faulty, it is advisable to use it as rarely as possible, and, especially, to avoid placing it in the highest voice, where it would be too conspicuous. It produces there a hollow and ill-balanced sound, not unlike that of a cracked vase.

bad   admissible

There are certain exceptions to this rule, which will be indicated when we study the connection of chords,[1] to be made use of, however, but sparingly.

We may mention here that it is quite permissible to double the bass of a chord of the sixth on the fourth degree, and this even in the first part, because in this case it reinforces the subdominant, which is a *tonal note*.

We will now consider the second inversions.

In **6-4** *chords,* inversions of perfect chords, the best notes to double are the bass or the fourth. In *chords of the augmented fourth and sixth,* a distinction must be made between those having for their fundamental the *chord of the diminished fifth* on the seventh degree of both modes, which have but one useful reduplication, that of the *sixth,* and those originating in the chord of the second degree of the minor mode, which contain two notes that can be doubled, the *fourth* and the *sixth.*

Various doublings of chords of **4-6**.

Fundamental chords.

Perf. maj. ch. Perf. min. ch.   Ch. of dim. 5th.

It is well to notice that these reduplications are rigorously logical : all of them reinforce *one of the tonal notes,* or else the *fundamental* of the chord, which is in conformity with the principle previously enunciated ; with the one exception starred in the preceding table where, since neither the bass nor its fourth could be doubled, on account of their tendencies in resolution, the only note remaining, the sixth, must be the one doubled, which here is on the second degree of the scale, a degree in some sense neutral, neither

1 See p. 223.

tonal nor modal, hence the least important and least characteristic of all.

In *dissonant chords,* which consist of four notes, in
writing in four parts one note cannot be doubled unless
another is omitted. This is never to be done except in the
fundamental chords, and not even in all of them. (Inversions are always used complete, otherwise it would be
impossible to recognise them.) The only note that can
be doubled here is the *bass,* with *omission of the fifth.*

This is very common in chords of *the dominant seventh,*
of the *major seventh,* of *the minor seventh,* of the *minor
seventh* and *diminished fifth;* more rarely in the chord of
the *seventh on the leading-tone,* and never in that of the
diminished seventh.

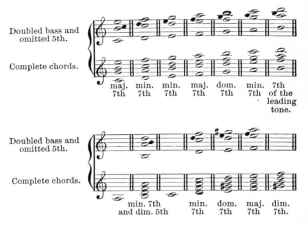

In writing in four parts, if we use *chords of the ninth*
with their five notes, one of these must be omitted, and
this is always their *fifth,* on the second degree of the scale.

In the sur-tonic chords, which contain five or six notes, any reduplication would be manifestly impossible; the notes less important are omitted.

Sur-tonic chords, complete, and with the omissions.

It is to be noted that the omissions usually affect the *second* degree; that is to say, the note least important either as to modality or tonality.

It is evident that the principle in itself is very simple: for notes to be doubled must be selected those of chief importance in the key or in the chord; tonal notes or the fundamental (that is to say, the bass of the chord in its fundamental position). For notes to be omitted, on the contrary, those of the least importance, or those least characteristic in the chord: a *chord of the ninth* if the ninth were omitted would become a chord of the seventh; a chord of the seventh, losing its seventh, would be nothing but a triad.

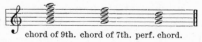

chord of 9th. chord of 7th. perf. chord.

Reduplication, therefore, can affect only a note of prime importance; omission, on the contrary, can be made only of an unimportant note, one easily imagined, guessed at, by the hearer.

All these chords, whether fundamental, inverted, complete, incomplete, having a note doubled or a note omitted, may have a great variety of positions; that is to say, the notes of which they are composed may change place, at the pleasure of the composer, always excepting the bass note, which must retain its position, or there would be not merely a change of position, but an inversion.

Here is a perfect chord:

However we may arrange its notes, double one of them, omit one, transport them to any octave,

it never ceases to be the *perfect major chord of C.* But if its bass be moved, and we have this:

or this:

for instance, it is now something else; the chord changes its character and its name; it becomes one of its own inversions, and must be *figured* differently.

This leads me to explain what is meant in harmony by the *figuring of chords.*

It is a system of abbreviations, itself very incomplete, which consists in writing *in notes* only the bass, and representing the other tones by figures or conventional signs.

In general use from the end of the sixteenth century to the beginning of the eighteenth, it is not improbable that it was invented by Vincent Galilei, father of the celebrated Galileo, who lived about 1550, and was a composer. After being long used to note, with deplorable insufficiency, entire scores, as in the time of Rameau, who believed that he had brought it to perfection, the *figured bass* was retained in the Italian school for the accompaniment of recitatives, consisting at that time almost exclusively of solid chords. At the present day it is scarcely known except to students of harmony, to whom it renders real service as a kind of shorthand, and especially in musical analysis.

The system is as follows:

Every figure placed above a bass-note represents, first, the interval numerically corresponding, and then, the chord of which it necessarily makes a part, the other notes being understood.

An accidental, placed at the left of a figure, acts upon it as upon a note. Standing alone, it indicates an altered third. A crossed figure indicates a diminished interval.[1] A little cross[2] preceding the figure designates the leading tone. Alone, it applies to the third. A dash after a figure, over two or more consecutive notes, indicates that the tone must be prolonged. The zero, employed alone, indicates silence;[3] associated with the other figures, it indicates the omission of a note of the chord. The simplest possible figuring is used, which is logical, since this is designed to be a kind of abbreviated writing, a harmonic stenography, so far as it goes.

Now the common chord is figured by a **3**, a **5**, or an **8**. (Some writers do not figure it at all, which is simpler.) With an altered third, the sign of alteration is enough, the perfect fifth is understood, as well as the reduplication if there is one.

The figuring with **5** is most common. Some authors reserve the **3** for the minor chord.

The chord of the sixth is figured by a **6**. If the sixth is augmented, an accidental is placed at the left; if it is the third that is augmented, the accidental is placed alone beneath the **6**.

---

1 [Indicates in England and Germany an *augmented* interval. ED.]

2 [Not used in England. ED.]

3 [Not used in England. ED.]

The chord of the fourth and sixth is figured $\frac{6}{4}$:

The chord of the diminished fifth is distinguished from the perfect chords by its crossed 5 ($\flat$); but its inversions are figured in the same way as the preceding,

without any possibility of mistake; first, because the degrees on which they stand indicate their nature and origin, and, secondly, because the sharps or flats show clearly, if there is need, the intervals which compose them.

The chord of the dominant seventh is figured $\frac{7}{+}$, which indicates that its third is the leading tone; its inversions: $\frac{6}{5}$ *diminished fifth and sixth;* +6, *sixth on the leading tone;* +4, *tritone :*

Here there is no need for sharps or flats, each chord having its figures and characteristic signs.

The chords of the *seventh on the leading tone,* and of the *minor seventh and diminished fifth,* formed of the intervals mentioned, are both figured $\frac{7}{\flat}$; their inversions are for the first: $^{+}\!\frac{6}{5}$, *fifth and sixth on the leading tone;* $^{+}\!\frac{4}{3}$, *tritone with major third;* $\frac{4}{+2}$, *second on the leading tone :*

for the second inversions: $\frac{6}{5}$, *fifth and sixth;* $\frac{4}{3}$, *third and augmented fourth;* **2,** *second:*

The chord of *the diminished seventh* is figured **7**; and its inversions: $^{+}\frac{6}{5}$, *diminished fifth and sixth* on the leading tone; $^{+}\frac{4}{3}$, *tritone* with *minor third;* +2, *augmented second:*

When there is occasion for it, accidentals are added.

Tritone with major 3d.   Tritone with minor 3d.

In the absence of any accidental, a figure is always understood to represent a note on the staff without sharp or flat.

Chords of *the seventh,* both major and minor, are figured by a **7,** a figuring unmistakable as is that of the perfect chords,—an accidental placed either before the **7,** or under it for the third, making known the nature of these intervals, where it is necessary to do so; the *fifth* always remains perfect, which dispenses with figuring; their inversions: $\frac{6}{5}$, *fifth and sixth;* $\frac{4}{3}$, *third and fourth;* **2,** *second:*

Chords of *the ninth* are the only ones which require three signs; they are figured $\frac{9}{7}$, with an accidental placed before the **9**, where it is necessary, to distinguish those of the *major* ninth from those of the *minor:*

Chords of the *sur-tonic* dominant seventh and of the *sur-tonic* dominant ninth, which certain schools call chords of the *tonic eleventh* and of the *tonic thirteenth,* are thus represented:

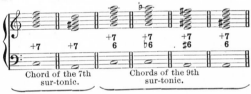

Chord of the 7th sur-tonic.   Chords of the 9th sur-tonic.

When figures are placed one above the other, or are presented in an unusual order, this is for the purpose of pointing out a position,— an intention which is but imperfectly fulfilled. Thus the group $\frac{3}{5}$ suggests clearly that the third must be above the fifth in the first part, but it can be translated in the following various ways, and in others still:

The form $\frac{3}{8}{\scriptstyle 5}$, although more definite, still leaves a choice among three:

It is evident, then, that figuring, while it clearly shows the chords and their composition, leaves great latitude, to him who interprets it, in the choice of positions, which it never shows except vaguely, and most frequently fails to indicate at all.

We will now speak of *positions*. They are not all equally good; the best are generally the most symmetrical, those where the notes are as nearly equidistant as possible.

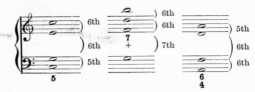

There is but one chord which permits absolute symmetry, this is 𝇈 (*the diminished seventh*)[1] formed of three minor thirds superposed.

(It is also strictly symmetrical if the order of these notes be inverted, producing a chord of the *augmented second* in an open position, instead of the fundamental, in a close one. We have then the superposition of three major sixths.)

The further we depart from complete symmetry, the less satisfactory is the position; at the same time, groupings like the following are still very acceptable:

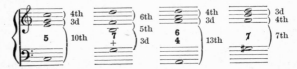

The fault most to be avoided is that of crowding the lower notes and scattering the higher; positions like the following are the worst, the most ill-balanced of all:

1 In future, chords will often be designated by their figuring, both for brevity and also to familiarise the reader with this system which is ingenious and often useful to the composer.

In choral music the greatest effects of strength are produced by grouping the tones in compact masses; and a rich, full sonority by symmetrical, spaced positions.

Now, in harmony, we are supposed to write always for voices. The four theoretic voices, or parts, are limited to the following average range:

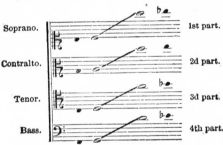

And the extreme tones, indicated by the black notes, should be used very circumspectly, the composer keeping as far as possible in the middle register of each voice.

Moreover, the parts should remain in their normal order, relatively to each other, so that no one should cross into its neighbour's domain; this is prohibited in elementary harmony, and is permissible only when it has the effect of giving a more elegant progression to the voices, or bringing into relief an interesting melodic design.

It is likewise forbidden that any two parts should meet

upon the same note, when unison would result, unless, however, by this unison, which is only feebleness, faults of a graver nature are avoided; in pure theory, the parts should no more be mixed than be allowed to cross; each should hold its place : the soprano and the bass being the exterior, the contralto and the tenor, the interior parts.

When there is an inequality, the greater intervals should be taken by the lower voices, and the less, by the higher (as in the series of the harmonics,— always the natural model), otherwise the sonority will either be dull and heavy, or else crude and harsh, and it may even have both faults at once, as in the fourth of the preceding examples. Certain other considerations must also be taken into account in selecting positions. Thus we should always, by preference, place *in the highest part*, which is the most conspicuous, one of the best notes of the chord : in certain chords this is imperative even : the major seventh, the minor seventh, and the leading tone seventh chords hardly allow the soprano to take any other than the third or the seventh; and their third inversions,— chords of the second, — any other than the second or the fourth. In chords of the fifth and sixth on the leading tone, of the tritone with the major third, or of the major dominant ninth, the disagreeable friction of seconds should be avoided by placing certain notes in the relation of sevenths.

Thus we have viewed chords in their individual character,— *chords in repose*, to speak technically. But the most interesting part in the study of harmony consists in the movement of these chords, in methods of linking them, of connecting them together, of grouping them to form phrases, sentences, and finally whole musical compositions. Techni-

cally this is harmonisation fully written out in distinction
to that indicated merely by a system of figuring. The
rules of harmonisation are those which concern the linking
together of chords.

GENERAL RULES OF HARMONISATION.

I.   Any *melodic interval* difficult to sing or disagreeable
to hear is forbidden; there are, then, only the following
allowed:

> The chromatic semitone;
> Major and minor seconds;
> Major and minor thirds;
> The perfect fourth;
> The perfect fifth;
> The minor sixth;
> The perfect octave;

and exceptionally, the augmented second, in the minor
mode, ascending only, and on condition that it be followed
by the tonic.

In general terms, the smaller intervals are the best.
(Some authors tolerate the skip of the major sixth,
especially ascending.)

Naturally, all compound intervals are forbidden.

Moreover, there must not be a seventh or a ninth in three notes, when these notes move in the same direction, unless the middle note is on a degree of the scale immediately preceding or following that of one of the outer notes.

Another melodic contour to be avoided is the augmented fourth in three notes in the same direction, ascending or descending, always with this exception : the augmented fourth in three notes ceases to be incorrect if the last note of the group, being the highest, then goes a diatonic semitone higher, or, if the last note, being the lowest, then descends a diatonic semitone; in a word, if this last note, whatever it is, obeys its leading tendency.[1]

II. Several *melodic* motions, taking place simultaneously, constitute the *harmonic* motion, which is *direct* or *similar,* when all the parts move in the same direction, ascending or descending.

The direct motion is not graceful, and, moreover, often occasions other faults ; it should, then, be rarely used ; in four parts it should be considered as totally prohibited, unless one of the parts proceeds chromatically, which, as a melodic motion, may be considered almost *nul,* since there is no change in the name of the note.

---

[1] The leading tone should ascend ; the subdominant, descend.

Also direct motion is tolerated when it ends on the fourth degree on which is a chord of the sixth.

Contrary motion occurs when parts move in opposite directions, some rising while others fall.

This movement is excellent: it should be sought and frequently employed.

Better still is the *oblique* motion, where one part, or more than one, remains stationary, while the others rise or fall.

When there is opportunity for choice, this should be preferred to the contrary motion.

In short, there is nothing absolutely forbidden except the parallel motion of the four parts, and even this has the exceptions indicated.

III.   When two parts proceed by direct harmonic motion, it is very bad and strictly forbidden that they should appear in two consecutive perfect fifths or two perfect octaves.   If, in two consecutive fifths, the first is diminished, the prohibition still remains; but if it be the second which is diminished, the impression produced is no longer disagreeable, and consequently this motion is allowed.

In the case of the octaves there is no exception.

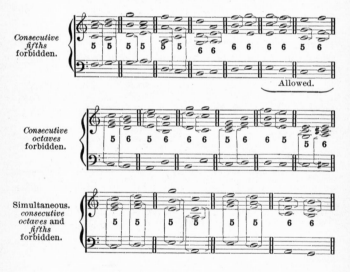

Two successive fifths are extremely harsh.   Two octaves give a feeling of harmonic poverty, naturally enough, since thus the number of parts is reduced, the two voices being each other's double.   The harshness of fifths is less easily explained.[1]   But it is a fact not to be denied, and they must be absolutely avoided.

---

[1] If the octave is the second harmonic, the fifth is the third. A succession of fifths is, then, almost as poor as a succession of octaves. Moreover, it is

IV. A like prohibition is in force when the parts progress by contrary motion, — a unison or a fifteenth succeeding an octave, a twelfth succeeding a fifth, or *vice versa,* being as displeasing in its effect as two consecutive octaves or fifths. The following forms of harmonisation, and all presenting the same faults, are, then, prohibited.

Octaves or fifths in contrary motion forbidden.

V. The harshness of fifths and the poverty of consecutive octaves, *sounded in direct motion,* are also perceptible, even when these intervals are separated by several notes, except in excessively slow movements. Arrangements like the following, therefore, must be rejected as faulty:

Separated octaves or fifths forbidden.

There is required an intermediate chord between the two octaves or the two fifths in order that they may cease to be disagreeable; and here figuring, for the first time, becomes for us a convenient means of analysis. Of the two exam-

harsh to the ear, because it involves the idea of two parts moving in different tonalities:

Key of G.

Key of C.

It would seem that the same censure might apply to a succession of fourths, but this is only in part true, that is to say, in respect to harshness; the fourth not being a harmonic of its fundamental, the impression of poverty is less; hence, the successive fourths are more admissible, though they are not to be especially desired.

We must, in fact, consider the *absolute* prohibition of consecutive octaves or

ples following, which are almost identical, the first is bad, containing two octaves; the second is good, because these same two octaves are separated not by a note merely but by an intermediate chord, which effaces the feeling of the first octave before the second makes itself heard.

The same is to be said of the fifths, which are faulty in the first example, but are not so in the second,

because a foreign chord interposes.

This rule is modified when the octaves or fifths occur upon the up-beat, where necessarily they have less importance; but the true purist will avoid them, as we shall see later, in the section on Counterpoint.

---

fifths, in modern composition, as the remnant of a violent reaction against early attempts at harmonisation of a very awkward character, in which nothing was used but fourths, fifths, and octaves, which to us at the present day seems both feeble and harsh,—intolerable, in a word.

The great modern composers do not hesitate, when it is needful in order to obtain a fine effect, to free themselves from this rule, whose rigour is indispensable only for the student,—a remark which would be entirely out of place in a work exclusively didactic.

It is undoubtedly true that a single fifth, emitted with a certain force, produces, alone, an impression of harshness, and that this disagreeable effect is increased when other fifths follow it; but I am convinced that the complete prohibition of two fifths, especially if separated by several notes, will be considered in the future as an exaggeration of the purism of our epoch. Composers will find ways of using them to advantage, and will derive from them new effects.

Tolerated,[1]
but
to be avoided.

The only case where consecutive fifths separated by a single note are fully permitted, and even upon the downbeat, is when they are syncopated, as in the following example:

Simple as this rule is, there seems to be great difficulty in its application, for very capable students, who are well advanced, are seen often to fall into this very serious fault of musical grammar which, from the beginning, has been pointed out to them as something specially to be avoided.

VI. Another objectionable movement of parts which must be avoided is that produced by hidden octaves, or fifths. The following is an example:

*Hidden
Octaves
or fifths*
forbidden.

and the prohibition may be thus stated: when two parts progress by direct harmonic motion, they must not end in an octave or a fifth.

To speak exactly, this rule, in all its rigour, affects only the first and fourth parts, losing much of its importance when one of the inner parts is concerned. Furthermore, it has a number of exceptions, which may be easily defined.

---

[1] It is important to observe the difference between that which, though an exception, is said to be *good* and that which is only *tolerated*.

The hidden octaves are permissible, and even commendable, whenever the highest part ascends a diatonic semi-
tone:

The hidden fifths are excellent when the bass ends on the
tonic or the dominant, while the higher part progresses by
similar motion an interval of a major or minor second.

They are also very tolerable when they occur between a
fundamental chord and one of its inversions, as:

When the inner parts are considered, there is occasion
for more subtle distinctions, which cannot be discussed
here.

VII. We have now to describe a class of faults in harmony altogether different from those previously mentioned.
We are no longer to consider two contiguous notes belonging to the same part, as in melodic motions, nor two simultaneous notes, like those produced by the octaves or fifths;
we have now the case of two notes belonging to different
parts, and to consecutive chords. (Two notes forming any

melodic motion are written on the same stave, horizontally: —————; two notes forming a harmonic interval are placed in notation one above the other, vertically: | ; those constituting *false relations*, with which we are now to be concerned, are situated obliquely towards each other, on a diagonal: \ or / .)

The *chromatic false relation* forms an interval of a chromatic semitone between any two parts:

It is the most disagreeable thing possible to hear and, moreover, extremely difficult to sing, for persons having a correct ear. Evidently, then, it should be avoided.

The same is true of the *false relation of the octave*, which is only the reproduction, at the distance of an octave, or of more than one, always on a diagonal line, of the chromatic false relation.

This also is forbidden because it produces to the auditor an impression of intolerable harshness, and also is extremely difficult of execution.

A single case authorises the use of notes thus placed: this is when one of the parts, between which the false relation is produced, is itself proceeding, melodically, by chromatic motion. In this case the harshness, if it be not entirely relieved, is so reduced that it becomes unimportant; and the difficulty of execution has entirely vanished, a melodic motion of a chromatic semitone, ascending or descending, being a very natural and easy motion, because it is so small.

The following are examples where the false relation, either chromatic or of the octave, entirely ceases to be faulty, and for the reason just given:

False relations permitted.

Indeed a progression of this kind should be considered as of superior advantage, since there are employed only very slight melodic motions which have just been mentioned as specially commendable.[1]

VIII. Although less disagreeable than the preceding, the *false relation of the tritone,* ♩, should as a rule be avoided. This is the relation between two notes successively emitted by two different parts, forming the interval of the augmented fourth; it is especially poor between the extreme parts (the soprano and the bass) and in progressions of the fundamental chords of the fifth and fourth degrees. The most objectionable instance of this is the following:

False relations of tritone, to be avoided.

It may be *tolerated* in the inner parts, where often it is even inevitable, and *admitted* without hesitation between the second and sixth degrees of the minor mode, for here it has no unpleasant effect.

1 Page 223.

2 It is a singular fact that these same chords, when inverted, produce an excellent effect.

Certain theorists prohibit this false relation only when it is produced by the succession of two major thirds, belonging one to the fourth, the other to the fifth degree, as:

We shall recur to this subject again in the examination of counterpoint,[1] where it is more strictly prohibited. Harmonists who avoid it show a certain refinement in so doing, and they are right, for their style gains in purity and distinction.

IX.—It frequently occurs, in the harmonisation of a series of chords, that the position which was good for one group does not suit the subsequent group, where it would occasion faults.

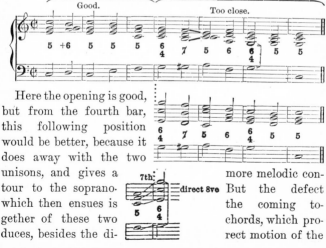

Here the opening is good, but from the fourth bar, this following position would be better, because it does away with the two unisons, and gives a tour to the soprano. which then ensues is gether of these two duces, besides the di-

more melodic con- But the defect the coming to- chords, which pro- rect motion of the

1 Section B of this chapter.

four parts, a melodic motion of a seventh in the soprano, and a concealed octave with the bass. In cases like this, and in many other instances, a *change of position* can be made, which con- sists, as its name indicates, in causing two positions of the same chord to occur consec- utively on the same note of the bass, as in the following :

In this way the two groups are well connected together, and everywhere produce a satisfactory progression.

This is what is meant in treatises on harmony, when it is said that "a change of position is often necessary to avoid faults and give more elegance to the progression of the parts."

In a change of position all melodic motions, without ex- ception, are permissible as is the direct motion of the four parts. Arrangements like the following are perfectly cor- rect, notwithstanding the faults that they seem to contain, because they present no difficulty of intonation, and are not disagreeable to hear :

Changes of position.

A special change of position which is frequently em- ployed is the *interchange of notes ;* a simple example will make this clear :

Interchange of notes.

As is shown in the last three bars, the interchange can also occur between a chord and one of its inversions; here the bass is also brought in. In this way it is possible by successive steps to arrive at a position very different from the point of departure:

Series of exchanges of notes.

etc.

Often, also, between the two notes which make the interchange, there is interpolated a note foreign to the harmony, which renders the motion of the parts more melodic:

This is the most elementary use of the *passing-note*, in regard to which we shall speak later. (This note, not making part of the harmony, is not to be figured.)

At this point an interesting remark may be made, although it is but indirectly connected with the subject; it is that, in an arrangement of notes like this, progressing harmonically by contrary motion, and melodically by single steps, if for any reason it is desired that this intermediate note should receive a chord, a chord of the sixth can be placed on it, and even with a doubling of the bass in the first part, a procedure which in almost all other cases is forbidden.[1]

1 See p. 211.

This is one of the rare instances where this reduplication is advantageous. Of course when harmonised, either in this or in any
other way, this note ceases to be a passing-note; there is no longer an
interchange, but there are three distinct chords, as also the figuring
plainly indicates.

X. Whenever the leading-tone occurs in a chord, it is
desirable that it should ascend to the tonic, if the tonic
belongs to the following chord:

In the same way, whenever the same chord contains two
notes which form an interval of the diminished fifth, or its
inversion (*tendency chords*), both must obey their tendency,
unless this brings about other faults of harmonisation. Of
course if one of the two is doubled, only one of the two

parts will follow this tendency, since otherwise there would be *consecutive octaves;* [1] but this doubled note must not be the seventh degree of the scale, the leading-tone.

These last rules are a sort of connecting link between those applicable to all chords, which we have already examined, and those peculiar to dissonant chords, which we have now to consider. Here the tendencies of the diminished fifth and of the augmented fourth, as also the obligatory motion of certain other notes, will acquire special importance, under the name of *resolutions*.

RULES OF HARMONISATION PECULIAR TO DISSONANT CHORDS.

XI. Every dissonant chord contains at least *one* dissonance,[2] which is the seventh in the original form of the chord, and becomes of course another interval in each of its inversions, without, however, ceasing to be the *dissonance*.

Now, to satisfy the laws of harmony, the dissonance must be resolved by descending one degree to a note of the following chord. This is called a *natural resolution*. Furthermore, whenever a dissonant chord contains a *consonance* with a strong tendency (diminished fifth or augmented fourth) which is almost a discord itself, this interval must, so far as is possible, be resolved according to its own tendencies.

The chord $^7_+$ contains two notes having obligatory progression : the seventh, a dissonance, which must descend ; and the third, which, being the leading-tone, must ascend.

---

1 See p. 226.

2 Chords of the ninth contain two, the seventh and the ninth.

These two notes form, also, in relation to each other, the interval of a diminished fifth, and hence tend to approach one another.

The only chords towards which natural resolution can be made are those which contain the notes necessary for the execution of these obligatory progressions; of these there are three in each mode.

(It might seem that there was also a fourth chord which would fulfil the same conditions, the chord of the sixth on the third degree, ; but it is not available here because, in whatever way the parts be disposed, there would always be caused the concealed octave, Now the concealed octave is never worse than when it is brought in by notes having an obligatory progression — dissonances or tendency consonances. In this case it must be absolutely prohibited, even in the inner parts.)

The natural resolution of inversions takes place in the same way, whenever, that is to say, the tones which have an obligatory progression, find, in the chord following, the notes towards which they are attracted.

XII. When these same notes having obligatory progression make part also of the following chord, they must remain as they are, in the same part, neither ascending nor descending. This is *non-resolution.*

(In this example, the slur ⌢ is used to point out the notes in a state of non-resolution, and the straight lines ⎯ or ⎯ to mark those which make their natural resolution.)

When an interchange of tones is made in a dissonant chord or among its inversions, there is always non-resolution of some notes. But those which form the last position must be regularly resolved.

XIII. There is, finally, a third method of connecting dissonant chords; this is the *exceptional resolution.* Here the note which normally should ascend (the leading-tone) is exceptionally resolved by descending a chromatic semi-tone. This chromatic semitone, being obtained only by means of a chromatic change, necessarily introduces an element foreign to the ruling tonality, hence it is evident that any exceptional resolution involves modulation.[1]

In the following examples, for the sake of clearness, are placed side by side, a chord with natural resolution, that with non-resolution, and that with exceptional resolution.

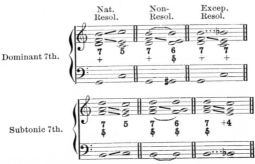

1 See p. 279

Diminished 7th.

(The straight line ——— indicates natural resolutions ; the slur ⌢ non-resolutions ; the dotted line ..... exceptional resolutions.)

The same is true in the case of chords of the ninth, which contain the leading-tone and two dissonances,—that is to say, three notes with obligatory progression, the first ascending and the two others descending, in natural resolution; in non-resolution, some of these remain stationary; in exceptional resolution, the leading-note descends chromatically. It is in all cases the same.

In order to bring out more clearly the homogeneity of the system, I have placed all these examples in the key of C major or minor. It thus is plainly seen that while the dissonance, which here is always the seventh of the fundamental chord, can occur anywhere in the scale, the notes with mutual attraction, forming the tendency consonance, never change place, and can be only the fourth and seventh degree; that is to say, in the above examples, the F and B.

The chords which remain to be examined as to resolution,

namely, those of the major and minor seventh, never unite
these two degrees:

hence there is only the dissonance to be resolved, descending always to the next note, if it occurs in the chord following, which is the *natural resolution:*

If, however, this dissonance, the seventh, is itself part of
the chord that follows, there will be *non-resolution :*

But there can never be, here, the *exceptional resolution,*
properly so-called, for this is an exception made to the normal motion of one of the notes of the tendency consonance,
which itself is not contained in chords of the major and
minor seventh.

In linking two chords of the seventh, by motion of a
descending fifth or an ascending fourth in the bass, in one
or other of these chords, the fifth must be omitted, and replaced by doubling the bass note:

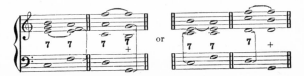

otherwise, the laws of preparation[1] and of resolution could not be obeyed without introducing consecutive octaves or fifths in four-part harmony.

For the two chords to be complete, there must be employed five voices or parts.

XIV. Another law governs the connection of dissonant chords: this is the *preparation of the dissonance,* by letting it be heard previously and in the same part, in the chord which precedes. The object of this is to diminish the harshness of the dissonance, accustoming the ear to the note which is to become dissonant, by presenting it, at first, as a consonance.

In earlier times, *preparation* was regarded as obligatory for every dissonance. Not until the close of the sixteenth century a bold innovator, Monteverde[2], who has had a great share in musical evolution, ventured to attack directly, without preparation, the dissonances contained in chords of the dominant seventh, the leading-tone seventh, the diminished seventh, and even of the dominant ninth, thus forming from these chords (which are all furnished by the harmonics) a special family,—intermediate between the consonant chords and the true dissonant chords,—called, of late, *natural dissonant harmony.*

This *mixed* group, if I may so call it, obeys the special laws of the dissonant chords as to resolution, but is excused

---

1 See sec. XIV., later.

2 See chap. V. It is probable that Monteverde himself had no idea of the immense scope of his discovery.

from preparation, and is thus associated, on the other hand, with the consonant chords.

Such is the theory at present accepted as authoritative; but I ought to add that its strictness is more and more relaxed every day, and that there are many composers of the modern school who have no hesitation in attacking dissonances of all kinds without preparation.

The reader will now understand why I did not venture to fix in the chapter on Acoustics [1] any precise limit between dissonances and consonances; this is a question of usage and habit, of what the ear will tolerate, of what it is accustomed to; and this has varied, varies now, and will continue to vary, in accordance with the individual tendencies of composers and also with the degree of harshness which the musical education of listeners will lead them more and more to endure. It is already easy to foresee that in a future not far distant the preparation of dissonances will fall into desuetude, and subsist only as an archaism.

At present and in the schools, in the study of harmony, it still remains obligatory for the more dissonant chords, namely, those of the major and minor seventh, and of the minor seventh and diminished fifth, which in certain treatises are called *chords with prolongation* (*accords avec prolongation*), and in others are classed as *artificial dissonant harmony*. Both terms are equally justified by the preceding explanations.

XV. It is evident that all the rules relative to preparation or resolution of dissonant chords in their fundamental position (which, for the sake of brevity, I have used as my only examples) apply equally to inversions of these chords. The notes change place with each other, but each note preserves the same tendencies, the same amount of dissonance, and should be treated in the same manner.

When all the above rules are well understood and strictly

applied, which is not always very easily done, the harmonisation is pure and correct, the musical effect satisfactory to the ear.

To impress these rules still further upon the reader's mind, I have prepared the following table, which seems to me to sum them up. I here consider the fundamental chords as divided into four groups:

The first, at the foot of the list, contains only the perfect major chord, the harmonic triad, the consonant chord *par excellence*.

The second contains the perfect minor chord and the chord of the diminished fifth, which are only conventionally consonant, the latter having relationship to the dissonant chords by the presence of the diminished fifth, which in the consonant chords is a tendency consonance, and in the dissonant, a dissonance.

The third group includes chords forming natural dissonant harmony,—the result, direct or indirect, of the natural phenomena of musical sound, and requiring resolution (according to the principles above stated) of part only of their notes.

The fourth, lastly, contains really dissonant chords, which must have not only resolution, but also preparation.

In white notes I indicate the chords of the major scale; in black, those of the minor; so that the two modalities shall be made apparent, and that the table may show at a glance all the elements of the present harmonic system. Reading upwards on this table, it will be seen how chords, at first consonant, free in all their motions, lose this freedom more and more by the addition of dissonances, which all demand resolution, while some, still further, require preparation.

(The *resolution* is shown by a line following the note, the *preparation* by a slur preceding it. The dotted lines designate the notes having a *tendency character*.)

The only chords omitted in this condensed table are the *sur-tonic chords*, explained on p. 207, which are subject to the same laws as are the chords from which they are derived. No preparation is demanded for them, because they belong to natural dissonant harmony; but they require resolution, in accordance with the principles governing all the chords of that group.

We will now resume, at the point where we left off,[1] our study of the modifications which a chord can receive without losing its individuality. We shall find that there are several of these yet to be examined.

One or more of the constituent notes of a chord may be held back, so that it is not sounded till after the others; this is called a *suspension*. Every suspension must be prepared and resolved by conjunct motion, a diatonic tone or semitone. The suspension may be from above or from below, resolving upwards or downwards. The former is much more in use, and is much more classic than the latter.

The most elementary logic would suggest that dissonant notes — themselves requiring preparation, like the seventh in the chords by prolongation — could not in any case be suspended, for they cannot be at once retarded and advanced. Usually, therefore, in a chord of any kind, it is a note making consonance with the fundamental that receives suspension.

The prevailing character of this musical device is amplitude, majesty; this character becomes the more evident where the movement is itself broad and tranquil; but it is adapted to all movements, giving them a certain degree of severity, even of rigidity, more valued formerly than at present, and, where it occurs in works of a generally modern character, having an archaic air.

1 Page 222.

It would not be possible to enumerate here all the varieties of suspensions, nor would it be useful to do so. The point of importance is to show their essence, their principle, and especially to avoid confusion between the suspension (*retard*) and the prolongation, which at first sight seem alike, both requiring preparation and resolution.

A very slight examination, however, will show the difference between the two. The prolongation creates a new chord, of which it is the characteristic element, *the seventh*, having its personality and its individual existence; on the other hand, the suspension is only a note foreign to the chord, requiring preparation because it generally introduces a dissonance, and destined shortly to disappear, giving place to the real note, whose advance it had momentarily *suspended*, hence its name.

I would not wish to fall into the same *naïveté* with the author of a dictionary which I possess, where exactly these words occur:

> "Violin, a small violoncello. (See *Violoncello.*)
> "Violoncello, a large violin. (See *Violin.*)"

But, reserving to myself the right later to say that an *appoggiatura* is merely a suspension without preparation, I can give no better definition of the suspension, than to call it a *prepared appoggiatura*. These two things explain each other.

In fact, something is occurring now, in relation to suspensions, which resembles what took place when, three hundred years ago, Monteverde enfranchised certain chords of the seventh from the formality of preparation. More and more composers are attacking dissonances directly, under the name of appoggiaturas.

From the point of view of classic harmony, every suspension should be prepared; and, indeed, there is no such thing as an unprepared suspension. I will mention here only those which are in current use, indicating their respective peculiarities.

In the consonant chords, any note of the triad can be suspended.

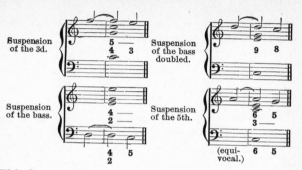

This last one is less used, because it may be confused with a chord of the sixth, as the figuring shows very clearly.[1]

In the inversions these same suspensions become, in the chord of the sixth:

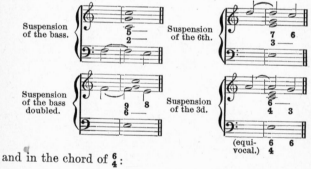

and in the chord of $\frac{6}{4}$:

---

[1] I give examples only in the perfect major chord; the use of suspensions is the same in the minor chords and in those of the diminished fifth.

Those which are equivocal (indicated by the double figuring) are much less employed.

In the suspension must be distinguished:

    1. The preparation;
    2. The suspension itself;
    3. The resolution.

The preparation must be at least as long as the suspension, else there would be an unequal syncope (the first part shorter than the second), which is absolutely prohibited in exercises of harmony.

The *suspension* must be on the down-beat.

The note of *resolution* must in no case and in no part be doubled by *parallel* movement; from this there would result, by reason of the attention which the suspension attracts to that note, concealed octaves of the worst kind, extremely disagreeable in effect.

Insufficient preparation.

Ill-placed suspension.

Doubling by direct motion of the resolution.

It is illogical, while a note is held back, that it should be heard in another part. This is always more or less harsh.

Some authors permit this license by way of exception, especially on the tonal notes and when the suspension is in the highest part, as in the preceding example; but it is purer harmony without this, and it is in general easily to be avoided.

In all dissonant chords, the notes forming consonance with the fundamental can be suspended.

On page 248, I have presented a table of suspensions possible in inversions of the consonant chords; here I will simplify by giving only examples in the fundamental position; it will be easy to find those of the inverted chords by interchanging the order of the notes.

In the chord of the dominant seventh:

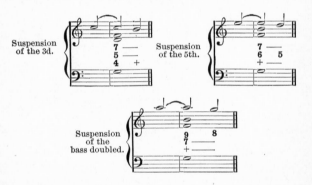

In the seventh chord on the leading-tone, or of the diminished seventh:

likewise in their inversions, and in many others that can easily be imagined.

To give briefly the characteristics of a suspension, we may say that it should form a prepared dissonance of the seventh or of the second, with another note of the chord; that it should occur on a comparatively accented part of the measure; and that it should be resolved descending diatonically.

Except in the direction of the resolution, the inferior suspension is the same; of this I will give some examples, though its use is rare, and in general, not classic:

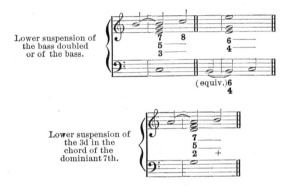

Lower suspension of the bass doubled or of the bass.

Lower suspension of the 3d in the chord of the dominant 7th.

The only case where a suspension from below is really in current use, is as a double suspension in the chord of the sixth. This arrangement is called by some authors the *adding of a fifth*. While the seventh, prepared, descends to the sixth, the fifth, also prepared, ascends to the same degree, and thus forms a suspension from below.

Double suspension ascending and descending.

Here we have two suspensions of the sixth, one from below, or ascending, and one from above.

The example is singular; in general, when two suspensions are simultaneous, they are parallel. The following are double suspensions in the more usual form:

Double suspension of the third and of the bass doubled.

The double suspension is very useful; it has no special rules other than those applying to single suspensions.

A suspension can be resolved into a chord other than that of which it holds back a note; in other words, the chord can change at the very moment of resolution, if the new chord contain the note required for this resolution.

Modulating resolutions of the suspension.

This is a sort of exceptional resolution, usually modulatory, in which, however, the suspension itself follows its normal motion.

I have thus, I believe, said all on the subject of suspensions, for which the limited extent of this work affords space.

In making use of this harmonic artifice, it must not be forgotten that the note called a suspension is itself foreign to the chord, and cannot separate two octaves or two fifths; one should, therefore, omit it from consideration, and examine whether without it the chord connection is according to rule; if it is not so, the fault is the same with the suspension as without it. Passages like the following are very disagreeable to hear, and should be carefully avoided:

The same examples are given below with the suspension omitted; the octaves or fifths then appear distinctly.

In certain cases the presence of the suspension authorises an irregular and unusual motion of the leading note; it descends a third, either to avoid the greater disadvantage of making the suspension heard with the suspended note, or that the chord of resolution be complete, as in the following example:

or, still further, itself serving as preparation for the suspended note, it loses at this moment its attractive tendency, which would cause it to ascend, and obeys only the law of the natural resolution of the suspension:

These irregularities, which are perfectly classic, are stated in all treatises on harmony.

More modern than the suspension, the *alteration* modifies the chord less profoundly. First, it is employed generally in the unaccented, or comparatively unaccented, part of the measure; then, it is usually preceded by the real note, which causes the hearer to have had in advance a perception of the chord in its normal condition. It is the melodic introduction of the chromatic element in a harmony which remains fundamentally diatonic; it is the partition of the space of a tone into its two semitones by a note foreign to the key, without any slightest idea of modulation or change of key being implied by this note, which preserves the character of a passing-note. This definition is long, but it will save further explanations.

Whenever between two consecutive notes there is a melodic interval of a major second,—of a whole tone, that is to say,—there is opportunity to introduce an alteration, either ascending or descending; but it is very far from being equally good and agreeable on all degrees, with all chords and in all circumstances. In contrast with the suspension, which is noble and solemn in its essence, the alteration is petty, affected, effeminate; the combinations in which its use is excessive become insincere and pretentious, lacking in frankness; the descending alteration specially has a morbid character, which is a reason for using it only when the intention is evident.

As in the case of suspensions, I will mention here only the most usual alterations. I omit also all explanation of details, the figuring being sufficient to show plainly the nature of each alteration, as well as the chord to which it applies.

1 Defective melodic movements, tolerated by reason of the impossibility of making a less faulty harmonisation.

1 See foot-note on page 254.

(1)

1 The bass, the dissonance of the chord, should be prepared and should descend one degree.

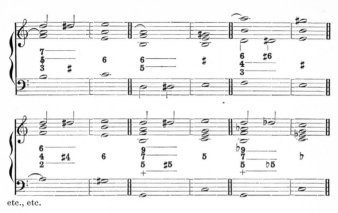

etc., etc.

Alteration may occur in more than one part simultaneously, making *double* and *triple* alterations:

It is also possible to use at once *suspensions and alterations,* and from this result very numerous and varied combinations:

which I can here only mention briefly.

Finally, new effects, often unforeseen and of great richness, spring from the *direct attack of the altered chord,* an entirely modern procedure, which will be used to the best advantage by those who have the most faithfully abstained from it in pursuing their technical studies, where all theorists condemn it, or at least strictly limit its use. Thus is explained the triad on the mediant of the minor mode,[1] omitted from our tables; it must be analysed as an altered chord directly attacked and obeying the law of resolution of ascending alterations, which fact withdraws it from the class of consonant chords, which are chords of repose, where each part can move freely.

It is sometimes called the chord of the augmented fifth.

We have already considered *notes foreign to the chord*, suspensions,— also, *notes foreign to the key*, alterations; we now come to *notes foreign to the harmony :* these are *passing-notes, appoggiaturas, anticipations, broderies*, in a word, all the ornaments which are purely melodic and have really no share in the harmonisation. These, however, must be understood, were it only in order to eliminate them in the harmonic analysis.

We will begin with the *appoggiatura*, whose definition will be readily understood; as we have already said, it is "a suspension without preparation." [2]   It is commonly placed on the accented part of the bar, as its etymology[3] indicates, or, at least, on a part which could receive the accent;[4] it may be *inferior* or *superior*, and correspondingly is resolved either ascending or descending to a note of the chord; if inferior, it is usually a diatonic semitone from the principal note; if superior, it may be a tone or a semitone from it.   Sometimes the two kinds are united, forming the double appoggiatura.

The following are examples of single and double appoggiaturas:

Simple appoggiaturas, lower and higher.

---

1 Pp. 191, 192, 194, 195, 196, 205.

2 Page 247.

3 Italian, *appoggiare*, to lean or *rest upon.*

4 Otherwise disposed, it is called a *weak* appoggiatura.

5 Melodic ornaments are not figured.

6 The dash before the figure indicates that the chord is emitted on the preceding note.

Double appoggiaturas.

There may also be two simultaneous appoggiaturas in two different parts; this corresponds to the double suspension, except in having no preparation.

Simultaneous appoggiaturas.

By reason of its melodic character, the appoggiatura, like the other ornaments, is most frequently used in the highest voice. This, however, is not an absolute rule; it can very well be placed elsewhere.

Other appoggiaturas.

The reader has already an idea as to the *passing-note*,[1] from the mention which has been previously made of it, in explaining the interchange of notes. It may be diatonic or chromatic, ascending or descending; also there may be several passing-notes, one after another.

Two notes at the distance of a minor second do not admit the use of this ornament; but, if they are separated by a tone, there can be introduced between them a chromatic note, either ascending or descending, which may be called either an alteration or a passing-note:

Between two notes separated by a third, there is room for a diatonic passing-note, or for two (or three) passing-notes of the chromatic scale:

If the two notes are separated by an interval of a fourth, there can be two passing-notes, if diatonic; or four, if accidentals are introduced.

Naturally, there is no objection to simultaneous passing-notes in different parts:

Passing-notes in several parts.

Same example with omission of passing-notes:

Passing-notes generally occur at the thesis, or unaccented part of the bar.

The *broderie,* or return dissonance, is kindred to the passing-note, from which it differs in that, instead of going on, it returns upon the principal note whence it came. It participates also, in some degree, in the character of the appoggiatura, although it occupies an unaccented portion of the bar; like the appoggiatura, if superior, it may be a tone or a semitone distant from the principal note, it may be diatonic or chromatic; but if inferior, is usually, according to modern feeling, at the distance of a semitone.

Broderies.

The old composers were very willing to place the broderie, when inferior, at the distance of a whole tone:

which is not without a certain charm.

It may be placed in any one of the parts, or simultaneously in two, or even in more.

Double or triple *broderies.*

This group of notes can be analysed (especially in a

rapid movement) either as a result of four simultaneous broderies, or as an individual chord, as is shown by the two figurings:

This ornament may be applied to any note whatever, whether it is a constituent note of the chord, a suspension, an alteration, or even a passing-note or an appoggiatura.

Suspension, alteration, passing-note, and appoggiatura with *broderies*.

Also, with a broderie in one part, another part may receive an alteration, a suspension, or any other harmonic or melodic device.

Also, there are double broderies, an inferior and a superior together, much resembling the double appoggiatura, with the difference that while the latter are in the accented, the former are in the unaccented portion of the bar.

Double *broderies*.　　　　Double appoggiaturas.

It is not usual to double a note having a broderie, unless it be either the tonic or the dominant.

Passing-notes and single or double broderies are ornaments frequent in classic works. The same is true as to the following, which should, however, be employed more carefully in pure scholastic style.

If from a broderie the return-note, the repetition of the initial note, is taken away, what remains is the *échappée.*

Broderies.   *Échappées.*

The *échappée* is, therefore, a curtailed broderie, with elision of the return-note, which remains as something implied; it can occur only in a very unaccented part of the bar or of the beat, and always in conjunct diatonic connection with the principal note, which precedes it and of which it is the ornament.

Also in the unaccented part is placed the *anticipation,* which as its name indicates is a note emitted in advance of the chord to which it belongs. It may be direct or indirect; this requires explanation.

What is called *direct anticipation* is the emission in advance of the same note which is about to appear, in the same part, in the following chord, thus:[1]

When, on the contrary, the note borrowed from the chord that follows does not remain, when the chord appears, in the part where it was anticipated, this is an *indirect anticipation.*

---

1 This is also called *port de voix.*

Direct or indirect, the *anticipation* is employed by preference in the first part, and in short notes; if too long, and thus assuming too great importance, it becomes pretentious and affected. It is allowable to anticipate simultaneously two parts, three, or even four,—that is to say, the entire chord.

In many cases, the indirect anticipation can, without any ill result, be identified with the *échappée*, from which it differs only in this, that it makes an integral part of the chord that follows.

Whatever may be the melodic notes,— appoggiaturas, passing-notes, broderies, *échappées*, or anticipations,—they must not serve to mask faults in harmonisation; it must always be possible, eliding them and replacing them by the real notes of which they are only the ornamentation, to reveal a harmonic framework of irreproachable construction.

The same is true, in instrumental composition, in regard to figures of any kind, diatonic or chromatic runs, chords broken or arpeggiated, intermingling of notes foreign to the harmony and hence invested with a purely ornamental character, even though they be long continued. All these are powerless to disguise a defective harmonisation, for when the notes of purely melodic character are omitted, there still remain the consecutive fifths or octaves, the false relations, etc., as is shown in the following examples, whose faults at once appear when these examples are played on the piano, or still better, are sung by four voices.[1]

---

1 The same is true as to most of the examples given.

Even more objectionable is it where the ornamental notes form, among themselves or in connection with the essential notes, defective groupings, as the following:

Under this head there are, however, some few and rare exceptions, in respect to which composers, even the best, are not agreed, and for whose application good taste and the artistic instinct, strengthened by observation and the frequent reading of classical works, are the only guides.

They must be considered as dangerous licenses, or at least as unsafe, and to be avoided by the student if he values purity of style.

By the intermingling of all these various artifices, by their association and combination among themselves in a thousand different ways, according to different plans of grouping, there results a veritable musical kaleidoscope of infinite variety, which constitutes the inexhaustible wealth of modern harmony. Notwithstanding the centuries that have elapsed since music was first written it is certain — however surprising this may appear to the unlearned — that all the formulas, simultaneous or successive, of which the seven notes and the seven signs of time-value are capable, with their numerous modifications, are still very far from being exhausted, and that there are many forms yet to be created, to be discovered.

It is with this material, then, that we construct harmonic phrases, having a complete and well-defined meaning, even in the absence of any melodic idea. Certain characteristic parts of these phrases have received special designations, which it is important to know, so that one can understand and analyse musical discourse, and also be able to recognise those cases where the rules now given must be applied in all their rigour, and those other cases where they may admit of certain modifications.

A *harmonic phrase* consists of a number of chords in logical sequence, ending with a cadence; a phrase may be separated into several parts, which are its *members*, each ending in a *cadence* of some kind. A number of associated phrases make a *period*, and then, a complete *musical discourse*, a *piece*, whose conclusion must also be a cadence, but in this case, only of the kind that is called a *perfect cadence*.

Here we see the importance of cadences, which are evidently one of those characteristic parts requiring special examination and study.

The cadence (from the Latin *cadere*, to fall) is the fall, the close, the ending, of every musical phrase or of its

members. Comparing the harmonic phrase with the gram-
matical, the chords are its words, and every cadence will
be, as it were, followed by a punctuation mark, which it
very distinctly suggests.

There are many kinds of cadences; two of them only
have a truly conclusive force,— the *perfect* or *authentic
cadence*, which corresponds to the period, and the *plagal
cadence*, which may be likened to the exclamation point.[1]
The *half cadence* suggests an interrogation point or a
colon : it calls for something more, and although logically
terminating a series of chords constituting a phrase, it
never gives an idea of completion, but the reverse. The
comma and the semicolon are, well represented by the
interrupted cadence, and the *broken cadence* suggests the
idea of a parenthesis.

We shall better understand these resemblances as we
study the subject further.

It is the motion of the bass at the moment when the
phrase ends, which determines the character of the cadence.

In the perfect cadence, the bass rises from the dominant
to the tonic.

The meaning here is the affirmative, conclusive. We
may note that the perfect cadence is formed by the two
principal generator-chords of the key, those of the fifth
and first degrees. If they should be preceded by the
chord of the fourth degree (which is done in what are called
formulas of cadences, as we shall shortly see), it would be
only the more fully conclusive,

---

1 It will be seen later (in Chapter V.) that the plagal cadence is nothing else
than the terminal, perfect cadence in the ancient plagal modes, where the fourth
degree was the dominant.

each note of the gamut being then represented in this group of chords exactly according to its relative importance :

The *tonic* three times;
The *dominant* three times;
The *subdominant* twice, or three times (according as the chord **5** or the chord **7** is used);
The *mediant, submediant,* and *leading-tone,* each once;
The *supertonic* once, or not at all.

Hence results the special and particularly satisfactory character of the perfect cadence; in a sense it sums everything up and makes a final conclusion, after giving for a last time the whole of the notes composing the gamut (its relative importance also being preserved to each note), with a chord itself formed of the purest and most natural tones of the scale, its best consonances, its first and simplest harmonics,— in short, with the perfect chord.

It therefore justifies well its name of the perfect cadence; and if we should examine in the same way the other cadences, we should see that the impression each one produces on us can be equally well analysed, and results simply from the manner in which the notes of the cadence are put together.

But this is a digression. To return to the perfect cadence, we conclude by saying that it is formed by two fundamental chords, one of the fifth degree, the other of the first, and that the motion of the bass may be, indifferently, ascending or descending; and with this we have all that we need to know about it.

Another cadence of a conclusive character, because also ending upon the tonic, is the *plagal cadence.* Here the

bass moves, ascending or descending, from the fourth to
the first degree, each of which bears a perfect chord.

It has, to modern taste, a sense rather less affirmative
than the preceding, because it does not contain the leading-
tone, which the ear is accustomed to require as guide to the
tonic. Accordingly, in music of the present day, it is
rarely employed except at the very end of a composition,
or at least, of a long period, and preceded by the perfect
cadence, whose meaning it serves to complete and affirm.
It is principally in sacred music, where the style is broad
and stately, that its use is retained as a sort of super-com-
pletion of the musical meaning. It is like a seal in addition to a signature.

If we invert the order of the chords of the perfect
cadence, and, instead of dominant-tonic, we say tonic-
dominant, naturally the meaning is also inverted and the
affirmative becomes the interrogative. This occurs in the
half or imperfect cadence (*cadence à la dominante*), of
which the following is the classic form:

But here the second chord, which has the stress, is alone
important; the one preceding it can be any other than
the tonic chord, without this cadence losing its proper
character.

The only essential thing is that the pause, the close of the phrase, should be on the chord of the dominant, which contains the leading-note; and it is this leading-note, remaining suspended, awaiting and asking for its harmonisation, which produces the interrogative sense characteristic of the half cadence.

The *interrupted cadence* is an unexpected progression, which avoids some regular cadence, of which it seems to be the fragment; the bass stops on its way towards the tonic:

The sense is neither affirmative nor interrogative, but simply suspensive.

The interrupted cadence is possible only within a phrase; it can never be the close of a composition, or of a period, or even of a whole phrase; it is nothing more than a comma.

Every other motion of the bass from the dominant to any degree whatsoever of the scale which is capable of receiving a perfect chord, but specially to the sixth, is characterised as a *broken cadence*. This cadence can have five different forms, of which three are major and two minor. Those given below in black notes are rarely used.

The meaning of this cadence (which may be compared to the semicolon) is generally considered as an unexpected breaking off of the musical phrase, hence its name.[1] It is also a half-cadence.

(There is still another, the *avoided cadence*, which is a product of the exceptional resolution; it will be defined under *Modulation*.[2])

By the *formula of the cadence* is understood a group of chords preceding it, and giving some hint of it. These formulas are infinitely various. I will indicate here — and only for the purpose of making clear the meaning of the word — some of the simplest and most commonly used of these formulas, adapting them successively to each one of the cadences above described; but it should be understood that this term *formula*, which will soon become obsolete, is applied to every group of chords so combined as to conduct the phrase to its fall, and to end necessarily in a cadence of some kind. Each school, each composer, has a certain number of favourite formulas.

Formula of perfect cadence.

1 In German it is called a deceptive cadence.
2 Page 285.

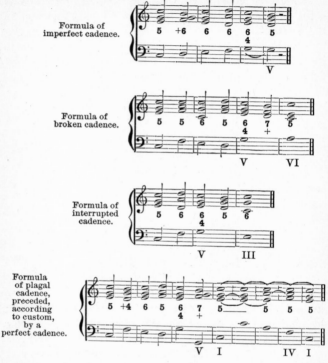

Formula of imperfect cadence.

Formula of broken cadence.

Formula of interrupted cadence.

Formula of plagal cadence, preceded, according to custom, by a perfect cadence.

(The same formulas may be read in the minor, by supposing three flats in the signature, and an accidental ♮ at all the Bs.)

In every cadence whose first chord contains the leading-note or the subdominant, the attractive tendency of these notes acquires greater strength than anywhere else, and the author can avoid giving them their proper resolution only in the somewhat unusual case of his proposing to lessen or enfeeble the special character of the cadence; a perfect cadence thus harmonised loses all its force:

It must be noted, then, that the need of resolution in notes having an obligatory motion is specially insistant in these cases.

In cadences and their formulas, a unison on the dominant, between the tenor and the bass, is permissible, provided it is brought in by a contrary or oblique motion:

also is tolerated a unison on the tonic when produced by contrary progressions:

lastly, there is further permissible even the hidden octave descending to the first degree, the highest part proceeding by conjunct degrees:

in this latter case, which, however, it is much better to avoid, the bass of the final chord is tripled, and the fifth omitted.

The plagal cadence authorises a unison, by oblique progression, between the tenor and bass, in its final chord.

The characteristic bass movements which, placed at the
end of a phrase, constitute a cadence, do not produce the
same impression if they are employed elsewhere; thus, in
the following example

there is a half-cadence at A, and a perfect cadence at B,
while the fragments *a* and *b*, though formed of the same
chords and the same notes, neither seem to be nor really
are cadences.   Likewise at *c*, the notes do not constitute
a broken cadence, because it is not the end of a phrase.

A harmonic procedure, much in use in the strict style,
consists in regarding a little group of chords as a model,
and repeating it several times, the repetitions ascending or
descending by equal intervals.   The repetitions are *progressions*, and the whole is a *sequence*.

It is apparent that the same model according to its progressions being spaced by one degree or by two or three
degrees, and being of an ascending or of a descending
character, can give rise to very diverse sequences.   Thus
the following, for example, can produce these
combinations:

and many others,— in very great number indeed, since not
only can the chords be changed, but they can be modified
in all the different ways by retardations and alterations
of both kinds, and there can be introduced into them all

the melodic artifices which have been already described, appoggiaturas, passing-notes, broderies, anticipations, etc.

Thus far, I have spoken only of unitonic sequences, non-modulatory,— that is to say, of sequences in which, from one end to the other, there are used only the chords of a single tonality.

But there are others which are called modulatory sequences, and the better to show the difference between the two classes I will here convert all the unitonic sequences of the preceding example into modulatory sequences,— although there will result from this transformation certain manifest errors, to which I will at once advert.

It will have surprised the reader to meet frequently, in the preceding examples, certain forbidden melodic motions[1] and various false relations.[2] *These licenses are permitted* in sequences, for two reasons: first, it is impossible to avoid them without impairing the characteristic symmetry of the sequence; and, second, in this special case there is no disagreeable effect nor any difficulty of execution. Also is tolerated the parallel harmonic progression of the four parts.

In writing a sequence it is, first of all, important to construct its model correctly, and then to take care that its first progression is faultless. After that there is only a mechanical transposition. But when the sequence ends it is important that its last chord should be connected with the chord that follows, in strict conformity to rules, the few licenses authorised for the sequence having no longer their *raison d'être.*

Before quitting this subject we must observe that sequences are not all equally symmetrical. Absolute in the modulatory sequences, symmetry is only relative in the unitonic, as any one may satisfy himself by examining closely the structure of the same sequence as represented in the two preceding tables. The unitonic sequence composed from the seven tones belonging to one key has each

1 Page 223.
2 Page 230.

of its progressions on a different degree; and as there are no two degrees formed from the same intervals, there can be only an approach to symmetry either in the horizontal relations of the notes (their melodic motions) or their vertical relations (the chords).

I reproduce here example *a,* of the unitonic sequences (page 275):

Let us now measure the vertical dimensions. The first chord of the model is a chord of the sixth, an inversion of the perfect major triad; in the first progression it is derived from the minor chord, and in the second, from a chord of the diminished fifth. The second chord of the model, the perfect major chord, becomes minor in the two following progressions, and is only restored to the major key in the third progression, to the F, the subdominant.

Similar irregularities occur in the horizontal proportions; I have indicated some of these in the example itself.

There is a symmetry to the eye, and also so far as the names of the intervals are concerned, but it does not extend to the characteristics which are its true measure.

We will now examine example *a* of the modulatory sequences (page 276):

Here, on the contrary, the symmetry is exact; model and progressions are all formed in the same way, from a chord of the sixth of major origin, and from a perfect major chord in its fundamental position; the melodic movements of one group are similar to those of the other groups; no difference can be found between the successive progressions, except that at each one the keynote is displaced with all its train, which makes it possible to preserve absolute symmetry, each note keeping its rank and functions in the scale. The same thing occurs in all the modulatory sequences.

To sum up what has been said, the unitonic sequence is a journey within the limits of a given tonality; the modulatory sequence is a journey through several tonalities which are more or less remote from each other.

The system of sequences is a procedure now somewhat antiquated, *rococo;* the modern school disdains it more and more, and considers a somewhat prolonged sequence as a *Rosalia.*[1] However, this study of sequences and their modulatory properties makes a natural transition to the subject of modulations, since sequences have now given us a first method of modulating.

Modulation occurs whenever, omitting one note, or more than one, from the ruling key, we substitute a note, or notes, bearing the same name, but belonging to another tonality, that is to say, chromatically altered.

For example, being in C major, for the F, substitute F♯, and the key is changed to G major.

Being now in G major, flat the B and E, and you have the key of G minor.

This is the entire mechanism of modulation, in principle extremely simple, but in practice, one may run against unexpected complications.

We must first observe that the best modulations, best because simplest and most natural, are those which take place between related tonalities,— those, namely, which

---

1 The term " Rosalia " is supposed to have been derived from an Italian folk-song beginning " Rosalia, mia cara," which is built upon such a principle of repetition as the author describes. The Germans use the term *Rosalia* and also *Schusterfleck*, i.e., cobbler's patch. [Three repetitions of a sequential model were called *Riverenze*, and more than three was thought bad by the eighteenth century " theorists." ED.]

differ from each other only by a single sign of alteration in the key signature.

These modulations are always effected by the simplest and most rapid means, which is plain when we remember that but a single note is affected in establishing the new scale.

The characteristic note which brings in these modulations is always, or almost always, either the leading-note or the subdominant of the new key.[1] Its simple introduction, as one of the constituent elements of a chord, displaces in the mind the idea of the note of the same name belonging to the key we leave, a note with which it must be in chromatic relation: and by this substitution modulation is effected.

In modulating from a minor key to its relative major, it is, on the contrary, the omission of the alteration of the leading-note which brings in the change. (See the sixth of the following examples.)

This succinct theory of the modulation into neighboring tonalities is clearly demonstrated in the examples given below.

I have presented each modulation under two forms: the first using only the consonant chords, that the framework may be apparent; the second, with other chords and various artifices of ornament. In both, one may discern the rôle of the characteristic note, this differentiating note which seems in a certain sense to prick you into the new key.

From C major into A minor.

Characteristic note G♯ 7th degree of A minor.

---

1 It is to be observed that these two notes form together the attractive consonance of the diminished fifth, and, in a sense, designate the seventh degree to which they belong in the two modes.

From C major into G major.

Characteristic
note F♯
7th degree
of G major.

From C major into F major.

Characteristic
note B♭
4th degree
of F major.

From C major into E minor.

Characteristic
note D♯
7th degree
of E minor.

From C major into D minor.

Characteristic
note C♯
7th degree
of D minor.

From A minor into C major.

Characteristic
note G♯ omitted
7th degree of A
minor (initial tone.

From A minor into E minor.

Characteristic
note D♯
7th degree
of E minor.

From A minor into D minor.

Characteristic
note C♯
7th degree
of D minor.

From A minor into G major.

Characteristic
note F♯,
7th degree
of G major.

From A minor into F major.

Characteristic
note B♭
4th degree
of F major.

Modulation into remote keys is effected by three means, namely, change of mode, the equivocal chord, and the enharmonic change.

A change of mode is to pass from major to minor, or *vice versa*, without changing the keynote; a simple chromatic modification of the third, and it is done:

The distance crossed by this change of mode is that of three alterations in either direction: C major, 0; C minor, 3 flats; A minor, 0; A major, 3 sharps.

The system of the equivocal chord is rather more subtle. Suppose that we are in the key of C; we play the perfect chord of the first degree; then, remembering that this chord is identical with the chord on the fifth degree in F minor, we accept the idea that the bass note is no longer a tonic, but is a dominant; and the modulation is made.

1st degree. 5th degree
from C. Maj. to F. min.

Here our path lies through four alterations, since in F minor there are four flats.[1]

The enharmonic change is, in a sense, an extension of the preceding. Disregarding the orthography of the chord as it is written, and considering only the actual sounds according to temperament,[2] we can often be transported to a very remote key.

C Maj.   *F ♯ Maj.*

In this example, the enharmonic change from F to E♯ takes us at one step across six alterations.

These are the rapid procedures, but we may also reach the same point by short successive stages, gaining one alteration at each step, that is to say, touching the intermediate tonalities which are nearly related among themselves,

1 The system of the equivocal chord is based, manifestly, on the fact that one chord may belong to several keys, occupying different degrees in each.

2 See p. 54.

Example of C minor into D major.

or finally, skilfully combine these different procedures to obtain a more unexpected or a more interesting result.

Example of C major into B♭ minor.

Another example, from A minor into E♭ major.

It is apparent that the resources in modulation are absolutely unlimited; the examples which we have given are among the most hackneyed.

Certain chords are especially apt for modulation. Such are the chords of $\frac{7}{+}$, whose mere succession in a motion of descending fifth or ascending fourth (an exceptional re-solution) leads from one dominant to another through the whole cycle of tonalities,

leaving the final chord at liberty to be of the major or of the minor mode.

By means of this series, which is simply a long modulatory sequence, one could modulate from any tone to any other, on the sole condition of choosing as point of departure the dominant of the initial tonality, and as point of arrival that of the tonality into which one proposes to go; also, it is possible to establish other similar series by means of inversions:

but it is evident how puerile such a procedure is. I have described it here only to have the opportunity to present the *avoided cadence*, which I proposed to describe under the head of modulations. This cadence is formed by any two consecutive chords taken from the preceding series, that is to say, two chords of the dominant seventh, at the distance of a fifth from each other; there is then a displacement of the dominant, whence results, besides a cadence, a modulation, a change of the tonic.

Avoided Cadences.

from C to F   from D to F

The following is the simplest form of an avoided cadence:

With it is given a like formula of the perfect cadence; it will be observed that the two differ only by a single chord, or rather, a single note, the one which causes the modulation to the subdominant, and is produced by the exceptional resolution[1] of the leading-note of the first chord of $\frac{7}{+}$.

Other chords very well adapted to modulations are chords of 7, which alone have this peculiarity: *all the inversions and the fundamental chord are homophonic among themselves in all their notes;* it is evident how well adapted these are to enharmonic modulations. And an excessive use has been made of them. Upon an instrument having fixed tones, a key-board instrument, for example, these four

chords , which represent, however,

four different states of the diminished seventh, are played on the same keys. Profiting by this complete homophony, one can, by means of a single chord, modulate into all the keys. For example:

1 See p. 239.

It will be observed that in these examples, which it is easy to complete, the initial chord is always the same; but any other chord of the diminished seventh can be taken as the point of departure. And since, moreover, all the chords of this family can be linked one to another by their exceptional resolution[1] or enharmonically,

and this either in ascending or in descending, their extreme usefulness is apparent for making an excursion through the entire extent of the scale of tonalities; but it is no less evident that a procedure so simple, so entirely within the reach of every one, must become extremely hackneyed; it is the omnibus of modulation,— to be used on occasion but not as a rule, if one stands much upon his dignity.

Another means of modulation, which has become rather childish, consists merely in the use of that harmonie

[1] See p. 240.

sequence, non-symmetrical and by contrary motion, which
has the effect of transporting you into any tonality, according to the particular chord on which you please to
stop.   Hackneyed as this is, this formula is certainly
ingenious :

Model.   1st prog.   2d prog.   etc.

It also is used equally well in the opposite direction :

and produces the same results, coming constantly, at each
moment, into the neighbourhood of one or another of the
twelve tonalities which the modern system of temperament
admits.

I cannot attempt to explain here, one by one, the various
methods of modulation.   A harmonist worthy of the name
should, however, possess them all, and use them with equal
facility.

He should, however, use them with circumspection ; for,
if from the absence of modulations results a literal *monotony* (in the etymologic meaning of the word),[1] their abuse

---

[1] *Monos tonos*, a single tone.

or their inconsiderate use leads to incoherence of musical language. The selection to be made is a matter of good taste, and of balance, and especially of pertinency. Modulation into related tones suits, in general, the expression of candid, simple feeling; into remote tones brings with it the idea of surprise, abrupt transition, and it is well to reserve this for effects of that special kind. But we shall recur to this subject in treating of *Composition*,[1] where it will be more in place.

There remain to be mentioned *pedals*, called also *pedal-points* and *organ-points;* and this will conclude all that there is space to say as to harmony in a work so condensed as this.

A *pedal*, in the harmonic sense of the word, is a tone sustained while chords more or less numerous are going on.

As its name suggests, the pedal derives its origin from organ music, where notes long sustained are committed to the lower key-board moved by the player's feet, and hence called the *pedal key-board*. But by extension, and to enrich the harmonic domain, it has come about that long-sustained notes are found also in the medium and higher regions, and the same name has also, somewhat inappropriately, been applied to them.

Thus we have the *lower pedals* (the only ones which justify their name), the *higher pedals*, and the *inner pedals*.[2]

In whatever register it is placed the pedal, by reason of the importance its long duration gives it, must be one of the principal notes of the key,— either the *tonic* or the *dominant*.

Specially noteworthy about it is this: during the duration of the pedal, there may go on above it, below it, and even across it (within limitations, however, for this involves the crossing of parts), chords to which it is not

1 See p. 343, *et seq.*

2 [What the author calls *higher* and *inner pedals* are called simply *inverted pedals* in English terminology. ED.]

regarded as belonging. It must make part of the first chord and of the last; but, as to the others, it suffices — to satisfy harmonic honour and the ear as well — that they progress in accordance with their usual rules.

The following are examples of pedals, perfectly correct, because the chords which follow while the note is sustained can be analysed, *the pedal being omitted*, with complete conformity to rule, and because, at the point of departure as well as at the point of arrival, the note makes part of the chord after the playing of which it is relinquished.

It will be observed also that the pedal, like any other note, may receive ornament of various kinds, and may itself skip an octave, being by no means obliged, in its character of pedal, to remain absolutely motionless, as might be supposed, and as, indeed, is usually the fact.

Pedal-point of the tonic, first in the lower part, then in the middle, lastly in the upper part.

Pedal-point of the dominant, first in the lower, then in the middle, then in the upper part.

Double pedal point of the tonic, in the lower and upper parts with broderies.

In fact, the *double pedal* of tonic and of dominant is frequently used.

When the student has acquired all this technical knowledge, it then remains for him to make the artistic application of it, and this requires, even for the most highly endowed,[1] a long experience and much observation.

An exercise frequently employed with excellent results, is the harmonisation in four voice-parts of some musical

[1] Some *exceptional* natures, however, are able to write purely by mere intuition, guided by the reading of noble and correct works.

composition where only the bass or the melody is given, requiring the student to understand his author's style, become imbued with his manner, and then supply the absent parts in a manner consistent with the epoch or school. This useful exercise, which draws its material from every style, from the epoch of fugues down to the very latest romantic compositions of the day, furnishes a vast field for study to those who comprehend that, carried to this height, a lesson in harmony is a little work of art.

The preceding pages can have done no more than give a glimpse of the interest attaching to these studies. Harmony is at once a science and an art. Of the science I have given the general outlines; but as to the art, that can be acquired only by long and laborious work. Having done this, a man finds himself possessed of pleasures entirely peculiar in their character, resulting from the analysis and dissection of the works of the masters, and from the criticism and comparison of the methods employed by them; pleasures purely intellectual, and having no relation, even the most remote, to the sensuous impression experienced by the amateur, however cultivated, who is not a student of harmony, as he listens to a musical work whose structure he cannot examine, however great may be the enjoyment that it gives him. It is entirely another thing. They are different orders of ideas, and from them spring modes of appreciation which also are very different.

The study of this art is long; it is somewhat difficult, though not so much so as is often believed, but it is attractive and captivating to the highest degree. It must be pursued tranquilly, with a mind at rest, without any haste. A minimum of two years of assiduous but quiet labour is needful for a man clearly to understand its difficulties and the procedures employed to overcome or evade them. As for the composer, he is studying harmony all his life, unconsciously, and daily discovers some new ingenious arrangement, some unforseen application. I speak here of the composer who has genius.

Numerous and remarkable books have been written for

instruction in harmony ; I mention at the head of the list given below those which are used in the Conservatory in Paris, and are, for this reason, most familiar to me :

REBER, *Traité d'harmonie.*

H. DUBOIS, *Notes et Études* (completion of Reber's work).

FR. BAZIN, *Cours d'harmonie.*

E. DURAND, *Cours d'harmonie.*

SAVARD, *Manuel d'harmonie.*

H. DUBOIS, *87 Leçons d'harmonie.*

A. LAVIGNAC, *Recueil de leçons d'harmonie.*

C. DARUTTE, *Technic du système harmonique.*

FR. RICHTER, *Traité d'harmonie* (translated into French by Sandré).

In English : HILES, H., *Grammar of Music.*

STAINER, J., *Theory of Harmony*, 1876; and *Composition*, 1880.

MACFARREN, SIR G. A., *Rudiments*, 1860 ; and *Six Lectures*, 1867.

ROCKSTRO, W. S., *Practical Harmony*, 1881.

JADASSOHN, S., *A Manual of Harmony* (translated by Th. Baker).

PROUT, E., *Harmony : Its Theory and Practice.*

RICHTER, E. F., *Manual of Harmony* (translated by John P. Morgan).

BROEKHOVEN, JOHN A., *A System of Harmony.*

CHADWICK, GEO. W., *Harmony.*

B.— Counterpoint.

Counterpoint is neither the preamble nor the complement to studies in harmony, though it is often so regarded. It is something different. Counterpoint is a study of the procedures, sometimes rudimentary, employed by the old composers, — procedures which have had such an effect upon musical development that it is perfectly correct to say that *the modern art could not exist without them.* Their undeniable traces are found in even the most advanced works of the present school, and this school often does no more than employ in a different way, after improving and enriching it, the apparatus, marvellous in its simplicity, which was our forefathers' legacy.

Whether the study of counterpoint should precede or follow that of harmony, or whether it should keep pace with it, is a question of pure pedagogy ; but it is absolutely certain that counterpoint should be mastered, sooner or later, by every student of music, were it but as a matter of archæology, and that no man should hope to become an accomplished musician and a composer of works having real value, without being first a strong contrapuntist. It is, so to speak, a dead language from which the present speech is derived, as important to the musician as Latin or Greek to the scholar. A knowledge of this language is, moreover, indispensable for the full comprehension of the works of such masters as Bach, Handel, Palestrina, and many others, who created its forms in accordance with the demands of their own genius. If it had no other claim than this, we could not neglect it; but, moreover, by the practice of counterpoint — whose rules are much severer and more positive than those of harmony — the composer acquires a peculiar suppleness, a facility in writing, and a light touch, which are a speedy recompense for the dryness of the study.

In what respect does counterpoint differ from harmony ?

In harmony, as we have recently seen, there is a material ready made to begin with, namely, chords; these we combine, modify, link together, — but they are always chords.

Counterpoint, on the other hand, recognises nothing of this kind; it begins with the mere note, and it associates one note to another or to several others without consideration of the chord thus formed, taking account only of the relation between these notes, that is to say, the interval. To combine notes one with another is its essence and aim; hence its name: note against note, point against point, *punctum contra punctum.* The chord is not a personality to the contrapuntist; he takes no heed of its name or its existence, and considers notes only in respect to their reciprocal distances, their consonance or dissonance, and their affinities.

In the present section we shall occasionally employ the names of chords, but it will be only for the purpose of being better understood by those who already have some knowledge of harmony.

Having called the reader's attention to this point, we shall now by a rapid statement of the principal rules of counterpoint make clear the general scheme of this primitive, but essentially robust, system.

Counterpoint is written in any number of parts, from two to eight.

Two or more parts, arranged to be executed simultaneously and thus produce a whole which satisfies the ear, constitute *simple counterpoint* in two parts, or whatever the number may be.

When the parts are so combined that they can be inverted without any disadvantage, the counterpoint is *double, triple, quadruple,* etc.; it is also called *invertible.*

When the different parts reproduce, one after another, the same melodic contour, either in unison, or at the octave, the fifth, the fourth, etc., this is *counterpoint in imitation.* This imitation may be *regular* or *irregular;* to be called regular, it must respect the position of the tones and semitones, and the resemblance must be complete between the *antecedent,* which proposes the melodic contour, and the *consequent* or *consequents,* imitating it; when irregular, it copies the model less closely, merely going over a like number of degrees, without regard to the character of the interval; the general design only is preserved.

Imitation may also take place *by augmentation* or *by diminution,* that is to say, in values greater or less than those of the proposed model; it may be *inverted* or *by contrary motion,* the consequent descending where the antecedent ascends, and *vice versa;* there is also the *retrograde imitation,* which reproduces its model in reversed order, beginning at the last note, and ending with the first, etc. These are diversions in counterpoint, sometimes degenerating into trivialities.

Most of these exercises are made upon a given part, called *plain song* or *plain chant,* also *cantus firmus;* this plain song is placed successively in the different voices, and parts of accompaniment are ingeniously produced, in constantly increasing numbers, with strict obedience to the following conditions:

SIMPLE COUNTERPOINT IN TWO PARTS.

First Species. Note against note.

1. Only consonances are employed.

2. The beginning is a perfect consonance, unison, octave, or fifth.[1]

3. The end must be a unison, or an octave preceded by the leading-note.

4. With the exception of the first and last bars, unison is forbidden; the crossing of parts is forbidden everywhere.

5. It is forbidden to sound the same note more than twice consecutively.

6. There must not be two consecutive octaves or fifths, or any progression in direct motion to an octave or fifth.[2]

7. Not more than three consecutive thirds or sixths are allowed.

8. The sixth on the fifth degree cannot be used unless it can be accompanied by a third; otherwise there would result an implied fourth,[3] and the fourth, being a dissonance, is not allowable, *even implied.*

9. The only melodic motions to be used are those of major and minor second, major and minor third, perfect fourth, perfect fifth, minor sixth, and perfect octave.[4]

10. False relations of octave and tritone are forbidden, except in the minor, between the third and altered sixth degree.

11. It is not allowed to modulate, except into related keys.

---

[1] In counterpoint, the fourth is a dissonance. The only consonances are the unison, octave, and perfect fifth (perfect consonances); the major and minor third and sixth (imperfect consonances). Every other interval is dissonant.

[2] This rule occurs also in harmony, but in counterpoint it has no exception.

[3] There would be a feeling of $\frac{6}{4}$.

[4] The smallest diatonic motions and the octave. No chromatic motions.

12. Repetition of the same melodic contours at short distances must be avoided.

Within the above limits the contrapuntist is entirely free, which does not save him, however, from feeling singularly hampered at first, and for some time scarcely able to move at all; but he becomes accustomed to this, and, later, takes great pleasure in what at first had appeared insupportable.

And let no one suppose that these rules are in any degree arbitrary; each has its good reason, which can be easily discovered; thus:

The prohibition of dissonances, consecutive or unprepared octaves and fifths, and of false relations, is for the avoidance of harshness; that of successive thirds or sixths, of repeated notes, of similar contours, is to avoid monotony; crossings of parts are forbidden to prevent confusion and a lack of balance among the sonorities of the different voices; the choice of the simplest melodic motions and of the most natural modulations compels a sober and simple style, and also avoids useless difficulties of execution. Nothing of all this is superfluous, it will be seen.[1]

Cantus firmus.

The same is true as to the following rules, concerning the other kinds. To avoid repetition I shall mention, henceforward, only *new* rules concerning each kind, it being understood that those already given remain in force, unless specially abrogated or modified.

---

[1] I give here only a single example; but the student is required to find at least six, placing the *cantus firmus* three times in the lower and three times in the upper voice. Exercises in counterpoint are generally from twelve to twenty measures in length. I have been obliged to restrict my examples on account of the dimensions of this volume; they aim only to give an exact idea of this kind of work.

Second Species.   Two notes against one.

The *cantus firmus* being written in whole notes, the counterpoint to be composed will have two half-notes to the bar.

1. The accented part of the bar must always contain a consonance.

2. The unaccented may be in consonance or dissonance.

3. Dissonances can be used only by conjunct motion with the note which precedes and the note which follows; that is to say, only as passing-notes or broderies.

4. Consecutive octaves and fifths on corresponding parts of bars are forbidden, even by contrary motion.

5. Between two up-beats are tolerated two fifths if one is diminished, especially if this be the second one.

6. The attractive character of the diminished fifth and augmented fourth must be remembered when they appear (as passing-notes).

7. The two parts must not be in the relation of seconds to each other, especially of minor seconds, except in case of broderie.[1]

8. The octave should rarely be employed, and notes must not be repeated.

9. It is usual to commence with a half-rest, followed by the octave, fifth, or unison.

10. The last bar but one should contain the leading-note, preceded by the submediant if the counterpoint is in the upper part, and by the dominant if in the lower. The last measure is necessarily an octave, a whole note.

(In many species there is a regular or conventional form of cadence.)

C. F.

---

[1] It is well also, though in general not mentioned in treatises on counterpoint, to avoid melodic contours of 7th and 9th *in three notes* by direct motion, with the restrictions indicated in the chapter on harmony. (See p. 224.)

Third Species. Four notes against one.

The *cantus firmus* remaining invariably in whole notes, it is to be accompanied by four quarter-notes.

1. With the exception of the down-beat, which can receive only a consonance, one may at will use consonances or dissonances, with this restriction, however, that the latter must proceed by conjunct motion, and be capable of analysis as passing-notes or broderies.

2. Octaves and fifths by parallel motion are allowable only when separated by at least four notes; those by contrary motion, if *absolutely necessary*, can be permitted after one or two quarter-notes.

3. Two fifths, of which the second is diminished, are sufficiently separated by one quarter-note.

4. The melodic motion of a minor sixth should be avoided.

5. The extreme points of a series of four quarter-notes, proceeding by conjunct motion, must not form the interval of the tritone.

6. It is usual to begin by a quarter-rest, followed by a perfect consonance.

7. The conclusion is made by letting the higher part ascend conjunctly from the subdominant to the tonic, the latter being a whole note; when the counterpoint is in the bass, the four quarter-notes of the last measure but one are the *leading-note, dominant, submediant, leading-note.*

(This formula is not invariable, but can be modified at will.)

Fourth Species.   Syncopated.

Here each measure must contain two half-notes, of which the second is syncopated with the first of the following measure; this arrangement can only be abandoned when it is impossible to preserve it,[1] except in the first and last measures.

1. The unaccented part of the bar always contains a consonance; by the rhythmic displacement it here becomes the accented.

2. The first can be at will consonant or dissonant; in this second case, it must be always capable of being regarded as a suspension, prepared and resolved as in harmony.[2]

3. Consecutive octaves and fifths are forbidden on the unaccented part of the bar, and are permitted on the accented.

4. It is forbidden to repeat a note previously syncopated.

5. The first measure must contain a half-note preceded by a half-rest.

6. The conclusion is made by the leading-note suspended, in the last bar but one, and the tonic, a whole note, in the final bar.

C. F.

Fifth Species.   Florid or figurate counterpoint.

This counterpoint, the most interesting of all to write, is an absolutely free mingling of the four species preceding, to which may be added, for further variety, dotted half-notes, and eighth-notes joined two by two; but no other rhythmic formula is admissible.

In each measure, according to the species that he employs, the contrapuntist will conform to its special rules. I have only, therefore, to give the rules for the dotted half-notes and the groups of eighth-notes, which have not yet been mentioned.

1 In this case syncopation can be deferred for one bar or, at most, two bars.
2 See p. 246.

1. The dot placed after the half-note must always complete its force in the measure following;[1] hence it could be replaced in writing by a quarter-note syncopated with the preceding half-note.

2. The eighth-notes must occupy the unaccented part of the bar, and not more than two can be used in each bar.

3. We begin, as in counterpoint of the second species, with a half-rest and a half-note in perfect consonance.

4. We end, as in the fourth species, by the leading-note suspended in the last measure but one (optional).

5. Good taste alone presides over the choice and blending of the different species; at the same time, sobriety is recommended. Syncopations and half-notes should be most frequently used, quarter-notes rarely, and very few of the eighth-note groups.

There are only these five kinds of simple counterpoint; but they can also be used with a large number of parts, as will now be shown.

SIMPLE COUNTERPOINT IN THREE PARTS.

First Species. Note against note.

From this point, the severity of the rules is constantly relaxed more and more, as the number of parts increases, which, of itself, produces, it will be readily understood, an

---

[1] This would not be the case in counterpoint in more than two parts.

always increasing difficulty; complete and absolute rigour cannot be enforced except in counterpoint in two parts.

It is important, however, to draw strong lines of demarcation between what is presented as *good*, what is *permitted as exceptional*, and what is merely *tolerated*.

The licenses which come under this last head should be used only when no other escape from some difficulty is possible.

This being said, once for all, we will go on with the examination of the varieties of simple counterpoint.

Counterpoint of the first species in three parts consists in accompanying the plain chant with two counterpoints in whole notes like itself. It is placed successively in each of the three parts, the lower, middle, and higher, and the attempt is made, in composing the other two parts, to employ in each measure three notes of different names;[1] where this is impossible, it is preferred to double the bass, — more rarely, the third,— never the fifth or sixth.

The rules to be observed are the same as in the first species in two parts, with the exception of the following slight modifications or allowances :

1. It is *tolerated* that a note occur three times.

2. Also a brief crossing of the voices is *tolerated*, except in the first and last measures, where it remains forbidden.

3. If one of the parts moves to a third with the bass, and another to a sixth, this arrangement must not last longer than through two consecutive bars.[2]

4. The first measure may contain the perfect consonances of unison, fifth, or octave, and the imperfect consonance of the third.

5. The last measure but one must present three different tones,— a complete chord,— and the last measure be, like the first, in perfect consonances or with a third.

---

1 Which forms a complete consonant chord ; this chord is always either in its normal position or in its first inversion, never the second $\binom{6}{4}$, which is prohibited as dissonant.

2 In other words, there must not be three chords of the sixth in the same position ; this would be monotonous and lacking in ingenuity.

Second Species. *Two notes against one.*

One part only may be written in half-notes, the other should be in whole notes, like the *cantus firmus.*

Each remains subject to the laws of counterpoint, whether in half-notes or in whole.

1. Dissonances are allowed only in the part that is in half-notes, in the unaccented portion of the measure, and by conjunct melodic motion.

2. The accented part of the bar must be consonant in all the parts.

3. Unison is tolerated in the up-beat.

4. The final formula may vary much; even the syncopation, borrowed from the fourth species, is authorised here.

Third Species. *Four notes against one.*

One part only is to be composed in quarter-notes; this is subject to the rules of the third species in two parts. The other, in whole notes, is treated as counterpoint, note against note.

1. As far as possible, three different notes in the three voices, in both the accented and unaccented parts of the bar,— at least in the accented.

2. Unison is tolerated in the last three quarter-notes of each measure, but it cannot be brought in by conjunct motion, which would produce a friction of the second.[1]

3. The crossing of voices is allowed.

4. No final formula is imposed.

The third species can be employed alternately with the second. In this case each voice obeys the laws of its own species.

1. Between the quarter-notes and the half-notes, two fifths of which the second is diminished can be tolerated, even if separated by only a single note.

2. Unison is permitted in the unaccented part of the bar; it is also tolerated in the up-beat except between the quarter and half-notes.

3. Each part should begin according to its own species; it is, however, permitted that the part in half-notes enter only at the second measure; in this case it may begin with a consonance.

4. The terminal formula may vary much; one may even break the rhythmic motion adopted in a part and use a whole note instead.

---

[1] See rule 7, p. 298.

Fourth Species.   Syncopated.

Here one part may be composed in syncopated and the other in whole notes, always obeying the special rules; but here there is much license, thus:

1. The fourth, without preparation, may be employed on the dominant, prolonged through two measures in the bass.[1]

2. The suspension of the leading-note in the bass may be accompanied by a major second and a perfect fourth, which become a minor third and a diminished fifth, when the suspension is resolved.[2]

It is, however, wise to make but a very moderate use of these two permissions, in respect to which all authors are not agreed.

One voice may be syncopated and one in half or quarter-notes, each part remaining subject to its own rules.

---

1 There results, however, from this a well-marked chord of $\frac{6}{4}$, which does not prevent this exception from being perfectly correct.

2 This gives an actual chord of the diminished fifth, up to this point absolutely prohibited, but whose employ will recur later.

Fifth Species.   Florid counterpoint.

One part or two can be written in florid counterpoint; in this latter case, the severity of the rules is still further relaxed.

1. The half-note on the accented part of the bar may be dotted.

2. Also a group of two eighth-notes may be placed on the weak part of the down-beat.

From this last rule it results that there may be two little groups of eighth-notes in the same bar; in this case they must never be in the same part. Also, it is true here, as in the case of two voices, that it is good taste to use the eighth-notes with extreme moderation.

Other combinations are possible,— one part florid, the other in half-notes, in quarter-notes, or syncopated, all of which are good practice for the student.

SIMPLE COUNTERPOINT IN FOUR PARTS.

First Species. Note against note.

Here, not only is it needful to have three different notes sounded simultaneously in each measure, but also, one of them must be doubled, to obtain the fourth voice. The selection of this note must be guided by the same principles as in harmony; first, the *tonal* notes, then the *second degree*, which may be called a neutral degree, then the *modal* notes, lastly, the *leading-note.*[1]

1. Except in the first and last measures, unison is not permitted.

2. On the other hand, crossing is allowed everywhere except in these two measures.

3. There must never be more than three thirds or three sixths successively between the same parts.

4. No voice is permitted to remain for more than three bars on the same note.

With the exception of these slight modifications, the rules are the same as for the same species in two and in three parts.

---

1 The bass in perfect chords, and the third or sixth in chords of the sixth, are the best for doubling.

Second Species.   Two notes against one.

The same rules, with the addition of No. 1, on p. 302;
also, the following:

1. The friction of the second is tolerated in the up-beat
when absolutely necessary.

2. Between two up-beats, octaves and fifths can be tolerated.

3. The same is true as to unison, if it cannot be avoided,
but only on the up-beat.

Third Species.   Four notes against one.

The same rules as for the three parts, with more tolera-
tion for the friction of the second.

There is also a combination of the second and third species, writing one part in half-notes and one in quarter, which does not call for distinctly new rules. Each voice remains subject to its normal progression, to its special principles, but with less rigour than heretofore; octaves and fifths are tolerated in the unaccented part of the measure; there even is permitted unison in whole notes, if in the two lower parts.

Fourth Species.   Syncopated.

Here, by special tolerance, the fourth may be attacked directly, in the unaccented part of the bar, provided it becomes the preparation for another fourth in the down-beat of the next bar, which is correctly resolved; hence, the bass note cannot change during this time.[1]   Also, it is allowable to use aggregations of four notes which are really chords of the seventh, but on condition that this

[1] See p. 305, rule 1.

seventh results from syncopation, and that its resolution is possible in the following note:

Finally, three species may be alternated: one part in half-notes, one in quarter-notes, one in syncopations, the whole upon the *cantus firmus* which remains in whole notes, so that, in reality, the first four species are all represented here. All the tolerances previously indicated may be utilised here, but the student should remember always that *perfection would be to dispense with these.*

Fifth Species. Florid counterpoint.

Here, of course, there can be one, two, or three florid parts, the plain song remaining, without change, in whole notes.

All the preceding rules should be observed, that is to say, each part must be considered subject, in each of its notes, to the species which momentarily rules it, both in its individual motions as well as in its relations with other parts, and only in case of necessity should the following privileges and exceptions be admitted.

(*Florid in one part.*)

C. F.

(Florid in two parts.)

C. F.

(*Florid in three parts.*)

It appears useless to describe in detail the rules of simple counterpoint in five, six, seven, or eight parts, for the reason that these rules can be inferred from those already given and their modifications.

It will suffice to say that the fundamental principles remain always the same as in counterpoint in two parts, the tolerances becoming broader as the number of voices increases, which has already been noted.

There is not and cannot be a strictly rigorous counterpoint except with a very limited number of voices, for the rigidity of rules must necessarily be lessened as the number of voices simultaneously employed grows larger, for this brings in inevitable complications, while, at the same time, it constitutes the interesting side of this kind of work.

Thus, in eight parts, in florid counterpoint, are permitted the following:

1. Octaves or fifths, between unaccented parts of the measure, and even on the down-beat, if they occur by contrary motion.

2. Those produced by the motion of syncopation, on the accented parts of bars, and even on the unaccented by contrary motion.

3. Two octaves (or unison and octave), even in whole notes, between the two lower parts, and by contrary motion.

4. Unison, except by direct motion.

5. Crossing of parts, except in the first and last measures.

6. Repetition of notes, in a part that is written in whole notes.

7. The *discreet* use of rests.

8. In case of need (but this is very hazardous) the meeting of a suspension and its note of resolution, etc.

With all these licenses it is still very difficult to write correct single counterpoint in eight parts, for there remain forbidden :

1. Octaves or fifths, between accented parts of the bar and by parallel motion.

2. Those caused by syncopation and occurring on the up-beat, except by contrary motion.

3. Parallel octaves or fifths between two outside parts.

4. The use of more than three consecutive thirds or sixths.

5. Repetition of notes, except of whole notes, etc.

It should also be said that the use of counterpoint in more than four or five parts has always been rare, and becomes more and more infrequent; it requires a great effort of combination, and the musical result obtained is very rarely in proportion to the amount of skill expended.

It is, in fact, scarcely practised except in the schools, and there merely as an exercise giving facility, and passing directly from the first to the fifth species. I shall not occupy further time in presenting all these various species.

The following is, however, an example, which I believe to be nearly correct, of florid counterpoint in eight voices, the *cantus firmus* being in the bass :

The parts *enter successively*, so as to present a tissue growing constantly thicker (and, also, thus showing themselves more distinctly in their individual character), up to the moment when the actual eight voices are together and unite to produce the effect of the whole.

Here it becomes difficult to preserve to each an independent progression, and to avoid conflicts among them; it is, however, possible,— for the great masters have done it, and admirable examples are not lacking of this marvel of combination.

An altogether peculiar species must be described here; it is the counterpoint with double chorus, one of the most attractive.

The eight parts are so arranged as to form two distinct choruses; each of these must produce, as far as may be, a complete whole, sufficient in itself, without, however, any one of its parts interfering with any part in the other

chorus. It is often interesting to make the two choruses answer each other, which authorises a more free use of rests than in counterpoint of any other kind.

Many great works of distinguished contrapuntists have been written on this plan, notably the famous oratorio of Sebastian Bach, *The Passion according to S. Matthew,* which has for accompaniment two distinct orchestras, while at times a *choral* forming a ninth part hovers over the whole, as shown in the illustration on page 316.

The reader who has gone over the preceding pages and has read the examples, will, I think, be no longer in danger of the mistake which, in the minds of many, represents counterpoint as a sort of corollary to modern harmony, but will clearly perceive that the two are entirely distinct technics.

The difference will become still more apparent in

DOUBLE COUNTERPOINT.

This counterpoint at first sight resembles florid counterpoint in two parts and is subject to the same rules; but, in addition,— and this makes its peculiarity,— it must be so constructed that the parts can be inverted, that is interchanged, taking the first for second, and the second for first, without any special incorrectness, whence arises the necessity for new and peculiar rules. This change of place must be borne in mind in composition, and whatever would become faulty by the new ordering must be avoided.

I will here describe double counterpoint *in the octave,* which is the simplest and, also, the most important form.

The fifth here must be guarded against because, in the inversion, it will be a fourth; it must therefore be treated as a dissonance, that is, prepared and resolved. The dissonance of the ninth, which, in simple counterpoint, may be only the suspension of the doubled bass, becomes impracticable, since from it would result a seventh requiring resolution in the bass, which is inadmissible.

Observe now, in detail, how each interval must be used so that the result is capable of reversal at the octave:

1. Unison is allowable only in the first or last measures or upon the up-beat or the weak part of the down-beat.

2. The second, as a passing-note or, prepared and resolved, as a suspension in the bass.

3. The third, not more than three times in succession; it would have an effect of poverty.

4. The fourth, as a passing-note or as a suspension.

5. The fifth, like the fourth.

6. The sixth, like the third.

7. The seventh, like the second,— that is to say, as a passing-note or as a suspension prepared and resolved.

8. The octave, as seldom as possible, except at the beginning and end.

9. The ninth, solely as a passing-note or broderie.

The other rules remain in force; no crossing of parts, no consecutive octaves or fifths, and as much variety as possible in melodic contours and groups of values.

When a counterpoint of this nature is composed with a few notes, moving within the space of an octave, it can be inverted in various ways, giving each of its parts to different voices, in the unison, octave, or the fifteenth, but it is still called double counterpoint in the octave.

If it exceeds this limit, the inversion at the fifteenth is the only one practicable without crossing of parts.

After double counterpoint in the octave, the most frequently employed are those in the *fifth* or twelfth, and in the *third* or tenth; then follow those having other intervals, seconds, fourths, sixths, and sevenths, rarely used and offering few resources. When the term double counterpoint is used without specifying the interval, the octave is always meant.

TRIPLE COUNTERPOINT.

This is chiefly in the octave, more rarely in the fifth or third. Here the problem is to construct the three parts so that any one of them can be in any position.

The rules are not materially different from those of double counterpoint; it is only that their application becomes more complicated and minute.

The relations of the intervals remain the same, but they must be examined, taking the parts two by two in all the positions they can hold relatively to each other, since, by inversion, any part may be bass, or inner, or highest voice.

The fifth, which by inversion becomes the fourth, is now absolutely prohibited as a true note, and can only be used as a suspension or as a passing-note.

From this total prohibition of the fifth, it becomes impossible — using the harmonic language — to furnish a single complete chord; for every consonant chord, normal or inverted, necessarily contains between two of its parts, a perfect fifth or fourth. The chord of the diminished fifth alone escapes this rule, by reason of its very imperfection: it contains neither a perfect fourth nor fifth; hence it is more frequently used here than in the preceding species. In triple counterpoint, as it is now practised in the schools, there are even admitted groups of notes which cannot be analysed harmonically except as chords of the seventh deprived of their fifth. This license is modern.

It is needless to say that the ninth is impracticable, because not invertible; that neither concealed octaves, nor crossings of parts, etc., are permitted.

QUADRUPLE COUNTERPOINT.

The same rules govern quadruple counterpoint, which differs from the preceding only in the number of its parts and the complications thence arising. But it has much importance in the construction of the fugue, of which we shall shortly speak, one of whose most valuable resources it is.

Here must be combined with the *cantus firmus* three other parts, so that the four voices — all having their own correct and elegant progression — can be inverted, can change place, without ceasing, however, to form a perfectly correct whole.

Some new tolerances now appear: thus, a succession of thirds or of sixths may exceed the limit of three notes; if it is unavoidable the parts may cross, but for as short a time as possible; rests are permitted, on condition that the re-entrance have some interest. With these exceptions, however, all the preceding rules of the various forms of counterpoint remain in force. These have been sufficiently made clear already.

INVERTIBLE COUNTERPOINT IN THE TENTH AND TWELFTH.

In the various invertible counterpoints that we have described, whether in two, three, or four parts, the change is produced according to the normal inversion of the intervals, that is to say, in the octave.

To obtain counterpoint invertible *in other intervals,* a fictitious inversion is arbitrarily made, which establishes new relations among the intervals and their inversions.

Thus for double counterpoint in the fifth or twelfth, we suppose the inversion of unison to be the twelfth, and establish these two reverse series of figures, of which each represents an interval, while the corresponding figure in the second series shows its inversion :

$$1. \quad 2. \quad 3. \quad 4. \quad 5. \quad 6. \quad 7. \quad 8. \quad 9. \quad 10. \quad 11. \quad 12.$$
$$12. \quad 11. \quad 10. \quad 9. \quad 8. \quad 7. \quad 6. \quad 5. \quad 4. \quad 3. \quad 2. \quad 1.$$

Here we considered the twelfth as the inversion of the unison; the eleventh, of the second; and so on.

This will give rise to but few new rules, for the octave becoming fifth and the fifth, octave, and these two intervals having similar laws as to their succession, they only need to be treated in the ordinary way. But it must be remembered that the sixth becomes a seventh, and is to be regarded as a dissonance, prepared and resolved, that its motion may remain correct and logical when the inversion is made.

For double counterpoint in the third or tenth, the double series of figures gives rise to very different observations.

$$1. \quad 2. \quad 3. \quad 4. \quad 5. \quad 6. \quad 7. \quad 8. \quad 9. \quad 10.$$
$$10. \quad 9. \quad 8. \quad 7. \quad 6. \quad 5. \quad 4. \quad 3. \quad 2. \quad 1.$$

Here the third is to be made the octave, and the sixth will become a fifth; the new law hence arising will be readily conjectured :

There must not be two consecutive thirds or sixths, since in the inversion these would become octaves and fifths.

As to the second, fourth, seventh, and ninth, which remain dissonances, they can be used only as suspensions or as passing-notes.

To obtain triple or quadruple counterpoints, either in the fifth or in the third, there is no other way than to *double* in thirds one of the parts, or both parts, of a double counterpoint of the same interval; this procedure scarcely deserves the name of counterpoint.

Counter-
point in
the tenth
in 3 parts.

Here, for example, the soprano doubles in thirds the bass voice.

The same in 4 parts.

Here the soprano and tenor of one part, and the contralto and bass of the other, produce a series of thirds.

In the 12th in 3 parts.

Here, the inevitable thirds are between the tenor and the bass.

The same
(transposed)
in 4 parts.

Here, be-
tween the
two male
voices, and
the two

female. This is childish.

There really is, therefore, no triple or quadruple counterpoint worthy of the name but that in the octave.

IMITATION.

In concluding this rapid survey of a style so rich in
combinations, and of such vitality that it even now vivifies
our great modern works, we have to examine, lastly, the
counterpoint in imitation, which offers to the composer
infinite and peculiarly fascinating resources.

It has already been said that there are imitations of
many different species; we will now examine these one by
one, with a few words of explanation and some examples,
to show the character of each.

Imitation, properly so called, consists in the musical act
of any one part reproducing more or less faithfully the
melodic design which another part has previously uttered.
When this reproduction is exact, when the spaces of tones
and diatonic or chromatic semitones of the model part are
represented in the imitating part by spaces identically
similar,— when, in a word, there is a perfect resemblance
in the contours of the two, the imitation is said to be
regular or canonical.[1] We may remark at once that this

---

1 Some authors say *constrained* imitation; and call the irregular imitation
free. This is only a verbal question.

absolutely perfect imitation can occur only at the unison, the octave, or the fifth.[1]   It is subject to all the laws of the simple florid counterpoint of the fifth species.

To render it invertible, there must be applied to it, further, the rules of double counterpoint.

1 The *regular* imitation in the fifth, either superior or inferior, can be made, of course, only by altering the seventh degree or subdominant of the imitating part; this is, actually, a transposition, and the two parts move in two keys, different, though nearly related.   If this detail be neglected, there can be an imitation in the fifth, but it will no longer be regular.

It is not difficult thus to combine regular imitations in three or four parts. Where they are of some extent, they take the name of *canon*, which is particularly appropriate when they are so conceived that a perpetual repetition permits each part to come in anew. The following is a correct example of the *perpetual canon:*

At any other interval than these, only *irregular* imitations can be formed, owing to the conformation of the gamut and the distribution of tones and semitones. Here the resemblance is less complete; a tone may correspond to a semitone, a third, major in the model, may be minor in the imitation, etc.; but the general aspect is the same, as well as the rhythmic disposition, which is sometimes sufficient.

The irregular imitation may also be written in double counterpoint, and it then becomes invertible.

In all the species of imitation, the part which furnishes the model is called the *antecedent*, and those which repeat the melodic design are *consequents*.

The antecedent may be in any part, and it may begin with the tonic, the dominant, or the mediant.

Continual repetitions of the same notes should be avoided, also repetitions of similar groups, and only a guarded use should be made of rests and crossings of parts. The only modulations permitted are those into related tones.

All the rules of florid counterpoint remain in force.

IMITATION BY CONTRARY MOTION.

To compose an imitation of this kind, there must be opposed to the scale in which the antecedent is written, a second gamut moving in the opposite direction, whence the notes for the consequent are to be taken.

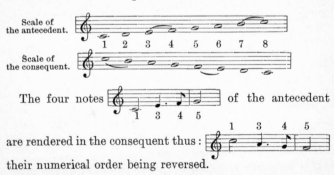

their numerical order being reversed.

Imitation by contrary motion can also be obtained by contrasting the two following scales:

which give as an answer to: the

notes : , always in virtue of the numerical order remaining the same in the two reverse series.

It is to be observed that in neither of these two systems is the place of the semitones taken into account; hence they are suited either to a major or its relative minor; but they furnish only irregular imitations.

If it is desired to obtain a *regular imitation by contrary motion*, there is this combination, where the tones and semitones agree exactly:[1]

By means of these scales, absolutely correct and faithful imitations in contrary motion are written; which, if long enough, may be called *inverted canons*.

But little need be said as to the other kinds of imitations, whose names carry with them their explanation.

In the *imitation by diminution*, the consequent employs time-values less than those of the antecedent, always, of course, observing the rhythmic proportions:

---

1 This minor scale is theoretically pure, without admission of any alteration.

The contrary is true of the *imitation by augmentation*:

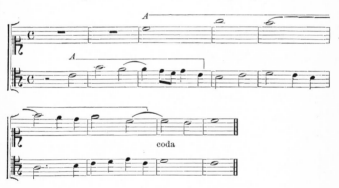

but this gives no occasion for new rules; it is a matter of
sagacity and ability on the composer's part.

Retrograde imitation (canon cancrizans) consists in
taking the last note of the antecedent as the initial note of
the consequent, and thus going backwards to the antecedent's first note, which becomes the consequent's last, no
modification being made in the time-values. This is no
more difficult than the preceding species.

All these various imitations can be written in three, four, five, or more voices; they can be combined among themselves, and they thus offer resources both interesting and unexpected; it will occur even that the consequent may become so different from the antecedent as to be unrecognisable except to the experienced ear.

Observe, for example, a *regular retrograde imitation by contrary motion and by diminution,*

whose interest certainly would escape any person not on the look-out for it; for, although presented here *entirely unconcealed, and with letters indicating its antecedent and consequent,* it must be very closely examined before the combination can be detected. I would suggest the experiment.

Such is, with all the apparent complication which its real simplicity allows, the mechanism of counterpoint.

Nothing can be clearer than its theory; but difficulties in execution arise at every step, the application of certain rules sometimes giving rise to different interpretations, and consequently to discussions between the most skilful contrapuntists.

In certain ancient treatises are found precepts more absolute; in others, more recent, are modifications, concessions to modern taste; the counterpoint here described is the severe, as it was practised by the old masters, only set free from the mediæval tonalities of which we shall have occasion to speak later.

Counterpoint might be defined as the art of juggling with notes; in fact, it will be observed *that all combinations which can occur to the imagination of the modern composer belong of necessity to one of these five species;* and that they always are (whatever be the supplementary licenses which one designs to allow himself) a fragment of counterpoint simple, double, triple, or quadruple, or an imitation, or some other artifice foreseen by the laws of the science. This is so true that no musician, however inexperienced, can design a melody, however insignificant, and apply to it an elementary accompaniment, without writing counterpoint, unawares,— as M. Jourdain talked prose; the question will be whether this prose conforms to the laws of grammar, syntax, logic, and rhetoric; and this is why the composer is obliged — if he cares that his style be pure and his musical language correct — to possess a thorough knowledge of the rules of counterpoint.

C.— Of the Fugue.

The fugue is the highest form of composition in counterpoint. All the *species* which have been described in the preceding section are used in it, and furthermore, the composition itself is required to have a certain form, a certain order in the modulations, a special build, from which there is no departure without infringing upon the laws ruling this form of musical composition,— a form generally considered dry, but in which a student will take the greatest interest, as soon as he penetrates the inmost details of its structure.

Inspiration, as we understand it in these days, there is none; neither to the heart nor to the senses does the fugue address itself but to the mind only, by the ingenuity of its procedures and the inexhaustible variety of its combinations.

A fine fugue can certainly, it is true, evoke an idea of the grand, the monumental, by its strong construction, its unity, and the harmonious proportions of its lines. Another fugue will appear subtle and ingenious, by the pertinency, or by the unexpectedness, presiding over the working up of its various artifices. But no other emotions are to be sought from it; the pleasure which it offers is purely intellectual, unimpassioned and without enthusiasm; we admire calmly,— reason and the spirit of analysis being called in. It is an edifice of sound, it is musical architecture; and that which renders supremely interesting the study of the fugue, now a thing of the past, is the knowledge that its solid framework is still the same on which are built the masterpieces of the present day,— a truth which will be better and more thoroughly demonstrated a little later, in the chapter where modern composition is treated of.

We will now first examine what constitutes *a fugue.*

A fugue is a musical composition entirely conceived in counterpoint, where everything is attached, directly or indirectly, to an initial *motif,* the *subject;* hence the unity of the work; variety is obtained by modulations and various combinations in canon or in imitation. The voices seem constantly flying from or pursuing each other, and this appears in the etymology of the name, *fuga* (flight).[1]

The constructive elements indispensable in every true fugue are: (1) the *subject,* or principal theme; (2) the *answer,* at the fifth, subject to special rules;[2] (3) the

---

1 [The fugue is a comparatively modern development of what is now called canon, and the latter was called fuga in the 16th century, the modern fugue development not existing till much later. Fugue in our modern sense has hardly been known more than 200 years, while its parent, the so-called " canon," has at least 600 years behind it. ED.]

2 See p. 336.

counter-subject, or *cou..:er-subjects* combined in double counterpoint with the subject; (4) the *stretto* (an Italian word signifying "narrow," "drawn together"), in which the subject and the answer are brought as close together as possible for the sake of heightening the interest.

Accessory elements are: (1) *episodes* drawn from the subject or counter-subject, and serving for transitions; (2) the *pedal,* either tonic or dominant, to strengthen the tonality at the moment of conclusion.

It is at once apparent how all the details are united to the subject, and derived from it.

But to see how these different elements may be utilised, we must examine closely the general plan of a composition of this kind.

PLAN OF THE FUGUE.

First comes the *exposition,* which consists in the enuncia tion of the subject and the answer, given *twice* in alterna tion, and, as far as possible, in different parts.[1]   Thus, where there are four parts, each one begins either with the subject or the answer; then it is used to accompany the new entrances, by means of the *counter-subject,* or simply by completing the harmony.   In this latter case it is called the part *ad libitum* (which does not prevent its being indirectly derived from the subject, for it is made expressly to serve as the latter's accompaniment).

Immediately after this, preceded by a brief *digression* or *episode,* comes the *counter-exposition,* a sort of reflected exposition, in which the *answer* is heard first, and then the *subject,*[2] each once only, and accompanied by the *counter- subject.*   Here, the composer, to avoid monotony, should be careful not to place each one of these elements in the same

1 Fugues are written in from two to eight parts. The school-fugue is gener- ally in four parts, which favours the distribution of the subjects and answers in the exposition.

2 Repetition might be avoided by sometimes calling the subject the *ante- cedent, proposition,* or *guide,* and the counter-subject, the *consequent;* but it is better to employ constantly the usual name. **The reader should, however, know that the other words are often employed.**

part which enunciated it in the exposition; inversions and reversals are always possible, since the subject and counter-subject are in double counterpoint.

Frequently the counter-exposition is omitted, and after the first episode a modulation is made into the related key, and the subject and its answer and their inseparable accompaniment of the counter-subject are again presented; this is always the first modulation.

After this, the tonality being well established, the composer makes excursions among the related keys,[1] by episodes becoming constantly more and more important, drawn from fragments of the subject or counter-subject, treated as *imitation* or as *canons*, utilising the various resources of counterpoint,[2] and combining the selection of tonalities in such a way as to end upon the dominant of the principal key. Then, a distinct *cadence* may occur, emphasised even by a pedal of the dominant; this, however, is not necessary, and the *stretto* may immediately begin, which is the most interesting part of the fugue.

Here, the subject and the answer must crowd upon each other, overlap in a way, and with increasing vehemence, if the nature of the subject permit; this is the pursuit, which grows eager and pressing; the episodes themselves participate in the action, and admit only of crowded imitations. Often there are several *stretti*, but every fugue requires at least one, which must be both harmonious and interesting.

After the *stretto*, which admits of but little modulation, and where, in any case, the subject and its answer are always in the principal key, comes the conclusion. Here we have the *pedal*, generally in the bass, its logical position, which repeats once more the *subject, answer,* and *counter-subject,* usually in *stretto,* and then follows the final *cadence, perfect* or *plagal.*

OF THE ANSWER.

We have said that the *answer* is subject to certain special rules : these will now be explained.

---

[1] See p. 279.

[2] Subject, *by augmentation, by diminution,* or *inverted;* the same as to the counter-subjects.

It must be said that there are two principal kinds of fugues: the *real fugue*, much the more ancient but less interesting; and the *tonal fugue*, based on the principle of tonality, which is the fugue of Bach and Händel, of Mendelssohn and Cherubini, [1]— the great fugue.

In the *real fugue*, of which we shall not speak further, the answer is merely a copy of the subject, transposed a fifth higher (or a fourth lower), whence results a perpetual canon, more or less rigorous, more or less free, often intermittent, which was the first to be called fugue.

Quite different is the answer in the *tonal fugue.* Here the scale is regarded as divided into two unequal parts, the dominant at the point between the two:

the principle is to answer the tonic by the dominant, and the dominant by the tonic; thus

The imitation is not exact, for the answer to a fifth is by a fourth, or conversely; but it is only thus that the answer is truly regular, according to the immutable laws of the *tonal fugue.*[2]

The following are examples of easy subjects, with their correct answers.

1 This is not to say that these composers never wrote *real* fugues.

2 [In England, real fugue simply means that the answer requires no alteration, and tonal fugue means that it does. The two kinds are otherwise just the same. ED.]

After this required change, which is called a *mutation*, the answer faithfully reproduces the subject, thus differing from it only by its *head;* this suffices, however, to distinguish them from each other, which was not the case in the *real fugue.*[1]

Moreover, it is understood that if the subject begin in C to end in G, for instance, the answer must begin in G and end in C,

whence results a sort of endless excursion back and forth between two tonalities, at the distance of a fifth from each other, characteristic of the *tonal fugue.*

It is needless to add that upon the subject depends the answer, and that a subject of a *real fugue* is not treated as a subject in a *tonal fugue.*

---

[1] This mutation of the subject and answer often involves a mutation of the counter-subject.

In respect to the counter-subject, it is essential in composing it, to make it as different from the subject as possible, both in the rhythm and in the melodic contour. Since all the episodes and all the combinations must be drawn from these two elements, it is by making them different from each other that the largest range for variety can be obtained. The obligation to write in double counterpoint, invertible, attains, though in another way, the same end, since it permits the parts to be inverted, and thus appear under new and varied aspects.

Two or even three counter-subjects may be employed, in that case combined with the subject in triple or quadruple counterpoint. Then the composition is sometimes called a fugue with three or with four subjects; but this designation is improper, a fugue having never more than the single principal theme.

Beside the *real fugue* and the *tonal fugue*, which are the two pure and classic types of the form, there are a quantity of others, more or less fanciful, such as the *free fugue*, the *imitative fugue*, the *irregular fugue*, whose names clearly suggest their nature. There is not space for us to describe these.

Notwithstanding the overture to the *Magic Flute*, and the *finale* of *Falstaff*, and a few other exceptional compositions, the fugue is not an operatic form: it can never be dramatic. Its home is the church; there, with the organ for auxiliary, it attains the *summum* of majesty. In the oratorio and in every composition of a religious character, nothing can fill its place.

This is not true as to compositions in the *fugal style*, or simply in counterpoint, which find their place everywhere. In studies of harmony, which are nothing else than first steps in the art of composition, great use is made of the procedures and artifices of counterpoint, such as imitation, double counterpoint and invertible imitation, but with less severity and the admission of chords of modern creation,— iridescent melodic contours.

In every work of strong construction may be found at
least vestiges of the general plan of the fugue, where this
plan itself is not the foundation of the work; moreover,
certain developments can acquire their true interest only
by borrowing from this style; and it is perhaps in the
lyric drama of our time that may be found its most striking as well as most unforeseen application. Such is the
rôle of the *fugue* and of *counterpoint* in the artistic evolution of music, which I hope soon to be able clearly to
demonstrate.

The principal works to be consulted on Counterpoint and Fugue
are those of : FUX (1660), MARPURG, ALBRECHTSBERGER, CHERUBINI,
FÉTIS and BAZIN. Also I would mention the *Traité de Contrepoint*
of E. FR. RICHTER (French of Sandré) where the *Church Tones* and
the style of *Protestant Chorals* are carefully studied. Some fugues
of BACH annotated with indication of subjects, counter-subjects,
episodes, etc., are published by Le Couppey. The reading of these
is instructive.

In English : translations of RICHTER's works.

HULLAH, J., *Grammar of Counterpoint,* 1876.

ROCKSTRO, W. S., *Rules of Counterpoint,* 1881. '

BRIDGE, J. F., *Counterpoint,* 1880 ; *Double Counterpoint,* 1881.

HILES, H., *Part-Writing, or Modern Counterpoint,* 1884.

AUGUST HAUPT, *Theory of Counterpoint, Fugue, and Double
Counterpoint,* translated by H. CLARENCE EDDY.

E. PROUT, *Fugue, Counterpoint, Strict and Free, and Double Counterpoint and Canon.*

CHAPTER IV.

ESTHETICS.

The human being comes into relations with the outside world by the agency of the senses. Among these, two are specially elaborated and have, so to speak, long range — *sight* and *hearing*. It is to these two only that the manifestations of art are addressed : to the sight, painting, sculpture, and architecture; to the hearing, music and poetry, which in the beginning were closely united and formed but one and the same art, then separated,— the one, by the aid of words to give exact form to thought; the other, to express with incomparable force the state of the soul. For this is the rôle of music : it depicts or it induces a state of the soul, without determining its causes; while poetry, the sister art, using articulate language, explains this state and comments upon it, like the explanations below a drawing. In truth they are each other's complement, and notwithstanding their occasional separations they tend always to re-union; for it is only by association that they can attain their highest intensity and penetrating power, still further augmented in the opera and the modern lyric drama by the scenery (in which painting, sculpture, and architecture are included, and with costume and ballet appeal to the eye). Here then, all the arts are united, converging towards the general effect; but if of these there is one which, left to its own resources, can transport us into an atmosphere purely ideal and intellectual, without doubt that one is music. We may say then, that, related though it is to physics and physiology, which are only its means of production, transmission, or perception; bound though it is to mathematics, which moreover rules the universe, music is the least material, the most ethereal of all the arts.

The plastic arts, sculpture and painting, represent to us natural objects with which we are familiar,—men and women, everything belonging to the animal, vegetable, and mineral kingdoms, every description of scene, historic, mythological, or purely imaginary, but in definite form; poetry addresses us in complete discourse, it gives language to its personages, a distinct individuality manifested in action; here again there is the visible channel by which influence reaches the mind. Much more mysterious is the action of music: *sounds* and *time-values*, sometimes even *silence*,—these are its sole means of action upon the human mind and with these it must awaken emotion.[1]

Considered alone, that is to say, deprived of all aid and free of any collaboration, doubtless the highest form of music is the *Symphony.* Here everything springs from the musician's brain; his imagination creates the leading idea and the secondary motives, with their developments, modulations, varieties of rhythm, the colouring of orchestration, without guidance or support from a sister art; and this complete emotional whole which he has translated into musical vibrations goes its way, across the molecules of air, to induce in the sensitive listener a condition of the soul analogous to that which presided over the creation of the work. Is there anything much more minute than a vibration of ether? Is there anything grander than the emotion produced by a fine symphony? The disproportion between the initial cause and the result obtained is very impressive, and gives truly a lofty idea of the power of art.

It is easy to understand the very strong desire which ardent natures feel in their turn to create works as grand and stirring as those which have filled them with passionate admiration. For this, it is not enough to understand

---

[1] We make no account of the kind of music called *descriptive*, which does its part by imitation of natural sounds, the *wind*, the *roll of thunder*, the *cries of animals;* this is artistic childishness.

how tones are produced, multiplied, combined,—which, as we have said, is the grammar. Quite another order of studies is requisite, and this it is not easy to define; for it differs essentially with each person's nature and character.

Let us attempt, however, to see how one may become a composer, or at least, may seek to become so; for to succeed is not within the reach of every man.

A. — Of Composition.

Though treatises upon musical composition are not unknown in catalogues, no man has ever written a work which teaches how to compose good music. A work of that kind, if such there were, might be abridged into two words: *have genius.*

With genius alone, it is possible to create grand and beautiful works; instances of this are not unknown; but how long and painful is the labour! The true condition for the production of healthy, robust works is to be able to unite with genius the treasures of acquired talent, of technic, and of erudition.[1]

If the reader will take the trouble to make some brief investigations, he will very soon become convinced that all the great masters who have done honour to the art of music are, above all, *great thinkers,* very learned in their own technic, but also very thoroughly versed in scientific or literary studies; philosophers of a high rank; in short, men who have something to say or to teach, new thoughts or grand emotions to communicate.

Genius is to art what the soul is to the body; the non-material principle which gives it life and governs it.

This is genius, which study can sometimes contribute to develop, but can never create in the individual who is not endowed with it by nature; it is without doubt a natural

---

1 A definition by Gounod, which I believe has never before been in print: " *Genius* is a tumultuous river always likely to overflow its banks ; *talent* builds quays for it."

gift, this faculty of conceiving and creating new forms which have the power of producing feeling in other minds. We shall never have classes in inspiration; and still, inspiration is contagious in a certain measure, and to frequent the society of men of genius, of great artists, is at least to favour its development if the germ exists latent in the soul.

On the other hand, talent is never inborn, but is acquired only by study, with the aid of time. The musician who has talent but lacks the spark of genius, may write well, may even attain a certain nobility of style, especially if he possesses the faculties of observation and assimilation; but he is evidently dependent upon his predecessors and employs only their procedures. If he attempt anything original, it appears at once that he is doing this by an effort, not spontaneously.

Talent is the necessary outfit for genius; the better the tools are, the more thoroughly genius can trust itself to them, and the more unhampered are its manifestations.

The man of genius *is in advance of his time;* he breaks out the path in which later those will walk who have admired him or, perhaps unconsciously, have felt his influence. For this reason he is rarely understood at first; he speaks a new language, we may say unknown by the public, to whom are addressed finally the manifestations of art; but once this same public has learned through him—more or less willingly, more or less rapidly—the new speech, it readily understands the men who follow this master, gleaning in his fields, exploiting what he has discovered. Hence the great successes of estimable artists of second rank, while the true genius is most frequently misunderstood in his time. Nor is this true in music only.

Since, then, genius is not taught, and scarcely can be defined, it is useless to speak longer about it; on the other hand, we can study the means of acquiring talent; these means are chiefly observation and practice.

By *observation* is meant the intelligent study, by hearing, reading and analysis, of the great works of different epochs and of all the schools. This analysis must occupy itself first and chiefly with the general form of the work, its plan and its proportions, then with the conduct of the modulations, finally with the minute details peculiar to each master.

The restricted scope of this work does not permit me to multiply examples. I will give, however, a few instances of this analysis, selecting them among the best-known works, which every student can easily procure.

By *form*, I mean the general plan of a work, the great outlines of its architecture, omitting the details of its working out, which belong to the domain of harmony or of counterpoint. The form thus regarded is the great framework, the musical skeleton; and if I insist upon this definition, it is because I believe it indispensable for the comprehension of what is to follow. Just as the form of a sonnet may be described thus: "Two quatrains, followed by two triplets," which in no way decides the length of the lines and leaves a good deal of freedom in the arrangment of the rhyme, so musical forms have their elasticity, and no more determine the number of bars than the number of notes. We speak here only of the general and comparative dimensions of a musical discourse, whose scheme we are now examining.

The principal important typical form of instrumental music is the *Sonata*. This is generally a work written for one instrument; when composed for two instruments, it is called a *duo;* for three, a *trio;* for four, a *quartet;* for five, six, seven, eight, nine, a *quintet, sextet, septet, octet, nonet;* but the general form remains the same. The Sonata for an orchestra is a *Symphony*, and when one instrument has solos, accompanied by the orchestra, the composition is called a *Concerto*.[1] Because of its importance we shall now describe the Sonata form in all its purity as it has been bequeathed to us by the classic composers.

The Sonata is a succession of movements of different characters, destined to be heard consecutively: the first

[1] In the Concerto, the form is a little modified. as will be shown later, but it is still the Sonata form.

and last must be in the same key,[1] the other movements in related tones, or in those so selected that the change of key will not offend the ear.

Every Sonata regularly constructed[2] contains a first movement called the *Allegro;* a slow movement, the *Andante* or *Adagio;* and an animated *Finale.*

Between the first and second movements, or between the second and third may be introduced a short piece— a *Minuet, Scherzo,* or *Intermezzo.* Such is the general scheme.

The first movement, the foundation of the Sonata, is required to have a certain construction which is its characteristic. It is made up out of two themes, two musical ideas: the *first subject,* and another phrase, generally of a graceful melodic nature, called the *second subject* or "character phrase." It is divided into two parts: the first must begin in the principal key, and end in the key of the dominant; (if the principal key is minor, the first part may end in the relative major); the second part brings about a return to the principal key.

We will now examine the first part. After the theme has been announced and the principal tonality well established, a short episode[3] leads to a cadence upon the dominant; by the device of equivocal chords, this dominant is considered as a tonic, and in this new key (the key of the dominant), which will persist till the end of the part, is presented the second theme; a new episode and a short coda follow, and this part is ended. The classic usage is to repeat it, probably that the listener may thoroughly grasp the two principal themes and lodge them in his memory.

We now come to the *second part.* This may begin in many ways. Here the composer is at liberty to give the freest scope to his imagination, and venture into remote

---

1 If the first movement is minor, the second may be in the major of the same key; but the converse of this is not allowable.

2 The purest classic authors have written *irregular* Sonatas.

3 This word has the same meaning here as in the fugue.

tonalities, but without forgetting that the subject must be brought in again and presented a second time, just as it was before, in the same key, and ending in the same cadence upon the dominant; here, however, there is no change of tonality, the dominant remains the dominant, and it is in the principal key, not again to be abandoned, that the second theme makes its second appearance. Then follow another episode, having only very brief modulations or not any at all, a coda strongly affirming the tonality, and the final conclusion, the peroration.

The following is the plan of an Allegro from a Sonata by C. P. E. Bach, who is considered as the creator [1] of the type; this Sonata is dated 1775.

First part.

—	Principal theme	. . . . . .	8 bars .	. *A major.*
—	Episode	. . . .	4 bars .	. —
—	Cadence on the dominant	. . .		—
—	2d theme	. . . .	4 bars .	. *E major.*
—	Episode	. . . .	22 bars .	. —
	(Passing modulations B major, A minor, D major, E minor.)			
—	Coda	. . . .	4 bars .	. —

Second part.

—	Developments of the first theme	. 39 bars .	. *E major.*
	(Passing modulations into F♯ minor, C♯ minor, G♯ minor, D minor, B major, G♯ major, C♯ minor.)		
—	Repetition of the principal theme	. 8 bars .	. *A major.*
—	Episode	. . . . 4 bars .	. —
—	Cadence on the dominant	. . .	—
—	2d theme	. . . . 4 bars .	. —
—	Episode	. . . . 20 bars .	. —
	(Passing modulations in E major, D minor, G major, A minor.)		
—	Coda	. . . . 4 bars .	. —

Total: 121 bars.

---

1 I say creator, as moulder of the type which has become classic, and not as inventor of the Sonata, which was invented by no one person, but took form by degrees under the efforts and innovations of many generations of composers. Long before C. P. E. Bach, the Italians had the *Sonata da Chiesa*, the Church Sonata, which opened with a largo and almost always ended with a fugue ; they had also the *Sonata di Camera*, Chamber Sonata, which consisted of a prelude

This is the plan of an Allegro, in its native—one might almost say, its naïve—simplicity. The purity of its outlines is especially admirable and also the fine skill of the modulations which, while bringing variety, surround like an escort the principal key, never going far away from it and thus contributing to strengthen the sentiment of tonality. It is also to be observed that this plan is not without some resemblance to the opening of a *tonal fugue*, where the subject moves from the tonic to the dominant, as here in the first part, while the answer, represented by the second part, returns from the dominant to the tonic. The use of episodes and the selection of keys which are touched upon in these digressions—for the most part minor, to give more relief to the themes—furnish further points of resemblance.

Numerous modifications *of detail* can be introduced into this plan without altering its principal lines. Two very often employed, and very advantageously by the composers who followed Bach, are given below:

1. A substitution for the cadence on the dominant and the equivocal construction which is its somewhat awkward result, of a cadence on the dominant of the *key of the dominant*, the key towards which we are moving;

2. Attack of the second part in a remote tonality, which causes surprise and marks still more clearly the division of the movement.

Other modifications have been devised and many others might be thought of, without, however, touching the great underlying principle: tonic-dominant, dominant-tonic, except in the case where, a Sonata being in the minor mode, it may be preferred to end the first part in the relative major, the nearest key of all. But this is a very rare case.

The Andante has a less clearly defined form. It is perhaps a mere Romance with its setting; it may be a theme

---

and many little dancing tunes, minuets, jigs, pavanes, and the like. Besides, not only had Sebastian Bach written many Sonatas, but I know one by Domenico Scarlatti, dated 1726, which is identical in form with the one analysed here. I have indicated the number of bars only in order to give an approximate idea of the importance given to each tonality; this is necessarily very variable.

with variations, as Mozart and Haydn often made it; and then there are the great Andantes of Beethoven, great Romances with many varied strophes, when each repetition of the theme is more and more richly ornamented; of this we have a model in the Sonatas, op. 22, and op. 31 (in G), in the Septuor, and in many Symphonies; finally, it may be nothing more than a simple introduction, longer or shorter, preceding the *finale* and connected with it.

For the *Finale*, the usual form is that of the *Rondo*, which may be thus conceived: a *principal theme* presented *three*, *four*, or even *five* times, more or less adorned or varied, each repetition being separated from the preceding one by an *episode*, the whole ending with a *coda*, making the conclusion.

The musical form, the *Rondo*, is derived from the poetical form, the *Rondeau*, in which a first verse forming a sort of refrain is repeated at regular intervals. The first Rondos were undoubtedly the musical setting of Rondeaux;[1] then this plan became introduced and acclimated into the instrumental style.

The following is an analysis of a finale in the rondo form; this is Weber's *Perpetual Motion*, the finale of his Sonata, op. 24. We notice here, as in every well-constructed work, the preponderance of the principal key, and the care with which the author has avoided repetition in his modulations, except for very short periods.

Principal theme (1) . . . . 15 bars	*C major.*
1st episode . . . . 34 bars	—
(Tonalities touched: C minor, A minor, D minor.)	
Principal theme (2) . . . . 15 bars	—
2d episode . . . . 68 bars	—
Modulations distinctly established into	*G major.*
and	*E minor.*
Principal theme (3) . . . . 15 bars	*C major.*
3d episode . . . . 105 bars	—
(Tonalities touched: C minor, A minor, D minor.)	
Distinct modulations into	*F minor.*

---

1 [It is, however, a fact that ancient Hymn tunes are found in this form, which were certainly not "the musical setting of Rondeaux." ED.]

Then into		*A♭ major.*
Then into . . . . . *.		*C minor.*
Principal theme (4)	8 bars (shortened) . .	*C major.*
4th episode	55 bars	—
(Passing modulations into A major, D minor, A minor, F major, A minor, D minor, E minor, then by a chromatic series of 7 chords, C minor, A minor, D minor, C minor, etc.)		
Principal theme (5)	6 bars (shortened) . .	*C major.*
Coda, non-modulatory . . .	10 bars	—

Total: 331 bars.

Haydn and Mozart have often given the example of finales not shaped as Rondos, but in the form of the first allegro, from which they then differ only by the gay and sportive character of the principal theme.

The little accessory pieces, the *Minuet* and *Scherzo*, have also their classic form, which is the same for both. They differ in character and movement, the Minuet being always in ¾ time, and having the ceremonious grace of the dance which it represents; the Scherzo (from the Italian *scherzare*, to joke) is light and sportive. It may be in 2-time or 3-time, but always in lively movement.

Their plan is most simple. A first part, very brief, ending either in the principal key or in that of the dominant, or else in the relative, so as to be taken up again; and a second part, often rather longer and finishing invariably in the principal key, form the bulk of the Minuet or Scherzo. Then comes the Trio,[1] built in the same way as the Minuet, with two repetitions also,—the Trio being in the same key, or in a related key, or in some other which was well-

---

[1] I feel bound to point out the origin of the word Trio, concerning which musical writers have been much puzzled.

In many of the Responsoria of Palestrina and Vittoria (xvi. century), written in four or five real parts, the middle part or *verset* is given to *three voices only*, often with this note : *verset in trio.*

A like arrangement is found in the Kyrie or the Credo in masses by the same masters or others of that epoch, with the evident intention of giving more richness to the effect of the whole ; later it was introduced into instrumental pieces, dance-music, and the name *Trio* remained attached to the middle portion of these little pieces, even when it was no longer justified by the number of instruments or of voices employed.

[J. S. Bach has also used the term in clavier music, and it is noticeable that the piece is always in three parts where this name is used. ED.]

suited; for after the Trio, the Minuet came again, but this time without repetitions. All this is a matter of tradition. Exceptionally, there are sometimes two Trios, separated by a return of the Minuet. In this case it is usual to write each in a different key. Also there may be a Coda.

The *Intermezzo* has no determinate form. These little pieces are *hors d'œuvre* of the Sonata. They fill a part like that of the ballet in an opera; they are a moment's diversion, after which the action goes on. I believe that Haydn and Boccherini were the first to introduce the Minuet, and Beethoven produced the first Scherzo; the Intermezzo is of more recent date.

There are many irregular Sonatas, in which the author strays from the classic plan while still preserving its spirit. Examples of this are the Sonata in C♯ minor, op. 27, one of the grandest conceptions of Beethoven's genius, which begins by an Adagio, followed by a very short Scherzo, the Finale taking the form of a first Allegro; also by Beethoven, the Sonata in A♭, op. 26, of which the first movement is an Andante with variations; the Sonata, op. 7, of Mendelssohn, whose four parts are connected without a break, the Finale ending by a recall of the beginning of the Allegro, like a snake biting its tail; Schumann's famous Quintet, whose peroration is a fugue in which the principal theme of the Allegro has the part of the subject, and that of the Finale, of counter-subject. There are many others among the great compositions, but they must all be regarded as exceptional, or, properly speaking, as works of free fancy conceived in a style resembling the Sonata, only bearing its name, however, for lack of any more accurate designation.

I have already said that all the great works of *chamber music*, from the *Duo* to the *Nonetto*, disclose the same plan.

In the Symphony it remains unchanged, but in larger proportions. The episodes are developed at greater length, the modulations are sometimes bolder; but the general conduct of the musical discourse, and the grand divisions remain the same. Who has not observed, moreover, that the great Sonatas of Beethoven, his Trios, give the impression of real Symphonies without an orchestra, whose missing instrumentation can be conjectured as in a faithful transcription?

The only frequent addition to the Symphony is that of an *Introduction* in a slow tempo, serving as prelude to the first movement, then taken up at once, as in the Pathetic Sonata of Beethoven, which thenceforward follows its regular course.

The Andante, the Scherzo or the Minuet, and the Finale, conform to the plans we have already described.

We now come to the *Concerto*.

Here the identity of design is a little more difficult to recognise, without, however, being doubtful on that account. The *Allegro de Concerto*, instead of being divided like that of the Sonata into two parts, of which the first is repeated, is divided into three *soli*, each preceded by a *tutti*, necessary to give the solo-player rest, to allow him to see that his instrument is in tune, if it be a violin or a 'cello; or, if he plays a wind instrument, to give him time to shake out the moisture condensed in the tubes,—a proceeding not elegant, but unavoidable.

The *first solo* is like the first part of the Sonata, announcing the theme in the principal key, then going on towards the dominant to give the second theme, and concluding in the same key.

The *second solo* corresponds to the beginning of the second part; it consists in modulated developments drawn from the two themes, in ingenious passages, unforeseen combinations often foreign to the subject, surprises, and the like.

The *third solo* corresponds to the remainder of the second part from the reappearance of the first theme to the *coda finale*. Towards the close of this last solo, or separated from it by a short *tutti*, is a pause on the dominant, indicated by a hold. At this place, the performer, if he be an improvisatore as well, is at liberty to introduce a *cadenza* of his own,[1] which may vary from a few passages showing his skill as a player, to a developed paraphrase of the whole Concerto. (The *cadenza* is an undoubted vestige of the traditions of the Italian school, where all vocal solos terminate thus.) The *cadenza* ended, the orchestra resumes and concludes.

The proportional length of the *tutti* has never been settled. In certain Concertos, the first *tutti*, preceding the entrance of the solo-performer, has almost the importance and the form of the first part of a Symphony;[2] in others, it is but a few measures, as if merely to call attention and impose silence; lastly, it is sometimes totally omitted, and the virtuoso attacks, alone and at once, the first solo.

Of the *Andante*, nothing need be said; it is the same as that of the Sonata.

(The Concerto does not include the Minuet; some modern attempts have been made to introduce the Scherzo.)

The *Finale* is generally conceived in the Rondo form, but always varied with *tutti*, whose utility is not merely to give the solo-performer a few minutes of rest, but also, by silencing for a short time the timbre of his instrument, to give interest to its return.

Like the *Allegro*, the *Finale* may contain a *cadenza*, intended to display the skill of the virtuoso.

Not to linger upon a description which is already long, I have thought it better to give entire, and with some details, the plan of a famous Concerto, showing its proportions; this will also aid the reader to comprehend fully what is included in the *analysis* of a work from the point of view of its architecture, and I shall have no need to return to this subject again in speaking of other forms of composition. Observe therefore the construction of Beethoven's Third Concerto in C minor (op. 37) for piano and orchestra. In the first movement, the sobriety of the modulations must be admired. The music is altogether in C, major

[1] Frequently the author, distrustful, takes the precaution to write the cadenza himself.

[2] As in the Concerto analysed on the next page.

or minor, in E flat, a related key, or in G minor, the key of the dominant; other tonalities are merely touched in passing; hence, the general effect is grand and imposing.

ALLEGRO.	Principal key	. . . .	C minor.
1st Tutti.	1st theme	16 bars	—
—	Episode	33 bars	—
—	2d theme	12 bars	E♭ major.
—	2d theme	8 bars	C major.
—	Episode	35 bars .	C major, then minor.
—	Coda	8 bars	C minor.
1st Solo.	1st theme	19 bars	—
—	Episode	33 bars	—
—	2d theme	16 bars	E♭ major.
—	Episode	19 bars	—
—	Coda	28 bars	—
2d Tutti.	Episode	7 bars	—
—	Modul. to the dom.	16 bars	G minor.
2d Solo.	Various developm'ts	60 bars	—
—	Transient modulations in F minor, D♭ major, C minor (principal key), B♭ minor, and return into		C minor.
3d Tutti.	Repetit'n of 1st theme	8 bars of orch. . .	—
3d Solo.	Episode	23 bars	C major.
—	2d theme	8 bars	—
—	2d theme	8 bars of orch. . .	—
—	Episode	19 bars	—
—	Coda	28 bars	—
4th Tutti.	With cadence on the dominant . .	13 bars	—
	Cadenza ad libitum.		
Final peroration		27 bars	C minor.
LARGO.	Principal key		E major.
Solo.	Theme	12 bars	—
Tutti.	Theme	12 bars	—
Solo	in dialogue with the orchestra and ending on key of . . .	14 bars	B major.
—	Trans. modulations in G major, A minor, E minor	14 bars	—
	Repetition of theme	12 bars	E major.
	with modulated variations		
Tutti.	Theme resumed . .	8 bars	—
Coda.	Concertante . . .	17 bars	—
RONDO.	Principal key		C minor.

Solo.	Theme (1) . . . 8 bars	*C minor.*
—	Short episode . . 18 bars	—
—	Theme (2) . . . 6 bars	—
Tutti.	Repetit'n of theme 23 bars	—
Solo.	2d episode . . . 71 bars	—
—	Dialogue with orchestra and modul. into	*E♭ major.*
	then direct return into	*C minor.*
—	Theme (3) . . . 32 bars	—
	(With cadenza *ad lib.* inserted.)	
Tutti.	Theme resumed . . 23 bars	—
—	3d episode . . . 109 bars	*A♭ major*
Solo.	Continuation of episode with mod. in F	
	minor (fugal) in E major, and return to	
	principal key	*C minor.*
—	Theme (4) . . . 8 bars	—
Tutti.	Theme resumed . 13 bars	—
Solo.	4th episode . . . 88 bars	—
—	with predominance of key of	*C major.*
—	Very brief modulations in D♭ major, E♭	
	minor, and return to the dominant . .	—
—	*Presto finale* . . . 50 bars	—
Tutti.	*Presto finale* . . . 6 bars	—

The choice for the *Largo* of the remote tone E major is evidently designed to cause a strong diversion and rest the ear from keys which, already largely employed in the Allegro, are to reappear in the finale: this is a very frequent procedure.

The first movement is in $\frac{4}{4}$, the second in $\frac{3}{8}$, the last in $\frac{2}{4}$; it is advantageous to seek variety thus in the rhythms.

Also should be observed, in the plan of the Rondo, the excellent proportion of the episodes, and the opportuneness of the modulations. The first episode, which is short, and, as it were, enclosed in the principal theme, remains in the initial key, which it helps to establish; the second, longer, goes on to the relative major key; the third, very largely developed, brings in for the first time the key of A flat, which, though related, has not been employed in the Allegro, and seems to have been reserved to produce variety here; then certain distant modulations are allowed; and the fourth and last, near the close of the movement, strengthens the tonal meaning by scarcely leaving at all the key of C major. Beethoven, moreover, is of those who love to affirm the tonality with energy at the moment of conclusion,—the finale of the Fifth Symphony ends with one perfect chord repeated through twenty-nine bars, preceded by six perfect cadences, and by fifteen other measures on the perfect chord of C major.

More frequently still than in the Symphony and the Sonata, it happens that the composer writing a Concerto makes sacrifices to virtuoso display, and adopts a free form, departing from the traditional plan in order to bring out the qualities of the solo instrument or of the player; this is a matter of course. The two Concertos of Mendelssohn for the piano, the same composer's Concerto for the violin, the Concertstück of Weber, are remarkable examples of exceptional forms. When the rôle of the orchestra has such importance that the solo instrument is no longer preponderant, appellations like this appear: *Concerto-Symphonique* or, even, Symphony with Viola solo, like the *Harold* of Berlioz, etc. Also there have been written *Symphonies Concertantes* for two instruments with orchestral accompaniment; there is even by Beethoven a triple Concerto for piano, violin, and violoncello (op. 56), which is never played, I know not why, for it is a very remarkable work. These are hybrid styles, connecting links, so to speak, between the Concerto and the Symphony, which as such are very interesting to study.

I have gone into such detail in respect to the form of the Sonata and kindred compositions, because of its preponderance in all the instrumental domain, from the mere solo for the harpsichord, piano, or violin, up to the complete development of the symphonic forces; but this type, important though it is, is not the only one that the student should know.

Another orchestral form is that of the *Overture*, which also it will be useful to analyse, although it is now but seldom employed (it would not do to take as a type the Overture of the *Magic Flute* which is an admirable symphonic Allegro in fugal style).

The Overture is midway between pure symphonic art and musical dramatic art, and derived from both.

Its object, usually, is to prepare the spectator for the emotions of the drama which is about to be performed in his presence, by placing him in the mood most suited to receive the impression vividly. Hence it is very often constructed out of the material of the work itself, or filled with allusions to its principal themes; sometimes, indeed, it becomes a veritable *Fantasia* upon the opera or opera-comique to which it serves as instrumental prologue. Its form cannot be fixed in advance, since it especially is modelled in accordance with the *scenario* of which it is but the prelude and commentary.

It is also needful to study the form of the operatic *Aria* at different epochs, although it is in the modern current no longer to write in this particular form. The Aria may have one movement or more; and many examples may be found in the famous scores which are vastly simpler to analyse than Sonatas and Symphonies. Also one must examine the construction of grand *Finales* of acts, and *ensemble* pieces in the various schools; they are more complicated and the differences are greater, but really require only time and some degree of a spirit of observation. It is well to know the manner and characteristic rhythm of the old dance-music, that one may not make such absurd blunders about them as, for instance, a *valse* in four-four time would be, or a march *prestissimo*. The following are some of these dance forms:

In duple time there are:

The *Gavotte* ($\frac{2}{2}$), in a moderate *tempo ;* it has two sections and a trio, like a minuet, and each phrase begins with the up beat; the trio is quite frequently treated like a musette, or piece for the bagpipe. (See later.)

The *Tambourin* ($\frac{2}{2}$), a very lively movement; it is divided into sections of 4, 8, 12, or 16 bars each, as a rule commencing with the up beat; the rhythm of the bass imitates a tambourine.

The *Jig* (*Gigue*) (⅝), very lively; the strains are of eight bars.

The *Sicilienne* (⅝), moderate; each beat is generally in this rhythm ♩♪♩.

The Auvergnaise *Bourrée*, the Rigadoon; its general plan is like that of the tambourin, but with different scansion; each member of the phrase begins on the weak part of the up beat.

The *Allemande* (²⁄₂ or ²⁄₄), a lively rhythm, but a little heavy.

In triple time:

The *Minuet*, described in the Sonata form.

The *Galliard* (*Gagliarda*), gay and spirited, though not rapid.

The *Polonaise*, stately and elegant, having this peculiarity, that each phrase and member of a phrase ends on one of the up beats.[1]

The *Chaconne* (*Ciaccona*), very rhythmic and not very rapid; it is a long series of variations, forming as it were, couplets.

The *Saraband*, slower than the minuet.

The *Courante*, slower than the saraband, notwithstanding its name.

The *Paspy* (*Passepied, Passa-mezzo*),[2] still more lively than the galliard; the sections beginning on the up beat.

Either double or triple measure:

The *Passacaille* (*Passacaglio*), much resembling the chaconne, but with slower tempo.

The *Pavan*, a stately dance of Italian origin.[3]

The *Musette*, whose bass is a pedal point single or double, but constant, like the drone of the instrument whence its

1 The Torchlight Dances of Meyerbeer are admirable instances of modern Polonaises. They are marches in triple rhythm. [But not in triple time. Military marches are frequently in ¹²⁄₈ time, viz., triple *rhythm*, but quadruple *time*. ED.]

2 ["The old English writers call it passa-measure, passing-measure, or simply, measure. It was a favourite dance in the time of Queen Elizabeth." Stainer and Barrett. Tr.]

3 [The original 16th and 17th century Pavan was always in duple time. ED.]

name; when it is introduced as a trio in a gavotte, it is necessarily in duple time; etc., etc.

Many I omit; indeed it would be impossible to mention all. I do not think there are any dance-forms in quadruple time, which seems reserved for *marches ;* on the other hand, solemn or religious marches have often been written in triple measure, and it is worth noting that the slow movement gains a special dignity from the fact that the stress comes alternately on the right and the left foot, as in the *polonaise.*

It must not be inferred from what has now been said, that every composition should as a matter of course be run in a known and adopted mould. Far from this, the composer remains at liberty to create new forms, and, as a matter of fact, good or bad he does create, every day; this is one of his functions, one of his duties. When they are good, these forms make themselves a place and remain, as new types, a lasting addition to the domain of art.

The student composer must be ever on the watch, for everywhere he will find something to learn, to store up for future use; but his investigations must be methodical, sagacious, prudent, or he will find his judgment, his artistic sense, false, whence would result the irreparable loss of his own originality.

One of the shoals most dangerous is the premature study of the great works of the modern *ultra-romantic* school (Berlioz, Wagner), a study towards which the young student is attracted as the moth to the fatal candle. These works must be known and admired, without doubt; but by *premature study* I mean that which is made before the student has obtained a thorough knowledge of the works and the principles of the classic school. Before he has done this, the neophyte is not in a condition to comprehend that which intuition already leads him to admire. Ignorant of the old forms, which he has never thought of analysing, he comes to regard as exempt from all plan, form, or logical structure, the works which — without being able to grasp their principles of construction, not knowing even that they have any — he proposes to take for his models, making disorder, henceforth, his own easy law. Having begun in this way, he will never become aware that these new forms, which are so seductive to him, are only trans-formations of earlier forms, that they also have their *raison d'être*, their logic, and conceal under extravagant and falla-cious externals, a solidly built skeleton wherein resides their vitality, their true strength.

The external appearances change, the basis remains the same. This, however, is not understood by the young mu-sician who reads these more recent works with feverish ardour, and, so to speak, intoxicates himself with them, not having as yet developed in himself a spirit of analysis by study of the earlier works, whose plan is more visible, more easily grasped. Those, only, who have been nourished upon the classics of their own time, can become, in their turn, the classics of the future, if so be that they have in them the spark of genius, the creative faculty, without which, whatever they do, they will never be more than musicians of talent, having a right to appreciation as such, but to nothing beyond.

There is not the slightest reason to fear that a thorough study of the classics will stifle inspiration, will restrict it by superannuated forms; examples in multitude prove the contrary.

Berlioz, who could not feel Wagner — which lack of ap-preciation the latter repaid in kind — had a real worship for Gluck and was proud to say that he had made Gluck his model. In turn, Wagner, indifferent towards Berlioz, was a fervent admirer of the author of *Armida*. Was there anything in common between Wagner and Berlioz? It would seem that each must have regarded the work of Gluck from a different point of view, since, equally admir-ing and enthusiastic, they carried out his ideas to results so divergent. Two painters, working side by side, see nature in different ways and produce entirely different landscapes.

Rossini, as I have said elsewhere, studied harmony by

writing out the scores of Haydn's quartets, of which he had only the separate parts; but it is not to be supposed that he did this as a copyist might do it. I have heard him frequently tell the story of this work: he first copied the part of first violin, or of 'cello, of a complete movement, and racked his ingenuity to conjecture how the three other parts were probably built: then he placed these three parts before him and copied them simultaneously, measure by measure, thus seeing the work constructed under his eyes. Was it not, with admirable models, the very same system of harmonic reconstruction which is practised at the present day in our Conservatories, under the name of *partimenti*, *basses* or *chants donnés?* Was it not, also, from the point of view of composition, a marvellous process of analysis?

Rossini, like Gounod, had a passionate admiration, a cult, for Mozart; yet the two men were most unlike, which proves, once more, that study does not involve imitation, and that young composers may analyse the processes of the old masters without fear of losing their own originality, if any they have.

No men among the present leaders of the French school have carried farther the study of the classics than Saint-Saëns and Massenet; but has any abatement resulted in their originality? By no means. They no more resemble each other than they do their models; but both are strong composers, because they have built upon ground of whose solidity they had first thoroughly assured themselves. Thus the complete musicians work, the men to whose genius are added talent and erudition.

There comes a time, however, when it is a duty to read the boldest works of the day; for the composer must be familiar with everything, and whatever may be his own preferences, he is not at liberty to remain ignorant as to the methods of any great school; indeed it is often by borrowing from musical literatures the most opposed to each other that he will finally form his personal style. When the moment has come, it is well to approach the Romantic School through those of its representatives who still offer marked points of contact with the great classics, and to take first the simplest of their works. If the young composer is a pianist, which it is well that he should be, he will advantageously begin with Chopin; then might follow Schumann, especially the *Scenes of Childhood*, the little collections of *Album Leaves*, the *Carnival*, and not till after these, the great chamber music, the Symphonies, and lastly *Paradise and the Peri*.

When the student reaches Wagner and Berlioz,—after whom there will be no further occasion to follow any definite order,—a good precaution is to undertake the systematic reading of one or the other, separately, following, at least very nearly, the chronological order of their productions,[1] to see the process of formation of their style, and to compel one's own mind to pass through the same phases with the master's. In the case of Wagner, especially, the works in his first manner should be studied first,—*Rienzi, The Flying Dutchman, Tannhäuser, Lohengrin*, before taking up *Tristan, The Mastersingers*, the *Tetralogy*, and *Parsifal*,—which not every musical brain, even the best organised, is capable of grasping.

To hear these great works performed, whose orchestration and stage-setting are so intimately connected with the composition properly so called, is of prime importance. Also they should be heard in favourable conditions and in their entirety, which is not easy for every one.

Only after this amount of experience will the neophyte be able intelligently and without presumption to express his preference for the maintenance of the earlier dramatic forms, or for the seasonableness of the Wagnerian reform, whose leading characteristics are as follows: 1. the intimate union of the scenic action and the musical woof; 2, the continuity of successive scenes; 3, the systematic employ of the *Leitmotiv* symbolic of a personage (or an object), of a state of mind, of a fact, of an action, whose invariable hieroglyphic, so to say, it becomes.

1 There is great profit in reading in this way the sonatas, the symphonies, and the quartets of Beethoven, who, in his third style is more truly romantic than classic. (See chap. V.)

I say with intention, "the systematic *employ*," not invention; for it does not seem to me proven that Wagner really
invented this procedure, of the highest expressive power
and of an incomparable luminous intensity. Examples of it
are seen of an earlier date. Is not the story of the Dream
(in the *Prophète*) based upon a marvellous orchestral allu-
sion to the Consecration Scene? Does not the whole score
of *Struensee* teem, from the very beginning of the overture,
with the most moving repetitions of an admirable symphonic phrase, which, after being carried through all the
groups of the orchestra, finds its explanation and its *raison
d'être* only at the very close of the work, in the scene of the
Benediction? If *Struensee* or the *Prophète* had been written this year it would be said that Meyerbeer had adopted
the new formula; why, then, not attribute to him the honour
of having a share in its development? And he is certainly
not alone. Were not overtures constructed by the use of
the chief *motifs* of the work really a sort of presentation of
personages and characters and principal situations? In the
domain of symphony, where it personifies an idea not yet
defined, but a fixed idea, nevertheless, there are numerous
anterior applications of this system, notably in the works
of Mendelssohn, Schubert, Schumann, and also of Beethoven. Is not the *finale* of the Quartet in F major, op.
135, with its curious epigraph:[1] *"Der schwergefasste Ent-*

schluss" quite as much a typical *motif* as it is a procedure
of imitation by contrary motion? In this way we may go
back to the true origin of the system, finding it, at last, *in
the fugue.*

---

[1] "The difficultly-taken Resolution."
[2] "Must it be? It must be! It must be!"

These *Leitmotive*, in their curious entanglements and their very interesting transformations, are treated by Wagner and his disciples—with all the resources of modern art added—exactly as the *subject* and *counter-subject* of a fugue are treated; instead of giving them these purely technical names, there is attributed to each one a conventional and philosophic significance, which determines its use in this or that part of the work, at this or that moment; but, with that exception only, they are worked out on the same principles, though modernised, which were employed in the ancient counterpoint. The only difference is that to their form is attached the definite and invariable idea of one of the heroes (in one instance, a bird, the Swan), or of an action, as the Supper,—or of a character, as the goodness of Sachs,—which allows them to be, notwithstanding the purely apparent complication of their combinations, actual clues guiding the experienced listener through the intricacies of the drama and rendering it extraordinarily clear. In this philosophic systematisation resides (so far as the *Leitmotiv* is concerned) the invention of Wagner, due in the first instance to Bach and the great classicists.

Much more important, and very much more *personal*, is that other part of the Wagnerian reform, which, abandoning the early division into detached movements, each forming a complete whole and often quite independent one of another, substitutes for it a division into scenes, borrowed from the drama, the cohesion of these scenes being further augmented and strengthened by the uninterrupted symphonic action, which follows the dramatic step by step, explains it, and comments upon it. This is truly an invention of genius, for there is no similar attempt of earlier date: the vast conception sprung, as a whole, from the brain of Wagner. Whether it forms a school, or will remain an isolated fact,—which, notwithstanding some recent applications of it, only the future can determine,—it must be saluted with the respect due to the very highest manifestations of the human intellect.

After having studied Wagner and Berlioz, and having

made sure that he well understands their two languages, so different one from the other, the student may then follow his inclination as to reading. He may even read very poor works, to have examples also of what he must not do. But he must not dread plunging again and again into the reading of the classic composers, for it is always there that the great instruction is to be found and the living germ of the future school.

Before finishing these exercises of analysis, I have to mention a fact singular enough to surprise and strongly attract the attention of observing minds; it is that, notwithstanding the uniformity inherent in our system of temperament, each key, major or minor, has peculiar characteristics. It was not by chance that Beethoven selected the key of E flat for the Heroic Symphony, and that of F for the Pastoral; it was in obedience to that mysterious law which assigns to each key a peculiar aspect, a special colour.

I do not assume to say that each key can express only the sentiments which I attribute to it; but merely that here it excels, it has its mastery, that its aptitude for their expression is peculiar.

Each person will regard this aspect according to his own personal temperament; to characterise it in any absolute way would probably be going too far; but, to my own mind, these are the preponderating shades of the different keys, major or minor:

C♯ Major: ?

F♯ Major: rugged.

B Major: energetic.

E Major: radiant, warm, joyous.

A Major: frank, sonorous.

D Major: gay, brilliant, alert.

G Major: rural, merry.

C Major: simple, naive, frank, or flat and commonplace.

F Major: pastoral, rustic.

B♭ Major: noble and elegant, graceful.

E♭ Major: sonorous, vigorous, chivalrous.

A♭ Major: gentle, caressing, or pompous.

D♭ Major: charming, suave, placid.

G♭ Major: gentle and calm.

C♭ Major: ?

A♯ Minor: ?

D♯ Minor: ?

G♯ Minor: very sombre.

C♯ Minor: brutal, sinister, or very sombre.

F♯ Minor: rough, or light, aerial.

B Minor: savage or sombre, but vigorous.

E Minor: sad, agitated.

A Minor: simple, naive, sad, rustic.

D Minor: serious, concentrated.

G Minor; melancholy, shy.

C Minor: gloomy, dramatic, violent.

F Minor: morose, surly, or energetic.

B♭ Minor: funereal or mysterious.

E♭ Minor: profoundly sad.

A♭ Minor: doleful, anxious.

Gevaert, in the first edition of his treatise on orchestration,[2] has given a similar table; I have not consulted it, but it has many points of similarity with the above.

If this curious fact were true only in relation to orchestral music, we should unhesitatingly account for it by the structure and fingering of the different instruments, the keys more or less sharped or flatted suiting each in different degrees; but where this thing becomes really marvellous is when it no less clearly appears in piano and organ music, and even in choral music, where it would seem that the tonalities must resemble each other exactly, being all mere transpositions of each other. But, if you play in C the *Berceuse* of Chopin, which is written in D flat, its beautiful poetic sonority would become crude and flat, almost common. In the same way, the *Funeral March* of the Sonata, op. 26, of Beethoven, which is originally in A flat minor, loses much of its dolefulness when it is transposed into A minor.[3]

It is impossible to say why this is so; but the fact remains. From it results the necessity of attaching importance in the first place to the selection of the principal key and making a choice in accordance with the general character of the proposed work; later, like considerations will influence the direction of the modulations, so that every episode may have its appropriate colouring. At the same time, this is not the only guide to follow, for the composer

1 [Berlioz (*Instrumentation*) also gives a table of characteristics of the keys. Ed.]

2 Ghent, 1863; p. 189.

3 As it is in a well-known collection: *Six Valses et une Marche funèbre.*

should never lose sight of the logic of musical architecture resulting from the relationship of tones, as established so magnificently by the grand structure of the fugue. I have said that the composer *should never lose sight of* this model of solid construction, and not that he must invariably conform to it; indeed there are occasions when he should intentionally desert it,—in a mad scene, for instance, where the wandering of the mind would be best depicted by the incoherence of tonalities the most dissimilar, combinations the most strange; or, in representing violent and opposing passions, passing from love to hate, from the mystic to the grotesque. But then it is genius itself, and not the coolly considered plan, which will require those bold and striking infractions of rules which will suitably represent exceptional situations and psychological conditions.

Nor is this all. The special technic must also have its influence upon the choice of the tonality, the individual character of the instrument or instruments for which one writes, the compass of the voice or voices to which such or such a design is to be entrusted, whose character may be changed completely according to the region, treble, alto, or bass,—brilliant, dull, or feeble,—of the interpreting agent, which also has its own colouring, peculiar to itself.[1]

Plainly, then, this is a question of by no means secondary importance, and merits the most careful attention.

In reading a work for analytical purposes, it is wise to take great care to understand the reasons which influenced the author's choice of this or that key, either for the ensemble, or for the various episodes.

We must know how to read before we can think of learning to write. If one knows a language thoroughly, he not only speaks it, reads it, and writes it, but he also thinks in it with no more effort than in his native tongue, and even dreams in it, which proves how natural, easy, and unconscious is his use of it. Thus the musician ought to surprise himself thinking and dreaming in music; unsolicited

1 See page 181.

rhythms and contours present themselves, groups of chords, modulations, captivating sonorities come into his mind, they take possession of it; he has only to put them on paper, and the creative work is done.

It is by this sign, this obsession of the mind, that he may know if he is mature enough, sufficiently developed, to undertake with some chance of success, the practical study of composition, a study as full of charm to him who has the creative faculty, as it is arid and discouraging to the poor fellow who has deceived himself as to his vocation, a case, alas! only too frequent.

The complement of analytical observation is practice, that is, the attempt to compose, oneself, — conforming strictly to the plan drawn from the composition analysed, seeking also to resemble it in the nature of the ideas, without puerile imitation, — another piece, having the same form, that is to say, able, if in its turn analysed, to receive the same technical description.

In practising this exercise, there is no occasion to seek for originality of ideas, but rather to give them a general resemblance to the manner of the author whose style and procedures are to be assimilated; but, also, the student must by no means think that he has produced a work of art; this is nothing more than a task, a study.

After having many times practised this double exercise of dissection and reconstruction, one may go on to other studies in the same general direction: take a theme of 8, 12, or 16 measures from an author, with or without its harmony, and develop it, afterwards comparing the obtained result with the original work ; or, take a poetic text which some author has already used, and treat it after his method, always for the sake of the subsequent comparison of the two, which constitutes the lesson, etc.

Practice like this makes both the hand and the mind supple, and if there are those to whom it is not necessary, there cannot but be many who will gladly avail themselves of these suggestions.

The student may, also, after having selected a theme which will serve the purpose, set himself the task of treating it in diverse styles and in different forms, varying it, transforming it, disguising it, to the point that it becomes unrecognisable. Excellent examples of diversions of this kind are given by Beethoven in the finale of his Ninth Symphony; by Schumann in his *Études Symphoniques;* by Bizet in the overture to *l'Arlésienne* (which is an overture in the form of an air with variations); and, most of all, by Wagner, in his latest works; also in *Manon* and in *Esclarmonde,* where Massenet has so well exploited—without doing it intentionally, and above all, while remaining sincere, extremely individual, and entirely French—the Germanic procedure of typical *motifs;* also, in the *Ascanio* of Saint-Saëns.

One of the things which young composers sometimes rather foolishly find embarrassing, is the application to composition of the rules of harmony.

It is, however, the simplest thing in the world, harmony being only a branch of composition. I begin by saying that these rules are all to be observed; not one can be omitted. But there is one which may be modified, the one concerning consecutive octaves, and these are the modifications:

1. It is allowed to double in octaves, in order to strengthen it, any part, or to triple or quadruple it, provided it be made perfectly clear that this is done with intention; that is to say, that it is not, for example, a doubling of two or three notes, which would be merely a blunder, but of the whole of a melodic contour which it is desired to strengthen, to bring out in relief.

2. It is always allowed to double in octaves the principal melodic part—even for no more than two notes—by any of the other parts (especially when there is a vocal or instrumental solo), provided this does not form octaves with the bass.

To this we may add that it is always permitted, from the

point of view of analysis, to suppose that the harmonic
parts are divided or united, so that a sequence of chords,
beginning in two parts, may, by the division of a part or
of more than one, become successively in three or four
parts, then in five or more, and inversely ; and it will be
easy to see that the composer is not restrained, hampered,
but rather is aided and guided by the laws of harmony and
counterpoint, which are really very elastic for him who well
understands them and has assimilated them.

The one essential thing is that it should be always possible to analyse the harmony and find its plan correct, the
slight modifications mentioned above being allowed, as absolutely indispensable for the orchestration.

Another subject of surprise to beginners in the art of
composition is that there could possibly be, that there have
been, and that there still are, scales differently constituted
from our European scales; the modes of the plain chant,
the ancient Greek tonalities, the Oriental scales, the five-
note scales of the Bretons, Scotch, Chinese, etc.

There are, however, in spoken language, things analogous, and quite as extraordinary, which appear to us so
natural that we give them no attention.

Thus, in French there are five vowels and two diph-
thongs : *a, e, i, o, u, ou, eu,* which are seven distinct sounds ;
but our neighbours the Italians, of Latin origin like ourselves, have never thought of using the sounds *u* and *eu,*
which their vocal organs could pronounce as well as ours
do, and limit themselves (except in certain dialects) to
the five sounds : *a, e, i, o, ou* (writing this last *u*). The
same is true of the Spaniards.

Inversely, alone in Europe the French use the nasal vowels:
an, en, in, on un ; the *e* mute is also peculiar to the French
language, while the Slav languages possess varieties of
sounds so foreign to our ears that it would be impossible to
represent them here, even employing figured pronunciation.
How many different shades, under the influence of different accents, the French letter *e* may take, and in English

the letter *a*, without any modifying sign at all, purely as a matter of custom! These delicate gradations in spoken sound are even much more subtle in Chinese and Japanese languages which, accordingly, serve much better than the European in playing upon words. An *a* or *e* a little more open in sound or a little closer, and the meaning of a word, or indeed of a whole sentence, is quite altered. These are surely differences more minute than the quarter-tones which certain theorists find in the music of the Eastern peoples.[1]

Let us examine the consonants. The English soft *th* and the Spanish *c* (*ceta*) are almost alike to a French ear; they are formed by putting the tongue between the teeth, and are not unlike what is called in French, *zézaiement;* this is a kind of lisp, which we do without very willingly, considering it as a defect. The modern Greek contains this sound, and writes it *th.* The German hard *ch* is almost equivalent to the Spanish *jota*, which is written *j;* this is a gutteral sound unknown to the French language. In France, the Tourangeau rolls his *r*'s, the man of the South burrs.

I limit these comparisons to languages of which the reader will have some idea; but it is clear from what has been said that the innumerable tongues spoken in the various regions of the world contain vowel and consonant sounds which any human lips could utter, after more or less prolonged study, but of which the need is not felt by ourselves, which we do not employ, of which we have not even an idea. The proof, if one were needed, is that there is not in the world any single alphabet capable of writing satisfactorily, even by the use of phonetics, all the words of every living language; and the same remark applies also to many of the dead languages.

The gamut of spoken sounds varies, then, with the epoch and the country. The same is true of the dialects of music. Each civilisation has adopted a scale or more than one, constituted, according to its degree of advancement, more

---

1 These so-called quarter-tones arise simply from the imperfections of instruments, or from a peculiar drawl, a kind of mewing, in singing.

or less arbitrarily or scientifically, outside of which every-thing is thought barbaric or abnormal.

But this is not true. There are other modes besides our scales — the major, the minor in its two forms, and the chromatic made enharmonic by our system of temperament. All the old modes subsist because they have been used and have had their logical *raison d'être*, and all the foreign modes should be known and studied.[1] And it may be that in a return to the use of these manifold melodic tonalities, with their inexhaustible wealth of expression and picturesqueness, combined and revivified by the ad-mirable technic of the present day, and embellished and adorned with the treasures of an ever-improving orchestra-tion, lies the near future of musical evolution.

I cannot conclude this section without exhorting the young composers of France to take care, above all things, to preserve to French art the characteristic qualities which have always been its glory, conspicous in all the great epochs, namely, clearness, elegance, and sincerity of expres-sion. This is the only way for them to be natural, and to succeed in creating a style and personality of their own; for whenever they wander from the inherent traditions of the race, from the genius of the language and from the true spirit of the country, they become only awkward imitators and plagiarists; they remind one of men speaking with difficulty and with a ridiculous accent some foreign tongue.

Wagner — not to be suspected of any special affection towards us — wrote as follows:[2] "I perceive in the French admirable skill in giving exact and elegant form to life and art; I have already said, on the other hand, that the Ger-mans, when they seek this perfection of forms, seem to me heavy and incapable." Other qualities they have, which, in us, would be faults; let us not seek to acquire these, but devote ourselves to the cultivation of our own.

[1] We shall have occasion to describe some of these in speaking of the history of Music, Chap. V.

[2] Letter to M. Monod, director of the *Revue historique*, Oct. 25, 1876.

Verdi gives us the finest example of a straightforward development of genius, constantly improving, from *Nabucodonosor* and *Ernani* up to *Falstaff*, without the slightest deviation, without borrowing anything from foreign schools, always remaining himself, always frankly Italian.

These are topics for serious meditation for all young men who have the noble ambition of adding their stone to the edifice of musical art; for the admiration, however ardent, of the masterpieces of a foreign musical literature, must never become so exclusive and absorbing as to destroy those precious qualities of charm, simplicity, and distinction, which are the appanage of our national style.

B.—Of Improvisation.

Improvisation is a composition which is instantaneous and leaves no trace of itself except in the memory. Here we find ourselves confronted by those two great factors, genius and talent, which we need not again define or compare. But in improvisation, even more than in written composition, is felt the importance of a logical plan guiding the inspiration, keeping it within the limits of musical good sense, and preventing it from going astray in aimless wanderings.

The only instruments truly adapted to improvisation are the autonomous, those forming, each in itself, a complete whole: in the first rank, the organ; after this, the piano and the harmonium; instruments with key-boards, in a word. It is possible, certainly, to improvise on the harp and the guitar, because these instruments can suffice alone; but it is scarcely practical. With the other instruments, strings, wood, or brass, and also with the human voice, there can be improvised only passages of virtuosity, cadenzas, more or less developed; this is not true improvisation as we have defined it. The perfect type of the successful improvisator is the organist, when he has under his hand a fine instrument which he knows how to use to its full range.

Then, improvisation is one of the highest musical pleasures; but it requires, besides complete technical skill and a fertile imagination always at command, much coolness, readiness, courage, and prompt decision, qualities difficult to find united, which is the reason that great improvisators are rare.

Except for very brief pieces, like short preludes, the musician should never attempt an improvisation without a plan determined, or at least projected, both as to the general scope of the movement and the tonalities to be used, with the degree of importance of each. This plan may be varied to any extent, but it must have been formed, and the improvisator must always remember whence he came and whither he is going, leaving nothing to chance or the mechanical habit of the fingers. It will frequently happen that, led away by his imagination or by some lucky find, he will for the moment desert his plan, but without forgetting it and tending always to come back to it again.

Also, he must never lose sight of the principal theme or the secondary themes upon which his improvisation is built, drawing from fragments of them the developments of which they are capable, making these fragments the subjects of the principal episodes, or of many new and unexpected *divertimenti*, and seeking constantly to create variety in unity; for the final impression which a beautiful improvisation should leave upon the mind is that of a work matured at length, strongly built, and written out at leisure. Such also it should appear when, by a system of musical stenography (which is yet to be invented), by Carpentier's melograph or Edison's phonograph, we shall be able to note it on the wing, that we may examine it in detail and with deliberation.

A test of the improvisator is the fugue. We hasten to say that it would not be reasonable to require one as elaborate, as rich in ingenious combinations as if it were coolly studied and written out; frequently it will be a free fugue, in which, however, there will be the general form, and all the characteristic constituent elements of this kind of composition. In all other forms of musical composition, on the contrary, the man of genius may find himself freer when unhampered by the limitations and delays of writing. This, notably, was the case with Beethoven, Mozart, Hummel, Mendelssohn, whose improvisations, it is said, were superior to their written works.

The exigences of the Roman Catholic ritual require the organist of the great organ to improvise almost constantly as he follows the service; consequently it is among the organists of our time that the greatest improvisators are to be sought; and this constant practice, developing spontaneity in them, gives to their written works generally a special freedom.

To become an improvisator, one must first of all understand thoroughly the art of composition, must be a skilled virtuoso upon his instrument so that he is unhampered by any difficulty of execution, and must have the natural gift of a fertile imagination. All this being so, it remains to acquire experience. For this purpose it is well to practise daily, but not for a very long time at first; select a theme, write it out, with or without its harmony, and place it before you on your musicstand, deciding, according to its character and rhythm, in what form it shall be developed, whether as a Prelude, the Allegro of a Sonata, an Offertory, a Minuet an Aria with variations, a Finale, a March, etc. A rapid analysis is made to see what are the fragments available for episodes and digressions, then fling yourself boldly into your work. An improvisator must habituate himself to avoid hesitation, even when he has lost his way, and to return as quickly as possible to the great lines of the plan on which he has decided. Later he will not need to write out the theme, his memory will furnish it.

Those persons, therefore, who suppose that the improvisator abandons himself uncontrolled to the chances of inspiration, that he rushes headlong into the unknown, have the falsest notion of his art that it is possible to hold, and the most unworthy, also. The great improvisator is, on the contrary, the most sagacious, well-balanced, level-headed of musicians; these conditions are indispensable.

I do not say that it never happens even to him, having attained the very height of virtuosity, to feel at times as if he were obeying the mere caprice of his mind; but his mind has come into such training that he could not, if he would, let himself be carried beyond the limits of good sense, and his very fingers would refuse to execute combinations which sound logic could not sanction.

In the case of a few rare individuals the faculty of improvisation is native, intuitive, existing in the absence of all technical knowledge; these are phenomenal cases, to be explained perhaps by the theory of anterior existence, — they are prodigies like the natural calculators, Jacques Inaudi or Vito Mangiamele. Even these musicians would do well to acquire some ideas of harmony and counterpoint that they might avoid errors otherwise than by the mere spirit of imitation or by routine.

To listen frequently to able improvisators, to attend their performances or the services of the Roman Catholic Church, would help much to develop the numerous qualities required for the exercise of this grand art; and also, the reading, the analysis, criticism, and repeated hearing of strongly thought-out works of all periods and all schools.

Let it be said at this point that usually opinions are too hastily formed in respect to any great musical production. I do not think there lives the musician capable of determining on a single hearing the exact value of a work in whose production months, or even years, have been spent.

Newspaper critics are forced, by the requirements of the public, to perform constantly this presumptuous *tour de force*. The man who required forty-eight hours for reflection, or a second hearing, would be regarded as incapable of rendering a judgment, or, at least, of doing his work in time. Hence we often see these critics obliged (according to the individual temperament of the man) either to modify an opinion expressed until it is almost unrecognisable, or else to persist obstinately in an error of judgment, lest he should seem to vacillate.

When *Faust* was first performed, a very famous critic of that day asserted that nothing in it would live except the *Valse* and the Soldiers' Chorus; later, another, of equal renown, accepted in *Tannhäuser* only the March (because he already knew it) and the Romance of the Star. Errors like these are repeated continually, because an opinion must be formed on the instant; I do not refer at all to questions of prejudice, of partiality, or of bad faith, which have no connection with the subject.

Before forming an opinion of a work it is indispensable to feel sure that one has completely understood it. So long as anything remains obscure, one should feel that possibly there may be beauty here accessible to a mind other- wise moulded than his own. It is fair to say of a thing that it is hackneyed, unsuited to a situation or a character, badly harmonised, badly orchestrated, and so on; for this opinion implies that the thing has been understood, or at least that the critic believes himself to have under- stood it. But it is unjust to say : " This is poor, for I do not understand it at all; I don't know what it means; consequently, it is worthless."

And besides, it is not necessary — far from it — that a thing should be understood by every one before it can truly be called beautiful.

I enter a lecture room where an orator is making an address in German which seems to fill his audience with enthusiasm; I listen with all my ears, but his address says nothing to me. Am I justified on this account in saying that his hearers are all deceived and that the address has no merit ? By no means, the fact is merely that I have the misfortune not to understand German.

If in this same hall it happened — most unfortunately for the lecturer — that all the audience were like myself, that all were ignorant of the German language except one man, that man alone would be the judge, and alone would have the right to say whether the address were good or bad.

It is the same in regard to music. Only he who is familiar with a given musical language can be permitted to say whether a work conceived in that manner, that style, has or has not real value; outside of this condition he can say but one thing, whether it pleases him or not, which is an altogether different matter.

Auber and Félicien David did not understand Wagner and Berlioz, nor did these latter understand each other; every man of the four spoke a different language.

Here a very natural objection presents itself. Music, it will be said, is, after all, addressed to the public; and if the public cannot understand it —?

Granted; but the manifestations of the highest art are addressed to an enlightened public, to that which has obtained by a certain amount of study the power to understand this special literature, and alone can fully enjoy it. For others, there is easy music, — that of the operetta and the café concert.

Certain superficial critics like to complain periodically that music seems to have become, in our days, a science based upon figures, mathematics, mental processes, and in this they think they see the negation of pure art, of inspiration. They prove in this way but one thing, — that they do not know the history of the art of which they constitute themselves defenders. In the time of Bach and of Handel, as also in the Middle Ages, when discant and counterpoint were the only music of any importance, music was an art vastly more mathematical than at present; it addressed itself to the mind, not to the senses, and could scarcely be understood except by those who had made it a study.

Now, most if not all of the procedures employed by living masters are borrowed from that great period; and borrowed is not even the correct word; it is a lawful inheritance which they have received from their predecessors, and they use it, accommodating it to the taste of the day, that is to say, obeying their own personal sentiment and feeling the influence of the artistic current around them, as well as the general movement of modern ideas. Thus it has always been and always must be. The grandest musical genius can create nothing without having a point of support in the works of his predecessors; for in music, as in every other thing, every man is some one's son. This is evolution.

To some, who liken artistic evolution to the changes in fashion, art seems to turn in a circle, passing successively through similar periods. To others, music appears to advance perpetually, rising to greater heights in every age. Both conceptions seem to me false or incomplete taken alone, and give me, on the other hand, an impression of truth if united into one formula.

To my mind, the progress of art through the ages may be represented by an ascending spiral which at each turn passes the same points of a vertical plane, but at different heights, forever drawing nearer to a point situated in the infinite, which is the ideal. It is the same spiral advance as that which leads the sun, with his train of planets revolving about him, while about them revolve their satellites, towards a point in the constellation Hercules, seemingly forever receding as he approaches, as the ideal forever recedes before the efforts of art.

Another subject of perpetual recriminations is the constant increase of sonority, an inevitable result of the progress of orchestration. It is certain that we no longer have the orchestra of Lully, nor even that of Boïeldieu. Berton saluted Rossini "il signor Vacarmini!" Rossini himself considered the works of the German school of his time as little else than noise. What would he say now, poor fellow?

Since that time, sonority has still further increased; there is much complaint, it is considered excessive; but we reconcile ourselves to it, and probably it will be further still increased.

From the purely symphonic point of view, this is no disadvantage. It is only in the musical drama that it might be feared the voices of the singers could not rise above the tumult, if it should please the composer to unleash at the wrong time his instrumental pack; but this will never happen to a man of talent and of experience in the art of orchestration, an art comparatively young but extremely progressive; and this fear is purely chimerical.

At the present time, in opera, the interest is divided between the stage and the orchestra nearly equally, leaning rather to the side of the symphony, contrary to what was the preference in the first half of the century.

A rapid glance at some points in the history of music will suffice to prove to us that the ideal has varied widely in different times and countries; that at present it is far from being everywhere the same, and that it is certain still further to vary in the future. On the other hand it appears to be indisputable that what is beautiful today cannot cease to be beautiful tomorrow, and that latitudes can make no difference here. The beautiful is unchangeable, it is eternal, it is world-wide: what varies is our manner of looking at it.

What, then, is the beautiful in music?

So many definitions have been attempted that I scarcely venture to propose mine; it would be this:

The beautiful in music consists in a fortunate harmony of proportions, and also in the penetrating intensity of the emotions it communicates.

These two conditions seem to me indispensable, and are each other's complement; I do not know a masterpiece worthy of the name which does not unite the two. It must, above all, stir, excite the soul, that is to say, awaken or depict emotion; also, it must bear calm analysis; only thus can it call out an admiration at once enthusiastic and rational — which means an admiration that will be lasting.

One may up to a certain point love music without understanding it, and even without seeking to understand it. In this case it is merely a gratification of the senses, a social diversion; music then becomes what is called an accomplishment, essentially frivolous and superficial.

But one cannot understand it without loving it; for the mere analysis of the emotions it arouses in us and of the procedures by which these emotions are produced, becomes a source of intellectual pleasures, pure and infinite, unknown to those who have not made it the object of special study, and for whom true music, the music of musicians, will remain always a sealed book.

CHAPTER V.

HISTORY OF THE ART OF MUSIC.

A. — The Ancients.

To sing is as natural for the human being as to speak; it therefore seems probable that the earliest men were the earliest singers.

Certain cries — of calling, of joy, of grief especially — have an evident musical character, and are susceptible of notation. The vocal manifestation, then, must necessarily and everywhere, in prehistoric times, have preceded all instrumental beginnings, even the most rudimentary.

Furthermore we may naturally suppose that in the beginning of every civilisation, the first instrument invented — or it would be better to say, discovered — must have been the simplest of all, something which mere chance brought to hand. And this was the fact; everywhere the reed, the flute made of a reed, was the first musical implement; the idea of blowing into it to clear it was very natural, and this was all that was necessary to produce a first instrumental sound.

The model of rhythm is furnished by certain natural movements, the alternate step, the beating of the heart, the throbbing of the temples; by respiration which, binary when one is awake, becomes ternary in sleep; by the regular gait of the horse, the trot and the pace in duple time, the gallop in triple.

Such are the points of departure which nature offers.

In its origins, music seems to have developed more slowly and with greater difficulty than any of the other arts, which less subtle and ethereal, responded to more urgent needs. Moreover, its beginnings are lost to us in thick darkness by the absence of written documents. In scarcely any other way than from the old bas-reliefs and fresco-paintings, or from papyrus-rolls, do we know that music was in very high honour among the Assyrians and the ancient Egyptians. By means of these we know the names and forms of their instruments which were numerous and well-made, but we have no idea as to the music thus produced. They had fine harps, with from three to twenty-two strings, perhaps more; lyres and guitars, with three and four strings, which they called *tambourah ;* many percussion-instruments of all forms and sizes,— sistra, bells, crotala, cymbals, single and double flutes, etc. Thus we see that the three great families of musical instruments, string, wind, and percussion, were already represented (but they had not made the discovery of the bow); and still, we are reduced to the barest conjectures as to the character of the music, sacred and profane, which was produced.

From this very remote antiquity nothing is discovered which gives any reason to suppose that the writing of music was known, either to the Egyptians, the Chaldeans, or the Syrians; and this is true, also, of the Hebrews, for the Talmud, which mentions everything, would not have failed to describe a procedure, however primitive in form, by which the chants of the ritual could be preserved intact. But the Talmud is silent on this subject, whence we conclude with something like certainty that in those remote ages, musical airs, probably of the most rudimentary kind, were handed down by oral tradition only, as is today the case with the Arabs and other oriental nations, even those quite advanced in civilisation.

(The Rabbinical notes are nothing more than *neumes,*[1] entirely indefinite, of which the key is lost, and hence their interpretation very doubtful.)

We know, however, that music was extremely important among the Jews, especially in their religious ceremonies,

1 See *Neumes,* p. 389.

for the Bible speaks of this constantly. Their instruments were evidently the same as those of the Egyptians, and rhythm must have been the chief point in their music, judging by their many percussion-instruments, and also by their uncommon taste for dancing. If we may believe Josephus, Solomon had made, for the dedication of the temple, two hundred thousand trumpets and forty thousand other instruments in gold or silver, to accompany the Psalms of David. I have not been able to verify this statement, but, even if it be exaggerated, it gives reason to believe that music, in Biblical times, was no secondary accessory. In war, the Jews used only trumpets, some straight, others curved.

It is odd to think that among the Greeks, at a time when poetry, painting, sculpture and architecture had attained the greatest heights, music was still in its infancy. They knew neither harmony nor even melody, as we conceive it; all musical interest for them consisted in rhythmic combinations and the union of these with prosody; music was the humble slave of poetry; it was rather a sort of rhythmed and droning diction, which must have gone well with the immobility of the tragic mask. As to instruments, their only use was to guide and sustain the voice of the declaimer, to give him the pitch, and to accentuate the rhythmic forms.

In Greece, music was never separated from poetry, and usually it was accompanied by dancing; in truth, the three arts united actually made but one, and that one had great expressive force. The personages of the chorus sang the rhythmic words, and danced as they sang; and it was this union which the Greeks called music, the Art of the Muses.

It always seems marvellous that a people who had *double* flutes, *double* trumpets, harps and lyres of many strings, never thought of producing two sounds at the same time, that they never, by accident, discovered harmony, having in other directions an artistic feeling so highly developed. Numerous controversies on this subject have sprung up.

But no text makes mention of any Greek use of simultaneous sounds, and (which is even a stronger proof) the Orientals of today, though they also have instruments capable of producing chords, and, through contact with European civilisation, have the example of our system, always cling to their purely melodic and rhythmic music. It must, therefore, be admitted that the Greeks practised homophony alone, which sufficed for their needs; and this gives yet another proof that the fact is not always the probable thing.

It is from the writings of the philosophers, Pythagoras (540 B. C.), Plato (430 B. C.), Aristotle and Aristoxenes (IV. Cent. B. C.), that we gain some vague idea of what Greek music must have been; it is certain that they knew the semi-tone, the tone, some say the quarter-tone, and they had the three systems, diatonic, chromatic, and enharmonic. The extent of their general scale was about three octaves, corresponding to the limits of the human voice. They had numerous modes, each constituting a different scale, which they divided into two parts, and of which the denominations and even the number vary according to different authors; the following is the list according to Alypios (IV. Cent. A. D.).

Low.	Medium.	High.
Hypo-Dorian.	Dorian.	Hyper-Dorian.
Hypo-Ionian.	Ionian.	Hyper-Ionian.
Hypo-Phrygian.	Phrygian.	Hyper-Phrygian
Hypo-Æolian.	Æolian.	Hyper-Æolian.
Hypo-Lydian.	Lydian.	Hyper- Lydian.

We also know the names of the strings of the lyre; the following series corresponds to the descending scale:

E.	Nētē.	⎫
D.	Paranētē.	⎬ Second Tetrachord.
C.	Tritē.	⎪
B.	Paramesē.	⎭
A.	Mesē (central tone).	⎫
G.	Lichanos.	⎬ First Tetrachord.
F.	Parhypatē.	⎪
E.	Hypatē.	⎭
D.	Proslambanomenos.	Added string.

For sol-faing they employed the syllables, *te, tu, tê, to,* applied equally in all the tetrachords.

In conclusion, the Greeks possessed a very complicated system of notation, formed by means of the letters of their alphabet, modified, inverted, etc., and varying for vocal or instrumental music. In this form have come down to us a few rare hymns or fragments, whose translation, in the present state of our knowledge on the subject, is unfortunately very uncertain.

It was not, however, in Greece, but in India that the idea of defining sounds by writing, had its origin. The Hindus designated the notes of the gamut by Sanskrit characters, and appear also to have known how to indicate time-values; but the interpretation of these signs is so vague that we can only say that there was a system, of which the present inhabitants of India have preserved nothing, not even the recollection.

The Persians, who called music "the science of circles," invented a sort of staff of nine lines, each of a different colour, in which one cannot but find a certain resemblance to our own, although ours is not derived from it.

As long ago as 2700 B. C., the Chinese represented the notes of their gamut — which appears vastly more complex than it really is — by ideographic signs resembling those of their language, and these they still have in use at the present day.

The Japanese, the Tonkinese, and the Annanites have had systems of the same kind, but have gradually abandoned them under the influence of European culture.

To return to the Greeks, it is absolutely certain that, before the time of Pythagoras, they had begun to employ the letters of the alphabet to designate musical sounds, and we know almost exactly the signs by which they represented, with comparative precision, values and rests, which were, as with us, in double or triple time, while China and Japan have known no other than the double time.

Imitating the Greeks, the Romans adopted first, in writing music, the first fifteen letters of their alphabet.

Originally the Latin music could not have differed materially from the Greek, which was its direct ancestor; there were the same scales, the same use of the lyre, the cithara, and the percussion-instruments, especially after the conquest of Greece. The flute and the trumpet were the favourites, but Nero, and other emperors after his time were pleased to sing, accompanying themselves upon the Etruscan lyre.

Two new instruments, no less different in character than they have been in destiny, yet founded on the same principle, of the air-reservoir, date from this epoch: the bagpipe and the organ. The former remained the popular instrument in Scotland, Brittany, and Italy, under various names; while the organ, according to contorniate medallions[1] preserved in the Bibliothèque Nationale and in many other museums, very early had its dozen pipes. It has increased remarkably since then; but the germ is there. Ctesibius (145 B. C.) is supposed to have been the inventor; perhaps, however, the first idea was Greek.

But an important event was about to take place, which was destined completely to overthrow the old systems and open to art a new road which it has followed definitely up to the present time; I refer to the advent of Christianity.

For dying Paganism, the plastic arts had sufficed, with the poetry that likened its gods to men. To dawning Christianity which, elevating the soul, freed it from material dross and opened to it infinite horizons, a new art was necessary, more powerful, more independent, above all, more penetrating; an art which, disdaining to depict or to represent objects or deeds, was capable of acting directly upon the soul, isolating it, making it captive, producing emotion unaided; an art no longer to be the slave of poetry, but its equal and its master, raising it to heights hitherto unknown and inaccessible, in the domain of the pure ideal, into which words cannot enter, for which they are insufficient.

---

1 These are bronze medals peculiar in the fact that they are encircled by a deep groove (*contorniate*). They were never used as coin, but were struck in commemoration of historic events.

Under the influence of this mighty afflatus, from its shapeless, earlier attempts came forth slowly and painfully the still primitive and uncertain art of the Middle Ages, which was destined to pass through numerous changes before itself giving rise to the modern art.

During the first eight centuries of the Christian era, the church chant remains exclusively homophonous. The most ancient Christian chants are those of the Psalms, which belonged to the Hebrew cult, and a few Greek or Latin melodies. S. Ambrose, Bishop of Milan (340–397), preserved four of the Greek modes, which later were called "the authentic modes," and attached his name to a first reform of the melodic liturgy, which he frees from superfluous ornament, retaining in it a rhythmic feeling of which the tradition is lost.

Later, Gregory the Great (540–604), proceeding to a new reform, excluded from the ritual certain chants which seemed to him unworthy, admitted, besides the four modes of S. Ambrose, four other modes, which take the name "plagal" or "collateral," and made the collection called the Antiphonary of St. Gregory, which is still in use, with, however, numerous modifications, in the Roman Catholic churches. From this time, the church-modes are eight in number; the authentic modes have their dominant on the fifth degree, the plagal on the fourth.

Agreement of the old Greek modes with the Church modes.

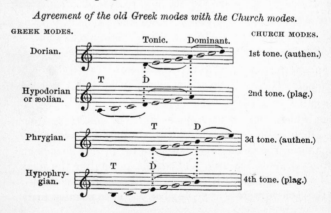

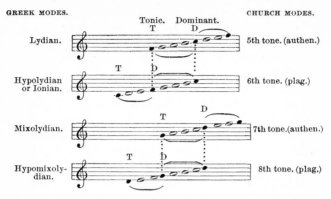

It was, also, during the pontificate of S. Gregory, to whom personally some authors attribute this reform, that the Romans reduced their notation to the first seven letters, which are also applied to the seven notes of the modern nomenclature:

A   B   C   D   E   F   G

A fact whose extreme interest will be apparent to everyone is, that these designations have been preserved intact across the centuries, that they are still employed in Germany and in England, and that we shall, later, find here the point of departure and explanation of the system of clefs as now in force; and the letters which are today over the strings of the piano are the last vestige of these dead civilisations.

B.— The Primitives.

Then followed, to last through the larger part of the mediæval period, an odd system, now incomprehensible, consisting of signs, a kind of hieroglyphics or abbreviations, which were called *neumes*, derived, doubtless, from the rabbinical notes, and having only a purely conventional meaning. The neumes did not indicate precise sounds on distinct degrees, but groups of sounds, not unlike the signs of the turn and the trill (∾ and ⌁) in modern notation; of these there were a large number. I have counted forty in an old MS.   The most eminent scholars in music have sought to decipher them, but not a man has been able to give them a satisfactory translation; the individual meaning of each is fairly well understood, but nothing indicates the connection among them or the point of departure of the tonality.

The Carthusians themselves, who have preserved intact, by tradition, the plain-chant of the eleventh century, were able to give me the translation of a few signs only; but it seemed to me interesting to record this, here.   The following table, prepared in accordance with the information given at the monastery of La Chartreuse, by one of the fathers who is very learned in liturgic music, contains:

1. The name of the neumatic sign;
2. The sign itself in the forms of the XI., XIII., and XIV. centuries;
3. Its signification;
4. Its translation into the characters of the plain-chant;
5. Its translation into the notation now employed.

The sounds not being fixed, but only indicating the vocal contour, I use no clefs and could not use any, since all these signs represent only kinds of vocal exercises, vocal feats, inflexions of all kinds, applied to a liturgic chant transmitted from age to age by oral tradition.   (The chant of the Carthusians differs considerably from the usual church chant.)

"Most of the neumatic signs are modified to indicate intervals and durations of the sounds they represent; they are also surmounted by certain letters indicating the tempo they should have; all these things, it must be confessed, render their reading very difficult, and have become at the present day a source of discussions and of varying interpretations among authors.

". . . It was not until the tenth century that the practice began of writing the neumes at different heights above the text, to indicate their respective places in the scale.   When Guido Aretino invented the staff,[1] he had at first no other idea than that of applying it to the neumatic signs in order to render it easier to read them."

Thus wrote the Rev. Father Charles Marie, a former

---

[1] We shall soon see that this is a mistake.

XI. XIII. XIV. centuries.

Name	Description
Virga..... Virgula.....	Long, isolated note, origin of the note with stem (of the plain chant).
Punctum...	Short, isolated note, origin of the "brevis."
Clivis, Clivus ... or Flexa	Two notes descending, with interval of second, third, fourth, or fifth; the first, long; the second, short.
Podatus....	The opposite of the *clivis*. Two notes ascending; the first, short; the second, long.
Torculus...	Three equal notes, the second always the highest.
Climacus..	A long note followed by two or three short notes descending, in successive or separated intervals.
Scandicus..	The opposite of the *climacus*.
Pressus....	Origin of the trill. Used at the end of phrases, in cadences.
Quilisma...	Origin of the *tremolo* or *vibrato*. A trembling on a note followed by a long higher note at an interval of a third, with a passing-note.
Distrophus.. Tristrophus.	Repetition of a note, according to the number of signs placed together.

prior of the Grande-Chartreuse, in a work now very rare: *Méthode de plain-chant selon les usages cartusiens.*

Of all the systems of notation known, this was certainly the most incomplete as well as the most barbaric up to the time when some one formed the idea of enriching it with a horizontal line, usually in colour, red or yellow, representing a given tone, above which or below which were placed the neumes, at distances greater or less which approximately represented the intervals.

In this single line we see the germ of the staff.

From these two elements, the names of notes designated in Greek or Roman letters and the line necessary to render intelligible the mediæval neumes, was destined by degrees to emerge the whole present system.

The manifest advantage of the one indicating line which made it possible for the neumatic signs to indicate intervals with some degree of precision, naturally suggested the idea that this precision and this advantage might be increased by using two lines; and, in fact, with two lines, widely spaced, it became possible to give a fairly satisfactory graphic representation of a scale of nine notes, more than was needed for the notation of church hymns.

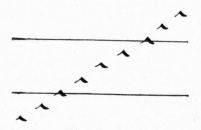

To determine the absolute height of the notes, there was placed at the beginning of each line one of the first seven letters of the alphabet, which gave a name to the sign placed on this line, whence, by comparison, the other signs received names. These were our clefs.

This road once open, there was no reason why the staff should not receive a third line, and then a fourth, which happened, to the great benefit of the clearness of the writing; on the other hand, the utility of the neumes, which represented, it will be remembered, groups of sounds and melodic formulas or ornaments, rather than the idea of one definite note, disappeared, in the adoption of a more precise and logical system; accordingly, they were gradually abandoned, and instead were used characters either square or lozenge shaped, ■ ◆, which are the real first notes.

These prolonged attempts to establish a complete notation show plainly enough how great was the interest attaching to the musical movement of the day, which had its centre in Rome. In 754, Pepin le Bref brought to the Abbey of Saint Médard two cantors, whom the Pope (Stephen II.) had given him to teach the Abbey choir. Not long after, in 784, Charlemagne, visiting Rome, took with him his own ordinary cantors, who were much scoffed at by their Roman brethren for their voices "like bulls." He obtained from Adrian I. some of the papal cantors to instruct his own. It is well known that Charlemagne founded two great schools of music,— one at Metz, the other at Soissons.

It was not, however, until near the ninth century that the first attempt was made at harmony (?) to place one note above another, but alas! in the relation of fourth, or of fifth.

This barbaric and primitive system, described and put in practice notably by the monk Hucbald of Saint-Amand (an enthusiastic musician, evidently) was called *diaphony* or *organum ;* in our time the word cacophony would seem more appropriate. We can see in it only an error which retarded the evolution of music by something like five centuries.

Accompaniments for the Gregorian plain-chant were written in two, three, four, and even five voices,— long series of fourths and fifths, without any fear of distorting its character and rhythm, for the diaphony was almost without tempo.

This continued till the thirteenth century, when the melodic sense appeared to progress more rapidly than the harmonic, though the diaphony was transforming itself into a system less brutal, the *descant,* which was nothing else than a first essay at counterpoint in two parts.   At this time lived :[1]

Adam de la Hale (about 1240), called the Hunchback of Arras.

Songs, motets, of a style still showing traces of diaphony, although with progress.

The *Jeu de Robin et de Marion,* which may be considered as the earliest type of the comic opera, was performed at the court of Naples, in 1285.

He appears to have been the first to employ the consonance of the third and its inversion the sixth, which brought into the descant a sweetness hitherto unknown ; he also essayed timidly the use of the perfect chord, but without entirely abandoning the system of consecutive fourths and fifths.   It was, however, an immense step.

Earlier than he came :

Guido d'Arezzo (XI. Cent.), born at Arezzo (Tuscany).

A Benedictine monk in the Abbey of Pomposa, about the year 1023 ; a learned musician, and especially occupied in teaching the liturgic chant.

There is, perhaps, no erroneous opinion more wide-spread than that which attributed to him the invention of the system of notation, as though he had conceived it as a whole and realised it all at once.   We have seen that the system grew up gradually, very slowly, in accordance with the unequally growing and very diverse needs of musical civilisation.

The truth is that he was struck with the difficulty that his pupils, monks like himself, sometimes even prelates, had in grasping and retaining the sound and also the relations of the notes, and devised for their use a pedagogic method which comes under the head of mnemonics.   He

---

[1] There are names of masters, ancient and modern, of theorists, composers, virtuosi, makers of instruments, that every musician ought to know because of the important services they have rendered to art, or of the splendour of their works, or, again, on account of their present conspicuousness. These persons will have special, but necessarily brief, mention, with an enumeration of their titles to the admiration, esteem, or gratitude of musicians.

selected a chant familiar to them all, or at least easily to be learned, in which each line begins with a different note and a different syllable, so that when this chant with its words was fixed in the memory, the position of each note was fixed also.

It was the hymn to S. John (which I reproduce here from an old MS. belonging to the chapter of the Cathedral of Sens,[1] with a translation into modern notation) that he employed.

The first six names of notes: *ut,*[1] *re, mi, fa, sol, la,* are all that the text of the hymn furnishes; but it is curious to observe, were it only as a coincidence, that the initials of Saint John, *Sanctus Iohannes,* S. I., on a *sol* and an *ut,* make a perfect cadence. (Notice the effaced letters.)

Near the beginning of the eleventh century, the notation used was almost the same as in the hymn just given; the principal figures of notes: ⌐ (*duplex longa* or *maxima*), ⌐ (longa), ▪ (breve), ♦ (semi-breve), had each twice the value of the following figure, and sometimes, thrice this value, as in our triplets. There were also certain accessory figures, indicating vocal ornaments, such as the *plicae*

⌐ ⌐ and the ligatures ⌐ ⌐, in which it is easy to

see a last remnant of the deplorable system of neumes. Rests, greater or less in length, were indicated by vertical lines extending a greater or less distance across the staff,

≡≡≡≡ which very likely are, with a totally different use, the origin of our bars of measure, which only began to be used with their present meaning in 1529.

However, this system of writing made its way but slowly; up to the twelfth century, and perhaps later, there are MSS. in neumatic signs. Also, there remains to us nothing of the music of the Mysteries, those curious manifestations of a naïve dramatic art, which drew its subjects from the sacred books, the Old or New Testament, and whose representations were given in the open air, amid natural scenery as is still done at Oberammergau (Bavaria). The great period of the Mysteries was from the X. to the XIII. century; from them is derived the Oratorio.

During that same period, apart from all religious art, our ancestors took pleasure in the *chanson,* martial, sentimental, or Bacchic, the latter often accompanied by dances, and supported by numerous instruments. At this time the nomadic poet-singers, known as *trouvères,* troubadours,

1 [The syllable *ut* is used in French notation instead of *do,* but is gradually giving place to the latter. TR.]

minstrels, bards, *trovatori, minnesingers,* carried *chansons, pastorelles, lais,* and *virelais,* from city to city, teaching the common people, no less than the highest personages in the land, to sing, and creating schools of *ménestrandie.* While schools of scientific music multiplied, the popular art also grew on every side.

The troubadours were not always very respectful towards religion. One of their favourite sports consisted in coupling, according to the rules of the counterpoint of that period, a hymn or chant of the church with some jolly chanson, so modifying each that, when sung together, they were not unmusical. Adam de la Hale (already mentioned) and many others have left deplorable instances of this exercise, profane or at least in bad taste.[1]

An attempt to have two or more melodies carried on at once was at that time the principal aim; the more these melodies differed from each other, the less suitable they seemed to be for each other's accompaniment, the more curious and interesting was the task; accordingly, elegance of the melodic contour was willingly sacrificed, and rhythm was torn to pieces when it did not serve for the desired combination. This study, which appears childish to us now, was useful in preparing for the advent of the fugue; and it differs only by its awkwardness from the applications of modern counterpoint.

The *chanson de gestes* and the *jeux partis* were works literary rather than musical; we have many collections of these, but unfortunately they are somewhat illegible as to the music, being for the most part written in neumes.

A fact characteristic of the epoch and showing that already the symphonic period was at hand, is the great increase in the number of instruments, as well as their improved quality, although not the slightest idea of orchestration yet appears. They were played simultaneously but with no other aim than to increase the volume of sound. There were varieties of flutes, the straight, the traverse,

---

1 It was, however, a step toward the independent motion of the parts, which is now sought and appreciated.

the beaked, the flageolet; in reed-instruments, the oboe, the chalumeau, the bombardo; many kinds of bagpipe, *musette, chevrette;* the brasses are represented by the horn, the cornet, the olifant, the trumpet, the buccina; there were many percussion-instruments, drums, kettle-drums, cymbals, triangles, bells, *carillons*, castanets; the strings were abundantly supplied by the rebec, the viol, the *gigue*, ancestors of the violin; and especially numerous were the instruments with strings plucked or struck,— the lute, *mandora*, guitar, harp, psaltery, *cembalo*, etc. Besides these, there were many more.

The ten-pipe organ of the Romans had made remarkable progress; as early as 951, there was an organ in Winchester which had forty keys, four hundred pipes at least, twenty-six bellows, and required, to be played, seventy bellows-blowers, and two organists who smote with their fists upon keys an ell long, like the Flemish chime-players.

There were also small portable organs called *régales, orguettes*, and *positifs;* in a word, to the manufacture of musical instruments much attention was paid.

During this period, composers were struggling with a monster who has been able to strike terror in periods more recent than the Middle Ages,— the interval, namely, of the augmented fourth, the *tritone*, which they used to call *diabolus in musicâ*, "the devil in music!" This *diabolus* of an interval (occurring only upon one interval of the scale, with its inversion, the diminished fifth (F–B, B–F), which appeared to them so strange and dissonant, that they dared not use it, except as a passing-note) hampered them in their composition as much as it did in their nomenclature; for, by reason of it, neither Guido d'Arezzo nor his successors were willing to give a name to the seventh note of the scale, which led them to adopt a mode of solmisation most inconvenient, that of mutations.

In brief, this was as follows: first, there was not a fixed and invariable sound of each note, as with us.

There were three hexachords, or series of six sounds, to which were applied indifferently the six names of notes, which we may represent to ourselves by our three (modern) scales of F, C, and G, deprived of the leading-tone.[1]

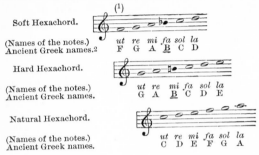

Soft Hexachord.

(Names of the notes.)   ut   re   mi   fa   sol   la
Ancient Greek names.[2]   F   G   A   <u>B</u>   C   D

Hard Hexachord.

(Names of the notes.)   ut   re   mi   fa   sol   la
Ancient Greek names.   G   A   <u>B</u>   C   D   E

Natural Hexachord.

(Names of the notes.)   ut   re   mi   fa   sol   la
Ancient Greek names.   C   D   E   F   G   A

It will be observed that in the soft hexachord the tone B is lowered; it is a B♭; in the hard hexachord it is a semitone higher, a B♮; lastly, in the natural hexachord, there is no B. Hence the old French expression, to sing *par nature, par bémol,* or *par bécarre.*

It is evident that while the melody remained within the interval of a sixth, this made no trouble; but as soon as it exceeded this limit, it was necessary to pass from one series to the other; hence came the mutations, giving rise to the most difficult complications. To sol-fa the following notes, that is to say, to pass from the natural to the hard hexachord, either in ascending:

ut   re   <u>mi</u>   <u>fa</u>   sol   re   <u>mi</u>   <u>fa</u>   sol   la
└—natural—┘   └—hard—┘

or in descending:

la   sol   <u>fa</u>   <u>mi</u>   la   sol   <u>fa</u>   <u>mi</u>   re   ut
└—hard—┘   └—natural—┘

it was necessary in ascending to attribute to the sound *la*

1 In present notation.
2 [Also modern English, American, German and Dutch. Tr.]

the syllable *re*, and in descending, to repeat the *la*, as I have shown in the previous example, where I have indicated the place of the mutation by an M, and have underlined the semitone *mi-fa*, the only one recognised at that time, whence the curious saying: *Mi contra Fa est diabolus in musicâ ;* for here was the unlucky tritone.

That the various functions belonging to the *la* as pivot of the system of mutations should be kept in mind, this note was called by all the names that it received in the different hexachords, joining to this triple designation the letter as well.   Accordingly, the note now called *la* (A), was in old times endowed with the imposing designation, *A mi la re.* The same was done also with the other notes, and in scores of much later date this usage is thus preserved: *"horns in C ut sol"* ; *"trumpets in A mi la."*

In writing music at this time, the staff was employed with points indicating the notes and some neumatic signs, but there was no rule as to the number of lines, which for a long time varied.

Notwithstanding all this embarrassing apparatus, the art made evident progress.   In the fourteenth century appeared the system of *faux-bourdon,* a series of thirds and sixths in three parts coming into use in the place of fourths and fifths ; this was rapidly adopted in France, Germany, Italy, and the Low Countries.

Less hard and brutal than the diaphony, it had, however, the disadvantage of extreme monotony.

Great composers became numerous at this time : **Jean de Meurs** or **de Muris** (1270–1320), better known as a theorist ; **Guillaume Dufay** (1350) and **Ockeghem** (1420), who seem to have been the creators of fugue ; and then, belonging, like them, to the Flemish or Gallo-Belgian school :

Desprès (Josquin), [about 1450–1521].   Born in Hainault.

Learned counterpoint with Jean Ockeghem, and wrote in this style, then in high repute, numerous masterpieces, such as masses, motets, chansons, etc., which were welcomed with enthusiasm by his contemporaries (among whom was Luther), and still remain objects

of admiration to learned musicians. His name is often written
Josquin des Près.

Arcadalt (Jacques), [about 1500]. Born in the Netherlands.

Madrigals, motets, church music, chansons, canticles in great
number; also masses.

Was maestro di capella at the Vatican, and later in the household of the Duke of Guise.

Lassus (Roland de), [1520–1594]. Born at Mons (Belgium).

Orlando Lasso is the name generally given him, although he is
sometimes called Roland Delattre; he was one of the greatest
musicians of the sixteenth century.

Choirmaster at S. John Lateran, Rome, from the age of twenty-
one; later, in the service of Duke Albert of Bavaria; he died insane, in Munich.

His works, admired by those who understand the style of his
time, consist of masses, psalms, motets; and then, in another
range of composition, of chansons and madrigals, all in large number, and of the highest archæological value.

Then, a famous Spanish musician,

Vittoria, [1540?–1608?]. Born at Avila in Spain.

Masses, psalms, motets, in a style resembling that of Palestrina,
for four, five, six, eight, and even frequently for twelve voices.

Goudimel (–1572), a Frenchman, who was the teacher
of the great Palestrina; **Clément Jannequin** (1480?), the
famous author of the *Bataille de Marignan,* a curious
descriptive work, often imitated.

About the same date lived in Germany:

Luther (Martin), [1484–1546]. Born at Eisleben (Saxony).

Music played an important part in his religious reform, for it
was his principle that "music rules the world and renders men
better."

He himself composed the music of many Protestant chorals, of
which one, *Ein' feste Burg,* particularly famous, gave Meyerbeer
important material for his score of *Les Huguenots.*

The Protestant Choral, which came into being after the
close of the mediæval period, differs essentially from the
Catholic plain-chant, in being always composed with the
idea of a polyphonic accompaniment, while the plain-chant,

whether of Jewish, or of Greek or Roman origin, only received this accompaniment as an afterthought, can do without it, and sometimes gains in dignity by the deprivation. These are, then, two manifestations of art which must not be confused with each other.

At this epoch, sacred vocal music, under the influence of secular music, was again loaded with *fioriture* in bad taste and with unsuitable ornaments. Music had become a speculative art; combinations of consonances and dissonances absorbed the attention; it was indeed not so much an art as a science, very interesting to the intellect, but leaving the heart untouched. The contrapuntists of that period had abandoned the system of their ancestors, and still delighted to couple with airs of canticles *chansonnettes* of the most frivolous, or even coarsest character. It is scarcely credible that whole masses were built on this plan, such as the mass of "the Man in Armour," the mass "With two faces and more," the mass of "Friend Baudichon," all of which derived their names from popular songs. This state of things very justly gave offence to religion, and was prohibited by the Council of Trent. Then came Palestrina's great reform.

Palestrina (Pierluigi), [1524–1594].   Born at Palestrina, near Rome, whence his name.

The greatest musical genius of his time. Must be considered as the creator of the true religious style, which he carried to perfection. To this day a model for all the great composers of sacred music.

The catalogue of his works would require many pages; it consists of masses (of which the most celebrated is the one dedicated to Pope Marcellus), motets, hymns, psalms, litanies, the Lamentations of Jeremiah, the Improperia, and also of madrigals in four and five parts, in the secular style of his time.

Neglecting the learned yet puerile combinations which had been in vogue, Palestrina returned to consonant harmony, and seeking only the satisfaction of the ear and a fine progression of the vocal parts, thus attained a fulness and a suavity up to that time unparalleled, which has never been surpassed in the art of writing for voices only. Exempt from all earthly passions, the Palestrinian style remains the purest type of liturgic polyphony.

Also we should mention, among the famous musicians of this period, **Clemens non Papa** (1480–1557), thus called, to distinguish him from the Pope, Clement VII. (his contemporary), author of masses and chants; **Claude Merulo** (1533–1604), organist at Venice and at Parma; **Hans Sachs,** shoemaker, poet, and musician at Nuremberg, one of the heroes of Wagner's *Meistersinger* (let us note in passing that Tannhaüser, Wolfram von Eschenbach, and Klingsor were also *meistersinger,* but living in the thirteenth century); then, some others who have left great names:

Cavalieri (Emilio del), [1550–1600]. Born in Italy.

One of the great Italian contrapuntists; now known only to scholars; his most famous work was his last: *la Rappresentazione dell' anima e del corpo,* which is very much in advance of the works of other composers of the same epoch. He was among the first to employ continuous figured bass, and introduced, if he did not invent, measured recitative.

Allegri, [1560?–1652]. Born at Rome.

Author of a great number of church works, of which the best known is the famous *Miserere,* which is still sung in Holy Week by the Sistine choir.

Frescobaldi, [XVII. century]. Born at Ferrara.

The most skilful organist of his time. He was organist at S. Peter's in Rome, and is believed to be the first, at least in Italy, to play tonal fugues upon the organ. His works are but little known, and are very difficult to read, being written on a double stave of fourteen lines; a number of them, however, have been translated, notably pieces for the harpsichord.

We may also note the progress of violin and other instrument-making:

Amati (Niccolo), [1596–1684]. Born at Cremona.

The most noted violin-maker of this name; there are also Andrea, Niccolo, Antonio, Girolamo, and Guiseppe Amati, all of the same family and nearly of the same date.

Magini, family of violin-makers of the sixteenth century.
(See article on THE VIOLIN, p. 128.)

Ruckers (Hans), [15— –1640].   Born at Antwerp.

Was the most famous of the makers of spinets and clavichords
in his time.   His son and grandson, both having the Christian
name of André, continued and further improved this manufacture.

Their instruments are extremely valued by collectors.

At this point it is interesting to observe the improve-
ments introduced into notation:

In the fifteenth century the system had been largely
improved; white notes had been substituted for black, and
each value had its corresponding rest:

Maxim:

Longa:

Breve:

Semi-breve:

Minim:

Semi-minim:

Fusa:

In the latter we find our eighth notes and sixteenth notes,
and their corresponding rests (the *soupir* and the *demi-*
soupir).

The staff has varied widely; in the remarkable work of
Ernest David and Mathis Lussy[1] from which I have de-

[1] *Histoire de la notation musicale* (Imp. nat., 1882).

rived much information, is given the reproduction of an organ piece by Frescobaldi, dated 1637, written on a double staff of fourteen lines, of which six are for the right hand, and eight for the left hand; also many other examples of the same style and the same epoch. It is also curious to see, in the same work, the series of changes of form through which passed, under the hands of awkward or fanciful copyists, the three letters, F, C, G, before becoming the clefs to which we are accustomed.

As for our accidentals, which would naturally be supposed of one date and the work of one person, they are of widely diverse origin.

The ♭ alone appears in books of plain-chant. It is found there from the year 927.

In some compositions of the fourteenth, or close of the thirteenth century, appears the ♯, but in a slightly different form.

The ♮ dates only from 1650 as cancelling the ♭, but not till the eighteenth century did it apply equally to the ♯.

The ♭♭ and the x are quite recent.

In the sixteenth century, the system of notation having acquired, one by one, as we have seen, all the organic requisites of perfection, no further serious modifications were made except by way of simplification, and in this direction something still remains to be done.

The most interesting of these attempts was the figured bass, a sort of short-hand, invented about 1580; this system of abbreviations, whose chief fault is that it lacks precision, leaving too much to the initiative of the performer, is now used chiefly as an assistance in teaching harmony, and has been described in the chapter on that subject.[1]

In the latter half of the sixteenth century, occurred an event seemingly unimportant, no doubt, at the time, which constitutes, however, one of the turning points in the history of music.

Secular art, keeping pace with sacred, had created the

1 See Page 215.

Madrigal, which is a step in the direction of the Opera.
This kind of composition is a vocal movement in three or
more parts, with or without accompaniment, always in
fugal style or in canon, by means of which the singers express or make known the sentiments of the actor on the
stage.   This was the only form of any importance, and
harmonisation also remained stationary until the day when
the mediæval *diabolus* found at last his master and his
Saint Michael in the person of:

Monteverde, [1568–1643].   Born at Cremona.

This composer was the first to attack chords of the dominant
seventh and ninth without preparation, thus making a new use of
the interval from B to F, or from F to B (the tritone).   By this
daring he created, without clearly understanding the importance
of his innovation, the present tonal system, based upon the tendency of the leading tone and the subdominant, which was destined shortly to dethrone the plain-chant; in him, therefore,
we must do honour to the actual inventor of natural dissonant
harmony,[1] without which the development of the impassioned,
dramatic style of music could never have taken place.

His works, quite incorrectly written, consist of a few operas, *airs
de ballet*, some church music, but especially, many collections of
madrigals for five voices, in which are seen to develop progressively, in the midst of much awkwardness, those audacities which
were to open a new road to expressive art and end in the modern
conception of tonality, with its system of modulations and its sen-
suously impassioned character.

This man of genius opened the way for the musical
drama, and in a general sense for all impassioned music.
The new chords which he introduced into the system, all
contain the *tendency-interval* of the diminished fifth or the
augmented fourth, the use of which is one of the strongest
expressive means in modern music; venturing to attack
without preparation the chords $\frac{7}{+}$, 7, $\frac{7}{5}$, and $\frac{6}{7}$, he was thus
led to practise modulation.   These two elements complete
the material needed for the formation of the dramatic
style, of which Monteverde is considered the actual creator,
a style whose development we shall now see to have been
rapid.

1 See p. 242.

In 1581, **Vincent Galileo,** father of the famous astronomer, filled with admiration for Greek tragedy, attempted
to revive it by having the characters in the drama sing
separately. It will be remembered that up to this time, in
madrigals as well as in mysteries, singing was always
choral or collective, in three, four, five parts. Galileo
called his new style "monody," and here began the *recitative*, lyric declamation. He was also a great theorist and a
skilful organist. The tube of the first telescope constructed
by his son, was, it is said, only an old organ-pipe, cast off,
and adapted by the young astronomer for his purposes, with
lenses fitted into it.

Only a work devoted to the purpose could claim to
enumerate all the great musicians of the sixteenth century,
whose fame has come down to us. I can but mention a few
of the most illustrious :

Carissimi, [1604–1674]. Born at Marino, near Rome.

Great numbers of masses, oratorios, cantatas, motets, and some
light and comic pieces. His style is more animated, vivacious, and
graceful than that of his contemporaries, and has had great influence upon musical evolution.

Cambert, [1628?–1677]. Born in Paris.

One of the founders of the French opera. He shared with the
Abbé Perrin the license of the *Académie Royale de Musique*,[1] at
the time of its creation in 1669, and had for his successor Lully,
1672.

Principal works : *La Pastorale* and *Pomona.*

About 1645 Mazarin introduced into France a taste for
Italian music, an event to be noted on account of its subsequent importance. Not very long after, in 1659, Cambert
performed at Vincennes, before the king, his *Pastorale,*
written with the assistance of the Abbé Perrin ; in 1669,
they had their *Pomona* represented with brilliant success.
Upon this they obtained a license to establish a theatre, in
the rue Mazarin, which was the cradle of the present Opéra,
or, at least, the first attempt of this kind made in France.

---

1 There was a third associate, the Marquis de Sourdéac, who had charge
specially of the scenery.

Cambert and Perrin did not long retain their license; they were ousted by Lully, a wily Florentine, and also a man of much ability and great artistic sagacity.

Lully, [1] [1633–1687].   Born in Florence.

Famous as a composer and as founder of the French Opéra, though here he was in fact preceded by Cambert ; apt at intrigue, much in favour with Louis XIV., and possessing, if not genius, at least great talent at a period when there was not one dramatic composer in France but himself, he had an easy success, obtaining from the king both honours and offices to his utmost desire.

He always asserted that he was by birth a Florentine gentleman ; but we find him, nevertheless, at the age of thirteen a scullion in the household of Mlle. de Montpensier, whence he was expelled for an act of impertinence.   His musical talent gained him admission to the king's band of violins, where he later distinguished himself as a composer, and was appointed leader at the age of nineteen of a band newly organised at the time, and called *Les Petits Violons*, which soon greatly surpassed the other.   This fact indicates his character and talent.   His life was a tissue of selfishness, avarice, and brutality, not to speak of his morals, which were far from correct ; but he retained the royal favour!

If he was quite unworthy of respect as a man, our judgment of him as an artist must be different, for he brought into France all the constituent elements of an art unknown there at the time, from which the opera as we now have it has been developed.

He wrote a score of operas, to which Quinault furnished the librettos, and had them orchestrated by his pupils in a primitive fashion ; important works in church music ; the music for most of Molière's ballets, in which he danced now and then (*le Roy y dansoit bien!*); and a great many instrumental compositions, dances, divertissements, and pieces for special occasions, which contributed to keep him very popular at court.

Mindful that the French nature seeks and appreciates, above all, clearness, simplicity, and correctness of expression, he had the wisdom to abandon the over-luxuriant ornamentation of the Italian style of that day, and produced works that are still interesting, and shine especially by truth of the declamation.

Alceste, Thésée, Persée, Armide, are his principal works.

Then follow **Campra** (1660–1738), born at Aix, creator

[1] The name probably, as Italian, should be Lulli, but he himself signed Lully.

of the opera-ballet, who produced *Hésiode, Idoménée, les Fêtes vénitiennes*; **Destouches,** with the ballet of the *Éléments ;* **Charpentier, Colasse, Mavais, Lalande, Desmarets,** and the great **Rameau.**

Rameau (Jean-Philippe), [1683–1764]. Born at Dijon.

Although he very early manifested a special aptitude for music and everything concerning it, he was nearly thirty-four years of age before circumstances permitted him to enter upon the career. He was first organist at Lille, then in the cathedral of Clermont.

Here he thought out his system of harmony, founded on the idea of the fundamental bass — a system which, with all its faults, now clearly evident, was nevertheless the work of a man of genius, and retains to this day great importance in respect to the harmonic structure.

He also wrote numerous works of instruction on this subject.

As a composer he left many celebrated works, among which may be mentioned : *Hippolyte et Aricie, les Indes galantes, Castor et Pollux, Dardanus ;* and many extremely interesting compositions for the clavichord.

He was already fifty years of age when his first work was played at the Opéra; but in the twenty-seven years that followed, twenty-two pieces of his were put on the stage, more or less important, and almost invariably successful.

However, notwithstanding all this vogue, he always regarded his theoretical works as his truest title to fame.

We have yet to mention :

Lotti, [1667?–1740]. Born in Hanover, of Venetian parents.

Organist, then chapel master at San Marco in Venice, from 1704 till his death. His works are operas, madrigals, masses, and much religious music.

Durante (F.), [1684–1755]. Born in the kingdom of Naples.

A pupil of Scarlatti, he has been considered the founder of the Neapolitan school. Among his pupils were Paisiello, Piccini, and Sacchini. He wrote principally church music.

Marcello (Benedetto), [1686–1739]. Born in Venice.

A noble Venetian signor, long a member of the Council of Forty, he is especially known musically by splendid *Psalms*, full of grandeur and Christian faith ; also by a few pieces of instrumental music, madrigals, and chansons. His musical feeling rebuked the exaggerated *fioriture* and ornaments of every kind that the *bel canto* spread profusely, to the detriment of expressive sincerity.

I know not why Berlioz, in his *Grotesques de la Musique*, saw fit to ridicule him on the subject of the splendid psalm, *I cieli immensi narranno*, in which he finds only "a song of cattle-dealers returning from market." (!)   Marcello merits no such treatment.

Porpora, [1686–1767].   Born in Naples.

A remarkable singing-master and author of many forgotten operas, whose titles have no interest. He had for scholars notably two of the most famous male soprani, Caffarelli and Farinelli, and he had great reputation in his life-time. He also was a composer of sacred music.

Leo, [1694–1746].   Born in the kingdom of Naples.

One of the greatest masters of the Italian school.   Operas, oratorios, and sacred music ; numerous vocal exercises.

and among composers exclusively devoted to sacred music, the choir-master **Dumont** (1610–1684), born at Liège, author of the *Five Royal Masses,* in one of which is the famous Dumont's *Credo,* a very beautiful composition, but archaic even at that time.

Buxtehude, [1635–1707].   Born in Denmark.

Admirable organ pieces, of which very few were published ; celebrated as an organist.

Couperin (François), [1668–1733].   Born in Paris.

Organist, clavichordist, and composer. Numerous compositions for the clavichord.

There were several other musicians of the same name, belonging to the same family.

Corelli (Archangelo), [1653–1713].   Born near Bologna.

One of the greatest violinists both as virtuoso and as composer. His church sonatas are the admiration of connoisseurs.

Tartini, [1692–1770].   Born at Pirano.

Possesses triple celebrity as violinist, composer, and acoustician, for he was the first to discover differential resultant sounds ; that is to say, the property that any two harmonics have, if perfectly true, of reconstituting and causing to sound, their fundamental tone, which he called "the third tone."   The mistake he made was, in proposing to build upon this single discovery a whole system of harmony, necessarily incomplete.

He composed remarkable sonatas for the violin, about fifty, of which the most famous is the *Devil's Trill ;* also a great number of concertos and of didactic works which were a very important contribution to the art of violin playing.

We mention next the great and famous singer

Stradella, [1645–1670?]. Born in Naples,
who, according to the legend, disarmed assassins, bribed to kill him, by the prestige of his talent as singer and composer. This story may be true.

In regard to the famous church Aria, said to be by Stradella, *Pieta Signore*, it cannot possibly be his, for it corresponds in no way to the style of his time, or to his own style. It is much more modern. Many have attributed it to Rossini. This also is an error. I have good reasons for saying that its author is *Fétis*, who proved himself in this case capable of a clever mystification as well as of a great musical work.

Also **Reinken** (1623–1722), organist and harpsichordist; **Froberger** (1637–1695); **Purcell,** the English composer; and the learned theorists, **dom Jumilhac, Père Mersenne, Kircher,** and **Doni,** to whom is attributed the substitution of the syllable *do* for *ut,* which latter is difficult in solmisation; and, finally, some instrument-makers:

Cristofori, [1653–1731]. Born in Padua.
He constructed at Florence (about 1711) a harpsichord whose strings were struck with hammers, preceding by a few years the invention of the piano, and very possibly contributing to it indirectly.

Stainer, [1620–1670]. Violin-maker. Born at Absom (Tyrol).

Stradivarius, [1644–1737]. Violin-maker. Born in Cremona.

Guarnerius, family of violin-makers, of the seventeenth and eighteenth centuries, natives of Cremona.
(See the article Violin, p. 129.)

This leads us to mention the great progress in instrument-making accomplished at this period.

To the numerous instruments already mentioned, must now be added: the violin, which, about 1520, had gained its final form and has remained the same ever since Stradivarius; viols of all sizes, and of shapes most curiously varied; the *violetta* (small viol); the viola da braccia, cor responding in size to the modern alto; the viola da gamba (original form of the violoncello, but with five strings [1]); the viola bastarda; the marine trumpet (*tromba marina*; but why *tromba*, and why *marina* no one can say), a single-stringed bow instrument, of gentle and melancholy tone (whence it may be urged that M. Jourdain was not so absurd as he has been considered); it would be better, perhaps, to call it melodious than harmonious, since there is but one string; however, this one string can produce harmonics.

The family of the lute and mandora gained by the addition of the graceful mandoline and the majestic *theorbo* or *archiluito* (close of the sixteenth century), with double neck and sculptural forms. The guitar and harp remained nearly the same, undergoing but few modifications. The reverse is true of the psaltery, which, by the addition of a key-board, like that of the organ, was progressively a spinet, virginal, clavichord, and, finally, *clavecin* or harpsichord (fourteenth to sixteenth centuries).

Flutes there were of all sizes; the largest as resonant as organ-pipes. The idea of completing the families (an idea to which there is a return at the present day) had led to the construction of treble bassoons, and bass oboes, notwithstanding the apparent contradiction of terms.[2] The cornets à bouquin played a great part (from these we long retained the serpent, whose place is now filled by the ophicleide or bass tuba). The family of brasses gained a mighty personality in the slide trombone (sixteenth century), first called a sackbut, and made originally in four types: alto, tenor, bass, and contra-bass.[3]

Towards the close of the fifteenth century,[4] pedals were

---

1 [Six, or (later) seven was the number. ED.]

2 [Less "apparent" than the author thinks. They were called by quite different family names, as Schalmey, Buzain. The latter is the origin of the corrupted form *Bassoon*, which is anomalous, and a mere blunder, having nothing to do with the word *Bass*. ED.]

3 [The four sizes of sixteenth century trombones are a peg too low: should be soprano, alto, tenor, and bass, the tenor being on A instead of in B♭, as now. ED.]

4 [Before the middle of this century, viz., 1448, Adam Ileborg's organ-book gives a notation for pedals in capital letters; *therefore*, organ pedals must have existed before 1448. ED.]

applied to the organ by Bernard **Mured**; at this period, and even earlier, pedal key-boards set in motion the chimes of bells which, from the campanili of cathedrals and the belfries of city halls, shed their harmony in silver drops over the Flemish cities. Purely instrumental music received a new impulse, and for the first time an idea of orchestral colouring begins to appear; fête and ballet orchestras were constituted; everything shows that the art of music having by degrees gained all the elements needed for its full development — the method of combining voices, the formulas of counterpoint, a system of harmony and a rational notation, truth of dramatic expression and a wealth of timbres — was now ready to climb boldly its mountain peaks.

And here we leave behind us the curious and interesting epoch of early endeavour, and the triumphal procession of the great classics begins.

Up to this time there has been no serious disadvantage in regarding musical development in the countries of Europe as in general homogeneous and coincident; but here it begins to be important to take into consideration the individual advance of the different nations, and to distinguish clearly the predominating tendencies of each school. This is not to say that these divergent tendencies now for the first time appeared; on the contrary, they had existed from the beginning. But now that music was in possession of all its technical elements, of its complete outfit, each country began to find its objective point more distinct than ever before, and perfectly corresponding to the national character.

Hence, the three great schools of European music, the French, the German, the Italian, which we shall henceforth consider separately, that we may study them more profitably and be better able to grasp the character of each.[1]

Germany is heir to the old contrapuntists; to her belongs scientific music,— profound and philosophic combinations.

Italy cultivates, above all things, melody; the art of

[1] The Russian school is of very recent date; it will be studied later.

singing specially attracts her; hers is the facile and seductive music.

France seeks purity of style, emotion and sincerity of expression.

To these three great schools are often attached individuals belonging to other nations, but who, either by natural bent or by the character of their musical education, or, indeed, as the result of long residence in a country, have espoused its ideas, and made it really their artistic fatherland.

It must not, therefore, cause surprise to find Italian names in the German school, or vice versa; it is not so much the name, or even the birthplace, as it is the temperament and the musical character of the individual, which must guide us in this classification. We shall find it open to discussion, moreover, since some composers have had many styles and received influences of the most diverse character.

We begin by the German School, the strongest, no doubt, at that epoch, and the one from which the other schools have borrowed most. Here we must expect to find solidity and boldness of construction, and profundity in combinations.

At its head stand the two giants, Bach and Handel, objects of admiration and veneration, who seem only grander as the centuries pass, and whose fame can never be lessened.

C. — German Classic School.

Bach (Johann Sebastian), [1685–1750]. Born at Eisenach.

One of the greatest musical geniuses of Germany, or indeed of the world, whose influence was immense in musical evolution and is still felt in all the schools.

An organist and clavier player of incomparable skill, he produced, in all forms of musical composition then known and in new forms of his own creation, a vast number of masterpieces (of which many have not even yet been published). In creative power he was probably unequalled.

In this work of really unknown extent, we can mention only

a few of the most celebrated compositions : Mass in B minor, motets, the S. Matthew Passion (oratorio for two choirs and two orchestras), and other oratorios ; Cantata for Easter and many other cantatas ; psalms and chorals in unknown number ; the Well-tempered Clavichord (a collection of preludes and fugues) ; many books of clavichord pieces (inventions, symphonies, fantasias) ; the Art of Fugue, Sonatas for Violin ; solos, duos, trios, concertos for various instruments, fugues, chorals, canons for the organ, toccatas, Prelude and Fugue upon the name of Bach,[1] etc. ; an immense amount of dance-music : courantes, sarabandes, allemandes, gigues, minuets, gavottes, etc.

He was twice married, and had eleven sons and nine daughters. Nine children survived him.

The Bach family produced an enormous number of musicians, both among the ancestors and the descendants of Sebastian ; not less than a hundred and twenty are enumerated who held with distinction the offices of Kapellmeister, organist, or cantor, in Cathedrals. I mention here those only who are known to us by their compositions :

Bach (Johann Ambrosius), [1645–1695]. Father of the celebrated Johann Sebastian.

Bach (Wilhelm Friedemann), [1710–1784]. Born at Weimar, eldest son of Johann Sebastian.

A remarkable improvisator, he left numerous works for the organ, clavichord, orchestra, or choruses, which have remained for the most part in manuscript.

Bach (Carl Philipp Emmanuel), [1714–1788]. Born at Weimar, second son of Johann Sebastian.

He abandoned in part the fugal and contrapuntal style of his father, was much more of a melodist, and established the form of the modern sonata, which Haydn, Mozart, and Beethoven were to raise to absolute perfection, and from which originates the model of the symphony. Thus he exercised — though his works are insufficently known at the present day — an important influence upon the development of the great forms of instrumental and symphonic music, and should be considered the connecting link between his father's severe school and the less austere style of the classical German school, of which he was the precursor.

Numerous compositions, religious and secular, vocal, symphonic, and instrumental, notably for the clavier.

[1] , according to the German nomenclature.
B   A   C   H

Bach (Johann Christian), [1735–1782]. Born at Leipzig, eleventh
and last son of Johann Sebastian.

Besides his church music and a few symphonies, he wrote
numerous operas, many of which have been performed in Germany, England, and Italy.

He was as much the pupil of his elder brother, Philipp Emmanuel, as of his father, and cultivated the melodic form.

The life of Johann Sebastian Bach, the descendant of a
veritable tribe of musicians, was calm and sedentary, consecrated to study, to composition, and to domestic life.

Handel, on the contrary, lived more in the world; hence
his style has more life, it is at once more interesting and
more dramatic, and it shows marked traces of the Italian
influence.

Handel (Georg Friedrich), [1685–1759]. Born at Halle (Saxony).

The exact contempory of Sebastian Bach, and not less illustrious
than he. Handel is often compared and associated with Bach, in
the public mind, so that a certain confusion between the two is not
uncommon, although they are entirely unlike in style.

Handel's characteristic is to be always majestic and solemn ;
even the least of his works has a stamp of grandeur, combined,
also, with extreme simplicity.

Born in Saxony, he lived first in Germany, then in Italy, finally
in England, where he settled permanently and spent the remainder
of his life ; his style received modifications from his various sur-
soundings, without ever losing its stateliness, which was, besides,
enhanced by the composer's life at royal or princely courts, as well
as by the repeated occasions for composition which private and
public solemnities of various kinds furnished him.

This style found its highest employ in the oratorio ; among the
most celebrated of his compositions are: *Israel in Egypt, Saul, The
Messiah, Samson, Judas Maccabœus, Susannah;* he also wrote
about fifty operas, on English, Italian, and German librettos,
which are at the present day forgotten, much sacred music, and
many instrumental pieces for the organ and harpsichord.

The English consider him as one of their national glories, though
England was only his country by adoption ; some go even so far
as to attribute to him the composition of *God save the King*, which
has no proof beyond similarity of style.

He is buried in Westminster Abbey.

These two extraordinary men, Bach and Handel, dominate not alone their epoch and their school, but the whole history of music.

During their lifetime,— and deriving much from Bach and from his son Emmanuel especially, though employing forms more elegant and brilliant,— appeared another great genius who was especially concerned with the development of the symphonic style:

Haydn (Franz Josef), [1732–1809]. Born at Rohrau (Austria).

He was at first only a choir-boy in the Cathedral of Vienna ; born of obscure parents (his father was a wheelright), he began his elementary musical education quite alone, by the reading of good books, living in extreme poverty, until a time when assistance came to him from various high personages, especially the princes Anton and Nicolaus Esterhazy, in whose household he held a place which combined the duties of a valet with those of a Kapellmeister.

He received some instruction from Porpora, the great singing-master, in exchange for menial services ; but his true teacher, as he himself said, was Philipp Emmanuel Bach, whose style and methods he made his own.

Haydn is considered the father of the symphony, whose type he fixed as it has remained to this day; in this form of composition he wrote no less than a hundred and eighteen works, of which twenty are well-known in France ; he also wrote many operas, now entirely forgotten, on French and German poems. But no oblivion has overtaken his two great oratorios, *The Creation* and *The Seasons*, which are masterpieces indeed. He also wrote much chamber music, in the form of quartets for strings, trios for piano, violin, and violoncello, sonatas for the piano solo, etc.; besides church music, notably the *Seven Words of Christ.*

The dominant note in the music of Haydn is its grace and spirit ; also must be admired his power of invention and his harmonic skill, rising often to audacity, considering the times in which he lived. He is a grand personage in musical history.

Haydn had a brother, **Michael Haydn** (1737–1806), organist and professor ; a man of very great talent, who has left important works of a religious character ; but his personality is quite lost in the fame of his illustrious elder brother.

I mention, at this point, Gluck, because he was born in Germany, in 1714 ; but the full development of his genius occurring during his French career, his place in this volume is among the French classics. It is appropriate, however, to mention here that his very important achievements in dramatic composition, in opera, were not without effect upon Mozart's work, and indeed upon theatrical art in general.

Mozart (Wolfgang), [1756–1791]. Born at Salzburg.

As a musical genius, the nearest to perfection that the world has ever seen, for he alone essayed every form of musical composition, and excelled in each. He left nothing untried: dramatic, religious, and symphonic compositions; oratorios, chamber music, songs, cantatas, psalms; he was familiar with them all, and everywhere scattered his marvels.

He resembles Haydn—with more heart and grace, and perhaps less subtlety and incisive power—in chamber music and symphony. As a melodist he is undoubtedly allied to the Italian school; and in his great works, to Gluck, by his sincerity and power of expression.

After being the most inconceivable of infant-prodigies,—since at the age of *five* he composed little minuets which his father noted down while the child played them,—between the ages of *six* and *ten*, he was taken by his father, a good violinist and Kapellmeister, on a tour through Austria, Germany, and then, through Belgium, France, England, and Holland, receiving everywhere, at courts and in the châteaux of the great nobles, the most flattering expressions of admiration,—which, unfortunately, took the form of kisses and caresses, and little gifts, rather than of minted coin; later, he visited the principal Italian cities, and returned to Paris in 1778, playing upon the harpsichord and the violin, composing sonatas, oratorios, and whole operas, at the request of great personages to whom he dedicated these compositions, everywhere exciting enthusiasm, but without ever obtaining any advantageous position.

Accordingly, at the age of twenty-three, he was obliged to accept the humble place of organist in Salzburg, his native city. It was only after this, that circumstances enabled him to begin his true career. In 1780 he wrote *Idomeneo*, which was performed at Munich with immense success; then followed : *The Abduction from the Seraglio, the Marriage of Figaro, Don Giovanni, Cosi fan tutte, the Magic Flute;* finally, *La Clemenza di Tito*, which was his last opera. A dozen symphonies, of which those in C major, D major, G minor, and E♭ major, are particularly famous ; a score of concertos for piano and orchestra (of which, one is for two pianos); concertos for violin, clarinet, bassoon, and horn, etc., represent his symphonic work. For the church he wrote a dozen masses, numerous psalms and motets, a famous *Ave Verum* for four voices, and the *Requiem Mass*, his last work, which was finished by Süssmayer, his pupil. Numerous quintets, quartets, and trios attest his worth as a composer of chamber music ; and, besides all this, he left an inexhaustible collection of piano pieces, sonatas, fantasias, variations, etc.

In all these varied styles of composition he surpassed all his predecessors, and the number of his works, according to a faithful catalogue, is six hundred and twenty-six ! He died at the age of thirty-six, and in a state of poverty so extreme that he was buried in the common vault. The scene was most pitiable : it was in the midst of a violent storm of wind and rain ; the few friends who had attempted to follow the remains abandoned their design ; alone, the grave-diggers completed their sad work ; and when, on the morrow, the widow desired to find the place of her husband's interment, no one could tell where it was ; and the grave of Mozart has never been known.

Up to this point we have mentioned only the masters of imperishable renown; on a level still very high, but of less eminence, we find the two following :

Steibelt [1765–1823].　Born in Berlin.

It is hardly conceivable to us now, that in 1799, in Vienna, this composer was a rival to Beethoven, and as such had numerous partisans ; this certainly was mental aberration, but the music of Steibelt merits more attention than it commonly receives at the present time.

He had many works performed at the Opéra or the Opéra-Comique, and also in England, especially ballets ; he wrote much piano music, many sonatas and concertos, and chamber music of real merit. He also had a successful career as a virtuoso artist.

One cannot but reproach him, however, with having invented, or at least introduced into France, the Fantaisie, a pot-pourri of opera themes, of detestable taste, and now happily fallen into desuetude.

Cramer (J. B.), [1771–1858].　Born at Mannheim.

A man of great reputation as a pianist ; a composer of many pieces in sober and correct style, excellent chamber music, and a remarkable collection of studies.

And now we return once more to the highest summits :

Beethoven (Ludwig van), [1770–1827].　Born at Bonn.

One of the greatest geniuses of the century. His principal domain is essentially instrumental. From simple sonatas up to symphonies, he has created only masterpieces.

Three styles or distinct epochs are generally recognised in his work as a composer. The first is evidently derived from Haydn and Mozart, whose work he continues on a broader scale. The second is extremely personal to himself, of a peculiar individuality; here he is seen in the plenitude of his genius. In respect to the third, opinions differ widely; some critics consider it as superior to the second in boldness of harmonic combinations and intensity of expressive power; others see in it a sort of glorious decadence, to be accounted for in part by the deafness which embittered half the life of this unfortunate musician. At least it is certain that he here rose to heights until that time unknown.

The manner in which Beethoven acquired musical instruction is not very well known. He was at first refractory, so that his father resorted to violence, and he was whipped to compel him to practice,— this, at the age of *five!* But after a year's study under the direction of Van der Eden he became enthusiastic as to music, and from this point his career began. Later he had Neefe for his teacher, who caused him to study Bach and Handel, for improvement in virtuosity; he now surprised all the musicians of his time (among whom was Mozart) with his marvellous aptitude for improvisation, an innate facility in his case, for as yet he had no knowledge of harmony or counterpoint; with him it was all pure instinct or the capacity for imitation.

As late as 1793 he received a few lessons from Haydn; but the old composer seemed to have no understanding of the genius that he had to deal with, and neglected his pupil. Then followed Albrechtsberger, a learned contrapuntist, who was really Beethoven's only master, except nature.

He frequently composed while walking on a pleasure jaunt. On his return home he would write down what had come to him, to be elaborated later with infinite painstaking. His eccentricity of manner was extreme, bordering on rudeness, though, both at Vienna and elsewhere, he was received in the most polished society, notably at the palace of the archduke Rudolf. This prince and Ferdinand Ries were his only pupils of any note.

His works are numerous: nine Symphonies, the last, with choruses; six Concertos for piano and orchestra; seventeen admirable Quartets for strings; many duos, trios, and sonatas; many other piano pieces; a famous Septet; *Fidelio*, an opera; many overtures: *Coriolanus*, *Egmont*, *Leonora* (*Fidelio*), *Ruins of Athens*; Choruses, Songs, *Ballet of Prometheus*, two masses, etc.

This great genius, although appreciated in his life, died, alas! almost as poor as Mozart.

The following musicians, men of talent, though of far less distinction than Mozart and Beethoven, may be regarded as their successors.

Hummel (Johann Nepomuk), [1778–1837]. Born at Presburg.

A pupil of Mozart from the age of seven, apparently only in piano playing ; later, he studied harmony, accompaniment, and counterpoint with Albrechtsberger ; finally received instruction from Salieri in composition, and from Clementi for the piano.

He was an astonishing improvisator and a remarkable performer. As composer, though he produced in all styles,—operas, church music, chamber music,—he is now scarcely known except by his piano music, elegantly written, resembling Mozart and Beethoven in the latter's first manner.

Ries (Ferdinand), [1784–1838]. Born at Bonn.

A pupil of Albrechtsberger in harmony and counterpoint, of Romberg for the violoncello, and especially of Beethoven (with whom he lived for nearly four years) in composition and for the piano.

His works are chiefly concertos for the piano, and chamber music in a style which much resembles Beethoven, and somewhat Hummel, his contemporary. He had little originality ; more talent than genius, but brilliancy and elegance.

Spohr [1784–1859]. Born at Brunswick.

His instrument was the violin, of which he may be regarded as the founder of a school.

The works of his that are chiefly known in France, are his chamber music, notably his quintets. He wrote, however, ten operas, of which some are popular in Germany ; a number of oratorios and masses ; fifteen concertos for the violin ; and ten symphonies, one of which is for two orchestras.

He was Hofkapellmeister to the Duke of Hesse-Cassel.

Czerny (Carl), [1791–1857]. Born in Vienna.

Had as pupils Liszt and Döhler. He composed a vast quantity of works of value, of which many are important,—masses and symphonies,—but scarcely anything of his is now generally known except collections of exercises and studies for the piano. Scarcely anyone is aware that this composer wrote more than any other has ever written, and that his works are really of interest. A complete catalogue of them would contain not less than *twelve hundred and fifty* numbered compositions.

Moscheles (Ignaz), [1794–1870]. Born in Prague.

A remarkable composer and improvisator, who had success throughout Europe. His works, principally for the piano or the instruments suited to chamber music, are a little neglected in our time ; he has written, notably, five concertos and a collection of studies still famous.

Nicolaï [1809–1849].   Born at Königsberg.

The author of many operas, of which one alone is well-known to us : *The Merry Wives of Windsor.*

Hiller (Ferd.), [1811–1885].   Born in Frankfort.

A great musician and erudite writer, long director of the Conservatory of Cologne.   He was generally hostile to Wagnerian ideas, and was one of the last German classics.

We mention also, among the conspicuous musicians of this marvellous epoch, but perhaps as virtuosi rather than composers :

Kirnberger [1721–1783].   Born at Saalfeld (Thuringia).

A pupil of Sebastian Bach, he has left charming compositions for the clavier.

Field (John), [1782–1837].   Born in Dublin.

The most famous of English pianists ; was the favourite pupil of Clementi, and studied counterpoint with Albrechtsberger.   Besides serious works, sonatas, concertos, now rather out of fashion, he is the creator of the charming form called *Nocturne*, which has contributed greatly to his reputation.

This composer belongs almost as much to the Italian as to the German school.

Romberg (Bernard), [1770–1841].   Born at Dinklage, near Münster.

The most famous of German violoncellists, and truly the founder of a school ; after having travelled widely and received great applause for his virtuosity, he was for two years (1801–3) professor in the Paris Conservatory.

His concertos for the violoncello are remarkable.   He has also written chamber music and even operas, which do not appear to have been successful.   ●

This epoch had also its great theorists : **Fux** (1660–1741), **Marpurg** (1718–1795), the Abbé **Vogler** (1749–1814), and especially :

Albrechtsberger [1736–1809].   Born at Klosterneuburg (Austria).

Numerous works of instruction on harmony, counterpoint, and fugue ; many sacred and secular compositions, motets, hymns, twenty-six masses, concertos, sonatas, etc.   He was a great scholar ; among his pupils were Beethoven, Hummel, Ries, and John Field.

D. — German Romantic School.

After this enumeration — which the limits of the present work have compelled me to make very brief and very dry — of the great German classics and of a few of their contemporaries, we must go back some years to mark the birth and development of the romantic art, whose germ is found in Beethoven's last works. While Hummel, Ries, and others followed that master in the purely classical order, it cannot be doubted that his genius exercised also a powerful influence over a very different school, in which Weber and Mendelssohn were file-leaders. With this latter school, forms, though still pure, certainly, are more veiled and draped with the garb of fancy; they are less rigid, the harmonic ordering is freer and more daring; the ensemble becomes more picturesque, more descriptive; everywhere is felt the sensuous tendency which was to lead to modern Romanticism.

At this period (about 1780), there was clearly a parting of the ways; a certain number of German masters strove to preserve intact the traditions of Haydn and of Mozart, whence Beethoven himself had departed; and they continued the purely classic art (which today has scarcely any representatives); others, more audacious, rushed boldly in search of new procedures more consonant with the literary evolution of the country, and these men, in their turn, became heads of a school at first criticised, then universally admired and approved.

Weber (Carl Maria von), [1786–1826]. Born at Eutin (Duchy of Holstein).

A composer full of originality, raciness, fire, and a fanciful poetry which is peculiar to himself.

The insufficiency of his technical studies is betrayed by awkwardness of writing and faults of composition, but the force of his genius is such that it engrosses the auditor's attention and compels his admiration. For the same reason, the execution of his works is often difficult and unsatisfactory, alike for voices and for instruments, with the single exception of the clarinet, which seemed to be his favourite timbre, and is employed by him most successfully, though we have no indication that he played it himself; with these slight drawbacks, his orchestration is rich, vigorous, coloured, and picturesque. He was one of the great composers of his time, and his expressive power deserves the more admiration because he had the disadvantage of lacking special instruction, and had to create for himself a new style.

Four famous operas: *Euryanthe, Der Freischütz, Oberon,* and *Preciosa*[1]; two others less known in France: *Abu-Hassan* and *Sylvana;* three Concertos for the piano (the third called *Concertstück*); two Concertos for the clarinet; a great Duo and Variations for piano and clarinet; a Trio; four beautiful Sonatas for the piano, two Polonaises, a Rondo in E♭,—such are his most important, most famous, but not his only, works.

Mendelssohn-Bartholdy (1809–1847). Born in Hamburg.

A remarkable symphonist, in whom thorough scientific knowledge is united to the highest distinction and the loftiest inspiration.

A pianist and organist of very great merit, he wrote superb sonatas for the organ, and, for the piano, concertos, sonatas, beautiful chamber music; but it is especially in the oratorio and the symphony that the marvellous qualities of his genius had their fullest scope.

The *Midsummer Night's Dream* music, the last three Symphonies, the Overtures, *Ruy Blas, Fingal's Cave, The Fair Melusina,* the Concerto for the violin, the two Concertos for the piano, the two Trios, the Sonata in B♭, and the Duo in D for piano and violoncello, as well as most of his *Songs Without Words* (a form of his own creation), must be considered as masterpieces.

Mendelssohn's orchestration is of the richest, fertile in picturesque sonorities and in ingenious musical devices.

Between Weber and Mendelssohn a composer of exquisite feeling finds his place; his compositions are all of a light style, it is true, but one must remember that he died at thirty-one:

Schubert (Franz), [1797–1828]. Born in Vienna.

A musician endowed with a very special poetic charm, especially excelling in songs (*lieder*) of which many are famous, such as the *Erl-King, Ave Maria, Serenade, The Young Nun,* and *Margaret at the Spinning Wheel.*

He also produced much admired chamber music and composi-

1 ["Preciosa" is not an opera, but a four-act play for which Weber composed incidental music. ED.]

tions for the piano, in which he shows himself as prolix as in his melodies he is concise.

Another poet-composer of the same date is Chopin. By turns chivalrous, elegiac, and impassioned, he is never frankly gay: he is an invalid dreamer, a sad exile, endowed with a singular fascination, the Alfred de Musset of music.

Chopin (Frédéric-François), [1810–1849]. Born near Warsaw, in the village of Zelazowa-Wola.

Great virtuoso and famous composer; he wrote for the piano only, with the exception of one Trio, and one Polonaise for the piano and violoncello, in which the part for the 'cello was *arranged* by Franchomme.

His works have a melodic charm and an exquisite poetry which we seek vainly in any other author. He left two Concertos, two Sonatas (the andante of the second is the famous funeral march), and a great many Polonaises, Mazurkas, Valses, Nocturnes, etc., with a remarkable collection of Studies, in all about eighty numbers of works known to pianists.

Although France was the country of his adoption, and indeed his family were of French origin, I do not hesitate to class him by reason of his affinities in the Romantic School of Germany.

On the other hand, though Meyerbeer was born in Berlin (1791), though he studied with the Abbé Vogler, I regard him as belonging to the French school, in which he found his definitive path and his fame. But I am perfectly conscious that, both in the case of Chopin and of Meyerbeer, others may think differently.

And now another great German genius appears:

Schumann (Robert), [1810–1856]. Born at Zwickau (Saxony).

Scarcely earlier than at the age of twenty did he enter upon serious study, with the idea of making music his career; up to this time he was destined for the law, which he was supposed to be studying at Leipzig, and later at Heidelberg, while in reality he only attended the lectures on philosophy, devoting the rest of his time to literature and social life. This lack of elementary technical studies made at the proper time, that is to say, in youth, is betrayed in his style by an indecision and vagueness of forms, as well as by numerous errors ; his works are not, as a rule, solidly timbered, well balanced ; his orchestration is rather colourless, lacking in force and splendour and light. These exceptions being made, one must admire profoundly the intense and heartfelt poetry even in his least works. His dreamy genius did not incline him toward the stage ; he did, however, essay dramatic production, notably in *Manfred* and in *Genoveva*, but with little success. His titles to fame are: the delicious oratorio, *Paradise and the Peri*, his songs, four Symphonies, a superb Quintet, and a Quartet (both in Bb) for piano and strings, and many pieces for the piano, of which the best known are the *Symphonic Studies*, the *Kinderscenen*, the *Davidsbündler* (*Tänze*), the *Noveletten*, the *Carnaval*, etc.

He died insane in a hospital near Bonn.

His wife was a remarkable pianist, by name Clara Wieck, who, after his death, continued to perform his music in public. She died in 1896.

Liszt (Franz), [1811–1888]. Born at Räding (Hungary).

He was at first a pianist, the most extraordinary and fascinating ever known, and one of the most wonderful of improvisators; yielding to the taste of the time he then composed Fantasias, arrangements or paraphrases upon fashionable operas, bristling with difficulties of execution so extreme that no one but himself could attempt to play them.

It was not until a later period that he began really to compose, bringing into his work the character of mysticism which was in his own nature. Whether as virtuoso or as composer, Liszt *pontificates* always ; moreover, he will not seek effect by simple means, taking pleasure only in complications. Hence those who are not his ardent admirers consider him as not exempt from a certain amount of charlatanism.

In 1861, he relinquished his office of Kapellmeister to the Grand Duke of Weimar, which he had held since 1849, to become the ducal chamberlain ; in 1865, he took lesser orders with the title of Abbé, and was ever after called the Abbé Liszt, not, however, abandoning his musical career.

One of his daughters married Wagner, of whom he was the ardent champion ; he was indeed as impassioned in his admirations and enthusiasms (Beethoven, Berlioz, Schumann, Wagner) as in his music and his playing. Differing estimates may be formed in respect to him, but certainly he was a man of genius, and his life one of the most curious and full of incident.

After the father-in-law, the son-in-law. Now comes to crown royally the efforts of the Romantic School, Richard

Wagner, the mighty innovator, the marvellous reformer of German dramatic art.

Wagner (Richard), [1813–1883]. Born at Leipzig.

The most discussed, most maligned, most adored of composers.

He has had two distinct manners. In the first, which produced *Rienzi, The Flying Dutchman, Tannhäuser,* and *Lohengrin,* it is manifest that he follows in the track of his predecessors, Gluck, Beethoven, Schumann, Mendelssohn, and Weber, while introducing into his way of writing a very personal, but by no means revolutionary element.

Where he becomes an innovator is in his second manner, characterised by the division of the dramatic work into scenes united with each other (which breaks up the old form of arias, duos, trios, etc.) and by the systematic and permanent employ of the *Leitmotiv* (already introduced in *Lohengrin*). On this new system are constructed *Tristan and Isolde, The Meistersinger, The Nibelung's Ring,* a trilogy with a prologue, requiring four occasions to be executed completely : (1) *Rheingold,* the prologue ; (2) *Die Walküre;* (3) *Siegfried;* (4) *Die Götterdämmerung;* and lastly, *Parsifal,* the master's final work.

Wagner, as a great musical genius, furnished with complete technical instruction,— as, also, a profound philosopher, and a poet, composing his own librettos, and superintending the *mise en scène* of his operas, even to the construction of the scenery — cannot be likened or compared to any of the great musicians of the past or present. His work is a colossal, unique, inimitable monument, which must be contemplated with the most respectful admiration.

There results from the two-fold means already indicated (the division into scenes and the Leitmotiv), to which has been given the name of the Wagnerian formula, an incomparable cohesion, unity, and expressive intensity, to which dramatic works written in separate pieces linked by recitatives can lay no claim. The musical drama of Wagner may be considered as cast in one piece, and, by comparison, operas written in the usual way, as works of mosaic or marquetry. The *difference* in these two procedures is apparent, without taking into consideration the question of superiority.

Wagner developed the art of orchestration, of orchestral colouring to a point before unknown, a point which is *apparently* its final limit; but in art there is no limit; progress is endless. I will not name the person, but it seems to me that there is now among French composers one who has surpassed Wagner in this very respect. Wagner, however, in addition to the new combinations that he devised among the various instruments of the classic orchestra,

introduced new elements, notably *tubas,* a family intermediate between horns and trombones, and the bass-trumpet, which figures
in nearly all of his scores, and singularly enriches the group of
brasses, without rendering his instrumentation any more noisy by
this, as the auditor will perceive for himself whenever he hears the
works of this composer well rendered,— a condition rare in Paris.

One must go to Bayreuth to appreciate the intensity of emotion
which can be produced by a Wagnerian drama, religiously played,
and religiously listened to, without the interruption of applause,
without the "Bravo! brava!" without calling for encores,— all
strictly prohibited there; with the scenery and the stage-setting
precisely as the master ordained it; with the invisible orchestra,
its sonorities deliciously melting into each other, *never noisy;* with
the auditorium in total darkness; instead of the *foyer* of the
entr'actes, a verdant, rolling country; instead of the prompter's
bell, a brilliant fanfare, sending to the four cardinal points of the
sky the principal Leitmotiv of the following act. All this is in-
toxicating; ravishing to the supreme degree.

This is not the place to express a judgment as to the man; but,
from the purely artistic point of view, we must admit that he who
was able to create this ensemble is in truth the greatest genius that
the mind can conceive of.

It is not going outside the family to place here, a little
in advance of his chronological position, another member
of the Wagnerian staff:

Bülow (Hans von), [1830–1894]. Born in Dresden.

Very remarkable as pianist, composer, and also orchestral
leader. As a composer, he derives from Schumann and Wagner,
of whom he was an ardent disciple; his masters for the piano and
musical technique were Litolff and Liszt. Though essentially belonging to the Romantic School, he has the classic sentiment
strongly developed.

By his works, not very well known in France, by his talent as
virtuoso and as Kapellmeister, as well as by his literary work, he
has played an important part in German musical evolution.

His wife, Cosima Liszt, one of the daughters of his master,
became later the wife of Wagner.

Before leaving Wagner and his immediate followers, it
is impossible not to put a question of the highest interest,
to which, however, only the future can give an answer.
Has Wagner really effected a reform, created a new and

national art, as he himself said; in a word, is he the head of a school?

Up to the present date, no successor is clearly announced. Certain composers, it is true, no less in France and Italy than in Germany, have adopted, or rather, have attempted, some of his procedures,—for instance, the use of typical *motives,* or the division of an opera into three acts, instead of the four or five usual before his time; advantage is taken of the progress in instrumentation due to him, and the new brasses which he introduced into the orchestra are employed; three flutes are used and three clarinets, families of instruments are completed; the division into separate numbers, united by recitatives, has been abandoned, and to it is preferred the more logical and vital one of scenes welded closely, without any break. But no man yet, by use of these *formulas,* to employ the word of today, has produced anything which can be considered as continuing the work of Wagner.

These isolated attempts prove one thing only : the world-wide resounding of the triumphal conflicts waged by this extraordinary man, so great a resounding that, through the whole musical world, every other man has been compelled to study in detail the processes whose sum constitutes the general Wagnerian technic; from this compulsory study has resulted for each a widening of his own horizon, a broader conception of what his mind was already conceiving; and in this way it is that Wagner, at least up to the present time, has had a powerful influence upon musical evolution. To continue him, strictly speaking, there must be a man of the same breadth of wing; and if this man exists, he will never be the imitator of anyone; rather, he also will be an inventor of new things. I range myself, then, very willingly, with those of Wagner's admirers who see in him an isolated fact, a necessary product of many centuries of German effort, whose ultimate expression he is, and not a reformer or the head of a new school. He is the culminating point of a magnificent mountain-chain, whose lesser peaks we have successively explored; there is no greater height beyond to reach; that which is to come after, will be something *different*.

We will now speak of a few other German composers who are of the school of Weber, Mendelssohn, and Schumann.

Heller (Stephen), [1815–1888]. Born at Pesth (Hungary).

One of the rare instances of a composer of great merit who has never written except for the piano. His works are filled with a quite peculiar poetic charm, which sometimes has a character of strangeness ; they should be known. At least as much as Chopin he merits the appellation of " the poet of the piano."

Gade (Niels Wilhelm), [1817–1890]. Born at Copenhagen.

Has produced numerous symphonies and works of chamber music, in a style which proves him to have strongly felt the influence of Mendelssohn, and still not without a personal note. I am only familiar with two sonatas for the piano and violin (but probably there are others), and the *Aquarellen*, for the piano, a collection of charming little pieces resembling Mendelssohn's *Kinderstücke*, the *Kinderscenen* of Schumann, and *Jeux d'enfants* of Bizet.

Raff (Joseph Joachim), [1822–1882]. Born at Lachen (Switzerland), of Würtemberg parents.

He was an extremely productive composer, especially in chamber music of every kind, and for all instruments ; much piano music, also, and even compositions very light in character, as his *Polka de la Reine*. In a more elevated style may be mentioned his eleven symphonies, having distinctive names usually, as *Im Walde*, *An das Vaterland*, *In den Alpen*, etc.; two *Orchestral Suites*, a little symphony (*Sinfonietta*) for wind-instruments, church music in great quantity, lastly, three dramatic works : *König Alfred*, four acts ; *Dame Kobold*, one act (1870) ; and *Samson*, which, I believe, has never been performed. To this must be added the music for the drama, *Bernhard von Weimar*.

He played the piano, violin, and organ, and, for principal masters or advisors, had Mendelssohn and Liszt.

Up to the age of eighteen, his studies were purely scientific.

Brahms (Johannes), [1833–1897]. Born at Hamburg.

A protégé of Schumann, who had for him the greatest admiration. Less dreamy and less poetic than Schumann, he had, on the other hand, more firmness and brilliancy, as well as great wealth of orchestral colouring.

His works are chiefly church music, a beautiful Requiem, four symphonies, much chamber and piano music, songs for one voice, or for several, etc. I am not aware that he ever essayed an opera. He is one of the leaders of the present school; and so also is

Bruch (Max). Born in 1838 at Cologne.

A pupil of Ferdinand Hiller, he began with two operas, which had only a comparative success, remarkable cantatas, symphonies, concertos, all grand in manner and of lofty character.

Svendsen (Johann Severin), [1840]. Born at Christiania.

Studied with his father and the violinist Ursin (a pupil of Léonard); studied harmony with Arnold at Christiania, then at Leipzig with Richter and Dr. Hauptmann.

His most important works are: op. 3, *Octet* for strings; op. 4, *Symphony in D;* op. 5, *Quintet* for strings; op. 8, *Sigurd Slembe*, symphonic overture; op. 9, *Carnaval à Paris* (orchestra); op. 11, *Zorahayde*, legend (orchestra); op. 15, *Symphony* in B flat ; op. 18, *Romeo and Juliet*, fantasia (orchestra); op. 19 and 21, *Rhapsodies Norvégiennes* (orchestra); op. 1, *Quartet ;* op. 6, *Concerto* for violin; op. 7, *Concerto* for violoncello; op. 30, *Quartet; Songs, Romances* for violin, etc.

Grieg (Edvard), [1843–1907]. Born at Bergen (Norway).

Studied first at the Conservatory of Leipzig, under the direction of Reinecke, Richter, Hauptmann, Moscheles, and Wenzel; much earlier, at the age of *six*, he had begun the study of the piano with his mother, an excellent musician. Later, in 1870, he had the advice of Liszt. He is particularly fond of employing national themes, or imitating their character, which gives his music a poetic charm, odd and picturesque.

He is specially known in France by the following works: *Concerto* in A minor for the piano; some songs, out of the many which he has written; *Peer Gynt*, an orchestral suite upon Ibsen's poem. Besides these, we may mention: op. 11, *Overture ;* op. 20, *Before the Cloister Gate* (chorus and orchestra); op. 27, *Quartet* for strings ; op. 40, a suite for strings, *Aus Holberg's Zeit ;* op. 42, *Bergliot*, melodrama; op. 50, *Olav Trygvason*, unfinished opera; op. 53, two *Melodies* for strings; op. 8, 13, 45, *Sonatas* for piano and violin; op. 36, *Sonata* for violoncello and piano; numerous pieces for piano, for two or four hands, etc.

Two composers are still to be mentioned whose lighter turn of mind leads to the supposition that they have not remained insensible to the seductions of the French school :

Flotow (Friedrich, Freiherr von), [1812–1883]. Born at Teutendorf in Mecklenburg.

Many pleasing operas and *Opéras-comiques: Stradella, Martha, L'Ombre.*

Suppé (Franz von), [1820–1895]. Born at Spalato (Dalmatia).

His works are not well known in France; I believe scarcely anything has been heard in Paris except *Fatinitza* (1876), *Poet and Peasant*, and *Boccaccio*.[1]

Many great virtuosos belong to the first half of the nineteenth century. Besides those who have already been mentioned as composers, the following should find place here.

Herz (Heinrich), [1806–1888]. Born at Vienna.

A remarkable virtuoso, author of works now out of fashion, but not without value; professor in the Conservatory of Paris, founder and manager of a great piano-factory and of a concert hall; publisher of most of his own works, Herz was able to carry on these multiple occupations with high artistic skill and indefatigable activity. He was, with Liszt, Chopin, and Thalberg, one of the four great pianists of his time.

Thalberg (Sigismund), [1812–1871]. Born at Geneva.

As a pianist he was faultless, calm, and distinguished. He had the most beautiful tone that has ever been heard, the art of making the piano sing, and drawing entirely new effects from the use of the pedals.

As composer, he invented passages of an entirely new form, placing the air in the medium register, and surrounding it with a halo of iridescent arpeggios; a procedure which has since been overused, but was nevertheless a lucky hit. He composed chiefly in the fantasia style, and his *Fantasias* on *Moïse, The Huguenots, Euryanthe, La Muette*, were long in favour. Among his original works may be mentioned his *Ballade*, his *Barcarole*, two *Studies* in A minor, etc.

Schulhoff (Julius), [1825–1898]. Born at Prague.

A virtuoso and composer of piano music; has been very much admired everywhere in Europe; many of his compositions have had great vogue: *Galop, Valses* in A flat and in D flat, a *Polonaise*, and other things.

[1] [Besides *Fatinitza* and *Boccaccio* mentioned, the following operettas by Suppé have been heard in the United States in English: *Donna Juanita* (1880), *Die Afrikareise* (1883), *Bellmann* (1887), *Die Jagd nach dem Glück* (1888). ED.]

Joachim (Josef), [1831]. Born at Kitsee (Hungary).

One of the most famous violinists of our time, and, besides, remarkable as an orchestral leader.

Wieniawski (Henri), [1835–1880]. Born in Poland.

Was a pupil of Massart at the Paris Conservatory, and one of the greatest violinists of the modern school. He wrote much concert music for the violin, notably a famous *Polonaise*.

Wieniawski (Josef), [1837]. Born in Poland.

Studied in the Paris Conservatory under the direction of Alkan for solfeggio, of Zimmermann and Marmontel for the piano, and of Le Couppey for harmony.

A virtuoso of great merit, he has also composed much for the the piano, in a style resembling both Chopin and Schulhoff.

Tausig (Karl), [1841–1871]. Born at Warsaw.

A pupil of Liszt, and one of the most wonderful of German virtuosos, especially in regard to technic.

It is not without interest to observe that the brothers Wieniawski studied in Paris, under French masters.

Here ends our examination of the German evolution of music. I have attempted only to give its general aspect, and indicate the most illustrious names. I shall also give, at the close of this chapter, as I have done hitherto, a list of special works where may be found fuller details.

I add here, merely by way of mention, a few names which will be of interest only to the specialist.

Chladni [1756–1829], acoustician. Born at Wittemberg.

Author of remarkable researches and discoveries as to the production of musical sound, and of an important *Treatise on Acoustics, Study of Vibrating Plates*, etc. ,

Berr (Friedrich), [1794–1838], clarinetist. Born at Mannheim.

A remarkable virtuoso, composer for his instrument and for military music; introduced into France the method of placing the reed *underneath*,— a change whose importance can be appreciated only by clarinetists, but is none the less important on that account.

Professor in the Conservatory in 1831.

Originator and director of the' Gymnase Musicale Militaire in 1836, in Paris.

Boehm (Theobald), [1794–1881], flutist. Born in Bavaria.

Inventor of the system of rings united by movable stems, now generally adopted for the flute, oboe, clarinet, bassoon, and their derivatives, which, by simplifying the fingering of these instruments, has fitted them for peculiar effects previously impossible to them.

Finally,

Mälzel (Johann Nepomuk), [1772–1838], mechanician. Born at Ratisbon.

Supposed to be the inventor of the metronome, but really only its improver; the true inventor seems to be Winkel (Amsterdam, 1812).

E.— Italian Classical School.

If now we transfer ourselves to Italy, at the period when Bach was living in Germany, we shall come into the presence of a musical art so different from his that it seems as if there were needed two distinct words to designate the two. The Italian School has had also its grand epochs and its justly famed masters; but to appreciate them, we must be able to place ourselves in the proper mental condition, and especially to avoid the error of judging these masters by comparison with those of other schools in which the ideal of the beautiful is differently placed.

Here, the principal, almost the sole, effort is towards beauty, purity, and elegance in the vocal contour; the melodic phrase, considered in and for itself in its application to singing and to the *tessitura*[1] of the voices; harmony is regarded as an accompaniment, always subordinated to the principal part, usually in plain harmony, in arpeggios, or in regular designs, but always secondary, the case being excepted of *ritornelle* or responses committed to the orchestra, in which, when the voice ceases, an instrument for the moment takes up the melodic design (this instrument is

---

[1] In Italian, *tessitura* is the main body of the notes in a given part, considered from the point of view of their different registers, whether they are dull or brilliant, more or less difficult to emit, " good notes " or bad; it might be translated by the words " vocal texture," including the idea " average range."

usually the violin), being accompanied by the rest; modulations are infrequent and simple, having no other object
than to avoid monotony or to place the phrase more advantageously for the voice of the singer. If by chance there is
a modulation into remote keys, this is to produce a great
surprise, a dramatic effect; and it succeeds in doing so,
but is considered an act of great daring. Little importance
is attached to the real meaning of words; the same air
will express love or despair, if its contour is pretty, attractive, and very vocal in its nature. This is the School of
Melody and of Virtuosity. Everything is subordinated to
that one solicitude.

Solicitude is not, perhaps, the word to use, for the
art of designing beautiful melodic forms seems a gift of
nature to the Italians. There is no suggestion of effort of
combination; "it comes natural," like the singing of a
bird; and this facility is one of the charms of the style.
Instrumentation necessarily can play but an insignificant
part, with rare exceptions; and it happens that the *maestro*,
with whom, to proceed chronologically, we begin the series,
is precisely one of those exceptions.

Scarlatti (Alessandro), [1649–1725]. Born at Trapani (Sicily).

Author of a hundred operas and a much greater number of
masses, not to speak of other church music and much chamber
music, all entirely neglected at the present day.

He possessed the feeling for orchestration to a degree remarkable for his time, and grouped instruments of various timbres with
great boldness and skill. He was perhaps the first to divide the
violins into four parts. He also modified the form of the recitative by orchestrating it, and created the aria type, long in use in
the Italian School, with a repetition of the initial theme (the da
capo) after an interposed episode.

If his works are forgotten, his life left traces important for the
future.

Scarlatti (Domenico), [1683–1757]. Born in Naples.

The son of Alessandro Scarlatti, he wrote some good operas and
a little church music, but owes his reputation specially to his skill
as harpsichordist and to his compositions for the harpsichord.

After being for four years Maestro di Capella at S. Peter's in

Rome, he was attached as harpsichordist first to the court of Portugal, then to that of Spain.

Several sonatas of his are known, and many pieces for the harpsichord are charming, but rather difficult of execution.

These two masters, especially the son, who is best known to us, have but little resemblance to those of their contemporaries of whom we have already spoken, but whose names I will again mention to make the story clear : *Leo*, pupil of the elder Scarlatti, of whom it is the chief title to fame that he himself was the master of Piccinni, Sacchini, Pergolesi, and other famous musicians, in the Conservatory of Naples, where his teaching, as well as his style of prodigious flexibility was highly appreciated, and where he had for successor *Durante*, another master of rare merit ; *Hasse* (1699–1783), who was one of the principal collaborators in the famous *Italian Solfeggi ;* and *Lotti*, who, about the same time, was Maestro di Cappella at S. Mark's in Venice.   These are the fathers of the Italian School. Soon after this time appeared the great

Pergolesi [1710–1736]. Born at Jesi.

He was especially famous for the *Serva Padrona*, a masterpiece of gaiety, and the *Stabat Mater*, a masterpiece of religious faith. The latter, which also was his last work, was paid for in advance by a religious brotherhood at the price of forty francs. This suggests the idea that he did not roll in gold, and that in his lifetime he was but poorly appreciated.

He died, unfortunately, before completing his twenty-sixth year, and it has only been of late that his worth has been appreciated.

We shall refer again to Pergolesi on occasions of the quarrels stirred up by the performance of his *Serva Padrona*, and in speaking of Italian influence upon the national style of France.   Then followed a few years later :

Jommelli (Niccolò), [1714–1774].   Born at Aversa, near Naples.

A great composer for both church and theatre; some forty operas and much sacred music are his principal works, known only to scholars,—and perhaps not to all of them even!

Piccinni [1728-1800]. Born at Bari (Southern Italy).

Pupil of Leo, and afterwards of Durante, he wrote many operas in the Italian style, which had great merit; but he encountered in his career, among his contemporaries, two very formidable rivals, Gluck and Sacchini, who relegated him to the background — not without serious strife, for he had faithful partisans,— but in what seems to be a definitive manner.

Later we shall speak of the famous quarrel between the Gluckists and the Piccinnists.

Sacchini [1734-1786]. Born at Pozzuoli.

Pupil of Durante, he had, himself, Berton for a disciple.

A musician of great merit, of a style at once noble and sweet, he produced much for the church and the theatre, but his works are, at the present day, quite neglected. He wrote an *Œdipe à Colone*, which was not performed till six months after his death, and whose antique beauty produced a deep impression; also a *Dardanus* and a *Rinaldo ed Armida* (1783), upon a subject already treated by Gluck in 1777, and by Lully in 1686, comparison with which, especially the former, was probably disadvantageous to him.

As we have seen, the first aim in Italy was the theatre, and after that the church ; now, however, we find a great musician entirely devoted to instrumental composition.

Boccherini (Luigi), [1740-1805]. Born at Lucca.

Very productive, and of a rare originality, this composer wrote three hundred and sixty-six works of chamber music, and twenty symphonies. He is especially famous for his *Quintets*, very numerous, exceeding a hundred and fifty, of which many are still unpublished and will probably so remain.

Paisiello [1741-1816]. Born at Tarento.

The list of Paisiello's operas contains not less than ninety-four! Out of this alarming number, I believe, are known in France only *La Molinara*, *Nina*, and *Il Barbiere di Siviglia*, which latter was cast into obscurity by Rossini's work of the same name.

There are also some forty masses, two Te Deums, a Requiem, and many church pieces.

Cordially patronised, like Paer and afterwards Lesueur, by Napoleon I., he was choir-master at the chapel of the Tuileries, and he wrote in 1804 a coronation mass for the Emperor.

He was made member of the Institute in 1809.

Cimarosa [1749–1801]. Born at Aversa (kingdom of Naples).

A pupil of Fenaroli and of Piccinni, himself a very prolific composer, he wrote more than eighty extremely interesting scores, of which one alone remains known to this day as a masterpiece: *Il Matrimonio Segreto.*

Salieri [1750–1825]. Born at Legnano.

A great admirer of Gluck, he received advice from the German composer and came more and more under his influence.

The circumstances in which was composed the opera of *The Danaïdes*, for which Salieri is specially celebrated, show the cordial nature of the affection existing between these two composers. Gluck, at this time an old man worn out with many labours, had received from the Opéra in Paris an order for *The Danaïdes*, of which he was at the time writing the libretto; this he gave to Salieri, who then composed the score, and went to Paris to direct the rehearsals in the character of the author's pupil, entrusted by the author with this duty, and with full discretion in executing it. Only after the success of the work was completely secured did Gluck unveil this affectionate deceit, in a letter declaring that Salieri was the sole and only author of the music of *The Danaïdes*.

His other works are far less known.

Among his disciples were Beethoven and Meyerbeer; in 1806 he became corresponding member of the Institute.

Zingarelli [1752–1837]. Born in Naples.

Author of a large number of operas, notably, a *Romeo and Juliet*, and of much church music. He was Maestro di Cappella at S. Peter's in Rome from 1804 to 1811. His works are characterised by more grace and simplicity than science.

We again interrupt the list of dramatic composers to inscribe in order of date the name of a great virtuoso, who, like Boccherini, produced only instrumental works, and, like him, has much in common with the German School, whose productions he must have thoroughly studied; it is, moreover, certain that in 1771, he heard Haydn and Mozart in Vienna, which may explain the fact.

Clementi (Muzio), [1752–1832]. Born in Rome.

A composer and organist; he published a hundred and six sonatas, for piano, with or without accompaniment, many short separate pieces, and the *Gradus ad Parnassum*, which remains to this day one of the fundamental works for classic instruction on the piano. John Field and Hummel were pupils of Clementi.

We return to the theatre with :

Paer (Ferd.), [1771–1839]. Born at Parma.

A prolific composer, but at the present time quite out of fashion. Of fifty operas, serious or comic, we know scarcely more than the *Maestro di Capella*. He was one of the musicians most valued by Napoleon I., to whose household he was attached from 1806; in 1831 he became Member of the Institute.

An excellent singer, and also the author of charming *ariettas*, now absolutely forgotten, in the Italian manner of Mozart, he delighted the Emperor by his ways of singing certain airs of Paisiello, which Napoleon particularly enjoyed. It is easy to understand that in those years when the crowns of France and Italy were united upon one head, very many things tended to a fusion of French and Italian art ; from this fusion, as also from a study of the great works of Gluck, came forth a genius which might be described as Franco-Italian, whose noble and stately style harmonised well with the artistic tendencies and the general taste of the epoch :

Spontini (Gasparo), [1774–1851]. Born at Majolati (Roman States).

La Vestale and *Fernand Cortez* are the two great works which make him famous; we may also mention *Olympie*.

Spontini's style is majestic, solemn, always noble and pure. Before attempting operas he composed many works in the Italian style, of which none remains.

He died a member of the Institute and loaded with honours, in his native village, whither he had desired to return, and in the arms of his wife, a niece of Érard, the great maker of pianos.

Some fragments of the *Vestale* and of *Fernand Cortez* are still in the répertoire of the Société des Concerts.

Another product of the same period, to whom the future was to decree less fame, is :

Carafa (Michele), [1787–1872]. Born in Naples.

A number of dramatic works, of which the best known are . *Masaniello, La Violette, Le Valet de Chambre.*

Professor of composition in the Conservatory, and member of the Institute in 1837; director of the Gymnase Musicale Militaire from 1838 till the suppression of this school in 1856.

He was the intimate friend and usual companion at meals

of Rossini, who, more profoundly Italian, was acted upon by French influence only as late as 1828: in the composition of *Comte Ory,* a little, and of *William Tell,* completely. Like most great men who have dominated their epoch, the Swan of Pesaro had many difficulties in the beginning of his career, and was obliged to do everything for himself. An indefatigable worker,—though having, in some way, I know not how, the unmerited reputation of an idler,— even in his advanced old age he wrote continually, often while talking, for the mere pleasure of writing, at his table, without aid of any instrument, and sprinkling each page before he laid it aside, with a fine pinch of snuff.

Rossini (Gioacchino), [1792–1868]. Born at Pesaro.

The most famous of the great Italian composers was the son of a poor vagrant musician and an obscure actress. He learned music by himself, by intuition and observation; his genius moulded his talent, for it cannot be attributed to the insufficient lessons he received from Padre Matteï of the school of Bologna. I have it from himself, and he was always willing to tell the story, that he learned harmony by writing the score to Haydn's Quartets. His greatest admiration was for Mozart, and he acknowledged willingly that he had often, especially in his earlier works, taken the German composer for a model. Thenceforward he surpassed his predecessors in purity of lines and in the elegance of the melody,—always admirably appropriate to the voice,— in the richness and boldness of the harmony which he learned from his German models, and in the interest and strength of his orchestration (which led his detractors to call him *Il Signor Vacarmini*), as well as by certain procedures peculiar to himself, such as the development of the *finales,* the repetition of formulas of cadence, and his famous *crescendo,* which excited the enthusiasm of dilettanti.

The triumphs of Rossini demonstrate that his genius was truly of his own time, and came just when the public were sufficiently prepared to admit his innovations; to this fortunate circumstance he owed it that his greatest success came in his lifetime, and that he died surrounded with honours and fame.

I will not attempt to give a full list of his forty operas, serious or bouffe, and will merely enumerate the principal ones, in their order of appearance: *La Cambiale di Matrimonio,* his first dramatic work (Venice, 1810); *L'Inganno felice; Tancredo* (1813); *Il Barbiere di Siviglia,* written in seventeen days (Rome, 1816) ; *Otello ; Cenerentola ; La Gazza ladra* (1817); *Mosè in Egitto* (1818); *La Donna del Lago* (1819); *Bianca e Faliero ; Maometto*

II. (1820); *Matilda di Ciabranó* (1821); *Semiramide* (1823); *Siège de Corinthe* (1826); *Le Comte Ory* (1828); and, lastly, *Guillaume Tell* (1829).

This last work was welcomed with amazement by the whole musical world. Rossini had, in truth, experienced a marvellous transformation. It is no longer Italian music; it is French art, with Italian grace and German solidity,— a new style, in a word, and so interesting that it made the faults of the libretto pardonable. After *William Tell*, Rossini declared that he would write no more, fearing that he should not do as well again. However, twelve years later, he produced a very beautiful *Stabat Mater*, which does not, however, eclipse that of Pergolesi, and, in 1865, a *Petite Messe solennelle*, for the opening of the house of his friend, Comte Pillet-Will, regent of the Banque de France; but he wrote no more for the stage.

In his old age he composed much piano-music, which his favourite pianists, especially Diémer, performed at the master's Saturday receptions.

He was *grand officier* of the Legion of Honour (1864), *Commandeur* of the Saints-Maurice-et-Lazare, decorated with almost all the foreign Orders, and member of the Institute.

Since 1830 the influence of Romanticism had made itself felt in Italy. Rossini, living in France, remained free from it, quietly following out his own personal evolution, in which he preserved to the last the classic character, notwithstanding his changes of style.

It was not the same with those of his fellow-countrymen who remained in Italy, becoming — although the separation was less marked than in Germany and in France — the Italian Romanticists.

F.— Italian Romantic School.

These composers are not very numerous, for it is a period of decline in Italian art. Many, however, do not merit the oblivion with which they seem to be threatened.

Donizetti (G.), [1797–1848]. Born at Bergamo.

Had for master in composition and harmony Matteï, of the Musical Lyceum of Bologna.

Numerous Italian operas, among others: *Anna Bolena, Lucia di Lammermoor;* a comic opera, *La Figlia del Reggimento;* and one more opera, *La Favorita*, still frequently performed. Also may be mentioned: *Maria Padilla*, *Linda di Chamouni*, *Don Pasquale*.

Mercadante (Francesco Saverio), [1797–1870]. Born at Altamura.

Author of a respectable number of operas (about sixty), he enjoyed great reputation in Italy and Spain, but had no success in France, where musicians, as a rule, know nothing of him except his name.

He also wrote much church music, cantatas, and many symphonies, in respect to which I am ignorant.

Bellini (Vincenzio), [1802–1835]. Born at Catana (Sicily).

A pupil of Zingarelli, in the Conservatory of Naples, from whom he seems to have retained very little; he was able to create for himself a style full of charm and expression. He wrote only operas. His principal works are: *La Straniera*, *I Capuletti ed i Montecchi*, *La Sonnambula*, *Norma*, *I Puritani*.

Ricci (Luigi), [1805–1860]. Born at Naples.

Ricci (Frederico), [1809–1877].

The brothers Ricci composed a number of Italian operas frequently in collaboration. Their principal success was the opera buffa, *Crispino e la Comare*, which was played first in Naples, then throughout Italy, in Paris at the Théâtre Italien, and then in many foreign cities.

We now come to that extraordinary man whose name is Verdi, who, after beginning with works of singular awkwardness, has gradually risen, always improving, without ever losing his national character and his individuality; and has been able, at the age of eighty-one, to compose his best work, *Falstaff*, a brilliant masterpiece, in which he shows not only that his Italian *verve* is very far from being exhausted, but also that he has been able to assimilate, even at his advanced age, all the most modern procedures — in form, in harmonization, and in orchestration — of all the schools; and this, while taking care — after the manner of the Italian School, whose most illustrious representative he without doubt is — to give the virtuosity of the singer every opportunity to display itself.[1]

[1] Verdi's is the only operatic career of the nineteenth century which bears comparison with that of the German master whose life began five months before Verdi's and ended nearly two decades earlier. Wagner's works illustrate the force of conviction working out its end in spite of obstacles ; Verdi's exemplify the development of high ideals in the midst of popular success. — Ed.

Verdi (Giuseppe) [1813–1901], composer. Born at Roncole.

He seems never to have had any real instructor, and to have trained himself by reading contemporary Italian works, which he then imitated in the most servile manner.

His first work performed was: *Oberto Conte di San Bonifazio* (Milan, 1839), where his inexperience is very manifest.

The following are the titles of his chief works: *Nabucodonosor, I Lombardi, Ernani, I due Foscari, Gerusalemme* (a transformation of *I Lombardi*), *Luisa Miller, Rigoletto, Il Trovatore, La Traviata, Les Vêpres siciliennes, Simone Boccanegra, Un Ballo in Maschera, La Forza del Destino, Don Carlos, Aïda, Otello, Falstaff* (1894).

For the church: his Requiem in memory of Manzoni, and four sacred pieces, including a *Stabat* (1898).

By the versatility of his genius and the absolutely youthful vitality of his talent, he appears as the superb culmination of the modern Italian School.

He was corresponding member of the Institute, Senator of the Kingdom of Italy, and received the Grand Cross of the Legion of Honour (1894) on the first performance (in Paris) of his *Otello*.

After this great genius, and before leaving the unrivalled Italian School,— till we return to it in the section on Contemporaries,— let us notice the many virtuosi whom it has produced.

We have already said that this school was above all, that of melody, of singing (*il bel canto*), and of virtuosity. Moreover, the Italian climate is the one among the climates of Europe which produces the best and warmest voices. Hence we seek here the greatest singers, the virtuosi of vocalisation. They are legion, and admirable; certainly no one can sing like them. But what we must also know is this, that Italian singing, at least up to the time of Rossini, and perhaps later, differs essentially from what we call singing in France; it is an art vaster — and especially freer — than with us.

In the old Italian School, the composer who wrote a vocal passage could never expect to hear it sung as he wrote it; his phrase is only the canvas upon which the singer embroiders, and has the right — I would almost say the duty — to embroider all the arabesques, all the vocalisation that seems to him suitable. The composer is therefore at the mercy of his interpreter, who exhausts all his ingenuity in completing the other's work, introducing the brilliant passages and cadenzas that are best suited to exhibit his talent and his voice. If the singer has tact and taste, the effect is good; if not, it is a succession of acrobatic feats and nothing more. This explains in a degree why the Italian composers took so little pains to make their melodies conform to the sentiments expressed by the words; it would be trouble wasted, the singer being sure to upset everything. This explains also the importance of singers in Italy, who thus became actual collaborators with the composer himself. The singer created the work almost as much as the author did; for, in this music where the melody was almost everything, he had the right to modify it at will, to change or disguise it, according to his own good pleasure. The composer supplied the rough sketch, the singer drew it to scale, and completed the work according to his own standard. We have therefore to consider the Italian singers, not as the respectful and obedient interpreters of the master's ideas, but as artists completing the master's work, in a sense, and with a last varnishing giving it the necessary prestige. Moreover, the Italian School, except in the person of its most eminent and latest representatives, is too feeble in its constructions to be able to do without this aid.

Among these fascinating singers, there were some of strange nature, whose talent must have been real, for it contributed their sole element of worldly success. I will name but a few :

Caffarelli [1703–1783], by his true name **Majorano**, soprano. Born at Bari.

One of the most wonderful of Italian singers; pupil of Porpora and of Caffaro, whence his name.

He had prodigious success and gained money enough to buy himself a small ducal estate and title, the dukedom of Santo-Dorato.

Farinelli (1705–1782), soprano. Born in Naples.

By his true name Carlo Broschi. The most wonderful male

soprano that has ever been heard; he was a pupil of Porpora, and had a European reputation.

Crescentini (1766–1846), soprano. Born at Urbania (Roman States).

One of the greatest dramatic singers of Italy; composed *ariettas* and vocal exercises still famous in instruction. This singer received from Napoleon I. the decoration of the Iron Crown of Lombardy.

The famous Italian *cantatrice* are past numbering; I mention almost at random:

Agujari (Lucrezia), [1743–1783], called *la Bastardella*. Born at Ferrara.

Mozart relates that her voice reached the high C (with five leger lines in the key of G). He heard her at Parma, in 1770.

Sontag (Henriette), [1805–1854]. Born at Coblentz.

One of the most famous prima donnas of the century; she began the theatrical career at the incredible age of *six*, and pursued it uninterruptedly with ever-increasing success, visiting Germany, Italy, France, Russia, finally America, where she died of cholera, in Mexico.

From 1826 to 1830, she belonged, with some intermittence, to the Théâtre Italien of Paris.

Malibran (Marie Félicité), [1808–1836]. Born in Paris.

Daughter of the famous singer Garcia, wife, by a second marriage, of the no less celebrated violinist, de Bériot, her brother was Manuel Garcia, professor of singing at the Conservatory, her sister was Madame Viardot, her son, Charles de Bériot, is now professor of the piano at the Conservatory, and her nephew, Paul Viardot, a very remarkable violinist. This is what may be called a family of artists.

She had an enthusiastic success in Paris, London, New York, Milan, Naples, Bologna, especially near the close of her too short career, for she died in the midst of her triumph at the age of twenty-eight. Her teacher of singing was her father, and she studied solfeggio and the piano with Panseron and Hérold.

Frezzolini (Erminia), [1818–1884]. Born at Orvieto.

Pupil of Ronconi and Manuel Garcia.

Had brilliant successes in Italy, London, Vienna, S. Petersburg, and finally in Paris, from 1838 to 1855.

Alboni (Marietta), [1823–1894]. Born at Cesana (Romagna).

A contralto voice, the most wonderful in its flexibility, its immense range, and the beauty of its timbre, that perhaps has ever existed. (See p. 73.)

Cruvelli (J. Sophia), [1826]. Born at Bielefeld (Westphalia).

By her true name, Sophia Krüvell, was celebrated in Italy, England, and in Paris, where she married Comte Vigier.

I continue my enumeration : **Tonelli, Mme. Catalani** (1779–1849), who was for a year Directress of the Théâtre Italien in Paris; **Pisaroni, Grassini,** Mesdames **Pasta,** Giulia **Grisi, Persiani, Borghi-Mamo,** and more recently the two sisters, Adelina and Carlotta **Patti,** whose brilliant successes everyone remembers.

Patti (Adelina), [1843]. Born in Madrid.

One of the last and most brilliant representatives of the beautiful vocal art of Italy, was a pupil of Strakosch, her brother-in-law, and went over the entire world, amid unparalleled triumphs which increased year after year. Her voice, an extremely high soprano, of crystalline purity, her prodigious talent in vocalisation, and her real merits as an actress fully justified the frantic admiration of dilettanti.

From 1861 to 1870 she sang in Paris at the Théâtre Italien. Beside the Italian music she attempted French opera, notably *Faust,* the *Huguenots,* and *Romeo and Juliet,* but here she was no longer in her element.

Among male singers, not less brilliant, we find :

Garcia (Manuel Vincent), [1775–1832]. Born in Seville.

A singer and composer, also a professor of music, he had manifold successes. At the present day he is only known on account of his pupils, of whom the most remarkable were his two daughters, Mme. Malibran de Bériot, and Mme. Viardot.

Rubini [1795–1854]. Born at Romano, near Bergamo.

A very famous tenor, who sang in all the great cities of Europe, and for more than twelve years in Paris; his successes may be judged by the amount of fortune he accumulated,— 3,500,000 francs!

Mario [1812–1883]. Born at Cagliari.

A charming tenor of the Italian school, very successful at the Opéra in Paris, then at the Théâtre Italien (1840), and also in England and America.

Tamburini [1800–1876].   Born at Faenza.

An admirable basso-buffo; also his son-in-law:

Gardoni (Italo), [1821–1882].   Born at Parma.

One of the most fascinating tenors that ever lived.

Ronconi, Zucchini, Scalese, Taglifico, and many others.

Many singers of foreign nationality, attracted by the charm of Italian singing, embraced the Italian career: besides Mme. Sontag, who was German, Mme. Malibran, French, and Sophia Cruvelli, also German, may be mentioned among these brilliant recruits: Mesdames **Mainvielle Fodor, de Méric Lalande, de Méric Lablache, de la Grange Jenny Lind;** and among the men, the famous **Lablache,** a Frenchman, **Agnesi,** a Belgian, **Tamberlik,** an Italian; and there are many others.

To form these admirable artists there were needed — besides the composers, who, however, were all singers and teachers of singing — special professors, themselves generally singers and also composers on occasion, so greatly in this art do all things hold together and mingle, with virtuosity for the pivot.   It is in this two-fold aspect that we must consider personalities like these:

Bordogni [1783–1856].   Born at Bergamo.

Professor of singing in the Conservatory in 1820, he is still known by numerous and elegant vocal exercises.

Banderali [1789–1849].   Born at Lodi.

Extremely well known by his vocal exercises.   Professor at the Conservatory from 1828 till his death.

Garcia (Manuel), [1805].   Born in Madrid.

Son of the great singer, and himself especially famous as an instructor; he was professor of singing in the Conservatory in Paris, where he has left important works.   Jenny Lind was one of his pupils.   He still lives in England.

Besides these, many others.

Instruction in harmony, on the other hand, could have but little importance in this school.   Accordingly, it is only modestly represented by:

Padre Martini [1706–1784].   Born at Bologna.

Very scientific composer and writer, has left masses, antiphons, litanies, and works on the history of music, often curious though very fanciful.

Padre Fenaroli [1732–1818].   Born at Lanciano (Abruzzi).

Author of a remarkable work on the accompaniment of the figured bass.

Cimarosa was one of his pupils.

Padre Stanislas Mattei [1750–1825].   Born at Bologna.

Known as the instructor of Rossini, Donizetti and others, to whom he could not have taught anything of great importance, if we may judge by the insufficiency of his works of instruction.

We have, however, some good exercises in harmony on the piano, of his composition,— what is now called accompaniment; and we know that he wrote much church music.

Association with all the great singers, and the admiration called forth by their vocalisation could not but stimulate, in its turn, instrumental virtuosity.   It did so; and, the progress in violin-making aiding, with makers such as:

Guadagnini (Lorenzo and Gianbattista).   Born at Piacenza in the eighteenth century.   (See in the section *Violin*, p. 135.)

Bergonzi (Carlo), [eighteenth century].   Born at Cremona.

Pupil of Antonio Stradivarius.   Known especially for his violoncellos.

it was especially violinists that Italy produced at this time:

Viotti (G. B.), [1753–1824].   Born at Fontanello (Piedmont).

The greatest violinist of his time and unquestionably founder of a school.   Among his pupils were Rode and Robberechts.

Twenty-nine concertos for violin, and a great number of sonatas, duos, trios, and quartours for strings came from his pen.

Full of modesty as an artist, Viotti never sought popular successes, but he enjoyed the highest consideration in the circles of distinguished amateurs.

He was for three years (1819–1822) director of the Opéra in Paris.

Paganini [1784–1839].   Born in Genoa.

The most wonderful of violin virtuosi, he invented new and

extraordinary effects, of which a few have been imitated by a limited number of players, notably Sivori, while the most of them have remained an undiscovered secret. There was certainly in his manner a studied eccentricity which has often been censured as charlatanism, and his manner of singing was not always in perfect taste; but the spell of his execution was so marvellous that more than one superstitious auditor attributed to him supernatural assistance. He had made a promise that he would reveal his secret before he died, but the promise was not kept.

One of his favourite effects consisted in removing three strings from his violin, and upon the remaining one to execute passages of the most incredible difficulty. This was acrobatic, rather than artistic, but it was surprising in the highest degree.

Sivori (Camillo), [1815–1894]. Born in Genoa.

A pupil and follower of Paganini; he had extraordinary success all over the world, not merely on account of his transcendent virtuosity, but also of the breadth and elevation of style with which he rendered the classic masters.

He was a great artist and a remarkable reader.

There were published in his lifetime some violin pieces of his composition, most of them Fantasias and of no great value.

Milanollo (Teresa), [1827]. Born at Savigliano (Italy).

A violinist, admirable especially by the expression and depth of the artistic feeling. She travelled repeatedly in Italy, France, England, Holland, Belgium, Prussia, Austria, and Switzerland, with ever increasing success. She had the good taste, even after her talent was unquestionably exceptional, to seek lessons on the violin, from distinguished masters, wherever in her journeyings she chanced to meet them; thus she was successively the pupil of Lafont, of Habeneck, of de Bériot,—to mention only the most famous.

She had a sister, Maria, who was her pupil and shared in her successes, but died young, in 1848.

Sighicelli (Vincenzo), [1830]. Born at Centa.

Son and grandson of violinists for five generations. He enjoyed a good deal of popularity in Paris for many years; at present he is rarely heard. He is the author of a number of estimable works for the violin.

If we add here the name of :

Bottesini [1823–1889]. Born in Lombardy.

The only virtuoso of the contrabass who has ever been heard of;[1]

1 [Except Dragonetti. ED.]

executed upon that unpropitious instrument the sweetest melodious passages and the most difficult; he obtained the harmonics with extreme facility. He was the Paganini of the contrabass.

we shall have mentioned, I think, the most conspicuous artists of that beautiful and fruitful Italian school which we disdain too much because we do not know it enough. In art we should be eclectic, and consider that a music which filled all Europe with enthusiasm for centuries cannot be totally devoid of charm. A knowledge of the Italian school and its method concerns us, moreover, from a more personal point of view. The common origin of the two nations and the two languages, the frequency of relations, the prolonged presence of Italian singers in Paris, all explain the manifold indebtedness of one school to the other,— an indebtedness which must be remembered, or otherwise, parts of the history of French music, which we shall now attempt to sketch,— would become almost incomprehensible.

G. — The French Classic School.

With **Rameau,** the greatest dramatic composer of his time (1683–1764), concerning whom we have already given (p. 409) some short biographical notes, we resume the study of the French school. It will be remembered that this admirable musician began by writing works of instruction, and only at an advanced age turned his attention to dramatic composition. With him, instrumentation takes color, the wood-winds seem to have a certain freedom, the melodic contour becomes more noble, and the harmony acquires a certain richness; in a general way he continues the system of Lully with wider scope. The same epoch saw, almost simultaneously, Bach in Germany, Scarlatti in Italy, Rameau in France.

During the lifetime of these composers, occurred the musical quarrel known under the name of *guerre des bouffons* (1752 and the following years). It happened thus:

Louis XV. and Madame de Pompadour were partisans of the French school, while the queen preferred the Italian. Hence : *le coin du roi, le coin de la reine.*

It must be remembered that the Italian ideal was the virtuosity of the singer ; the *bel canto* with its *fioriture* and *fanfreluches.* French art, on the contrary, tended to develop itself in the path it has always followed, that is to say, in a dramatic direction, seeking truth in the expression of feeling. The idea was suggested of comparing a French work with an Italian work ; a passionate discussion as to their merits and comparative value followed, and the victory remained with France, so that the poor *bouffons* had to depart with all their belongings. This victory, however, was not of a definitive character, for the battle had not been honestly fought.

The Italian school was admirably represented by the masterpiece of one of the greatest masters (the *Serva Padrona* of Pergolesi), to which the French school opposed a work of secondary merit, due to the comparatively unskilful and certainly mediocre pen of Jean-Joseph Cassanea de

Mondonville [1711–1772].

This composer gained but one success, and that absolutely ephemeral and due to royal protection, with *Titon et l'Aurore.* Although of very poor quality as a musician, he belongs to the history of music because he was chosen as a sort of champion by Louis XV. against the Italian school, which had the favour of the queen.

Under these conditions it is evident the *bouffons* should have had an easy victory ; not that their art was of a higher quality than our own (which we do not admit), but because of the crushing superiority of their champion. Then an act of treachery was done : on the morning of the performance of *Titon,* the king's gentlemen and his courtiers took complete possession of the hall, leaving no place for the partisans of the Italians, and it was this audience, with minds made up to praise, that gave the work of Mondonville a reception whose applause the future was obliged to decide unmerited. The dispute, therefore, was destined to recommence, and that very speedily.

A few years later, rises the grand figure of Gluck. Although a German by birth, and having received his musical education in Italy, he is so French in the character of his genius, he so follows in the track of Lully and Rameau, that I have no hesitation in ranking him among the most illustrious representatives of our great national style.

Gluck [1714–1787]. Born at Weidenwang (in the upper Palatinate).

Brought up in a station of life akin to domestic service, in 1736 he was little better than a vagrant musician, roving from village to village and from church to church, to sing and to play the violin. Between 1740 and 1760 he wrote much, of which there seems to be but very little left. From this time on, however, he composed successively: *Orfeo*, *Alceste*, *Iphigénie en Aulide*, *Armide*, *Iphigénie en Tauride*, five immortal works, which have determined the direction of musical dramatic art,— not to speak of a number of other important productions which have now fallen into oblivion, and are to be found only on the shelves of the great libraries.

His principal successes were in France, at the court of Marie Antoinette, who in her youth had been for a short time his pupil.

It was in Italy, in 1762 and 1767, that he wrote, to Italian librettos, the first version of *Orfeo* and of *Alceste*. In a preface to the latter work, he explains that it is his intention to put an end to singers' exactions and the excessive compliance of composers; to bring back music to its true function, namely, the production of feeling,— in a word, the entire programme of French dramatic opera. Accordingly, it is not surprising to see him fail in Italy and in Germany. Before coming to the Opéra in Paris, he took care to secure the good will of the journals and of well-known authors like Rousseau, and also the efficacious support of the queen, Marie Antoinette, who gave him her protection, perhaps even invited him.

Here, then, in 1774, he produced *Iphigénie en Aulide* and modified *Orfeo* and also the Italian *Alceste* by adapting to them French librettos. Here, too, he composed *Armide*, in 1777.

During this time had awakened — after a truce of fifteen years — the old quarrel between the partisans of Italian vocalisation and those of lyric declamation. This time, there was pitted against Gluck a rival of importance, Piccinni, of whose worth we have already spoken. The two masters treated, each in his own way, and with a libretto of his own selection, the same subject, *Iphigenia in Tauris;* and about 1779 the two works were performed with equal care. Then ended forever the famous strife between *Gluckists and Piccinnists;* the latter were defeated notwithstanding the real merits of melodic grace which their champion opposed to the classic grandeur and dramatic feeling of Gluck. Such was the epilogue to *la guerre des bouffons.*

Gluck has been considered by all the great masters who followed him — to whatever nation they belonged — as having opened new and broad paths for dramatic musical manifestation; and Mozart, Rossini, Verdi, as well as Wagner and Berlioz, have never thought of denying the fact of his influence upon them. He enriched the orchestra with new effects and new timbres; he introduced into the opera harmonic procedures which had never been attempted before, outside of oratorios; his melody became particularly declamatory and expressive; and, finally, rhythm took an almost Greek importance, which it has never lost.

A pupil of his was Salieri, who, in turn, was one of the masters of Beethoven and of Meyerbeer; and it is singular to see that the latter, seventy-seven years later, followed exactly in the footsteps of Gluck, as if by a sort of artistic heredity. Born in Germany, he studied in Italy, and only found his definitive form and perfect expansion in the French opera, as his illustrious musical ancestor had done.

But we will not anticipate. For the moment we have to enumerate a few artists, certainly of fair merit, but dwarfed into extreme insignificance by the formidable personality of Gluck, whose contemporaries they were.

Philidor (F. A. Danican), [1726–1795]. Born at Dreux.

More famous as a chess player than as a musician. He was the first to carry on several games at once without seeing the boards. However, it is certain that at the Opéra, as well as at the Comédie Italienne and at the Opéra-Comique, he had great successes, and that he was one of the first musicians of his time.

Monsigny [1729–1817]. Born near Saint-Omer (Pas-de-Calais).

Notwithstanding his well-merited successes, we must regard Monsigny as a distinguished amateur endowed with exquisite sensibility, rather than as an accomplished artist; he had no special erudition, and in his work all depends on musical instinct, which he possessed in a very high degree.

This opinion only heightens the merit of his works, simple, naïve, sincere,— of which *Rose et Colas* and *le Déserteur* are the best known at the present time. He was a member of the Institute during the last three years of his life.

Gossec [1733–1829]. Born in Belgium.

A remarkable symphonist, a theorician and professor of great talent, appointed inspector of the Conservatory at the time it was established, and afterwards member of the Institute.

His works are totally unknown at the present day, notwithstanding their great number and their real value.

Grétry [1741–1813]. Born at Liège.

A musician rather inspired than instructed in his art; a member of the Institute from its beginning, inspector of the Conservatory for some months. His work was especially for the Opéra-Comique; the most famous of his compositions are: *Le Tableau parlant*, *Les Deux Avares*, *Zémire et Azor*, *Le Magnifique*, *La Rosière de Salency*, *L'Epreuve villageoise*, *Richard Cœur de Lion*, *La Caravane du Caïre*, *L'Amant jaloux*.

Martini [1741–1816]. Born at Friestadt (in the Palatinate).

His true name was Schwartzendorf, and he must not be confounded with the learned Padre Martini. He was a graceful and facile musician, scarcely known except by two opéras-comiques, *Le Droit du seigneur*, and *Annette et Lubin*, and especially by a romance: *Plaisir d'Amour*, a graceful type, whose success has been very lasting.

Dalayrac (N.), [1753–1809]. Born at Muret (Languedoc).

Studied harmony with Langlé, who was himself a pupil of Caffaro; between 1782 and 1804 he composed about fifty opéras-comiques, of which the best known are: *Nina, Camille ou le Sou-*

terrain, Gulistan; also a quantity of short romances in the style of the day.

I should mention here the name of an amateur, who has become more famous than many artists :

Rouget de l'Isle [1760–1836]. Born in Lons-le-Saulnier.

Author of many romances and patriotic airs, of which he wrote both words and music, among them the alluring *Marseillaise,* destined to play the part we know in the history of France. At the time this was composed (1792) he was an officer of engineers in garrison at Strassburg.

Lesueur (Jean-François), [1760–1837]. Born near Abbeville.

After being choir-master of Notre Dame de Paris in 1786, then of the chapel of the Emperor Napoleon in 1804, he was appointed member of the Institute in 1813. He had been inspector of the Conservatory since its foundation and later was professor of composition. He wrote many remarkable religious works,— masses, motets, the Emperor's Coronation March, as well as a great number of operas in a style no longer interesting.

Perhaps his chief title to fame is that he was the instructor of three famous pupils: Berlioz, Gounod, Ambroise Thomas.

Cherubini [1760–1842]. Born at Florence.

Was considered by Beethoven, Haydn, and Méhul as the first dramatic composer of his time. From a multitude of works we may name: *Lodoïska, les Deux Journées, Faniska,* masses, and other church music.

Member of the Institute, professor, then director at the Conservatory from 1821 to 1841; among his pupils were Zimmerman, Auber, and Halévy; he left a *Treatise on Counterpoint and Fugue,* which contains perfectly correct precepts, but arranged entirely without precision or clearness; and also excellent solfeggios.

Méhul [1763–1817]. Born at Givet.

His great dramatic works, in which we may trace the influence of Gluck: *Euphrosine et Corradin, Stratonice, Phrosine et Mélidor, La Caverne, Le jeune Henri, Ariodant, l'Irato, Les Aveugles de Tolède,* and lastly *Joseph,* give him a place among the greatest composers of the French School.

He was one of the four inspectors appointed to organise the Conservatory.

Méhul is more directly a follower of Gluck than are any of the French masters whose names come between, even Lesueur and Cherubini, who, after Méhul, have most resemblance to that incomparable model. With him the opéra-comique attains to the same elevation of style as the grand opera, in no way distinguishable from it except by the substitution of spoken dialogue for recitative. Méhul's *Joseph* is still in the repertoire of all the great German opera-houses.

Onslow [1784–1852]. Born at Clermont. Of English origin.

After some fruitless dramatic attempts, he specialised himself in chamber music. He has left sonatas, duos, trios, quartets, a sextet for strings, and a remarkable collection of *quintets*, by which he has remained famous.

We now return to seek the origin of musical Romanticism in France.

H.—French Romantic School.

Its first representative is also one of the purest fames in the history of French music, one of the composers whose numerous successes had the widest appreciation, and whose style, always very correct, has only lately begun to go out of fashion.

Boïeldieu (Fr. Adrien), [1775–1834]. Born at Rouen.

With the exception of a few songs and some instrumental pieces, now forgotten, he wrote only for the stage.

Le Calife de Bagdad, Ma Tante Aurore, les Voitures versées, Jean de Paris, le Nouveau Seigneur de village, le Fête du village voisin, le Chaperon rouge; and lastly, *la Dame blanche,* which is still performed.

In the work of Boïeldieu all the inherent merits of the French style are seen — clearness, simplicity, sincerity, *esprit,* and cheerfulness. The harmony is very carefully written, very pure, and the instrumentation interesting; the ensemble is always elegant and well arranged. His long vogue is therefore deserved. Less important was:

Nicolo [1775–1818]. Born in Malta.

His true name was Isouard, Nicolo being only the Christian name. A composer of agreeable and easy music, he has left many *opéras-comiques*, among which may be mentioned: *les Rendezvous bourgeois*, *le Billet de loterie*, *Joconde*, *Jeannot et Colin*, which have had a lasting reputation.

The study of the French Romanticists brings us down, through one of the finest periods of art, to the present time. But we shall reserve for a separate chapter and special grouping those of the contemporary masters still in the midst of their militant career.

Immediately after the author of the *Dame Blanche,* we find in an uninterrupted succession the composers of *la Muette*, *le Pré aux Clercs*, *le Prophète*, *la Juive*, *le Châlet*, and *les Troyens*.

Auber (Daniel François Esprit), [1782–1871]. Born at Caen.

A pupil of Ladurner for the piano and of Cherubini in composition; the following are his principal operas:

Maçon, *la Muette*, *Fra Diavolo*, *le Dieu et la Bayadère*, *le Philtre*, *Gustave III.*, *le Cheval de bronze*, *le Domino noir*, *les Diamants de la Couronne*, *le Premier Jour de Bonheur*.

Auber is one of the most prolific dramatic composers of the French School, the cleverest, perhaps, and the most elegant. Grace and fineness are his characteristics. Once, exceptionally, in *la Muette*, he showed another aspect of his talent, for there, ardour, patriotic enthusiasm, and an almost Italian fire and spirit, become the dominant qualities. He was director of music in the imperial chapel of the Tuileries, for which he wrote a number of religious works; member of the Institute in 1829, and director of the Conservatory from 1842 to 1871. He died during the Commune.

Hérold (Ferdinand), [1791–1833]. Born in Paris.

A pupil of Fétis in solfeggio, of Catel in harmony, of Kreutzer for the violin, of Ad. Adam for the piano, of Méhul in composition, he obtained, in 1812, the prize of the Institute.

His most celebrated works are three *opéras-comiques: Marie*, *Zampa*, and *le Pré aux Clercs;* a style clear, elegant, facile; an orchestration rich and coloured; much piquancy in the melodic construction.

Meyerbeer (Giacomo), [1791–1864]. Born in Berlin.

It was at Darmstadt, about 1810, in the school of Abbé **Vogler,** where there was little interest in any other than scientific and religious music, that Meyerbeer began his serious studies in composition. Up to this time he had been only a skilful pianist, having been a pupil of Clementi, and was already celebrated, though so young; having, besides, a marvellous faculty for improvisation. Under Abbé Vogler he learned counterpoint and fugue, and the rules of composition in the German style. Nothing remains except the titles of a few (*Jephta's Gelübde,* oratorio; *les Amours de Tévelinde,* monodrama; *Alimelek,* opéra-comique,) of the dramatic or instrumental works of this first period of production (1813 and subsequent years).

Having by nature, and also as a result of the direction of his studies, the greatest reluctance for anything outside of German Art, he, however, made, by advice of Salieri, a journey to Venice, there to study the manner of employing the voice; and he became so enamoured of the school of Rossini that he abandoned his first style to write henceforward in the Italian manner. Among the works of this period, six or eight in number, only three are memorable, *Margherita d'Anjou* (1820), *l'Esule di Granata* (1822), and *Il Crociato* (1824, Venice), which established his reputation in Italy.

A second and splendid metamorphosis occurred when, in 1831, he produced in Paris, at the Opéra, *Robert le Diable,* in the French style, still following Rossini — who had become his intimate friend — in this new evolution; then came in succession: *les Huguenots* (1836) *Ein Feldlager in Schlesien* (1844), — which in 1854 became *l'Étoile du nord,* — *le Prophète* (1849), *le Pardon de Ploermel* (1859), and, lastly *l'Africaine,* which was not played until after the author's death, and into which it is probable he would have introduced some changes at the rehearsals, as was his constant practice.

Meyerbeer was elected associate member of the Institute in 1834.

Halévy (Fromental), [1799–1862]. Born in Paris.

Pupil of Berton and of Cherubini. Grand prix de Rome, in 1819.

His most important works are: *la Juive, l'Éclair, Guido et Ginevra, la Reine de Chypre;* but we should not forget : *les Mousquetaires de la Reine, la Fée aux Roses, la Magicienne, Jaguarita,* works which had their period of success, and largely merited it. At present we have in the Opéra repertoire only *la Juive,* and some fragments of *Guido* and *l'Éclair.*

Halévy was professor in the Conservatory; first of harmony and accompaniment, in 1827; later, in 1833, of counterpoint, fugue, and composition.

He became a member of the Institute in 1836, and perpetual secretary in 1852.

Adam (Adolphe), [1803–1805]. Born in Paris.

A pupil of Reicha and of Boïeldieu, second prix de Rome in 1825.

Le Châlet, le Postillon de Longjumeau, le Brasseur de Preston, Giselle, le Diable à quatre (ballet), *le Toréador, la Poupée de Nuremburg, Si j'étais Roi, les Pantins de Violette, Giralda,* etc. Many masses.

Member of the Institute in 1844.

Professor of composition at the Conservatory in 1848.

Berlioz (Hector), [1803–1869]. Born at La Côte-Saint-André (Isère).

One of the greatest and saddest examples of the man of genius unappreciated in his time.

Pupil of Lesueur at the Conservatory, he obtained the grand prix de Rome in 1830. He had studied previously under the direction of Reicha, but in reality retained, from the instruction of these two masters, only a few of Lesueur's ideas on methods,— which are frequently recognisable in his works, — and created for himself an entirely personal style, a result of his philosophic studies and the contemplation of the older masterpieces, those of Gluck particularly.

The principal works which he has bequeathed to our admiration are: *Benvenuto Cellini, la Prise de Troie, Béatrice et Bénédict, les Troyens à Carthage,* operas; *la Damnation de Faust,* legend; *l'Enfance du Christ,* oratorio; *Symphonie fantastique,* the symphony of *Harold en Italie* (with viola solo), the symphony of *Romeo and Juliet, Symphonie funèbre et triomphale;* three overtures: *les Francs-Juges, Waverley, Le Carnaval Romain.*

The studies of Berlioz were slow, painful, disconnected, and ill-conducted. It would suffice to read his Memoirs to be convinced of this, even if it were not written on every page of his works. where there is not to be found a trace of true science or of acquired skill, except in orchestration. One may state the fact without any irreverence, for it simply shows in Berlioz the triumph of inspiration and of will, and compels admiration for what in him is indeed admirable.

This estimate by no means depreciates him, as thinker and man of genius; it raises him, on the contrary, upon a pedestal altogether peculiar.

We have from his pen a remarkable *Traité d'instrumentation et d'orchestration,* followed by *Le chef d'orchestre.*

Although much undervalued by his contemporaries, Berlioz died an officer of the Legion of Honour, a member of the Institute, and the wearer of innumerable foreign decorations; he was also librarian of the Conservatory, and member of the musical jury in the Paris Exposition and also in that of London.

We come next to a peculiar type which stands alone in the history of French music : —

David (Félicien), [1810–1876], composer.   Born at Cadenet (Vaucluse).

Studied elementary music in a school in Aix, where he was afterwards choir-master; he then came to Paris, and studied harmony with Reber, the organ with Benoist, and composition with Fétis.

Having united himself with the Saint-Simonians, he accompanied, on their dispersal in 1833, the group which went to preach the new doctrine in the East.

This circumstance decided his career.   He became a musical Orientalist; not merely that he introduced into some of his works really Oriental themes, which any one may do,— but rather in the special colouring or turn of mind which resulted from a residence of nearly three years in Egypt, whence he brought back an Oriental style, conventional, it is true, but marvellously effective in producing the Oriental impression desired for Western ears, giving them an illusion of the East.

At this time he produced: *Le Désert, Christophe Colomb*, symphonic odes; *Le Perle du Brésil, Lalla Roukh*, opéras-comiques; *Herculanum*, grand opera; and many songs published in collections or separately.   His style is unusually poetic.

He became Member of the Institute in 1869 and titular librarian of the Conservatory from the same date until his death, six years later.

He was pre-eminently a dreamer, a poet, and a man of unpretending character.

At this time began the early successes of

Thomas (Ambroise), [1811–1896].

Who was destined to outlive nearly all of the associates of his youth.   Born in Metz, he began his studies in solfeggio at the age of four, under the direction of his father, and on the piano and violin when about seven.

In 1828, under the direction of Cherubini, he was received as a pupil at the Conservatory, of which, in 1891, he became the head; and received instruction there from Zimmermann on the piano, from Dourlen in harmony, and from Lesueur in composition; especially, however, from Kalkbrenner on the piano, and from Barbereau in counterpoint and fugue.

It was as the pupil of Lesueur and Barbereau that he obtained, in 1832, the grand prix of the Institute, by his cantata *Hermann et Ketty*.

From his residence in Rome he brought back a *Messe de Requiem;* to the same period belong a *Quatuor* and a *Quintette* for strings (1833–1836).

Then began the marvellously fruitful period of production of dramatic works by this illustrious composer: —

La Double Échelle, opéra-comique, one act (1837); *Le Perruquier de la Régence,* opéra-comique, three acts (1838); *La Gipsy,* ballet in two acts (in collaboration with Benoist) (1839); *Le Panier fleuri,* opéra-comique, one act (1839); *Carline,* opéra-comique, three acts (1840); *Le Comte de Carmagnola,* grand opera, two acts (1842); *Le Guerrillero,* grand opera, two acts (1842); *Angélique et Médor,* opéra-comique, one act (1843); *Mina,* opéra-comique, three acts (1843); *Betty,* ballet in two acts (1846); *Le Caïd,* opéra-comique, two acts (1849); *Le Songe d'une Nuit d'été,* opéra-comique, three acts (1850); *Raymond,* opéra-comique, three acts (1851); *La Tonelli,* opéra-comique, two acts (1853); *La Cour de Célimène,* opéra-comique, two acts (1854); *Psyché,* opéra-comique, three acts (1857); *Le Carnaval de Venise,* opéra-comique, three acts (1867); *Le Roman d'Elvire,* opéra-comique, three acts (1860); *Mignon,* opéra-comique, three acts (1866); *Hamlet,* grand opera, five acts (1868); *Gille et Gillotin,* opéra-comique, one act (1874); *Francoise de Rimini,* grand opera, five acts (1882); *La Tempête,* ballet in two acts (1889).

To these works for the stage must be added a *Cantata* performed in Rouen, in 1875, at the centenary fête of Boïeldieu, *Hommage à Boïeldieu;* a *Messe Solennelle* (1857); a *Marche religieuse* for the grand orchestra (1865); *Motets,* and a quantity of songs and romances; also choruses, really important works, many of which are famous: *Le Tyrol, La Nuit du Sabbat, Le Carnaval de Rome, Le Chant des Amis, L'Atlantide, France,*— which have done much to raise the intellectual musical level of the masses, as well as to make the author's name famous among the people.

Before being called to the directorship of the Conservatory, M. Thomas had been professor in the same institution from 1856 to 1870, giving instruction in counterpoint, fugue, and composition. Among his pupils,— many of whom have become famous,— I will mention only those who have received the honours of the Institute. Th. Dubois (1861), Bourgault-Ducoudray, Massenet, Sieg, Ch. Lefebvre, Salvayre (1872).

It was in 1871, after bravely fulfilling his duties as citizen during the siege of Paris, where I saw him on guard with the commander's cross on his overcoat of *garde national,* that he was appointed director of the Conservatory.

A member of the Institute since 1851, Ambroise Thomas was the first musician who ever received the grand cross of the Legion of Honour, which was bestowed upon him on the 16th of May, 1894, on occasion of the thousandth performance of his *Mignon* at the Opéra-Comique.

Shortly after, on the 16th of October, his illustrious friend Verdi (who had just received that honour himself), brought to him from the King of Italy the grand cordon of the Santi Maurisio è Lazzaro, the Italian equivalent to the Legion of Honour. M. Thomas died on February 12, 1896.

Maillart (Aimé) [1817–1871]. Born at Montpelier.

Pupil of Guérin for the violin, of Elwart in harmony, then of Leborne for fugue and composition, he obtained in 1841 the grand prix de Rome.

His dramatic works are; *Gastibelza, le Moulin des Tilleuls, la Croix de Marie, les Dragons de Villars, les Pêcheurs de Catane,* and *Lara.*

Litolff (Henry Charles), [1818–1891]. Born in London.

His father was French, his mother English.

In artistic temperament, he was not unlike Liszt. A great pianist virtuoso, fiery, impassioned, like Liszt a composer of the Romantic school, he unfortunately differed from the Abbé in the matter of success, of which he had very little, and perhaps also, he differed in possessing a less elevated tone.

He wrote for the theatre, the orchestra and the piano ; we may mention his concertos and symphonies; the overture of the *Girondins; Héloïse et Abélard,* operetta; *la Belle au Bois dormant,* pantomime; *l'Escadron volant de la reine,* opéra-comique.

Lacombe (Louis), [1818–1884]. Born at Bourges.

By his true name, Louis Brouillon, he was a pupil of Zimmermann, Czerny, and Barbereau. He is less than unappreciated, he is unknown, notwithstanding the unquestionable merit of his works, among which should at least be remembered: *les Harmonies de la nature, l'Ondine et le Pêcheur ;* two dramatic symphonies, *Manfred* and *Arva ;* an opéra-comique, *la Madone*; and *Winkelried,* a posthumous work. Some piano music of his has alone been successful, and even this success was quite ephemeral.

Offenbach (Jacques), [1819–1880]. Born at Cologne.

Creator of the genus *operetta,* which resembles the opéra-comique and the Italian opéra-buffa, his scores are full of talent and merriment, but sometimes lacking in distinction: *Orphée aux Enfers, la Belle Hélène, les Deux Aveugles, la Chanson de Fortunio,* etc. A musician by instinct and without musical education, he never succeeded in any higher kind of music; although at times, as in *les Contes d'Hoffmann*, he attempted it.

He is, however, one of the most entertaining artists that ever lived. And now we come to a very grand figure of the French School, a master whom each should salute with uncovered head. I refer to:

Gounod (Charles), [1818–1893]. Born in Paris.

Pupil of Halévy, Lesueur, and Paër, he obtained the grand prix de Rome in 1839.

His career is too recent in men's memories for me to need to sketch it here. I will only give a list, nearly chronological, of his principal works: *Sapho*, grand opera (1851); *la Nonne sanglante;* *le Médecin malgré lui*, opéra-comique; *Faust; la Colombe; Philémon et Baucis; la Reine de Saba; Mireille; Roméo et Juliette; Polyeucte; Cinq-Mars;* the music for two dramas, *les Deux Reines* of Lejouré, and the *Jeanne d'Arc* of Barbier; then, in another style, many masses, some for full orchestra; much church music, two symphonies, four collections of twenty songs each, which have become almost popular; a charming little poem, *Biondina;* the oratorio of *Tobie;* the fine lament, *Gallia; Rédemption, Mors et Vita;* a number of songs with English or Italian words, and even piano music and a method for the cor-à-pistons. Like Mozart, whom he adored, his last work was a *Requiem.* He died suddenly while playing it to his family and some friends.

This great genius, who was also a philosopher and a man of profound learning, will retain the place which he has valiantly won in the history of French music, to whose progress he has so greatly contributed, and of which he will remain one of the great glories. His nature, at once mystical and ardent, opened to art paths new, unexplored, and most fruitful,— followed out in our day by many, and destined long to affect the entire French School.

The funeral of Gounod, member of the Institute, grand officer of the Legion of Honour, was at the State's expense, and marked by great official display,— a just tribute to his merit.

Franck (César), [1822–1890]. Born at Liège.

Pupil of Zimmermann for the piano, and of Leborne in counterpoint, in the Conservatory of Paris, where he was later, from 1872 to 1891, professor of the class in organ music.

The following is a list of the principal works of this great musician, who trained numerous and enthusiastic students, and may be considered as distinctly the founder of a school:

Ruth, Biblical eclogue; Rédemption, a symphonic poem; Rebecca; les Béatitudes, oratorio; les Eolides; masses, offertories, organ music, etc.

Belgium claims the honour of his birth; he is the descendant of Bach by his scientific knowledge, of Gluck by his power of lofty expression, and of the German Romanticists by his harmonic methods; while he is French in the clearness, purity, and simplicity of work. Moreover, as an individual characteristic, he has a nobility, an elegance of form, an incomparable sweetness, which render the work of this great master imperishable. He was also a wonderful improvisator.

Massé (Victor), [1822–1884]. Born at Lorient.

Pupil of Zimmermann and Halévy, grand prix de Rome in 1844; his principal works were: la Chanteuse voilée, les Noces de Jeannette, Galathée, la Fiancée du Diable, Miss Fauvette, les Saisons, la Reine Topaze, la Fée Carabosse, la Mule de Pedro, Fior d'Aliza, Paul et Virginie.

He taught composition at the Conservatory from 1866 till his death; also from 1866 he was a member of the Institute.

Gevaert (François-Auguste), [1828]. Born at Huysse (Flanders).

A musician of profound learning, author of numerous and remarkable works of instruction: Traités d'instrumentation, Cours méthodique d'orchestration, Histoire et Théorie de la musique de l'antiquité.

Since 1872 he has been director of the Conservatory at Brussels.

Principal works: le Billet de Marguérite, les Lavandières de Santarem, opéras-comiques; Quentin Durward, lyric drama; le Diable au moulin, le Château-Trompette, le Capitaine Henriot (1864); les Deux Amours; choruses, religious music, a cantata on a Flemish theme, Jacques Arteveld, etc.

Lalo (Edouard), [1830–1892]. Born at Lille.

Began by writing chamber music and two symphonies, which attracted but little attention; then an opera in three acts, Fiesque, which has been much talked of, but has never been performed; then a Symphonie espagnole, for violin and orchestra, which, performed by Sarasate, obtained a very great success; then a Rapsodie norwégienne, a Concerto pour piano, Namouna, a ballet; much admired songs, a remarkable Divertissement for the orchestra, etc.; but it was only in his old age, or nearly so, that he had at last the satisfaction of seeing his Roi d'Ys, written long before, put upon the stage of the Opéra-Comique.

Delibes (Léo), [1836–1891]. Born at Saint-Germain-du-Val (Sarthe).

A musician essentially elegant, author of ravishing ballets, he was at first a choir-boy at the Madeleine in 1848, then pupil of Le Couppey, Bazin, and Adam, at the Conservatory.

Endowed with great facility of writing, he produced rapidly many short works which cannot here be enumerated, but made a brilliant success by his ballet, *La Source* (1866), written in collaboration with a young Russian musician, M. Minkous. From that time his career was established. He produced successively: *l'Écossais de Chatou; la Cour du roi Pétaud;* the ballet *Coppelia* (a gem of orchestration); *le Roi l'a dit,* opéra-comique; *Sylvia,* a ballet; then *Jean de Nivelle, Lakmé, Kassya,* of which he witnessed the first performance only.

The style of Delibes is always elegant, distinguished, charming. He is the direct successor of Hérold and of Ad. Adam, but with more *verve* and orchestral knowledge, and a prodigious facility of musical invention.

In 1881 he was appointed professor of composition at the Conservatory, and held this office until his death. Member of the Institute in 1885.

Guiraud (Ernest), [1837–1892]. Born in New Orleans (Louisiana).

Pupil of Marmontel, Barbereau, and Halévy, he obtained, in 1859, by unanimous vote, and at his first competition, the grand prix de Rome, which, by an occurrence unique in the history of this prize, his father had obtained, also, thirty-two years before, in 1827.

This distinguished musician, whose manner so well represented the merits of the French School — raciness, fire, elegance, and clearness — but whose career was too quickly ended, left but a limited number of works, all very personal and characteristic: *Sylvie* (1864), *En Prison, le Kobold, Gretna-Green* (ballet), *Madame Turlupin, Piccolino.*

Besides his dramatic compositions, *Suites d'orchestre,* of which one has for *finale* the famous *Carnaval,* which is also in the *Piccolino;* and an interesting little *Traité d'orchestration* which was one of the last things he wrote.

Member of the Institute, elected but a few months before his death in 1891.

The French Romantic School reached one of its highest points in the personality of the famous and so keenly regretted

Bizet (Georges), [1838–1875]. Born in Paris.

Pupil of Zimmermann in harmony, of Marmontel for the piano, and of Halévy in fugue and composition; grand prix de Rome in 1857.

This remarkable musician, whose name is today one of the most famous in the history of the French School, although he died at the age of thirty-seven, was one of the first in France to recognise the genius of Wagner, and to seek to assimulate his methods; this is apparent in most of his works, of which the following is a nearly complete list: *les Pêcheurs de perles* (1867), *la Jolie Fille de Perth, Djamileh, l'Arlésienne,* and *Carmen* (1875), the two latter really masterpieces.

Besides dramatic compositions, we may mention the beautiful overture of *Patrie,* a charming collection of twenty songs, and a few piano pieces.

His style, clear and melodious, remains truly French in its elegance and purity of lines. Only in the general plan and the employ of *Leitmotive* are recognisable those Wagnerian tendencies which he loudly proclaimed at a time when to do this required no little courage.

Chabrier (Emmanuel), [1841–1894]. Born at Ambert.

After having, at his father's wish, studied law in Paris and received his degree at the age of twenty, he was for some years attached to the Ministry of the Interior. This implies that his studies in music were those of an amateur. So far as is known he had but one teacher, Aristide Hignard, who himself had obtained, in 1850, for the second time, a second prix de Rome,— a modest and very distinguished musician.

Chabrier's first work was an opera-bouffe in three acts, *l'Étoile* (1877); then followed *l'Education Manquée,* one act (not orchestrated); then *Dix pièces pittoresques,* for the piano (1881); and *Trois Valses romantiques* for two pianos (1883); in the same year *le Credo d'Amour,* for the voice, and the famous *Rapsodie España,* for the grand orchestra, which called attention to him. Then appeared in succession: *la Sulamite* (1885); *Habanera,* for the piano (1885); *Gwendoline,* grand opera, two acts (1886); *Chanson pour Jeanne,* a song (1886); *le Roi Malgré lui,* opéra-comique, three acts (1887); *Joyeuse Marche,* for orchestra (1890); *l'Ile heureuse, Toutes les fleurs, les Cigales, la Villanelle des petits canards, la Ballade des gros dindons, la Pastorale des cochons roses,* piano and voice (1890); the *Bourrée fantastique* for the piano, and lastly, *A la musique,* chorus for female voices (1891). I believe this list is complete.

Godard (Benjamin), [1849–1895]. Born in Paris.

Pupil of Hammer for the violin, and of Reber in harmony.

A musician of rare merit who repeatedly gave evidence of real genius, yet never was able to produce a true masterpiece, perhaps because his work was too hasty and his brain too crowded with ideas. He did not mature his compositions, giving them to the public just as they were first written, without change or addition. Hence the inequality of his production, subordinated to the moment's inspiration, each being in the condition in which it was at first thrown off.

His principal work is *le Tasse*, by which he made himself known, obtaining, in 1878, at the age of twenty-eight, the prize of the City of Paris; then came *Jocelyn, le Dante, Pedro de Zalamea, les Guelfes*, concerning which the last word has not yet been said. At the time of his death he had finished, but not entirely orchestrated, the score of *la Vivandière*, destined for the Opéra-Comique. The first performance of this composition took place in 1895, shortly after his death, the orchestration having been completed by Vidal.

He also wrote remarkable orchestral works: *la Symphonie gothique, la Symphonie orientale, la Symphonie légendaire, la Symphonie-ballet, les Scènes poétiques*, two *Concertos*, one for violin, and one for piano; much chamber music of great interest; songs, and an astonishing quantity of piano music.

This enumeration, with all its faults, has brought us, step by step, into the heart of the modern school, so that, the history of music being thus made by the history of musicians, we shall have no occasion to define present tendencies.

Also, on the subject of actual contemporaries, the reader will permit me an extremely moderate expression of opinion. Without this reserve I should risk falling into many serious mistakes, which later I should be the first to deplore. In my judgment, it is only when an artist has finished his career, that we can — taking into consideration his entire work, seeing to what height he has been able to rise— cautiously allow ourselves to assign to him some sort of definite rank in the musical hierarchy. Also I should fear to be influenced by considerations of personal sympathies, taking from the needed independence of judgment; and, most of all, I desire not to place myself in the attitude of the critic, for which I do not feel myself fitted. Consequently, from this time forward, the reader will find, with rare exception, nothing more than names and dates and definite facts.

I. — Contemporaries.

A school which can have had the grief of losing in less than twenty years, these six men: Gounod, Thomas, Franck, Lalo, Delibes, and Bizet,— certainly gives no evidence of a period of decline. The brilliant series continues in our day, and the French school may be justly proud to count in its ranks such names as these: Reyer, Saint-Saëns, Massenet, Paladilhe, Théodore Dubois, members of the Institute; Victorin Joncières, Widor, Weckerlin, Alph. Duvernoy, Pugno, Lepot-Delahaye, Diaz, Vincent d'Indy, Fauré, S. Rousseau, Boellmann, Messager, Bruneau, William Chaumet, A. Coquard, Chausson, Missa, de Boisdeffre, Albert Cahen, Canoby, Gouvy, de la Tombelle, Ch. René, Chapuis, Mme. la Comtesse de Grandval, Mlle. Augusta Holmès,[1] Mlle. Chaminade, — whose names have figured on the play-bills of the Opéra and the Opéra-Comique, or on the programmes of the great symphonic concerts; and these also who have been pointed out to the attention of the public by the premier grand prix de Rome: Boulanger, Gastinel, Deffès, Ad. Barthe, Bourgault-Ducoudray, Lenepveu, Pessard, Ch. Lefebvre, Maréchal, Salvayre, Paul Puget, the brothers Hillemacher, André Wormser, Véronge de la Nux, Georges Hüe, Pierné, Marty, Vidal, Xavier Leroux, Charpentier,[2] Erlanger, and others.

Some of these have already taken rank, and others are becoming masters in their turn.

While a certain number of light and graceful composers, — Lecocq, Audran, Jonas, Planquette,[3] Serpette, Banès, Vasseur, Varney, Victor Roger, cultivate, under the designation of operetta, a pleasing kind of music, much resembling what used to be the opéra-comique, we have also, pledged to the consecrated style, great improvisators, — Th. Dubois, Widor, Guilmant, Gigout, Boellmann, Fissot, Pugno, Dallier, Sergent, Loret, Samuel Rousseau, Pierné, Galeotti, and others.[4]

[1] Died January 28, 1903. — ED.   [2] See Appendix.   [3] Died, 1903.
[4] De Bussy. — ED.

Besides the preceding names, we must mention further, among those who seem to have devoted themselves specially to the symphonic order of music, or else to chamber music: Ch. Dancla, Sauzay, Mathias, Garcin, G. Pfeiffer, Taudou, E. Bernard, Thomé, de Maupeou, Claudius Blanc, Paul Lacombe, Perilhou, Chevillard, Dolmetsch; and then pianists of the highest rank, at once professors and composers: first, Marmontel, who may well be called the father of the present generation of pianists, (for all or nearly all, from Planté to Delafosse, Jules Cohen, Wieniawski, Diémer, Fissot, Alph. Duvernoy, Lack, Thomé, Wormser, Galeotti, as well as Bizet, Paladilhe, Th. Dubois, Guiraud, Delahaye, Bourgeois, Bellaigue, Pierné, Ch. René, make part of the legion of his disciples), Ravina, Ch. Delioux, Mathias, Ch. de Bériot, Alph. Duvernoy, Delaborde, Georges Pfeiffer, Diémer, Fissot, Pugno, of whom the larger number have been or are professors at the Conservatory, and are very often applauded, either as composers or performers, at the great symphonic concerts; Colomer, Th. Lack, Thomé, Wormser, Adolphe David, Antonin Marmontel *fils*, and the brilliant group of young pianist virtuosi: J. Phillippe, Falcke, Falkenberg, Delafosse, Risler, and these two admirable artists, Mme. de Serres (Caroline Rémaury), and Francis Planté, who, as amateurs, are sometimes heard at concerts for charitable objects; and among instrumentalists, great artists, such as Sarasate, Marsick, Rémy, Nadaud, Berthelier, Paul Viardot, Laforge, van Wœfelghem, Delsart, Loys, Rabaud, Cabassol, Cros-Saint-Ange, Hasselmans, Taffanel, Hennebains, Gillet, Turban, Garigue, Brémond, and others.

It is manifestly impossible for me to mention them all, this book not being a directory, or a biographical dictionary. I only seek to give, by names *chosen* among those that are best known, the musical physiognomy of our time, as I have done that of past epochs, superficially.

The best traditions of the lyric stage are preserved and transmitted by singers who will remain famous: Gilbert Duprez, Faure, Mme. Viardot, Mme. Carvalho, and Mme. Krauss.

We now come to the present members of the Section of Music of the Institute:

Reyer (Ernest), [1823]. Born at Marseilles.

The most important works of Reyer are, in the order of their production: *le Sélam* (1850), *Maître Wolfram, Sacountala*, ballet, *la Statue, Erostrate, Sigurd, Salammbô*, all works of wide scope, of lofty and imposing style, stamped with a sincere and worthy artistic conviction, and bearing on every page the author's sign manual.

His only instructor seems to have been Mme. Farrenc, his aunt,[1] a great musician who never received the appreciation she deserved, and whose works are at this day totally forgotten; she left, however, a good number of important compositions, symphonic or instrumental, especially chamber music, and it is easy to understand that she was capable of conducting a musical education of the very highest order.

At the same time there is nothing of her strictly classical manner in the style of her distinguished pupil and nephew, who seemed rather to attach himself to the school of Berlioz, his friend and intimate, and the object of his very high admiration.

Member of the Institute in 1846.

Massenet (Jules), [1842–1912]. Born at Montaud (Loire).

This indefatigable and fruitful composer, one of the most brilliant and many-sided members of the French school, obtained the grand prix de Rome in 1863, in the class of Ambroise Thomas, after being the pupil of Reber in harmony.

Since that time he has composed an astonishing series of well-known works, of which I will name only the more conspicuous, following always their chronological order:

Don César de Bazan, opéra-comique, three acts (1872); *Marie Magdeleine*, sacred drama, (1873); *Les Erynnies* (for the tragedy of Leconte de Lisle), 1873; *Ève, mystère* (1875); *Le Roi de Lahore*, grand opera, five acts (1877); *La Vierge* (1880); *Hérodiade*, grand opera, three acts (1881); *Manon*, opéra-comique, five acts (1884); *Le Cid*, grand opera, four acts (1885); *Esclarmonde*, opéra romanesque, four acts (1889); *Le Mage*, grand opera, five acts (1891); *Werther*, lyric drama, four acts (1892); *Thaïs*, comédie lyrique, three acts (1894); *Le Portrait de Manon* (1894); *La Navarraise* (1894); *Sapho* (1897); *Don Quichotte* (1911).

Besides these dramatic works, seven *orchestral suites, Biblis, Narcisse* (for soli, choruses, and orchestra), many collections of songs, almost all famous: *Poèmes d'amour, d'Avril, du Souvenir,*

1 Mme. Farrenc was professor of the piano at the Conservatory from 1842 to 1872.

d'*Octobre*, *Pastoral*, d'*Hiver*, and an infinity of other pretty or beautiful things.

He was appointed professor of composition at the Conservatory and member of the Institute during the same year, 1878.

Saint-Saëns (Camille), [1835]. Born in Paris.

Had for masters Stamaty for the piano, Maleden and Halévy in harmony and composition, and Benoist for the organ.

His first successes were as pianist, and he then rapidly acquired a high reputation as an organist. He is especially a wonderful and incomparable improvisator.

He writes with equal facility music of all kinds; I will enumerate here only his most celebrated works:

Chamber music: two *Trios*, a *Quatuor*, a *Quintette*, a *Septuor* (with trumpet); symphonic works: three *Symphonies*, of which the third, in C minor, is perhaps the finest masterpiece of orchestration that was ever written; four *Poèmes symphoniques : le Rouet d'Omphale*, *Phaéton*, *la Danse macabre*, *la Jeunesse d'Hercule;* *Marche héroïque* in memory of Henri Regnault (written during the siege of Paris and at first called *la Délivrance*); five *Concertos* for the piano, three *Concertos* for the violin, one *Concerto* for the violoncello; *Tarentelle* for flute, clarinet, and orchestra; *Suite algérienne.*

In church music: *Messe de Requiem*, *Messe solennelle*, *Ave verum*, chorus for four voices; psalm *Cœli enarrant.*

In the oratorio or cantata style: *Oratorio de Noël*, *les Noces de Prométhée* (for the exposition of 1867); *le Déluge*, *la Lyre et la Harpe.*

Finally, for the stage: *la Princesse Jaune* (1872); *Samson et Dalila* (1876); *le Timbre d'Argent* (1877); *Étienne Marcel* (1879); *Henry VIII.* (1883); *Proserpine* (1887); *Ascanio* (1890); *Phryné* (1893); *Déjanire* (drama) (1898). Also an immense quantity of pieces for one piano or two pianos, and collections of songs. His facility in writing is marvellous.

He has been a member of the Institute since 1881.

Paladilhe (Émile), [1844]. Born near Montpellier.

Grand prix de Rome at the age of sixteen (in 1860), an unparalleled occurrence. As instructors he had, first, his father and dom Sébastien Boixet, organist of the cathedral of Montpellier, and then, at the Conservatory, Marmontel, Benoist, and Halévy.

His compositions are chiefly these: one mass with orchestra, two symphonies; *le Passant*, one act (1872); *l'Amour africain*, two acts (1875); *Suzanne*, three acts (1879); *Diana*, three acts (1885); *Patrie*, five acts (1886); *les Saintes Maries de la Mer*, sacred legend in four parts; and a hundred *Melodies*. Also should be added,

Vanina, four acts, a work entirely completed, but as yet unpublished.

Member of the Institute in 1892.

The directorship of the Conservatoire remained vacant for nearly three months after the death of M. Thomas, within which time it was offered to Massenet and Saint-Saëns, and declined by both. Finally in May, 1896,

François Clement Theodore Dubois was appointed to the post. M. Dubois was born Aug. 24, 1837 at Rosney. He received instruction as a lad at Rheims and then became a pupil of the Conservatory. Marmontel taught him pianoforte, Bazin harmony, Benoist organ, and Ambroise Thomas fugue and composition. He won the prix de Rome in 1861, and after his return from Italy, four years later, he was appointed choir-master at the church of Ste. Clotilde. For this church he wrote the oratorio *Les Sept Paroles du Christ,* one of his finest works. He became professor of harmony at the Conservatory in 1871 and six years later Saint-Saëns's successor as organist at the Madeleine. Among his most important works after *Les Sept Paroles du Christ* is another oratorio, *Paradis perdu,* with which he won a prize at a musical competition instituted by the city of Paris in 1878. For the stage he has written *la Guzla de l'émir* (1875), *Le Pain bis* (1879), *La Farandole* (ballet, 1883), and *Aben Hamet* (1884). He has also composed much for orchestra and choir, being inclined strongly toward the serious forms.

And lastly I feel that I must mention here, although he does not wear the coat with green palms, but because he has shared with two members of the Illustre Société (Massenet and Th. Dubois) the honor and the heavy responsibility of instruction in composition at the Conservatory :

Lenepveu (Charles), [1840]. Born at Rouen.

Pupil of Savard in solfeggio and in harmony, of Ambroise Thomas and Chauvet in fugue, counterpoint, and composition; premier prix de Rome in 1865.

Professor of harmony at the Conservatory in 1881, and professor of Composition in 1893.

Principal works: *le Florentin,* opéra-comique, three acts, written in 1868, performed in Paris in 1874; *Velleda,* opera, four acts (London, Covent Garden, 1882, with Adelina Patti in the chief rôle); *Jeanne d'Arc,* lyric drama (Rouen, 1886); *Iphigénie,* grand lyric scene; *Méditation,* soli, choruses, orchestra (Société des concerts, 1886); *Hymne funèbre et triomphal* (Rouen, 1892); *Messe de Requiem*, a fine *Laudate*, and many *Mélodies* or *Scènes Lyriques*, some of which have a well-merited popularity.

Such are some of the conspicuous personalities of the present French school, in the vitality of which we may have a just confidence.

It would be supremely unjust not to recall the names of some, at least, among the more prominent virtuosi who were the interpreters of the great French masters of our century, and of whom many were themselves composers of talent; also, names of eminent theoricians or professors, whom we have mentioned from time to time, in speaking of pupils of theirs, who in turn became masters. This will be done as briefly as possible, deploring inevitable omissions.

Nourrit (Adolphe), [1802–1839]. Born at Montpellier.

One of the celebrated opera tenors, he studied with Garcia, keeping the secret from his father, Louis Nourrit, who was himself a tenor at the Opéra but had decided that his son should follow a mercantile career. For five years the father and son, who resembled each other so much as to occasion mistakes as to identity, played together in the same rôles; after the retirement of the elder Nourrit, Adolphe for more than ten years was the leading tenor of the Opéra, and created the first rôles in all the great works of Auber, Meyerbeer, Rossini, and Halévy.

He died by his own hand at Naples in a moment of despair at the slight enfeeblement of his vocal powers.

Roger (Gustave), [1815–1879]. Born at Saint-Denis.

One of the most charming of French tenors; his début, in 1838, was made in Halévy's *l'Éclair;* he then passed rapidly on to the Opéra, where, in 1849, he created the *Prophète.* His career was brilliant but short. An accident received while hunting, compelled the amputation of his right arm. A vain attempt was made to supply an artificial arm, but he was obliged to relinquish the stage and devote himself to teaching. Made professor of singing at the Conservatory in 1869, he trained many brilliant pupils.

Kalkbrenner (Fréd.-Guill.), [1784–1849]. Born at Cassel.

Was at first the pupil of his father, himself a composer and writer, and then of Ad. Adam for the piano, and of Catel in harmony.

His great successes as a performer, both in France and Germany, did not lead him to neglect composition, and we have numerous works of his for the piano, either alone or accompanied by other instruments.

Ritter (Théodore), [1836–1888]. Born in Paris.

A remarkable virtuoso, as interesting in his rendering of the classics as he was brilliant in the performance of his own works.

Kreutzer (Rodolphe), [1766–1831]. Born at Versailles.

A famous virtuoso; from childhood a protégé of Marie Antoinette. He was appointed professor of the violin at the Conservatory, almost at the foundation of that establishment; then conductor of the orchestra at the Opéra in 1817. Beethoven dedicated to him one of his most remarkable sonatas for piano and violin. He himself composed a great deal of music and even operas.

Baillot [1771–1842]. Born at Passy, near Paris.

One of the great French violinists; must be regarded as the creator of the present school of violinists.

His reputation was European; and he was as remarkable in chamber music as in pieces of pure virtuosity.

He left a large number of compositions which are little known at the present day; also a Method, *l'Art du Violon*, the most distinguished work that has ever been written on the subject.

Rode [1774–1830]. Born at Bordeaux.

There have been published ten famous concertos of his and some chamber music.

He was a great virtuoso, successful in all the principal cities of Europe; the First Consul attached him to his household orchestra as violin soloist; he was a pupil of Viotti.

Bériot (Ch.-Auguste de), [1802–1870]. Born in Louvain.

A remarkable virtuoso and a composer for the violin. A fine *Méthode de Violon*, seven *Concertos*, arias, fantasias in great number on the most notable operas of his time, *Études*, and *Sonatas* for piano and violin, etc. He was the husband of Mme. Malibran, the famous singer.

Servais [1807–1866]. Born at Hal.

One of the most remarkable of violoncello virtuosi. After a long series of triumphs, he died in 1848; professor at the Conservatory of Brussels, where his eldest son has succeeded him.

He wrote *Concertos*, *Études*, *and Fantaisies* for the violoncello.

Alard (Delphin), [1815–1888]. Born at Bayonne.

A pupil of Habeneck for the violin, of Fétis in composition.

Numerous works for the violin: *Fantaisies*, Methods, works of instruction, *Études.* He was professor at the Conservatory from 1843 to 1875.

Léonard [1819–1890]. Born at Bellaire (Belgium).

A famous Belgian violinist, and professor at the Conservatory of Brussels. He had immense success throughout Europe, especially in Paris, where he died; he was a pupil of Habeneck.

Vieuxtemps [1820–1881]. Born at Verviers.

Received a few lessons on the violin from Ch. de Bériot, and in composition from Reicha. He made repeated tours in Europe, exciting admiration everywhere, both by his talent as a performer and his merit as a composer.

His *Concertos*, his *Élégie*, his *Polonaise*, and others of his works, were long in the repertory of every violinist.

During this period of French art, the organ school is brilliantly represented:

Lefébure-Wély [1817–1870]. Born in Paris.

Pupil of Zimmermann for the piano, of Berton, Adam, and Halévy in composition, of Benoist and Séjan for the organ; he was, above all, a remarkable improvisator, full of charm and flavour, and not without science; he had successively the great organ at Saint-Roch, the Madeleine, and Saint-Sulpice.

He also composed much for the organ and the orchestra, as well as for the piano and the harmonium; his works are in a pleasing and elegant style.

Lemmens (1823–1881). Born at Antwerp.

The most distinguished of Belgian organists, professor of the organ at the Conservatory of Brussels. He wrote much for his instrument and the church; he also trained many and remarkable pupils.

Lastly, we should mention among those who, while themselves composers, were especially distinguished by their works on instruction or by the influence which their ideas have had upon the development of art, a certain number of great theorists and professors. To do this, we must go back to the beginning of the eighteenth century, the epoch of the absurd *querelle des bouffons.* Among the writers and disputants who threw themselves into this conflict figures in the foremost rank the author of the *Confessions,* whose musical career is all that we shall mention in this place :

Rousseau (Jean-Jacques), [1712–1778].   Born in Geneva.

A musician without elementary musical instruction, a feeble reader, most deficient as a harmonist, he had the gift of melody; and this is the only thing to admire in his compositions, which were few in number. I can scarcely mention anything except *le Devin du village.*

His first intermeddling in musical affairs took place in 1742, when he made a proposition to the Académie des Sciences to adopt a new system of musical writing, in which figures should be used instead of notes. This change, without the least utility, seemed to him useful solely because his ignorance was such that he did not grasp the ingenious simplicity of the system of notation, and saw nothing in it but futile complications.

Later, about 1750, he was employed by Diderot and d'Alembert in the preparation of the articles on Music for the *Encyclopédie,* which is to be regretted, for they contain numerous errors, and are not on a level with the other parts of this great work.

Fétis (François-Joseph), [1784–1871].   Born at Mons.

Pupil of Rey and of Catel in harmony, and of Boïeldieu on the piano, at the Conservatory of Paris.

Although he composed much, it is specially by his writings on music that he remains famous. His *Biographie universelle des musiciens* has been of use in the preparation of this work.[1] It is particularly valuable in furnishing dates and facts; its opinions are open to discussion.

He was professor of composition at the Conservatory from 1821 to 1833, at which latter date he accepted the direction of the Conservatory at Brussels.

K. — The Russian School.

While we have felt at liberty, by reason of their affinities, and for the sake of simplifying, to fuse together the Belgian and French schools; while we have left in the shade the Spanish school, which, to say the truth, really does not exist; and have neglected a few English com-

[1] As also the *Supplément* to the *Biographie,* published in 1880 by the eminent critic and bibliophile, Arthur Pougin.

posers, little known in France, and to be considered rather as isolated instances[1] than as members of a school; we are obliged to proceed differently in the case of the school now to be considered, which presents a distinct character, resulting from the nature of its origin, and could not be classed with any other.

The Russian school is still young; it has not yet had a century of existence, and from its birth, so to speak, it was in possession of the mighty technic created by centuries of effort by the three great European schools, with their immense modern resources and their powerful orchestration.

Moreover, its masters are not, in general at least,— as they are in France, Germany, and Italy,— true *professionals;* Russian musicians are usually learned and scientific men, and men of rank and social prestige, who begin as amateurs and then are drawn in to the artistic whirl; this being with us a very rare (though when it does occur it is often a fortunate) occurrence.

It is easily understood that men of a high intellectual level, well informed as to all that is done elsewhere in music, and, on the other hand, possessing a literature, religion, and manners which differ notably from those of Central Europe, must have created a national art of quite peculiar character, and much more precocious than the arts with whose genesis and very slow development we have now been occupied.

The people's song has always been known in Russia, since, as we have already said, song is as natural as speech to the men of every land; and there, as elsewhere, it has acquired, by the force of things, and outside of any intentional artistic interference, a character peculiar to itself. Hence, the Slavic melodies or *mélopées*, without author, true songs of the people; hence, also, the typic side, now rough, now full of languor, of the Russian music, which makes its principal charm,— its true picturesque originality. As to procedures of execution, of writing, they cannot be different from those we have already examined;

[1] Balfe (1808), Macfarren (1813). Wallace (1814), and more recently, Mackenzie. See Appendix, pp. 506, 507.

for, if they were, the Russian school would be behind the rest, *which it is not.* It has taken rank among distinct schools, and though lacking a past, it appears to have a future clearly before it. This is proven by the merit of its representatives, of whom some leading individuals will now be mentioned, in their rank of date.

Let it be well understood there are no Russian classics to be looked for; the school begins in the midst of Romanticism; and up to the time of Glinka, the true father of this youthful school, Russia was tributary in the matter of music to Italy and to France.

Glinka (Michel), [1804–1857]. Born at Nowospask (government of Smolensk).

After receiving at the Seminary of the Nobles a solid literary and scientific training, he studied the piano with Field and Ch. Mayer, harmony with Dehn, a German (who had also Anton and Nicolas Rubinstein as pupils, and thus had an important share in the development of Russian musical art); and for singing and the violin, Glinka had an Italian master.

In both meanings of the word, he is first among Russian musicians. His best known work is *A Life for the Czar* (1836), but his talent shows its fullest blossoming in *Ruslan and Ludmilla.* Also there is a *Jota Aragonesa* and *A Night in Madrid*, souvenirs of a journey in Spain, and built on Spanish motifs; *Kamarinskaïa*, composed on Russian popular airs, etc.

His works are rich in harmony, skilfully orchestrated for the period, and his frequent and systematic use of popular motifs happily accentuates the local colour and the essentially national character.

In addition to music, Glinka studied with great interest geography and natural history.

Dargomizsky [1813–1867]. Born in a village in the government of Toula.

Principal works: *la Roussalka, Esmeralda, The Triumph of Bacchus* (opera-ballet), piano pieces, dances, songs, etc., and *The Stone Guest*, posthumous, whose orchestration was completed by Rimsky-Korsakow.

He is regarded in Russia as the head of a school. In France he is nearly unknown, and I regret to speak of him only from report. His family were rich, and he had received a general training and education of the most careful description.

Rubinstein (Anton), [1829–1894]. Born at Wechwotynez (Moldavia).

Among the theatrical works of this composer and pianist, I may mention: *Dimitri-Donskoï* (1852), *Tom the Fool, The Revenge, The Hunters of Siberia, The Children of the Heath, Feramors, The Demon, The Maccabres, Nero, Kalachnikoff, the Merchant of Moscow, The Vine* (ballet in three acts), *The Parrot, Among Robbers, Sulamite, Moses* (1894), two oratorios, *The Tower of Babel* and *Paradise Lost*, the great *Ocean Symphony* and sixteen other works of the kind which place him in the front rank of symphonists.

Grand and beautiful works of chamber music, vocal melodies, and concertos.

His teachers were Villoing at Moscow, for the piano, and Dehn at Berlin, in composition. The advice of Liszt was not without effect in his development.

The most inspired as well as the most wonderful and profound of modern pianists, Rubinstein belongs, by the character of his virtuosity, to the great German school, and reminds one of Beethoven, to whom he had some slight personal resemblance. He is a colossal artist, a genius of the broadest wing, but perhaps more Russian by birth than by artistic tendencies.

Since 1862, he had been director of the Conservatory of Saint Petersburg, of which he was, also, the founder.

He had a younger brother :

Rubinstein (Nicolas), [1835–1881]. Born in Moscow.

Received nearly the same musical education as his brother, with the same masters, and appeared in his youth to have more facility than the elder (according to Anton himself), but his too short career was less brilliant on the whole.

Although practising composition very creditably, he gave himself up to teaching while still very young, and this finally absorbed him completely, notwithstanding his great success in Russia as a virtuoso. Unlike his brother he travelled but little in foreign countries; but Paris knew him as conductor, pianist, and composer in 1878, when he was conductor of the Russian concerts at the exposition.

In 1859 he established symphonic concerts in Moscow, and in 1864 a conservatory.

Borodine [1834–1887]. Born in Saint Petersburg.

Has left two symphonies, full of interest, originality, and elegance, richly orchestrated; also an opera, *Prince Igor*, a posthumous work, finished by Rimsky-Korsakow and Glazounow.

Cui (César), [1835].   Born at Wilna.

Many operas: *The Prisoner of the Caucasus*, *William Ratcliff*, *Angelo*, *The Flibustier;* much piano music and songs in great number, all in a very original and personal style, energetic and extremely distinguished.

With Rubinstein and Tschaïkowsky, he makes the third in the list of Russian musicians who are well-known in France.

A remarkable peculiarity is that his songs are really models of French prosody.

He holds the rank of General in the army, and is professor of the art of fortification in the Military School of Artillery and Engineering in Saint Petersburg.

Balakireff (Mily Alexélivitch), [1836].   Born at Nijni-Novgorod.

A direct successor to Glinka, with the same love of using national popular songs.

Principal works: *Overture on Russian Themes; a Thousand Years*, a sort of cantata or ode-symphony, written and performed in 1862, on occasion of the thousandth anniversary of the founding of the Russian empire; *Overture and Entr'actes* for *King Lear; Islamey*, an original fantasia for the piano, etc.

Even more, perhaps, than Glinka, he is the apostle of patriotic Russian music, but he came later, was only a disciple of the elder composer, and Glinka remains the unquestioned file-leader of the Russian school.

Balakireff has written nothing for the stage.

Moussorgsky [1839–1881].   Born at Toropetz.

A charming and fruitful melodist, who makes up for a lack of skill in harmonisation by a daring, which is sometimes of doubtful taste; has produced songs, piano music in small amount, and an opera, *Boris Godounoff*.

Tschaikowsky (Pierre), [1840–1893].   Born at Voltkinsk.

Among his numerous works are : *Voyevode*, *Jeanne d'Arc*, *Eugène Oneguine*, three other operas, the fantaisie *Francesca da Rimini*, fantaisie-overtures *Romeo and Juliet*, and *Hamlet*, Russian Masses, chamber music, concertos, and six symphonies, of which the last, the *Pathetique*, with the superb *Andante lamentoso*, with which it concludes, has become world-famous.

He had completed his studies in law, served three years in the ministry of justice, and was nearly twenty-one, before he entered on his musical studies under Rubinstein and Zaremba.

Rimsky-Korsakow [1844].   Born at Tichwine.

The Maiden of Psikow, *The May Night*, *Snegourotchka*, a fantastic opera, many remarkable symphonies, *Sadko*, *Antar*, etc.

He is a naval officer, and at the present time leader of all the marine bands of the Russian Empire.

Glazounow (Alexandre), [1865].   Born in Saint Petersburg.

Pupil of Rimsky-Korsakow.   While quite young, he produced many remarkable symphonies, of which the first, written in 1885, is called *Stenka Razine*, very interesting in its orchestration; then, *The Sea*, *The Forest*, and much chamber music.

I do not think that, up to the present time, he has attempted opera, but he assisted Rimsky-Korsakow in completing the *Prince Igor* by Borodine.

He is considered by many the most brilliant representative of the young Russian school, in its latest form.

In conclusion, I mention this fact, that the author of the Russian Hymn is an army officer, General Lvoff, who has also written an opera, *Undine*.

Russian virtuosi are known and admired in France.   We have only to remember the successes, past or present, of Jean and Edouard de Reszké at the Opéra, of Mme. Essipoff, of the pianists, Sapelnikoff, Paderewski,[1] the brothers Wieniawski, of the young violinist Petchnikoff, of Davidoff and Brandoukoff, 'cellists, as also the performances of the strange choir of Wladimir Slaviansky D'Agrenef, and the little orchestra of *balalaïkists*[2] of B. Andreef.

Religious music in Russia merits attention, and differs totally from our own; it is composed entirely of unaccompanied choruses, of rapid chanting, a sort of mysterious whispering, which has a strange fascination.

We would earnestly recommend the reader to visit sometimes, at hours of service, the Greek church of the rue Daru, and take note of the curious arrangement of voices: the men sing in four parts; the boy-voices double them, an octave higher; and the contrabass voices, an exclusive

[1] See Appendix.

[2] The balalaïka is the common Russian guitar; it is triangular in form, and its three strings are tuned in different keys, which permits peculiar effects, often very pleasing.

product of the Slav races, strengthen the bass, an octave lower. From this results a diffuse sonority, perfectly equal, much resembling an organ with stops of eight and

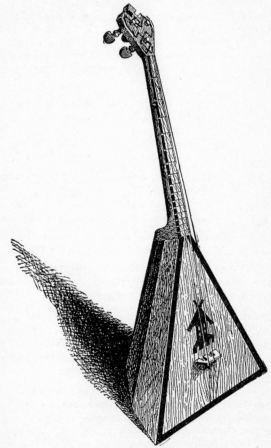

Fig. 94. BALALAÏKA. Height, about 2 feet.

four feet in the manual and sixteen feet in the pedal; so much so that many persons suppose there is a concealed organ. A detail to be noted is that the contra-bass voices which go down to the A♭ below the staff, reserve these solemn notes for the great ceremonies!

PRINCIPAL WORKS TO BE CONSULTED FOR THE HISTORY OF MUSIC.

In French:

FÉLIX CLÉMENT, *Histoire de la musique;* 1885.

H. LAVOIX FILS, *Histoire de la musique.*

— *Histoire de la musique française.*

ARTH. COQUARD, *De la musique en France;* 1891.

LAURE COLLIN, *Histoire abrégée de la musique;* 1884.

KASTNER, *Parémiologie musicale.*

MATHYS–LUSSY, *Histoire de la notation.*

— *Le Rythme musical.*

CLÉMENT, *Dictionnaire lyrique;* 1869.

FÉTIS, *Histoire generale de la musique;* 1876.

— *Biographie des musiciens;* 1865.

POUGIN, *Supplément au précédent;* 1880.

GEVAERT, *Histoire et Théorie de la musique grecque;* 1881.

COUSSEMAKER, *Histoire de l'harmonie au moyen âge;* 1842.

—   *L'Art harmonique aux* XIIe *et* XIIIe *siècles;* 1865.

—   *Drames liturgiques au moyen âge;* 1852.

DINAUX, *Trouvères, Jongleurs et Ménestrels;* 1843.

LAVOIX FILS, *Histoire de l'instrumentation.*

BRENET, *Histoire de la symphonie;* 1882.

CHOUQUET, *Histoire de la musique dramatique en France;* 1873.

POUGIN, *les Vrais Créateurs de l'opéra français;* 1881.

BERLIOZ, *Voyage musical en Allemagne;* 1850.

LAVOIX ET LEMAIRE, *Histoire du chant.*

ADAM, *Souvenirs d'un musicien;* 1857.

—   *Derniers Souvenirs d'un musicien;* 1859.

BERTRAND, *les Nationalités musicales;* 1872.

BOURDELOT, *Histoire de la musique;* 1743.

CASTIL-BLAZE, *Dictionnaire de musique moderne;* 1828.

F. CLÉMENT, *Histoire de la musique religieuse;* 1866.

GEVAERT, *les Origines du chant liturgique;* 1890.

DOM JUMILHAC, *Art et Science du plain-chant.*

TARDIF, *Essai sur les neumes.*

KASTNER, *la Danse des morts;* 1852.

THOINOT–ARBEAU, *Orchésographie.*

J. TIERSOT, *Histoire de la chanson populaire en France;* 1889.

LAJARTE, *les Curiosités de l'Opéra;* 1883.

SOUBIES ET MALHERBE, *Histoire de l'Opéra-Comique;* 1887.

SOUBIES, *Soixante-sept ans à l'Opéra en une page;* 1893.

—   *Soixante-neuf ans à l'Opéra-Comique en deux pages;* 1894.

LASSABATHIE, *Histoire du Conservatoire;* 1860.

MÉREAUX, *les Clavecinistes;* 1867.

MERSENNE (Le Père), *l'Harmonie universelle;* 1636.

BRENET, *Histoire de la symphonie;* 1882.

ELWART, *la Société des concerts;* 1860.

—   *Les Concerts populaires;* 1864.

DELDEVEZ, *la Société des concerts;* 1887.

BELLAIGUE, *Un Siècle de musique française;* 1887.

—   *D'Année musicale;* 1886, 1887, 1880, etc.

CLÉMENT ET LAROUSSE, *Dictionnaire lyrique des Opéras.*

C. SAINT–SAËNS, *Harmonie et Mélodie;* 1885.

POUGIN, *Dictionnaire historique et pittoresque du théâtre.*

RUBINSTEIN, *la Musique et ses représentants;* 1892.

WECKERLIN, *Musiciana.*

—   *Nouveaux Musiciana.*

—   *La Chanson populaire en France.*

SOUBIES, *Précis de l'histoire de la musique russe;* 1893.

BERLIOZ, *les Grotesques de la musique.*

—   *Les Soirées de l'orchestre.*

From the foregoing works I have taken needed material, and in them the reader will find much more extended details, as well as in the innumerable biographies of celebrated musicians, of which I cannot even give a list here.

In German[1]:

AMBROS, AUGUST WILHELM, *Geschichte der Musik.*

BRENDEL, FRANZ, *Geschichte der Musik.*

RIEMANN, H., *Geschichte der Musik seit Beethoven.*

In English:

HENDERSON, W. J., *The Story of Music.*

HUNT, H. G., *Concise History of Music.*

LANGHANS, W., *The History of Music in Twelve Lectures,* trans. by J. H. Cornell.

NAUMANN, EMIL, *The History of Music,* trans. by F. Praeger.

ROCKSTRO, W. S., *General History of Music.*

THE OXFORD HISTORY OF MUSIC.

HOGARTH, GEO., *Memoirs of the Opera.*

HOPKINS AND RIMBAULT, *The Organ: Its History and Construction.*

MATHEWS, W. S. B., *A Hundred Years of Music in America.*

RIMBAULT, E. F., *The Pianoforte: Its Origin, Progress, and Construction.*

SHEDLOCK, J. S., *The Pianoforte Sonata: Its Origin and Development.*

WEITZMANN, C. F., *History of Pianoforte Playing and Pianoforte Literature.*

HOPE, ROBERT CHARLES, *Mediæval Music.*

STAINER, JOHN, *The Music of the Bible.*

CHAPPELL, WILLIAM, *Old English Popular Music.*

ENGEL, CARL, *An Introduction to the Study of National Music.*

WALLASCHEK, R., *Primitive Music.*

AMBROS, A. W., *The Boundaries of Music and Poetry.*

BERLIOZ, HECTOR, Selections and translations made by William F. Apthorp.

WAGNER, RICHARD, *Art Life and Theories.* Selections and translations by Edward L. Burlingame.

HANSLICK, EDWARD, *The Beautiful in Music,* trans. by Gustav Cohen.

GROVE, SIR GEORGE, *Beethoven and His Nine Symphonies.*

STREATFIELD, R. A., *The Opera.*

EDWARDS, H. SUTHERLAND, *History of the Opera.*

GROVE, SIR GEORGE, *Dictionary of Music and Musicians.*

MACFARREN, *Musical History.*

---

[1] The German and English lists have been added by the American editor.

Not to revert again to France, which has everything to hope from her young generation of composers,—without going further with the history of the Russian school, except to add to the names already mentioned that of Arensky, a young musician of brilliant promise,—we see the foreign musical nations well armed for the peaceful contests of the future. Belgium may join to the already famous names of Gevaert and Peter Benoit, those of Mathieu and Gilson; Germany can bring forward, as followers of Brahms, Max Bruch, who seems to be its present leader, Goldmark, (composer of *The Queen of Sheba, Merlin*, and other operas), Ignace Brüll, and Humperdinck; Norway has Grieg and Svendsen;[1] lastly, Italy is brilliantly represented by Sgambati, a great composer and remarkable symphonist, whose works are, unfortunately, not generally known in France; Boïto, the librettist of Verdi's latest operas, who is himself the admirable composer of *Mefistofele ;* Mascagni, whose *Cavalleria Rusticana* is well known in Paris; Puccini, whose operas include *Manon Lescaut, La Bohème*, and *Tosca ;* Leoncavallo, best known by his *I Pagliacci ;* Franchetti, Tasca, and Spiro Samara, the latter a Greek, and, I think, for a time, pupil of Delibes.

I do not believe that in any age or country has been gathered a group of artists of so much talent,—taking into account the number of individuals, as well as their personal merit—as that which we see around us at the present time.

This is in part due no doubt to the extreme diffusion of musical education in our day; and, for the same reason, never before have artists been in the presence of a public so enlightened and so able to comprehend them.

And therefore, notwithstanding the great and splendid examples we have of men of genius attaining the height of honours, of brilliant musicians whose labours are crowned with success; notwithstanding the charm and fascination

---

[1] [And Christian Sinding, who is likely to turn out greater than his colleagues mentioned by our author.] ED.

which music possesses for noble minds,—it is wise to dissuade young men without fortune from entering upon this career, if they regard it merely as a comparatively easy way to earn their bread and are not drawn to it by attraction that it is impossible to resist. Quite on the contrary, this career is most ungrateful and perfidious, and the facts as to musicians, not destitute of merit, who drag out a miserable existence, who literally suffer with hunger, are truly heartbreaking. When one has been for twenty-five years professor in that great artist-manufactory which is called the Conservatory of Paris; when one has seen with his own eyes the frightful number of students who have fallen to the level of the *bal public* and the *café concert*, from having misunderstood or overestimated their abilities; when one knows how many there are who live by infrequent lessons at twenty sous the ticket where there is one who will ever see his name on a play-bill, it becomes a duty to warn the rash aspirant, seeking to enter on this path of danger, without having the stamp of genius on his brow.

I am asked, how shall any one know whether or not he has genius.

The reply is simple.

He will not know, for no man can understand himself—whatever may be said to the contrary. Genius is without self-consciousness. He will not say: "I have in me the making of a great musician;" for this would be a sign,—alas! far too frequent—of presumption merely. He will not have in view celebrity,—scarcely the desire for applause,—never the idea of lucre. No; he will almost always be modest, often very timid, timorous even. But he will be cuirassed with triple brass; and advice the most discouraging, the most alarming (like mine, for example), will have no effect at all upon him; will not disturb his inward certainty; will not make any change in his line of conduct; for genius is indomitable. Such a man as this will go straight on, turning a deaf ear to all the advice that mistaken well-wishers offer, to deter him; he will go forward against wind and tide; he will suffer, if need be, all privations, indifferent to all solicitudes as to the material life; he will courageously undergo checks and mortifications; he will struggle against persecutions, prejudices, and the spirit of clique,—having always for his sole aim, not fame, which must come unsought and later; not success, which is ephemeral; not fortune, which is despicable; but only his personal Ideal,—that which sums up for him according to his own conception, the beautiful; and after the beautiful, —the most beautiful! Genius is a fate; and no human power could have stayed the step of great, poor Mozart, in the glorious path which was to bring his body to a pauper's grave, and his fame to immortality.

APPENDIX

MUSIC IN AMERICA
THE PRESENT STATE OF THE ART OF MUSIC

BY
H. E. KREHBIEL

Music in America.

The musical composers of America are unable as yet to point to a distinctive element in their music as segregating it from the mass of good music the world over. No claim has been made by them, or by any discriminating critic for them, that they have created what may be called a national school in the sense that school means a distinctive style of expression. The characteristics of the French school rests upon its attention to the rules of French prosody and deference to declamation — in short on a recognition of the values and rights of the French language. This element surely entitles it to be called national, but it also limits the music which from this point of view is to be looked upon as distinctively French to that which is joined with words — chiefly the opera. Recognition of this principle furnishes all the justification that there is for calling Gluck a French composer. In the purely instrumental branch of the art the French composers are eclectics, who have assimilated what seemed good to them from all the schools of Europe. They furnish in this respect a parallel to the composers who have grown up in America, who stand as yet in marked contrast with the composers of Russia, Bohemia, and the Norse countries, in that they have not made essential elements out of the rhythmical and melodic peculiarities which distinguish their Folk-songs and dances from those of the other peoples of the world. The way to the utilisation by the Americans of such elements (as well as of others for which the mass of the people have shown a predilection, as evidenced by the popularity of the songs of the day) has recently been pointed out, however, and it is not presumptuous to say that an American school of matter as well as manner may invite attention early in the twentieth century.

At present we can only direct attention to some of the men of American birth who have carried highest and most valiantly the banner of music, as the term is understood

among the peoples of Europe. The education of these men
for the greater part has been conducted along German lines.
Many American *virtuosi* have studied in Paris, but American composers, as a rule, have studied in the conservatories
of Leipsic, Munich, and Berlin, if they have studied abroad
at all. The result has been that the ideals of Germany
have prevailed amongst the composers themselves, just as
German tastes have been cultivated among the American
people who do not make, but only listen to music. (Of
course here, reference can only go to that element of the
people which supports the musical art — not to the vulgar
mass which confounds the emanations of the so-called
music-hall with music. With them, this book has nothing
to do). This statement, however, should be read in a
liberal spirit. The cultivation of orchestral and choral
music (to which departments we look for the manifestation
of its highest forms) has grown with particular luxuriance
within the last three decades. In the programmes of the
concerts of magnitude given in the chief cities of the
country, there do not appear signs of a desire to favour
any one school at the expense of another. Not Paris, not
Vienna, not London, nor any of the capitals of Germany
can show such early and zealous cultivation of the French
and Russian symphonists as New York; but the great
masters of the symphony and its allied forms have been
Germans, from the father of the symphony, Haydn, down
to Brahms, and it was as inevitable as it was natural that
the patrons of the large orchestral organisations which have
their homes in New York, Boston, Chicago, Philadelphia,
Pittsburgh, and Cincinnati, and thence have carried the
musical evangel through the country, should know more
of Haydn, Mozart, Beethoven, Schubert, Schumann, Mendelssohn, and Brahms, than of any single master of any of
the other schools. Until the last decade of the nineteenth
century was reached, the reverse of this was true of the
opera; but opera is an exotic in America, while the symphony and oratorio are become strong native growths.

We see in the careers of the most notable composers of

America that they have in a manner kept pace with the changing ideals of Germany. He who may be styled the dean of the faculty by virtue of the length and dignity of his career, and the opportunities for influence which his position as Professor of Music in Harvard University has brought him, is

John Knowles Paine, born in Portland, Me., on Jan. 9, 1839. His early studies were carried on in his native home, but in 1858 he went to Berlin where he remained three years devoting himself to the study of the organ and composition. He aimed to become an organ virtuoso, but probably realised soon after his return that the organist is of necessity a sedentary individual, and was willing a year after his return from Berlin to settle down at Cambridge as instructor in music at Harvard. In 1876 a professorship was created for him, and he has been the incumbent of the chair ever since, the meaning of the professorship of music being that the art has been put upon a level with philosophy, science, and classical philology. When Mr. Paine came from Europe he was an unyielding adherent of classical ideas, and these he exemplified in his earlier compositions, an oratorio entitled *St. Peter*, and a mass in D; but a liberalising process set in a few years later and bore fruit first in his second symphony entitled *Spring*, a symphonic poem on Shakespeare's *Tempest*, and best of all, in the incidental music to the *Œdipus Tyrannus* of Sophocles, which he composed for a performance of the tragedy by students of Harvard University in the spring of 1881. He has written other choral works in the large forms since, but this remains his masterpiece.

A composer, the lines of whose career began like Mr. Paine's and for long ran parallel, saving the fact that he never became associated with an institution of classical learning, is

Dudley Buck, born in Hartford, Conn., on March 10, 1839, who went from Trinity College in his native town to study music at the Leipsic Conservatory under Hauptmann, Richter, Rietz, Moscheles, and Plaidy. In Dresden he also perfected himself in organ playing under Johann Gottlob Schneider, one of the last of the old-school German organists. Like Mr. Paine he began his professional career as a concert organist, but soon found that the field was not wide enough to keep him occupied. So, after sojourns in Chicago and Boston, he came to New York as assistant conductor of Mr. Theodore Thomas's orchestra, and in 1876 took up his residence in Brooklyn, where he has since lived, caring for the music of a church, teaching, and composing. The works which have made him most widely known are his contributions to the Protestant church services and his organ compositions, but he has also written cantatas for men's and mixed voices, one comic and one grand opera, overtures, a symphony, and two choral works of the large dimensions of an oratorio, one, a setting of scenes from Longfellow's *Golden Legend* and of Edwin Arnold's *Light of Asia*. Mr. Buck's leaning is toward a blending of the learned forms with the easily comprehended, which circumstance has given his music great vogue with church choirs.

A composer whose work, before he became professor of music at Yale University, was in the direction of Mr. Buck's, though inspired by greater ambition and newer knowledge, is

Horatio W. Parker, a pupil first of his mother, then of George W. Chadwick and Stephen A. Emery, and finally of the professors of the Munich Conservatory. Mr. Parker was born in Auburndale, Mass., on Sept. 15, 1863. He has also been associated with the music of the church ever since his return from foreign studies, and his masterpiece, though he has written chamber music, orchestral music, and secular cantatas also, is the oratorio *Hora Novissima*, which is surely one of the finest products of American composition.

In **Mr. Chadwick**, already mentioned as one of the teachers of Mr. Parker, there is noticeable a tendency which promises to disclose something idiomatic which, if pursued, will eventually give characteristic colour to the American school. At present the fruits of this tendency are not obvious enough to excite special comment, though they are noticeable in a symphony in F and a quartet for strings in E minor, which are among the latest of his compositions. Mr. Chadwick was born on Nov. 13, 1854, at Lowell, Mass. He studied at home and in Boston, then gave instruction in a small college town in Michigan, Olivet, and thus earned the money which carried him to Germany in 1877. Two years he spent with Reinecke and Jadassohn in Leipsic, and one with Rheinberger in Munich. His thoughts turned to American subjects even while he was a student, and he introduced himself as a composer, in Boston in 1880, by conducting a performance of his overture *Rip Van Winkle*, which he had written while studying at Leipsic. His most important works since, exclusive of those already mentioned, are two overtures respectively entitled *Thalia* and *Melpomene*, his second symphony in B flat (the one in F is his third), the Columbian ode, written for the dedication of the World's

Fair in 1893, a dramatic cantata, *The Lily Nymph,* and *Phœnix expirans,* a setting for solos, chorus, orchestra, and organ of a mediæval hymn.

A composer whose entire training, literary and artistic, was gained in the United States, and who has taken his place in the front rank, is

Arthur Foote, born March 5, 1853, in Salem, Mass. He is a graduate of Harvard University, and his studies in harmony, counterpoint, and composition were made partly under Prof. Paine and partly without help except the books. His songs appear oftenest of all his compositions on American programmes, but he has written also for chamber music, for orchestra, an overture, two suites, a symphonic prologue, *Francesca da Rimini,* and three works for chorus and orchestra.

The extreme romantic tendency is not found in the compositions of any of the men thus far enumerated. For that we have been obliged to wait for two young composers, who have been closely identified in manner of thought and in the source of their inspirations. They are

Edward Alexander MacDowell and **G. Templeton Strong.** The former was professor of music in Columbia University, New York. The latter has spent all of his professional life in Germany and Switzerland. Both were born in New York City, Mr. Mac-Dowell on Dec. 18, 1861, and Mr. Strong on May 26, 1856. Mr. MacDowell studied at the Paris Conservatory from 1876 to 1879 under Marmontel and Savard, and thence went to Germany where he fell completely under the influence of Joachim Raff. He is a believer in idealised programme music, and indulges in none of the crasser materialistic methods which mark the music of his colleague, such as the symphony, *Sintram,* the fiftieth of Mr. Strong's numbered work, which is dedicated to Mr. MacDowell. Mr. Mac-Dowell has a graciously poetic fancy and a refined sense of orchestral colours, qualifications which are eloquently published in his symphonic poems, *Hamlet, Ophelia,* and *Lancelot and Elaine,* as well as in his orchestral suite in A minor, op. 42. In a second orchestral suite he has paid tribute to the movement toward nationalism by making use of themes drawn from songs of American Indians, but in a manner characterized by great freedom. In this he may be said to have done in a most dignified, elevated, and refined manner, what Louis Moreau Gottschalk (born in New Orleans in 1829, died in 1869) did for salon purposes when he utilised negro and West Indian dances, and what Dr. Dvořák urged upon the young American composers, both by precept and example (symphony "From the New World," quartet, op. 96, quintet, op. 97).

There are many other native American composers who deserve mention, but it has been thought wisest to confine the detailed list to those who are most widely recognised as representative men. In a supplementary list of names merely, there should appear those of Frank van der Stucken, Arthur Bird, Henry Holden Huss, Edgar Stillman Kelley, W. W. Gilchrist, Arthur Whiting, George E. Whiting, and George F. Bristow. Finally it ought to be noted that though scarcely more than half a dozen American composers have achieved fame abroad, all Europe has resounded for a generation with the names of her singers, of whom it will suffice to mention Emma Albani, Clara Louise Kellogg, Annie Louise Cary, Minnie Hauk, Emma Thursby, Antoinette Sterling, Lillian Nordica, Marie van Zandt, Emma Nevada, Emma Abbott, Emma Eames, Sibyl Sanderson, and Ella Russell.

The Present State of the Art of Music.

Without departing so widely from the view-point of the author as seriously to disturb the symmetry and equilibrium of his book, the American editor deems it needful and proper to augment the fourth edition of this work with a survey of the field of musical composition as it presents itself to his mind a decade after Professor Lavignac wrote the original work. It was but natural that the author should have been somewhat more generous to the French School than to others in his discussion of contemporary composers. He wrote for his own people. The editor has already considered music in America, and in this concluding survey finds occasion to devote particular attention to the English and Bohemian schools. While continuing his story of musical evolution, it seems to him a duty to take enough of a retrospective view to fill some gaps in the preceding record, especially in the case of certain men who, though no longer young, and in no manner the peers of all the masters signalized by special discussion, are yet the representatives of contemporaneous music in a larger sense than they were ten years ago.

The two marked tendencies in musical composition in the opening years of the twentieth century are towards that form of poetic, characteristic, or descriptive expression for which Liszt, Berlioz, and Wagner pointed the way on the one hand, and the employment of national, or, more properly, popular idioms on the other. In the exposition of the first tendency, I am compelled, not without regret, to recognize mastery in manipulation rather than beautiful invention. It is manner, not matter, that is dominant, as is always the case when an art, in the course of its development, reaches the stage of great virtuosoship. At the head of those who have attained supreme technical mastery in the art of musical expression I place

Strauss (Richard). Born in Munich, June 11, 1864.

He is the son of a musician who was long a French-horn player in the Court Orchestra at Munich. His father was a strong conservative and so remained in spite of his long and intimate association with Wagner and Wagnerism. His influence secured for the son a firm grounding in the classics and made him an adept in the free handling of forms when the time came for him to leave the beaten paths. The young man was faced in the new direction by association with Alexander Ritter, a nephew by marriage of Richard Wagner and a vigorous champion of that master's theories. Strauss began composing at the age of six years, and at seventeen had placed a string quartet and symphony to his credit, besides a large number of pieces of a smaller *genre*. The first of his works which made its way into the world was a *Serenade* in E flat for wind instruments. This was produced in various German cities by Hans von Bülow, who, despite his own modern leanings, directed the steps of his protégé to the feet of Brahms. A second symphony, in F minor, which betrays this classic-romantic feeling, had its first performance in New York on December 13, 1884, under the direction of Theodore Thomas. Soon after, his thoughts underwent a change, the parting of the ways being marked by a symphonic fantasia entitled *Aus Italien*. Thereafter his progress toward the ultra-radical style, exemplified in the latest of his compositions, was rapid, and marked by the following tone-poems which serve as milestones along the road which he has travelled : *Macbeth, Don Juan, Tod und Verklärung, Till Eulenspiegel's lustige Streiche, Also sprach Zarathustra, Don Quixote,* and *Ein Heldenleben.* Though his highest significance lies in his symphonic poems, Strauss has composed in all the forms, among his works being also two operas, *Guntram* and *Die Feuersnot*, which embody the Wagnerian system, chamber music, and a large number of songs, many of them of marvellous eloquence of expression.

The compositions of Richard Strauss, since he achieved individuality of style and purpose, mark the latest phase in the development of the programmatic idea in instrumental music. The guiding principle of Berlioz was delineation of mood by means of music in its absolute estate aided by moderate freedom in the handling of established forms, together with a strong infusion of realism. In the use of a fundamental and recurrent theme (*L'idée fixe*), he sought, moreover, to give greater pregnancy to the delineation of the underlying poetical conceit as also by abolishing multiplicity of movements substituting symphonic poems for symphonies, and seeking unity in variety by characteristic modification of the fundamental musical thought. Strauss has greatly extended the application of this principle, and, by exercising the utmost freedom in the use of all imaginable devices of composition, especially polyphony and orchestral color, in which department he is an original inventor of marvellous fecundity, as he is also in the development of climaxes, and frankly enlisting ugliness, not merely for the sake of contrast, but also as an independent agency of expression, has extended the scope of programme music into regions never dreamed of before. Soul states, the progress and warring of emotions, and the external phenomena of nature no longer suffice him; the whole world of conscious existence, physical and metaphysical, he has chosen for his domain. Nevertheless, it may be said that his art, with all its marvellously heightened capacity for expression, is yet as naïve, as dependent on external suggestion, as the music of the programmatic composers of three centuries ago. In his Biblical sonata which purported to tell the story of Gideon, Kuhnau asked his listeners to accept a theme as the symbol of the dry fleece and the wet ground, and its inversion as signifying the wet fleece and the dry ground. In *Also sprach Zarathustra,* Strauss seeks to satirize science with a fugue and to indicate that he leaves the riddle of the universe unsolved by sounding C as the root of the chord of B major.

Amongst the German composers who have been strongly influenced by the modern tendency, but have not been carried to the extremity exemplified by Strauss, are Friedrich von Hausegger, Max Schillings, and Felix Weingartner. The last, by original bent a radical, by culture become a classical romanticist, by choice chiefly active as a conductor, has not only kept the waters of the musical pool in violent agitation with his baton, but has also found time to compose operas (*Sakuntala, Malawika, Genesius*), symphonies, symphonic poems, chamber pieces, etc., and to write several polemical books of excellent suggestiveness. Notable instrumental writers, who have established reputations in the later day, or, if earlier, have maintained themselves before the public, are Felix Draeseke August Klughardt, Jean Louis Nicodé, Hans Huber, Georg Schumann, and

Bruckner (Anton), [1824–1896].

He was the son of a schoolmaster in Upper Austria, and, though largely self-taught in the field in which he achieved his greatest distinction, became one of the most eminent of European organists and ablest contrapuntists of the time. He succeeded his teacher in composition, Sechter, as Court Organist in Vienna in 1867, and became professor of organ playing, harmony, and counterpoint at the Conservatory. A born pedant and pedagogue, he was yet a warm adherent of Wagner's cause, and permitted Wagnerian *melos* to tincture his nine symphonies to such an extent as to create the impression that he was deficient in invention and inspiration. One of the finest of his works is a *Te Deum* which has been performed in America.

An associate of Liszt, Von Bülow, and Draeseke in Weimar when they and their coterie were in the thick of the fight for Wagnerian principles about the middle of the nineteenth century, and one who won a large posthumous fame through the strikingly original charm of an opera, was

Cornelius (Peter), [1824–1874].

It was because of a court and social cabal against his opera, *Der Barbier von Bagdad*, which Liszt insisted on bringing out in 1858, that the latter laid down his office as Conductor of the Court Opera at Weimar. After this incident, Cornelius left the Thuringian town, and through the influence of Wagner received the appointment of reader to King Ludwig II of Bavaria, and professor of harmony and rhetoric at the Royal Music School at Munich. He composed a second opera, *Der Cid*, and was at work on a third, *Gunlöd* (afterwards completed by Lassen), when he died. Cornelius was his own librettist, an excellent translator, and a clever poet. Some of his songs, especially *Ein Ton* and his *Weihnachtlieder*, enjoy a considerable vogue.

In the department of operatic composition, which, since Wagner, has occupied the attention of German musicians almost as much as it has that of the French, three men have succeeded in making more than temporary hits. They are Carl Goldmark, Wilhelm Kienzl, and Engelbert Humperdinck.

Goldmark (Carl). Born in Keszthely, Hungary, May 18, 1832.

He received his musical education at Vienna, where he gave his first concert in 1858, playing a pianoforte concerto of his own composition. He cultivated the instrumental forms with assiduity, and had already attracted attention as a brilliant orchestral writer by his concert overtures, *Sakuntala* and *Penthesilea*, and his symphony (more properly, symphonic suite), *Ländliche Hochzeit*, when, in 1875, he produced an opera, *Die Königin von Saba*, which made him famous the world over. Since then he has written other operas, viz., *Merlin*, *Das Heimchen am Herd*, *Die Kriegsgefangene*, and *Götz von Berlichingen*. He has also written some admired chamber music ; and three overtures, *In the Spring*, *Prometheus Bound*, and *Sappho*, have won almost as much favor as the earlier works of their class.

Kienzl (Wilhelm). Born in Waizenkirchen, Austria, January 17, 1857.

His classic studies, which fitted him for some commendable literary work which he has placed to his credit, were pursued at the University of Prague. With them, and his earlier Gymnasial studies, he combined music, at first under local teachers, finally with Liszt at Weimar. The early part of his professional career was that of a musician who was also a man of literary culture. He wrote essays, edited the writings of others, lectured, gave concerts, conducted opera companies, singing societies, and concert orchestras, became *Hofkapellmeister* at Munich, and finally was able to settle down to thoroughly congenial labors at Graz. He had composed two operas, *Urvasi* and *Heilmar der Narr*, which had been well received in Germany, when he achieved an extraordinary success with *Der Evangelimann*, an opera that had been produced at over 170 theatres at the beginning of 1903.

Humperdinck (Engelbert). Born at Siegburg, near Bonn, September 1, 1854.

It was his original purpose to become an architect, but while pursuing his scientific studies at Cologne, he was persuaded by Ferdinand Hiller to take up music. He entered the Cologne Conservatory, where he remained four years, Hiller, Gernsheim and Jensen being among his teachers. He then went for two years to Munich, where at the High School for Music Rheinberger and Franz Lassen were his instructors. He became intimate with the Wagner household at Bayreuth, and assisted the great man in preparing *Parsifal* for performance, and gave musical instruction to his son Siegfried. He occupied but a small part in public attention until December, 1883, when he produced his opera, *Hänsel und Gretel*, which soon ran around the world like wildfire, receiving general recognition as the most successful of the many attempts that had yet been made to employ the Wagnerian system in operatic composition. Humperdinck's departure from Wagner consisted in the substitution of fairy tale for myth as the subject-matter of his drama. He also borrowed from and copied the manner of folk-tune with charming effect, marred only by excessive heaviness of orchestration, which seems out of consonance with the people and the spirit of his play. After the wide and unequivocal success of *Hänsel und Gretel*, Humperdinck essayed a novel form of musical play based on the ancient conception of melodrama (using the term in its proper sense). In *Die Königskinder* he carried on the dialogue in a species of "pointed" speech, using the speaking voice with an occasional cadence and having it flow rhythmically over an orchestral part developed out of symbolic melodies, or typical phrases, in Wagner's manner. This he intersperses with vocal and instrumental numbers. Other attempts along the line of fairy tale as the basis of lyric drama are seen in *Dornröschen* and *Die sieben Geislein*. A *Moorish Rhapsody* for orchestra by this composer has been favorably received.

Characteristic elements of the folk-music of Hungary and strains from the synagogal music of the Jews tincture the music of Goldmark, the latter element having agreeable appositeness in the score of his operatic masterpiece. These folk-song elements, however, are not sufficiently pronounced to place the composer in a distinctively national school. He is an eclectic. Very different is the case of a number of Bohemian composers who, inspired largely by political bias, which led them to cling tenaciously to their language and other native institutions which compulsory national affiliation threatened to tear away from them, and also a fondness for the rhythms of their national dances, created a Czech school of composition which has won all but universal admiration. Bohemia had once been renowned for its culture, but the Golden Age of its music, like that of England, lay in the distant past. Excellent composers, and still more excellent performers, came from within its boundaries in the eighteenth century, when Prague provided the audiences for which Mozart wrote by expressed preference; but the country did not compel special attention to itself as an original producer of musical work until the compositions of the chiefest of her modern musical sons came, tardily, into notice. This was

Smetana (Frederich Bedrich). (Pronounced Smay-tah-nah, with the accent on the first syllable.)

He was born in Leitomischl on March 2, 1824, and died in a mad-house on May 12, 1884, after ten years of agonizing sufferings due to a mysterious auricular malady. This malady manifested itself at first in an occasional whistling in his right ear, which gradually grew more and more intense, and was aggravated by a continuous buzzing and acute whistling " in the form of the A-flat major chord of the sixth in a high position." He made these acoustical diagnoses himself, and left a mournful record of the fact in one of the finest — certainly the best known — of his works, a string quartet in E minor, entitled *Aus meinem Leben*, in which he attempted a musi-cal portrayal of his experiences. The finale contains a long-drawn E as a premonition of the calamity which came upon him in 1874 and ended in total deafness and insanity. Despite the dreadful drawback, he composed some of his finest works at this period, — the quartet already mentioned, a series of symphonic poems of a descriptive character entitled *Má Vlast* (My Fatherland), an opera, *Tajemstvi* (The Secret), and other compositions. He had already carried off a prize of 1,000 florins with an opera, *Libussa*, written for the dedication of Czech National Theatre in Prague, which did not take place until June 11, 1881. Smetana was present on the occasion but could not hear a note of his music. His operas are *Libussa*, *Braniboři v Cechách* (The Brandenburghers in Bohemia), *Prodana nevesta* (The Bartered Bride), *Dalibor*, *Dvě Vdovy* (Two Widows), *Hubicka* (The Kiss), *Tajemstvi*, and *Certova Stena* (The Devil's Wall). Of these operas, *The Bartered Bride* has won suc-cess in Germany, Austria, and England, and its overture, a scintil-lant piece of contrapuntal work, has long been popular in Ameri-can concert-rooms. His symphonic poems are *Wallenstein's Camp*, the series comprehended in *Má Vlast*, *Richard III*, and *Hakon Jarl*.

The foremost representative of the Bohemian school, since Smetana, is the present director of the National Con-servatory at Prague.

Dvořák (Antonin). Born at Nehalozeves (Mühlhausen), Septem-ber 8, 1841. Died at Prague, May 1, 1904.

His father was an innkeeper and destined his son to be a butcher. But, like thousands of Bohemian children, he had learned to play the violin from the village schoolmaster, and at sixteen years of age, making his own choice of a profession, he left his home and went to Prague to study music. He became a pupil of the Organ School and supported himself by playing the violin in a band which provided entertainment at popular resorts. Later he became a member of the orchestra of the National Theatre, and when a new building took the place of the old one which had been destroyed by fire, he wrote the overture, *Husitzka*, long the best known and most admired of his works in America, for the opening. In this overture he paid tribute to the historic past of his country by employing a theme from an ancient Hussite hymn. In 1875 he received a stipend from the Austro-Hungarian government to enable him to devote himself to composition, and within five years his name had been borne throughout Germany and to the principal cities of England and America, by his *Slavonic Rhapsodies* and *Dances*. The production of a beautiful *Stabat Mater*, in London in 1883, enlisted the interest of the English Festival authorities, and he turned his attention for a while to choral work, composing a dramatic cantata, *The Spectre's Bride*, for the Birmingham festival of 1855, an oratorio, *St. Ludmilla*, for Leeds in 1886, and a *Requiem* for Birmingham in 1891, in which year the University of Cambridge conferred upon him the degree of Doctor of Music. For three years, 1892–1895, he lived in New York, where, his attention being drawn to a popular type of American melody which had sprung from the slave songs of the Southern states, he composed a symphony, his fifth, entitled *From the New World*, a quartet (op. 96), and a quintet (op. 97), to illustrate the value of Afro-American elements in serious composition. Returned to his native land, he was made director of the conservatory at Prague, and after putting out four orchestral ballads, or symphonic poems, based on Bohemian legends, *Der Wassermann*, *Die Mittagshexe*, *Das Goldene Spinnrad* and *Die Waldtaube*, some chamber pieces and smaller works, he settled down to operatic composition, a field in which he had made half a dozen essays before he came to America.

Dvořák has been a voluminous composer, and many of his works, like a setting of Drake's *Ode to the American Flag*, betray his besetting sin, which is want of careful reflection and self-criticism. He is a fluent melodist in the Schubertian vein, an ingenious harmonist, and a most brilliant colorist. I have mentioned but a small fraction of his works, not even all the important ones. His five symphonies have been played in New York, the last oftener than all the others put together. The American quartet proved so popular that the Kneisel Quartet of Boston, the first organization to play it either in private or public, performed it no less than ninety times in one season It also figured largely on the programmes of the Bohemian

Quartet, whose second violin, Josef Suk, a pupil of Dvořák in composition, is following closely in the footsteps of his master in the utilization of Bohemian elements. He and Zdenko Fibich (1850–1900), together with Dvořák, have been the brightest ornaments of the Czech schools of which I have set down Smetana as the creator, though he had been preceded by many composers, one of whom, František Škroup, is credited with writing the first Bohemian opera. Of the forms found in the national music of his country, Dvořák has introduced the wild dance called *Furiant* into instrumental music and the elegiac *Dumka* with fine effect. A similar utilization of folk-song and folk-dance elements is found in some of the compositions of Ignace Jan Paderewski (born in Podolia, Poland, November 6, 1859), who handles Gypsy themes with great vigor and vividness in his opera, *Manru,* and strikes fire with native rhythms and intervals in his *Fantasie Polonaise* for pianoforte and orchestra.

Out of the list of French names marshalled on page 468 I lift one for special mention, not so much because its bearer has done more credit to the art of music than his fellows (in serious accomplishment he cannot be said to take precedence of D'Indy, or of De Bussy in the employment of those superficial and glittering extravagances too frequently used to cloak poverty of ideas), but because by a striking success he has added one more to the works which keep French opera alive on the foreign stage. It is

Charpentier (Gustave). Born at Dieuze, June 25, 1860.

He began his studies at Tourcoing, whither his parents had removed after the Franco-Prussian war. Thence he went to the Conservatoire at Lille, where his progress was so pronounced that the municipality of Tourcoing gave him a pension of 1,200 francs to enable him to study at the Conservatoire in Paris. There Massenet was his teacher in composition, and in 1887 he won the *Prix de Rome*. The first, and finest, result of his Italian sojourn was the orchestral suite, *Impressions d'Italie,* which made the round of the concert-rooms of Germany and America before he attracted wider notice with his opera, *Louise,* which, after reposing several years in his desk by the side of three other operatic scores, *Marie,*

Orphée, and *Tête rouge*, was brought forward at the Opéra-Comique in February, 1900. Its success was instantaneous, and it rapidly made its way into the opera houses of the continent.

Charpentier, who bears a surname that has honorable prominence on the roster of French composers (see page 409), is the musical poet *par excellence* of Montmartre and the humble and Bohemian phases of Parisian life. The story of his opera is that of a working-girl of Montmartre for whom the charms of a loose life with a painter in the city outweigh filial affection and all considerations of religion and morals. It ends with a heart-broken father hurling his dying curse at the city whose myriad of gay lights shine up to his humble home from the valley below. Into its web and woof the composer has woven some of the street cries of Paris, a proceeding which he had already followed in his *Couronnement de la Muse*, written in 1897 and performed at Lille the next year. It was composed for a Montmartre festival; but even this was not the beginning. From the Villa Medici he sent not only his picturesque *Impressions d'Italie*, but also a symphony-drama, *La Vie du Poète*, for orchestra, soli, and chorus. In the last movement of this work he introduced "all the noises and echoes of a Montmartre festival, with its low dancing-rooms, its drunken cornets, its hideous din of rattles, the wild laughter of bands of revellers and the cries of hysterical women." This is realism as bald as the smashing of crockery in the *Till Eulenspiegel* of Richard Strauss; it is also nationalism of a sort, but of a very different sort than that cultivated by the group of British composers who must now have some attention.

In Sir Alexander Campbell Mackenzie, and Hamish McCunn, we have two British composers who have taken up the Scotch idioms into their music and given them artistic utterance; in Charles Villiers Stanford, an Irishman who has succeeded in weaving the melodies of his native land into a symphony which is admirable in every respect; in Samuel Coleridge-Taylor, a unique type who has unconsciously betrayed influences which seem to have come from his African father as well as those which have surrounded him from his birth in the land of his English mother. Frederick H. Cowen, born on the island of Jamaica, educated in London, Leipsic, and Berlin, has not only composed operas, oratorios, cantatas, and pianoforte concertos which belong to the large mass of absolute music, but has also given utterance to folk-idioms in a *Scandinavian* and a *Welsh* symphony. Charles Hubert Hastings Parry (for whom a critic must stop to pay a tribute richly deserved for his literary work in behalf of music), Sir John Frederick Bridge, Sir John Stainer, Sir John Goss, and many other British musicians amongst those living and recently dead, have perpetuated the solid traditions of English church music. Mackenzie, Stanford, and Cowen have composed operas and seen them live out their short lives on the public stage, while one of their contemporaries and colleagues, aided by an exceptionally brilliant literary collaborator, was creating a type of operetta which from several points of view stands as high at least as the works of Offenbach, Planquette, and Suppé. I refer to

Sullivan (Sir Arthur Seymour), [1842–1900].

He was born in London and as a lad was chorister in the Chapel Royal. He was the first winner of the Mendelssohn Scholarship in the Royal Academy of Music, and studied there under Bennett and Goss; then at the Leipsic Conservatory, 1858–1861, under Moscheles, Hauptmann, Plaidy, and Richter. His music to Shakespeare's *Tempest* won enthusiastic recognition for his talents on his return to his native land, and he began the conventional career of the English composer under exceptionally favorable circumstances. He composed cantatas, oratorios, songs, and incidental music for plays by Shakespeare, but finally found the forte which was to lift his individuality of style into eminence in the comic operettas which he wrote in collaboration with W. S. Gilbert. These works stand as models of scintillant wit and genial humor, keen satire kept within the bounds of good taste, ingenuity of construction, wealth of graceful melody of a frankly English type, neatly introduced, cleverly handled, and effectively embellished with harmony and orchestral effects. The best of them are *Trial by Jury, H. M. S. Pinafore, Pirates of Penzance, Patience, Iolanthe,* and *The Mikado.* Of Sullivan's works in the more serious department I mention as peculiarly worthy of notice *Kenilworth*, *The Martyr of Antioch*, *The Prodigal Son*, *The Light of the World*, and *The Golden Legend.*

There remains for mention a composer in whom many English hopes are centred because of the instance which he has given of the compelling force of an individuality developed by original choice and persistent devotion to self-conceived ideals. The man is

Elgar (Edward William). Born at Broadheath, June 2, 1857.

He is practically self-educated, an *autodidakt*, as the Germans say. He took a few private violin lessons in London, but did not study at any of the continental conservatories, enroll himself at any of the British schools of music, or go down to any of the British universities for either a scholastic or a musical degree. Only at the festivals of Worcester, Hanley, Leeds, and Hereford, and at Queen Victoria's Diamond Jubilee celebration in 1897, had works of his been heard. For the rest he was only a modest, hard-working musician, who had taught himself all he knew about the higher branches of the art, who could play the organ, pianoforte, violin, and bassoon, had conducted small amateur organizations of instrumentalists and choristers, had sat among the second violins at festivals which were afterwards to be proud to claim his works, had composed all manner of pieces, and for four years had been organist of a church in Worcester. Suddenly he burst upon an astonished nation with an oratorio, *The Dream of Gerontius*, the performance of which in England, America, and Germany lifted him at once to a pinnacle of fame which can only be maintained by work of the highest character. For the Birmingham festival of 1903 he has written an oratorio entitled *The Apostles.* An overture, *Cockaigne*, and a series of orchestral variations which have been heartily enjoyed in Germany and the United States, have added to his reputation.

INDEX.

NEW POPULAR EDITION, WITH APPENDIX

Containing tables, etc., of the Opera Season 1908-11.

"The most complete and authoritative . . . pre-eminently the man to write the book . . . full of the spirit of discerning criticism. . . . Delightfully engaging manner, with humor, allusiveness and an abundance of the personal note."—*Richard Aldrich in New York Times Review.* (Complete notice on application.)

CHAPTERS OF OPERA

Being historical and critical observations and records concerning the Lyric Drama in New York from its earliest days down to the present time.

By HENRY EDWARD KREHBIEL, musical critic of the New York *Tribune*, author of "Music and Manners in the Classical Period," "Studies in the Wagnerian Drama," "How to Listen to Music," etc. With over 70 portraits and pictures of Opera Houses. 450 pp. 12mo. $2.50 net; by mail, $2.68. Illustrated circular on application.

This is perhaps Mr. Krehbiel's most important book. The first seven chapters deal with the earliest operatic performances in New York. Then follows a brilliant account of the first quarter-century of the Metropolitan, 1883-1908. He tells how Abbey's first disastrous Italian season was followed by seven seasons of German Opera under Leopold Damrosch and Stanton, how this was temporarily eclipsed by French and Italian, and then returned to dwell with them in harmony, thanks to Walter Damrosch's brilliant crusade,—also of the burning of the opera house, the vicissitudes of the American Opera Company, the coming and passing of Grau and Conried, and finally the opening of Oscar Hammerstein's Manhattan Opera House and the first two seasons therein, 1906-08.

"Presented not only in a readable manner but without bias . . . extremely interesting and valuable."—*Nation.*

"The illustrations are a true embellishment . . . Mr. Krehbiel's style was never more charming. It is a delight."—*Philip Hale in Boston Herald.*

"Invaluable for purpose of reference . . . rich in critical passages . . . all the great singers of the world have been heard here. Most of the great conductors have come to our shores. . . . Memories of them which serve to humanize, as it were, his analyses of their work."—*New York Tribune.*

***If the reader will send his name and address, the publishers will send, from time to time, information regarding their new books.

HENRY HOLT AND COMPANY
PUBLISHERS   NEW YORK

" The most important biographic contribution to musical literature since the beginning of the century, with the exception of Wagner's Letters to Frau Wesendonck."

—H. T. Finck, in the New York Evening Post.

(Circular with complete review and sample pages on application.)

Personal Recollections of Wagner

By ANGELO NEUMANN

Translated from the fourth German edition by Edith Livermore. Large 12mo. 318 pp., with portraits and one of Wagner's letters in facsimile. $2.50 net; by mail $2.65.

Probably no man ever did more to make Wagner's music dramas known than Angelo Neumann, who, with his famous " Wagner Travelling Theatre," carrying his artists, orchestra, scenery and elaborate mechanical devices, toured Germany, Holland, Belgium, Italy, Austria and Russia, and with another organization gave " The Ring " in London. But the account of this tour, interesting as it is, is not the main feature of his book, which abounds in intimate glimpses of Wagner at rehearsals, at Wahnfried and elsewhere, and tells much of the great conductor, Anton Seidl, so beloved by Americans. Among other striking figures are Nikisch and Muck, both conductors of the Boston Symphony orchestra, Mottl, the Vogls, Von Bulow, Materna, Marianna Brandt, Klafsky, and Reicher-Kindermann.

It is doubtful if any book gives a more vivid and truthful picture of life and " politics " behind the scenes of various opera houses. Many of the episodes, such as those of a bearded Brynhild, the comedy writer and the horn player and the prince and the Rhinedaughter are decidedly humorous.

The earlier portions of the book tell of the Leipsic negotiations and performances, the great struggle with Von Hülsen, the royal intendant at Berlin, Bayreuth and " Parsifal." Many of Wagner's letters appear here for the first time.

ILLUSTRATIONS.—Richard Wagner : Bust by Anton zur Strassen in the foyer of the Leipsic Stadttheater.—Angelo Neumann : From a picture in the Künstlerzimmer of the Leipsic Stadttheater.—Anton Seidl : Bas-relief by Winifred Holt of New York. Replica commissioned by Herr Direktor Neumann. —Hedwig Reicher-Kindermann—Facsimile of letter from Wagner to Neumann, received after the news of Wagner's death.

If the reader will send his name and address the publishers will send information about their new books as issued.

HENRY HOLT AND COMPANY

34 WEST 33RD STREET   NEW YORK

SOME FORERUNNERS OF ITALIAN OPERA

By W. J. HENDERSON, Musical Critic of *The Sun,* Author of "Richard Wagner, His Life and Dramas," "The Art of the Singer," etc. 12mo, 243 pp. $1.25 net.

The contents cover early Liturgical Drama, the Sacre Rappresentazioni, Birthplace of the Secular Drama, The Artistic Impulse, Poliziano's "Favola di Orfeo" (five chapters covering the work, the performance, music, solos and orchestra), Frottola Drama to Madrigal, Preponderance of the Spectacular, Influence of the Taste for Comedy, Vecchi and the Matured Madrigal Drama, the Spectacular Element in Music, and the Medium for Individual Utterance.

"A delightful introduction to Mr. Apthorp's 'The Opera Past and Present'. . . . A landscape full of varied charms. . . . Highly suggestive and full of instruction."—*New York Tribune.*

"The writer has studied his subject exhaustively. . . . Of Mantua's intellectual atmosphere, its activity and importance as a literary and musical centre, the author gives a vivid picture."—*Nation.*

"Chapters which show patient research and an exercise of a finely critical faculty. . . . Scholarly, and contains much that is new in the way of conclusions. While it is chiefly historical and critical, it is written in a manner that holds the attention and the picture of life and manners will entertain the general reader."—*Boston Herald.*

THE WIND-BAND AND ITS INSTRUMENTS: Their History, Construction, Acoustics, Technique and Combination.

By ARTHUR A. CLAPPÉ, formerly on the faculty of the Royal Military School of Music, and sometime teacher of music at the U. S. Military Academy, West Point. With some 90 cuts of instruments, etc., 36 examples in musical notation in the text and 30 charts for fingering, etc. 12mo, 208 pp. $1.50 net. By mail, $1.60.

(Illustrated circular on application)

Of value to students, and of interest to music lovers. It includes quaint bits of history and apt comparisons and is written, says *Musical America,* in a "fascinatiing style."

"Those who hope to see the military music of this country improved —and there is abundant room for improvement—will welcome it. . . . Ought to attract the attention of every student of music, every amateur who desires to be well informed, every orchestra conductor who wishes to obtain a complete insight into the construction and technic of wind instruments, and every bandmaster who hopes to be really a master. . . . A small, compact, and remarkably clearly written book. . . . He has discussed with discernment such matters as the duties of the bandmaster, the qualities of tone color and the dynamics of wind bands, their general technic and their ensemble. . . . An important contribution to the literature of musical technics and should become a standard authority."—*W. J. Henderson in the New York Sun.*

HENRY HOLT AND COMPANY

PUBLISHERS   (VIII'12)   NEW YORK

ARCHIBALD HENDERSON'S THE CHANGING DRAMA

Its Contributions and Tendencies. By the Author of "George Bernard Shaw: His Life and Works," "European Dramatists," etc. 12mo. $1.50 net.

The pioneer book in English in its field. While a number of good books, taking up important dramatists and discussing them one after another, are available, this is probably the first that describes the significant changes and movements in the drama of the last half century, illustrating them by the work of leading dramatists and by apt citations of and quotations from their plays. The author, publicist as well as dramatic critic, aims to show the expression of the larger realities of contemporary life in the drama, the widening of social influence of the stage, the new technic, form, and content of the play, the substitution of the theme for the hero, the conflict of wills for that of arms, etc. In short, to give a brief but authoritative general survey with a more detailed appraisal of some of the chief creative contributions.

The chapter headings indicate the content and scope of the work: Drama in the New Age; The New Criticism and New Ethics; Science and the New Drama; The New Forms—Realism and the Pulpit Stage; The New Forms—Naturalism and the Free Theatre; The Battle with Illusions; The Ancient Bondage and the New Freedom; The New Technic; The Play and the Reader; The New Content; The Newer Tendencies.

The author, though an American, has also studied the drama in the theatres of Great Britain and the Continent, and has before this demonstrated that he is a dramatic scholar and a keen, clear-eyed, entertaining critic. His articles have appeared in *La Société Nouvelle, Mercure de France, Deutsche Revue, Illustreret Tidende, Finsk Tidskrift, T. P.'s Magazine,* etc., etc.

Maurice Maeterlinck said of his "Interpreters of Life" (now incorporated in his "European Dramatists"): "You have written one of the most sagacious, most acute, and most penetrating essays in the whole modern literary movement."

"It is a really great work," said Professor William Lyon Phelps of "George Bernard Shaw: His Life and Works."

Of his "European Dramatists," *The Dial* said: "The criticisms of their work are keen and lucid, and have the advantage of coming from one who has studied the plays exhaustively."

HENRY   HOLT   AND   COMPANY
PUBLISHERS   vii'14   NEW YORK

Hale's Dramatists of To-day

Rostand, Hauptmann, Sudermann, Pinero, Shaw, Phillips, Maeterlinck

By Prof. EDWARD EVERETT HALE, Jr., of Union College. With gilt top, $1.50 net. (By mail, $1.60.)

An informal discussion of their principal plays and of the performances of some of them. A few of those considered are *Man and Superman, Candida, Cyrano de Bergerac, L'Aiglon, The Sunken Bell, Magda, Ulysses, Letty, Iris,* and *Pelleas and Melisande.* The volume opens with a paper "On Standards of Criticism," and concludes with " Our Idea of Tragedy," and an appendix of all the plays of each author, with dates of their first performance or publication.

Bookman: " He writes in a pleasant, free-and-easy way. . . . He accepts things chiefly at their face value, but he describes them so accurately and agreeably that he recalls vividly to mind the plays we have seen and the pleasure we have found in them."

New York Evening Post: " It is not often nowadays that a theatrical book can be met with so free from gush and mere eulogy, or so weighted by common sense . . . an excellent chronological appendix and full index . . . uncommonly useful for reference."

Dial: " Noteworthy example of literary criticism in one of the most interesting of literary fields. . . . Provides a varied menu of the most interesting character. . . . Prof. Hale establishes confidential relations with the reader from the start. . . . Very definite opinions, clearly reasoned and amply fortified by example. . . . Well worth reading a second time."

New York Tribune: " Both instructive and entertaining."

Brooklyn Eagle: " A dramatic critic who is not just ' busting ' himself with Titanic intellectualities, but who is a readable dramatic critic. . . . Mr. Hale is a modest and sensible, as well as an acute and sound critic. . . . Most people will be surprised and delighted with Mr. Hale's simplicity, perspicuity, and ingenuousness."

New York Dramatic Mirror: " Though one may not always agree with Mr. Hale's opinions, yet one always finds that he has something interesting to say, and that he says it well. Entertaining and generally instructive without being pedantic."

The Theatre: " A pleasing lightness of touch. . . . Very readable book."

Henry   Holt   and   Company

Publishers

New York

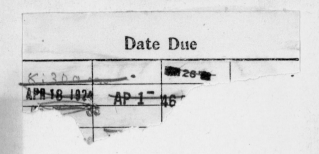